Social Support and Motherhood

The Natural History of a Research Project

ANN OAKLEY

BLACKWELL
Oxford UK & Cambridge USA

Copyright © Ann Oakley, 1992

The right of Ann Oakley to be identified as author of this work has been asserted in accordance with the Copyright, Designs and Patents Act 1988.

First published 1992

Blackwell Publishers
108 Cowley Road
Oxford OX4 1JF
UK

238 Main Street
Suite 501
Cambridge
MA 02142
USA

British Library Cataloguing-in-Publication Data

A CIP catalogue record for this book is available from the British Library.

Library of Congress Cataloging-in-Publication Data

A CIP record for this book is available from the Library of Congress. ISBNs: 0 631 1827-3 X; 0 631 18274 8 (pbk.)

Typeset in 10 on 11½pt Garamond by Acorn Bookwork
Printed in Great Britain by T. J. Press (Padstow) Ltd., Padstow, Cornwall

This book is printed on acid-free paper

Contents

Acknowledgements

This book has been a long time in the writing, and the research which it describes also has a long (and continuing) history. Many people have had to listen to stories about both the research and the book – different stories over the years, as the problems each has posed have developed, changed, resolved, or given rise, like the phoenix from the ashes, to new flights of fancy. I am grateful to everyone who has provided a listening ear: to everyone, in short, who has given *me* social support. This includes my friends and family, and colleagues in the three research units where the study was conceived, gestated and born: the National Perinatal Epidemiology Unit in Oxford, the Thomas Coram Research Unit and the (now) Social Science Research Unit in London. Without the help and support of Sandra Stone, in particular, the project's own pregnancy outcome would have been a very different story. The role of Lynda Rajan who worked with me on the study from its early stages, and those of the four research midwives are described in this book; they, too, gave unsparingly of their commitment and help. Penrose Robertson worked with flair and imagination on the computing side of the study. More recently, Jackie Lee deserves thanks for helping with the preparation of the manuscript, and Gill Bendelow for help with the bibliography. I owe a fundamental intellectual debt to Iain Chalmers for drawing my attention to the importance of the experimental method. None of these people are, of course, responsible for the product of the book's final text.

All of us who have been involved in carrying out the various stages of the research owe a particular debt of gratitude to the organizations which had the vision and faith to fund it: to the (then) Social Science Research Council, the Department of Health, the Iolanthe Trust, the Institute of Education, and the (now) Economic and Social Research Council. Those who did not understand or appreciate what we were trying to do may be unhappy to find their names recorded later in this book; but non-funders, like 'negative' research findings, are as much a part of the 'natural history' of a research project as funders and positive results.

My greatest thanks must go to the women who took up the challenge of taking part in the research – both in the pilot study, and in a fully fledged 'trial' of social support. Without *their* support, there would have been no study to do, and no book to write. Moreover, their commitment to the study demonstrates the possibility of fully informed experimental studies on women's health issues which this book argues are essential to breaking down the unhelpful divide between different ways of thinking about research, about knowledge, and about the behaviour of bodies and selves in a social, gendered world.

The author and publishers gratefully acknowledge permission to reproduce the paper 'Social Support and Pregnancy Outcome', by Ann Oakley, Lynda Rajan and Adrian Grant, which appeared in the *British Journal of Obstetrics and Gynaecology*, February 1990, Vol. 97, pp. 155–162. Thanks for permission to reproduce material are also due to Iain Chalmers for table 3.1; to Alison Macfarlane for figure 1.2; and to Raymond Illsley, David Rush and Margaret Stacey for material in Chapter 4. Some of the material in chapters 6, 10 and 11 has already been published in the form of journal papers; a list of these can be found in appendix II.

Note on Numbers

This is a book which challenges the divide between quantitative and qualitative research methods. Because of this it uses both. As certain characteristics of quantitative methods are commonly felt to be less easily accessible than those of their qualitative peers, some comments about the way in which numbers are deployed may be required.

I have tried to use these so that they are intelligible to those not trained in the science of deciphering them. In the process, however, I will inevitably have sacrificed the refinements needed to satisfy those whose domain they are. For example, in order to aid readability, most of the tables show percentages rather than percentages and figures, with the total figures on which the table is based being given at either the top or the bottom. I have not attempted to standardize the statistical techniques used – indeed, the sprinkling of different techniques illustrates that very disciplinary and epistemological divide which is the book's main theme (and which is discussed in more detail in Chapter 9).

I apologize for these sins of omission and commission to those who will notice them. Some other comments are needed both about my general use of numbers and for those whose forte is not the domain of numeracy and statistics. Where data from the Social Support and Pregnancy Outcome study are quoted, the total numbers in different tables and for different variables sometimes differ, since the exact numbers depend on the particular data source (interview, questionnaire, midwives' records, hospital case-notes, etc.) drawn on. For the same reason, references to other studies may quote different sample numbers in the text and in particular tables. Research is an untidy exercise in which the same full information is rarely available for every research participant. In interviews and when completing questionnaires, for example, not every participant answers every question researchers ask. In the tables, percentages have been rounded up to total 100, and they omit people for whom information is missing for that question or variable (because they did not answer the question, or for some other reason).

The main statistic used in the tables in this book is the chi-square. This is a test used to evaluate the probability of an apparent difference between groups found in a piece of empirical research occurring by chance. In other words, it provides a rough measure of the extent to which the difference in question can be believed as 'real'. The 'p'-value shown in the tables is the probability of that particular difference occurring by chance. If the probability is shown as <0.05, the chance is less than 5 in 100 that the difference is not genuine. P-values are shown on the tables in this book when they are less than 0.1. Where no p-value is shown, there is no 'statistically significant' difference. Chi-squares cannot be used for averages or means, so, where it is necessary to perform a similar exercise for means which look different, a *t*-test may be used instead. Some means show standard deviations or standard errors: these provide information about the range of values in the populations used to calculate the means. A few tables show confidence intervals or limits, or odds ratios: these are other ways of estimating the probability of an apparent difference being due to chance or not.

The use of statistics is not a substitute for other ways of appreciating social events and processes, but it is an aid to understanding the social world and to interpreting the quantitative statements all of us make. In this sense, some understanding of statistical thinking is necessary to the task of bridging different modes of knowing and understanding.

Introduction

This book has three aims. One is to provide an account of a research project concerning the health and wellbeing of women and their babies that began in 1983 and continues today. The second aim is to contextualize this account within 'a sociology of the research process' (Platt 1976) that centres on the telling of a story about how and why the research came into being, and what happened when it did. Both the descriptive and the analytic aims of the book are grounded in its third major focus, which is an epistemological one, concerning the status and gendering of knowledge in the contemporary capitalist world.

The story unfolded in the book, and the details of the narrative it encloses, link a wide variety of different concerns about knowledge, policy and practice in the contemporary industrialized world. Some of the major issues addressed in the book are:

1   What 'is' health? How far do variations in the social environment, including people's social relationships and networks, 'explain' differences in health status between individuals and groups?
2   What are the possibilities and limits of professionalized medical care as a strategy for promoting health?
3   When women have children, what is the role of professionalized health care on the one hand, and of the social environment on the other, in helping them to do so?
4   To what extent do professional definitions of the 'normal' distort people's experiences of their bodies and their social identities, and what has the concept of 'risk' to do with this?
5   What is the epistemological basis of the methods used by social scientists to advance knowledge? What 'is' knowledge, anyway?
6   Why are methods of contributing to advances in knowledge commonly divided into quantitative and qualitative? How does this division work in practice?

7 What is the relationship between social science research, academic knowledge and public policy?

'The real problem'

When I say this book will address these issues, I do not mean it will provide any easy answers. Like Martin Hammersley (1989: 6) in his account of the origins and dilemmas of the qualitative method in social science, I warn the reader now that there is no point in turning to the end of this book to find solutions to the problems posed – the reader will be disappointed. The issues themselves are enormous in scale and relevance, and it would be arrogant to suppose that my own perspective on one research project (this book) could untangle some of the most difficult questions of our time. What I am doing, rather more modestly, is following Wright Mills's (1959) injunction to deploy a sociological imagination in connecting private troubles to public issues, and, in perceiving their common ground, to identify some of the crises of ideology and practice confronting contemporary culture. From this point of view, then, the book's aim is to expose complex problems rather than provide simple solutions. It is not that there *are* no solutions, but that the nature of the problems exposes the falsity of the premises on which the questions are based. You cannot have a solution which works if the problem it addresses is not the 'real' problem. Or, to put it differently, 'reality' may be considered to be the problem.

To anticipate the argument set out later in the book: the knowledge systems of western postcapitalist societies have reached a crisis in their model of *how* the world is to be known and *who* is to know it. It is *this* crisis that joins others – the growing debate about the relevance of medicine to health, the crippling dependence of modern societies on the power of the legal profession to arbitrate behaviour, the waning light of sociology/social science itself in contemporary political discourse and institutions of academia, the redefinition of the university as a profit-making enterprise, the continuing insurgence of feminism in drawing attention to gender inequality – all these features of life are connected through a confusion about what knowledge 'is' and how it is to be attained. In naming this a 'confusion' rather than a 'conspiracy', I wish to distance myself as a feminist social scientist from those who say that either capitalism or patriarchy is to 'blame' for the present situation. Social systems that appropriate the labours of some to give others spurious power are not likely to be those in which the ownership and nature of knowledge are openly and freely debated, except in the sense identified by Walkerdine and Lucey (1989: 29) that 'successful' socialization involves transmission of the illusion of autonomy – the child must *believe* itself to be free. But this does not mean that those who point out the fallacies of capitalism and the phallacies of patriarchy successfully circumvent the problem by identifying one or other institutional structure as responsible for this.

The *particular* confusion within the general one which occupies a good deal of the argument of this book hinges on the relation between subjectivity and objectivity. According to western philosophical tradition, what exists in a person's mind – is subjective – is separable from what exists in reality – is objective. But 'subject' also means one who is not independent, who is under the authority of others; and 'reality' also means 'of or pertaining to the king ... that which pertains to the one in power' (Frye 1989: 79). The student, black and women's movements of the 1960s and 1970s articulated the subjectivity/objectivity relation as *political* – institutional power structures were shown to be closely associated with the ideologies and content of knowledge. To the challenge of claiming the 'personal is political', academic discourse responded in a variety of ways. Sociologists learnt to get their tongues around 'symbolic interactionism' and 'ethnomethodology', and to place positivism and functionalism firmly in the past. But now the political revolutions of the sixties are themselves in the past, we stand amidst the fragments of two languages wondering where to go next. The 'new' language of postmodernism (combined at times with the ambiguous, if not frankly derogatory, 'postfeminism') provides an apparently fresh technical categorizer, but its texts tend to obscurantism, and it is, in any case, the domination of the 'isms' we need to escape.

'The turning-point'?

Physicist Fritjof Capra calls this 'the turning-point': the moment of potential cultural movement caught between two alternative paradigms of knowledge. While one asserts the supremacy of the mind–body divide – the model of a rational, analytic science based on a mechanical view of the natural world – the other suggests a more subversive philosophy – the language of political revolt, which speaks of values masquerading as facts, and of people's entrapment and consequent alienation in political and economic systems they did not create. Table A lists two paired columns of words which signify the paradigm clash to which Capra refers. To his own list of terms, I have added others which represent the themes around which the argument of this book is organized. Table A thus stands as an important thematic conceptual divide to which the text will refer many times. It is headed 'The habit of thinking in dichotomies' after an essay by the US philosopher Susan Sherwin (1989) on the shortcomings of traditional philosophical methodologies. Sherwin says:

> Dichotomous thinking forces ideas, persons, roles and disciplines into rigid polarities. It reduces richness and complexity in the interest of logical

Table A 'The habit of thinking in dichotomies'

Social	Medical
Art	Science
Subjective	Objective
Experience	Knowledge
Observation	Intervention
Qualitative	Quantitative
Interpretation	Enumeration
Synthesizing	Analytic
Process	Structure
Practice	Theory
Emotion	Reason
Feeling	Thinking
Mind	Body
Spirit	Matter
Intuition	Intellect
Nature	Culture
Primitive	Civilized
Feminine	Masculine
'Soft'	'Hard'
Women	Men
Nurses	Doctors
Midwives	Obstetricians
Normality	Abnormality
Health	Disease
Care	Control
Co-operation	Competition
Connection	Separation
Community	Institution
Family	Work
Private	Public
Value	Fact

neatness ... Moreover, the creation and use of dichotomies seem to be important elements in the very structure of patriarchy – the institution of patriarchy involves power relations that rest on the assumption of fundamental and unbridgeable differences between the sexes reflected in multiple forms of polarity. (Sherwin 1989: 32)

Either/or thinking puts an embargo on both/sometimes-the-one, sometimes-the-other, possibilities. It is endemic in many areas of life. As Sherwin says, either/or is a cultural (but not the biological – see Oakley 1972; Laqueur 1990) basis of gender differentiation. The paralleling and confirming of social gender dichotomies with the home/work, private/ public divisions of an economic system is an extremely powerful force ensuring the longevity of these.

Capra's argument, invoked by his own unease as a working physicist with the discontinuity between modern physics and the dominant view of knowledge, is that civilizations pass through cultural transformations in which certain world views and constellations of beliefs and practices disintegrate to be replaced by others. Examples of such transformations are the rise of civilization with the invention of agriculture at the start of the neolithic period, the development of Christianity and the transition from the Middle Ages to the Scientific Age. Western civilizations, Capra maintains, are currently facing a crisis which is marked by three transitions in particular: the decline of patriarchy, the economic transition from fossil-fuels to solar energy, and a shift in cultural values away from 'the belief in the scientific method as the only approach to knowledge' (Capra 1983: 31). It is *only* within such a context as Capra describes that the trials, tribulations and successes outlined in the rest of this book become, as a whole, comprehensible. While each can be explained in particular terms – the Social Science Research Council turned the social support project down because they ran out of money, the research midwives were unhappy with the ethics of random allocation because they had insufficient training in the scientific method, medical audiences to the research findings came up with allegations of bias because the project 'director' made no secret of her allegiance to the political importance of subjectivity – yet these fragmented explanations do not tell a story with a coherent beginning, a middle and an end. They assume the whole to be a sum of its parts. But every whole is more than that; every story is more than a list of characters, scenes, dialogues and happenings. *The narrative strength of a story is the way these features interact to produce a set of meanings which make sense/ are generalizable beyond the story itself.*

Social Support and Motherhood is not a book that reports the results of research in the way in which this is conventionally understood. One paper which does this is reproduced as Figure 9.1. Others have been published, and are available to anyone who wants to pursue particular areas of data and their analysis (see appendix II for a list). What this book tries to do is tell a story about the unfolding of a particular research project in a particular cultural context. In so doing, it attempts to abstract some general lessons about the activity of research in the real world. As Dorothy Smith (1988) argues, there is no theory about the world which does not begin in someone's everyday experience. Even the grandest theories start as seedlings in the soil of human beings' efforts to survive and produce their own identities and futures through a multitude of 'trivial' labours. The Platonic idea of knowledge which contends the necessity of *transcending* the everyday, the mundane, in order to arrive at things which can be universally known, has successfully blinded us to this simple experiential fact. We must go back, then, to what it is like to be researchers and to do research if we want to understand more about the limits and possibilities of knowledge in our time.

1

Social Origins

To include epistemological questions concerning the validity of sociological knowledge in the sociology of knowledge is somewhat like trying to push a bus in which one is riding. (Berger and Luckman 1971: 85)

The main problem with retrospective interpretations is that subsequent experience can play the trick of laying new meanings on old events. In part this is because the need to make a coherent, seemingly planned story of one's life constantly overwhelms the more honest ambition of describing it as it was. As it was is usually a series of false starts and premature stops, a mix of ill-assorted and conflicting ideas, and of feelings and intellectual insights all jumbled together in an unholy melting-pot. Memory is unfortunately but endearingly opaque, leading us to dissemble instead of revealing.

Bearing this qualification in mind, it seems to me now that the Social Support and Pregnancy Outcome (SSPO) study, as it was ultimately called, had its origins in six sets of observations about social relations. These were that:

1   Science, including medical science, may be regarded as a 'social' product – its content and practice reflect the social backgrounds and motives of its practitioners, rather than existing in some pure, uncontaminated, ahistorical mode.
2   The professional ideologies, status and organization of the medical profession militate against recognition of the universe and impact of the 'social' in health care.
3   The survival and health of mothers and babies are consistently worse in socially disadvantaged as compared with socially advantaged groups.
4   Differences in social position and experience, especially as mediated by stress, are linked with different fates of mothers and babies.
5   Social support is good for health.
6   Being researched may in this sense be health-promoting.

The rest of this chapter expands these six observations as a prelude to describing the background and beginnings of the study.

'Knit your own incubator'

For twenty years from 1965 to 1985 I worked as a contract researcher, for the last five years of this twenty-year period with other such researchers in the National Perinatal Epidemiology Unit (NPEU) in Oxford. The NPEU was a new unit set up in 1978 through a joint initiative of the Royal College of Obstetricians and Gynaecologists and the British Paediatric Association, and funded by the Department of Health to carry out epidemiological research 'with a view to providing information which can promote effective use of resources in the perinatal health services' (Hansard, 5 July 1978). A major reason for the unit's establishment was to consider whether or not a fourth national survey of perinatal mortality should be carried out. Since the earlier ones had been undertaken in 1946, 1958 and 1970, 1982 was looming as the next twelve-year interval for the fourth in the series. One of my first tasks as the unit's advisory social scientist was to comment on the desirability of a fourth survey from a social science point of view. My conclusion was that the evidence was insufficiently strong to justify the effort: the problem was not that we needed more data to understand patterns of reproductive health and illness, but that we needed to make better use of the data we already had (Oakley 1979b).[1]

The next major project on which I worked was funded by the Wellcome Trust and concerned the development of antenatal care in Britain. The notion of medical care as an important influence on the *social* process of becoming a mother had emerged in work I had previously carried out on first childbirth (Oakley 1979a; Oakley 1980). At the NPEU I was exposed to a complementary debate – one about the extent to which medical care could itself confidently be said to influence the *physical* processes of reproduction. Which obstetric procedures had been shown to be effective and safe, and which had not? An alarming number had not (see Chalmers et al. 1989a). As the NPEU set out on its path to becoming an internationally renowned repository of wisdom about evaluation in perinatal care – and in particular a proponent of the use of randomized controlled trials – government reports and pressure groups were vociferously making some rather simplistic claims about the state of Britain's perinatal health services, and about the therapeutic power of modern medicine. Britain's record of baby deaths was described as a 'holocaust' (Court Report 1976), and 'guestimates' cited 10,000 British babies as dying or being handicapped every year as result of shortfalls in the maternity services (Social Services Committee 1980). Many of the recommendations put forward in the Social Services Committee's report on *Perinatal and Neonatal Mortality* to correct this state of affairs pushed for more, and especially more centralized, high-technology, medical care, despite lack of evidence that these would be appropriate or effective solutions, and on the shaky assumption that medical care could compensate for or override the health-damaging effects of material disadvantage.

Interventions in human life designed to benefit may also harm. Until the 1980s, there was virtually no information on the frequency of handicapping disorders in children that might have their origin in the perinatal period (Chalmers 1981; Chalmers et al. 1980). The accelerating trend in many countries in the increasing 'salvage' of small sick babies led to suggestions that more expenditure on specialist neonatal care – the 'knit an incubator' campaign of pressure groups such as the Spastics Society – would automatically reduce deaths and illness among babies. The acronym BLISS of one such group, Baby Life Support Systems, identified the technological support of the special care baby unit – the first resting place of 1 in 20 British babies in 1964 but of 1 in 5 in 1977 (Richards 1980) – as a primary target of maternity services policy. Scepticism among researchers and epidemiologists regarding these claims – technology could not solve all the problems some babies were born with – equalled the missionary enthusiasm of the maternity pressure groups, and the battle cries of (some) neonatal paediatricians. The leap from the laudable goal of preventing baby deaths to the dubious recommendation of increasing expenditure on mechanized birth and postbirth care exposed the mendacious logic of the Cartesian medical model itself: the silly idea that death is the only suffering worth avoiding, and the nonsense of arguing that the health of babies placed in jeopardy by hazardous social conditions may easily be restored by expensive hospital machines (see Hack and Fanaroff 1986; Heinonen et al. 1988, for discussions).

A number of different studies starting in the 1970s began to suggest that one result of the increasing survival of low-birthweight babies through the use of high-technology medical care was that rates of cerebral palsy were increasing (Hagberg et al. 1984; Powell et al. 1986; Stanley and Atkinson 1981; Stanley and Watson 1992). Another possible consequence was a transfer of death from the immediate period after birth to later in infancy (Heinonen et al. 1988). In other words, paediatricians were keeping more small babies alive for longer, but some of these merely died later, while others survived with mental and physical impairment. In societal terms, as various commentators have pointed out, this may seem far from an advance. To the families involved, it represents a multilayered trauma, in which the agony of watching a tiny baby subjected to a series of intensive 'therapeutic' manipulations, only eventually to die and grow up disabled, is mixed with the impertinence of a medical system which allows no parental input to medical decision-making, and stereotypes mothers[2] as uncaring, and psychiatrically abnormal if they dare to suggest a peaceful death as preferable to a suffering life – for the child as well as the family (see Guillemin and Holmstrom 1986; Levin 1990).

Quantifying the biological and the social

Perinatal mortality, birthweight and social class are the three key concepts linking the social to the medical in this debate about appropriate strategies for promoting the health of mothers and babies. Figure 1.1 gives the definitions. Table 1.1 shows the most recent available figures for social

---

A *Perinatal mortality*

$$\text{Perinatal mortality rate} = \frac{(\text{stillbirths plus deaths at 0–6 days after live birth}) \times 1000}{\text{Live births} + \text{stillbirths}}$$

Stillbirth = 'A child which has issued forth from its mother after the 28th week of pregnancy and which did not at any time after being completely expelled from its mother breathe or show any other signs of life.[a]

B *Birthweight*

'The first weight of the fetus or newborn obtained after birth. This weight should be measured preferably within the first hour of life, before significant postnatal weight loss has occurred.'

Low birthweight: less than 2500 g, i.e. up to and including 2499 g.

Recommended weight classification for perinatal mortality statistics: by weight intervals of 500 g, i.e. 1000–1499 g, 1500–1999 g, etc.

C *Social class*

Class		Typical occupations
I	Professional	Doctors, lawyers
II	Intermediate occupations (managerial and lower professional)	Teachers, managers
III	Skilled occupations This is often subdivided into:	
IIIN	Non manual	Clerks, shop assistants
IIIM	Manual	Bricklayers, coalminers below ground
IV	Partly skilled occupations	Bus conductors, postmen, traffic wardens
V	Unskilled occupations	General labourers, dustmen

Unclassified: the armed forces, students, those about whom there is no informa-tion, those whose occupations do not fit into the classifications.

Figure 1.1 Definitions of perinatal mortality, birthweight and social class, England and Wales

[a]The Stillbirth (Definition) Act 1992 lowered the limit to 24 weeks.
Sources: Births and Deaths Registration Act 1953; World Health Organization, *International Classification of Diseases*. Ninth Revision, Registrar-General, *Classification of Occupations*, 1980.

class, low birthweight and perinatal mortality in England and Wales in 1989. The low-birthweight rate goes from 4.9 in social class I to 8.0 in social class V, a rise which is paralleled by a near-doubling of the perinatal mortality rate from 5.8 to 10.2. The pattern underlying the figures shown in table 1.1 is that, for the *same* birthweight, babies in working-class households are twice as likely to die as their middle-class counterparts. Though the figures in 1980 were slightly different from those shown in table 1.1, the general pattern was the same. The trend is for perinatal mortality to fall over time, but for the social class differences to be maintained (Social Services Committee 1988). There is no similar trend towards a falling incidence for low birthweight, nor any suggestion of a disappearing social class differential. The conjunction of a stable low-birthweight rate with a falling perinatal mortality rate is, of course, evidence of the trend already mentioned towards increasing survival for small babies.

While use of these terms 'social class', 'birthweight' and 'perinatal mortality' can yield information which is useful to the debate about how health is produced, it is equally important to understand how history has produced the terms themselves. Social class, for example, is a designation introduced by nineteenth-century statisticians and intended to describe cultural as well as occupational differences between individuals. The concern was to find a way of differentiating people by social class which would, in the aggregate, produce a picture of the different social classes having the greatest mortality differentials possible (Macfarlane and Mugford 1984). Given this, it is hardly surprising that occupationally based class *does* differentiate. What social class differences do not do is to *explain* anything. The 'reification' of the *analytical* construct of class into

Table 1.1 Social class, low birthweight and perinatal mortality, England and Wales, 1989

Social class	Low birthweight rate[a]	Perinatal mortality rate[b]
I	4.9	5.8
II	5.3	6.9
III non-manual	6.1	7.4
III manual	6.6	7.7
IV	7.0	8.9
V	8.0	10.2
Other	5.2	10.2
Total	6.1	7.7

[a]Low-birthweight births as a percentage of all live and stillbirths.
[b]Stillbirths and deaths in the first week of life per thousand live and stillbirths.
Source: OPCS, *Mortality Statistics: perinatal and infant: social and biological factors*, series DH3, no. 32 (London: HMSO, 1989)

something substantive-in-itself diverts attention from the ways in which the social and material circumstances of individuals provide different constellations of risk. Furthermore, the debate about why the designation 'social class' is so predictive of life chances was, and is, largely a debate about the lives of *men*. In the most widely used measures of social class, including that of the British Registrar-General, men are assigned a social class directly on the basis of their occupation, but women and children are only assigned an occupationally based class because of their membership of a family 'headed' by a man. Thus, as Hilary Graham has pointed out:

> when we talk of 'working-class men', 'working-class women' and 'working-class children', we are not using categories that are equivalent. Working-class men are men in manual occupations: working-class women are women fathered by, married to or living with men in manual occupations. Working-class children, similarly, are children living with a man with a manual job. Only when the woman lives alone is the ascription 'working-class' likely to describe her occupational status. (Graham 1986: 42)

The narrowness of current 'social class' definitions was recognized by the OPCS in 1989 in the form of a recommendation that social class be renamed 'occupational skill groups', a strategy which would, of course, leave untouched the conceptual and practical problems inherent in tying social location to employment status.

As concepts, both 'social class' and 'birthweight' were important landmarks in the epistemological terrain supporting the foundations of the SSPO study. While social class is a *social* category, birthweight is seen as a distinctively *biological* one. In the pre-industrial era, and in small-scale rural societies today, babies are not greeted by being subject to *quantification*. The reasons why they began to be so are explored in chapter 9, which takes a closer look at the social construction of birthweight today as 'objective fact'. But the same point holds for birthweight as for social class: once babies begin routinely to be weighed, birthweight becomes an explanatory variable in its own right, a thing which explains other things. People begin to speak as though a baby's physical weight, its quantity, contributes an important and predictive item of knowledge about it, just as the 'fact' that someone is working or middle class is considered informative and explanatory, without anything else being said. Sub-categories of birthweight are subject to the same reification process as the principal category itself. The initiative of dividing babies into two weight classes – 'normal' and 'low' – was taken by a Finnish doctor working in Germany in the 1920s who observed that the effect of being born too small was somewhat different from that of being born too early, and that 2500 g might be a convenient point of division between the two groups (see chapter 9). This observation about the importance of low birthweight (LBW) led to the near-universal designation of biological features of populations in these terms. In 1980, the World Health Organization

(WHO) attempted a world view of the incidence of low birthweight. The figures updated a few years later showed the world LBW rate[3] as 16.0 per cent – that is, 16 out of a 100 babies were quantified at birth as weighing less than 2500 g. Asia was the region with the highest percentage – 19.7 per cent, three times the lowest, 6.5 per cent for Europe (WHO 1984; see Puffer and Serrano 1987). As a matter of fact, there remains a difference of opinion about what the exact dividing line between normal and low birthweight ought to be; it was a matter of continual irritation in our study that we had to remember the disagreement that obtains in the UK at the present time between the Department of Health and the Office of Population Censuses and Surveys – while the former defines LBW as 2500 g or less, OPCS defines it as less than 2500 g.

The amount a baby weighs is often taken in conjunction with the length of its gestation in arriving at estimates of what birthweight 'means'. Pregnancy, too, has been subdivided within the technical language of medicine into 'normal' and 'abnormal' – here into 'term' and 'preterm'. Preterm babies are defined as babies born before 37 completed weeks of pregnancy. A small baby born early is considered more normal than a small baby born at the end of pregnancy; that is, its reduced size is attributed to (explained in the light of) its premature exit from the womb. A small baby born at the end of pregnancy may be designated 'small for gestational age' (SGA) or suffering from 'intrauterine growth retardation (IUGR). Of the four groups produced by combining the two criteria of gestation and birthweight – preterm and LBW, preterm and normal birthweight, term and LBW, term and normal birthweight – babies who are born at term but are of LBW have the poorest chances of survival.

Two significant 'facts' about birthweight are shown in table 1.1: being born at less than 'normal' birthweight is more likely if you come from a working-class family, and is associated with a greater risk of death around the time of birth. But the stigma of low birthweight follows one through life: LBW babies who survive are more likely than normal-birthweight survivors to suffer from neurological abnormalities, mental retardation, 'low' intellectual and educational achievement/subnormality, to be ill as children, have later onset of puberty and 'poor' physical development generally (Illsley and Mitchell 1984). In 1989 a group of Swedish doctors tracking the blood pressures of male army conscripts found the risk of high blood pressure to be significantly raised in men who had been low-birthweight babies, and especially in those who had been defined as growth-retarded at birth (Gennser et al. 1988). In Britain, researchers following the health of babies born in the 1946 and 1970 birth cohorts found a similar inverse relationship between systolic blood pressure and birthweight. This was present at age 10 but had strengthened by age 36 (Barker et al. 1989).

Like birthweight, perinatal mortality has become a universal descriptor of life and death events. The first-identified use of the term was in the

1940s, when it was argued that deaths during the first week of life lay on a continuum with those before birth (Peller 1947–8). Some of the causes of both were the same. Thus, it would make sense to link them analytically – 'make sense', that is, to the emergent profession of obstetrics, which was during this period demarcating an area of physical existence over which it wished to claim unique expertise.

The concepts of social class, birthweight and perinatal mortality all, then, arise at particular historical moments, as part of the armamentarium developed by power elites (politicians and health professionals) claiming control over the quality and quantity of populations by being able more precisely to measure their component parts.

The focus on low birthweight

The condition of LBW symbolizes much of the debate about the present, future and meaning of the perinatal health services in the 1970s and 1980s. Arbitrarily divided from their 'normal' peers by the finer points of hospital scales and official statisticians' calculations, LBW babies appear ideologically both as exemplar and proof of biology's operation in determining the social (obstetrical) product, and of medicine's parallel rhetoric in claiming – in the pursuit of the 'perfect' baby – to repair or mask all known biological flaws. This is one reason why low birthweight as a conceptual category holds such an attraction for maternity care policy-makers concerned with the goal of improving the operation of the maternity services. It also helps to explain why sociologists interested in the dynamics of social relations in health and illness are drawn to the concept of birthweight categories; why, in short, LBW was to become a main focus of the research described in this book.

The debate hung around the key concepts of social class, birthweight and perinatal mortality in the period when the study discussed in this book was conceived and gestated was one which tended to reiterate a highly problematic set of claims: (1) that LBW could be prevented by better, earlier and more appropriate antenatal care; (2) that the background for this was the proven effectiveness of medical antenatal and delivery care in promoting the health, and saving the lives, of mothers and babies; (3) that the background for *this* was the proven effectiveness of professionalized medical care as a means of promoting the health of populations; and by implication (4) that the contribution of LBW to the whole picture of social inequalities in health could effectively be disregarded, as medical care is not designed to treat problems of social inequality.

Three considerations in particular underlie these claims. The first is the tendency within the medical system to tackle problems, whatever their aetiology, by increasing the input of medical care on the assumption that such problems *are treatable* by such means. The assumption that LBW itself can be prevented by more medical care suggests – if we are to follow the habit of dichotomous thinking – that LBW is a biologically caused condition, a fault in the mechanism of the body correctable by the doctor-as-repair-man. The second consideration, which is related to the first, is the *technological* imperative within medicine: the tendency to devise, institute and routinize technologically based strategies for obstinate problems on the assumption that any technology is better than no technology, and a lot of technology is better than a little. Thirdly, there is the pervasive effect of competition between specialities within medicine. The obstetrician's interest is in delivering a live child, preferably one that survives for a week after birth and so does not enter the stillbirth or perinatal mortality statistics, which are yardsticks of the obstetrician's professional competence. The neonatal paediatrician's interest is in keeping the child alive for a long enough period – four weeks – for it not to appear in the neonatal mortality statistics. Babies' lives are thus shifted analytically between statistical categories in the interests of health professionals' claims to expertise.

Even a cursory glance at the stability of the LBW rate over time (figure 1.2) shows that, whatever obstetricians and midwives have been doing in the name of antenatal care, this has not succeeded in altering the incidence of LBW (except for possibly preventing it rising). Health professionals have tried many specific strategies, as well as routine, or routine-intensified, antenatal care to prevent LBW. Specific strategies have included such old-

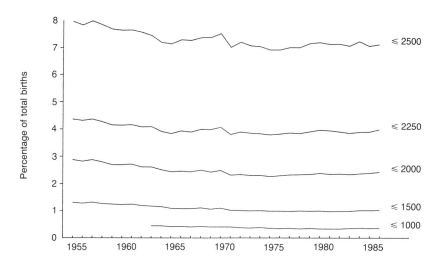

Figure 1.2 Incidence of low birthweight, England and Wales, 1955–1986
Source: DHSS, summaries of LHS 27/1 low birthweight returns

fashioned notions as bed-rest, as well as the more modern ones of serial cervical assessment, cervical cerclage, and electronic monitoring of uterine activity, as well as progestogen, antibiotic and tocolytic drugs. Most of these interventions have been targeted on women at risk of having preterm babies (see Chalmers et al. 1989b; Lumley 1988). More mundanely, routine antenatal care is said to be designed to identify and prevent problems. Indeed, that is its rationale. But, contrary to what most people believe, antenatal care – the system we all know and love whereby pregnant women attend for medical examinations and testing at the pre-set intervals of monthly to 28 weeks, fortnightly to 36 weeks and weekly thereafter – is not the outcome of a carefully controlled scientific evaluation showing it to be a safe, appropriate and effective way of promoting maternal and infant health. Rather, antenatal care routines are an extension of the practices in which a Ministry of Health survey of local authority antenatal clinics of the 1920s found practitioners at the time to be engaged (Ministry of Health 1929). The basis of medical antenatal care is not scientifically proven value, but merely a description of practices as they happen to have evolved.

From the status of medical innovation in the period from about 1915 to 1930 in Britain, antenatal care passed to the status of standard procedure without any kind of formal evaluation. During the 1930s, some unease was voiced about the effectiveness of antenatal care when maternal mortality (deaths of mothers due to childbearing) appeared to be rising in parallel with the numbers of antenatal clinics. But the national birth surveys of 1946, 1958 and 1970 all appeared to confirm the importance of antenatal care to health by drawing attention to the correlation between numbers of antenatal visits and perinatal mortality rates. Interpretation of this correlation as causality was and is common, despite evidence that women who do not attend for antenatal care, or who do so late in pregnancy, tend also to be those with multiple social and/or medical problems, and despite the very obvious rider that some whose babies die give birth to them after a curtailed pregnancy which itself imposes a limit on the number of antenatal visits that can be made (see Oakley 1984).

The medicalization of health

As John McKinlay (1981) has shown, the career of antenatal care is characteristic of the development of many medical innovations. Once having achieved standard procedure status through the enthusiasm of practitioners and policy-makers, such techniques are unlikely ever to be evaluated, as widespread belief in their efficacy leads to claims that evaluation would be unethical: it is argued that it would be unfair to withhold the benefits of the treatment from one group of people – a requirement of such evaluation – in order to establish the effectiveness it is 'known' to possess.

The belief that medical antenatal care is the best means to promote maternal and child health is congruent with a dominant ideology of our times – that health is, first and foremost, a medical product. This notion has been widely questioned by McKeown, Cochrane and Illich, among others (McKeown 1976; Cochrane 1972; Illich 1975). Environmental improvements expressed in the medium of rising living standards are important in securing increased survival and life expectancy in populations, with medical care having a limited impact in terms of specific innovations such as antibiotics, blood transfusions and immunizations. A repeated paradox found when examining historical data is that the rates of deaths due to diseases for which new drug therapies are found often seem to be on a downward curve before the therapy is introduced. One example is puerperal fever, a common cause of maternal mortality for many years. Case-fatality rates for puerperal fever showed a decline before prontosil, the first sulphonamide, was made available (Colebrook and Kenny 1936). Other examples are deaths from smallpox, diphtheria, whooping cough and measles, which were decreasing in virulence well before the immunization era (Mercer 1985). Indeed, a very similar argument could be put for the context in which obstetricians began in the 1970s aggressively to tackle by means of interventions such as induction of labour and serial ultrasound scanning the problem of high perinatal mortality; the rate at which babies died fell consistently in all countries through the 1970s and 1980s, while different obstetric fashions came into practice in different places (Macfarlane and Mugford 1984). Congruent with this lack of fit between medical practices and public health is the discrepancy between expenditure on medical care and death-rates (Cochrane 1979), and the further paradox dubbed by its discoverers 'the anomaly that wouldn't go away' (St Leger et al. 1978) – namely, that the populations with the lowest mortality rates are also those with the fewest doctors.

Recent historical work (Szreter 1988) has criticized the 'McKeown thesis' by drawing attention to the fact that rising living conditions emerge as significant for negative rather than positive reasons – because of what medical interventions cannot explain rather than because of what social conditions are known to do. But, while it can be argued that McKeown may have underestimated the effectiveness of directed human change in instituting important public health reforms in the congested and insanitary conditions of early industrial conurbations, the importance of the main negative point still stands: the curative power of medicine must be *proved*; it cannot be *assumed*. The fact that 'science' cannot prove that medicine produces health is a major weakness of the quantitative paradigm (the right-hand column of table A). It is also the case that we 'know' almost nothing about the contribution medical care may make to the *quality* of people's lives. The preoccupation with death-rates as a measure of health has simply been overwhelming.

Caring for the poor women?

Buried in the pro-medicine views of groups such as the Spastics Society and the House of Commons Committee on Perinatal and Neonatal Mortality in the late 1970s and early 1980s was some awareness that women who used the maternity services had been complaining about them for some time. Indeed, the Social Services Committee report summarized these comments and their significance by saying:

> it is not enough, in our survey of perinatal and neonatal mortality, to concentrate solely on the physical wellbeing of the mother and her baby. The emotional support provided by the maternity services, although more difficult to define, is also of major importance. We would regard a mother who has produced a healthy baby but looks back on her pregnancy as an experience she does not wish to repeat as evidence of a failure on the part of the maternity services. (Social Services Committee 1980: 91)

Medical care can be a significant source of stress. Some of the key themes that stand out in a very large literature of 'consumer' studies amassed in the UK, North America and elsewhere in the postwar period are the fact that care is experienced as depersonalized – women feel they have the status of objects on an assembly line; lack of continuity of care – never seeing the same doctor or midwife more than once or twice; bland reassurance (or silence) in place of information; over-use (and under-justification) of technologies such as ultrasound scanning and induction of labour; the anxiety engendered by antenatal visits; organizational problems such as long waiting times and lack of childcare facilities; and the tendency of health professionals to ignore women's reports of social problems and complaints of what may appear to be 'minor' symptoms. According to a recent review, 'A common finding of many of the studies of women's views of care throughout the childbearing period has been the lack of respect shown by the caregivers, both to the women themselves, and to their family commitments and responsibilities' (Reid and Garcia 1989: 133–4).

Most of this literature dates from the 1960s, which was the beginning of the era of modern obstetrics, with its emphasis on increasing hospital-delivery rates, growth in centralized care, and the 'need' for new types of monitoring to survey the progress of pregnancy. Delving into the history of antenatal care before this produces some quite markedly contrasting examples. As I have argued elsewhere (Oakley 1984), women's responses to antenatal care, when taken together with the professional rationale of expanding the territory obstetricians can claim to know more about than anyone else, add up to a situation in which 'control' rather than 'care' has become the motif of the maternity services. There are, of course, exceptions to this rule, and the position of midwives is in some difficulty because of it. None the less, any informed reading of both sides of the case suggests that antenatal care has increasingly lost its 'care' component and become a package of other things – surveillance, monitoring, social control. Since most obstetricians are men and all the users of the maternity services are women, the gender-based dichotomies listed in table A also apply here. When placed in the context of other power relations, we have, then, a situation in which a patriarchal structure contextualizes the way the antenatal services are provided and used – the discourse of encounters between doctors and 'their' patients.

The gender inequalities of medical encounters are only one of several types of inequality which inform these: others are inequalities of race, class and heterosexism. One of these – class inequality – was an important reason for the research design of the Social Support and Pregnancy Outcome study. As table 1.1 demonstrated, the ratio of perinatal deaths is about 1:2 in favour of middle-class households. This direction of difference holds for other reproductive outcomes, including miscarriage, congenital malformations such as neural tube malformations and oral clefts, and preterm delivery (Oakley et al. 1982). Anyone who faces the task of unravelling the many factors associated with membership of different social classes that may be responsible for these different rates must feel daunted at the range of circumstances that need to be considered: direct and indirect effects of employment and household work; disposable income and its distribution within the household; housing conditions; access to and use of educational, health and welfare services; nutrition (including smoking and alcohol); selective movement between classes (the argument that those in poorer health move 'downwards' and vice versa); changes in the definition and social grading of occupations over time, and in the sizes of different classes. Once again, these class differences in reproduction form part of a much broader picture of class differences in health, illness and mortality (see e.g. Hart 1986; Sagan 1987; Smith et al. 1990).

Studies show both that stressful life events and circumstances are unequally distributed among social class groups, and that these are implicated in a range of reproductive difficulties, including preterm delivery, low birthweight, the need for obstetric intervention in delivery and the need for specialist medical care after birth (see Oakley et al. 1982, for a review). The concept of stress, though problematic, because ambiguously defined and used, none the less provides a promising theoretical tool in bridging the divisions of the two models shown in table A. So far as pregnancy is concerned, the idea that mothers' stressful experiences may expose fetuses to harm receives support from a large group of studies, some of which are discussed in chapter 2. In this context, women's responses to antenatal 'care' may not in themselves be health-promoting. For example, Wendy Farrant's (1980) study of antenatal blood tests showed how such tests may be experienced as anxiety-creating, and thus lead to increased smoking and alcohol consumption. The recognition that medical 'care' may involve stress for the mother goes back a long way, though its inclusion in twentieth-century obstetric textbooks conflicts, as Emily Martin (1987) shows, with the medical construction of women's bodies as 'involuntary' birth machines.

What seemed to emerge quite clearly, then, from my research on antenatal care, within the context of the NPEU's epidemiological work, and within the general framework of the hyperbolical media and pressure-group emphasis in the late 1970s and early 1980s on the dire state of Britain's maternity services, was that whatever research did next should in some way bring together the two sides of table A. It should be an attempt to integrate medical and sociological understandings of a phenomenon that both is social and has been made medical, that captures both the intellectual imagination and the attention of policy-makers and politicians – in short, the problem of why some women become mothers more easily than others, and why those who have difficulty are more likely to live in conditions of social and material disadvantage. The appeal of such a study was twofold. One, it promised an enhanced understanding of the 'problem of low birthweight' as conceived by medical science. Two, it offered a framework for achieving something of importance to social science, in the integration of so-called 'qualitative' and 'quantitative' research methods.

At this point the vast universe of literature on social support was virtually unknown to me. But I had an idea, born of another set of experiences, that seemed to me at least worth testing within this context.

'I've really enjoyed having someone to talk to'

Writing up a previous project at the end of the 1970s on women's transition into first-time motherhood, I was struck by the particular insight that the process of interviewing itself could be seen as a socially supportive experience. Most of the women interviewed for this project had said how good it was to take part in the research, and to have had a chance to talk about the things that concerned or delighted them. Some went further in answer to a question about whether the research had affected their experience of becoming a mother: their answers are shown in table 1.2. Nearly three-quarters said their experiences had been altered by the research, most commonly because they had thought about these more, or found it reassuring or a positive relief to unburden themselves of critical feelings and experiences. The women in the study also asked a great many questions of their interviewers. The categories of questions are shown in table 1.3. This to me was evidence of two important aspects of the research

Table 1.2   The impact of research on participants: 'transition to motherhood' study

Impact of research	*% of women*[a]
Has the research affected your experience of becoming a mother?	
No	27
Yes	73
Thought about it more	30[b]
Found it reassuring	25[b]
A relief to talk	30[b]
Changed attitudes/behaviour	7[b]

[a]Total number of women = 66.
[b]Percentages do not add up to 100, as multiple answers were possible.
Source: Oakley 1979a

process: one, that it revealed a great need for information that was not being met by the health professionals the women were seeing; two, that the ability to put these requests to an interviewer might be one dimension of the generalized social support a research interview offered.

As a consequence I argued (Oakley 1981a) that women interviewing women may be regarded as a contradiction in terms. Interviews possess a

Table 1.3   Questions asked by interviewees of interviewers: 'transition to motherhood' study

Questions asked	%
General (N = 214)	24
Of which:	
Personal questions	61
Questions about the research	24
Advice questions	15
Information requests (N = 664)	76
Of which:	
Medical procedures	31
Organizational procedures	19
Physiology of reproduction	15
Baby care/development/feeding	21
Other	14

Total number of women = 66.
Source: Oakley 1979a

dual, and double-edged, status: as a research tool – a way of collecting data – and as a *social* relationship. In the study of the transition to motherhood, these insights were confined to the situation of women researchers interviewing women. Both the women interviewed and those doing the interviewing shared social characteristics because of our structural social position as a 'minority' group. These perspectives on interviewing contrasted with the textbook model, in which interviewers are agents of objectivity and data-gathering machines, and interviewees agents of subjectivity or data-yielding machines.

In 1992 it is not unusual to find sociologists openly discussing experiences of social science interviewing which deviate from the strictures outlined in the research methods textbooks. Far from finding interviewing a difficult exercise in which the interviewer must struggle to achieve rapport and obtain data, at the same time as maintaining 'distance' and striving for 'objectivity', many researchers find that encouraging other people to talk about themselves is relatively easy and enjoyable, and that its success does not hang on the maintenance of social distance within the context of a hierarchical relationship (see e.g. Finch 1984).

Others (see e.g. Malseed 1987) have since pointed out some of the weaknesses in my initial statement of the case for a different view of interviewing – for example, the fact that my own identity as a white middle-class woman may have encouraged certain sorts of mutual identification over others. As Janet Finch (1984: 85) has said, the 'siding with' the subject that is characteristic of feminist interviewing is 'entirely consistent with major traditions in sociological research, in which . . . the sociologist sides with the underdog'.[4] But the essential difference is that a feminist researcher doing research on women shares the powerless position of those she researches; this carries the corollary of an emotional as well as an intellectual commitment to promoting those interests. 'How else can one justify having taken from them the very private information which may have been given so readily?' Finch asks. She finds unconvincing the argument that justifies disclosure of private information on the grounds of adding to knowledge, and rather more comfortable the notion that this is a means to the end of creating a sociology *for* women (rather than one *of* women – see D. E. Smith 1979).

The tendency for social research to act on and transform the social world at the same time as studying it has always been regarded as one of the main ways in which the 'science' element in 'social science' cannot be regarded as equivalent to that in the natural sciences. Sociologists speak disparagingly of the 'Hawthorne effect' as the best-known – and certainly the most frequently quoted – example of this. The Hawthorne study carried out in the USA in the 1930s concerned the productivity of factory workers. Researchers were interested in finding out if brighter illumination would raise productivity. At first it seemed as if this were the case, but the same effect was then obtained with lights of a lower intensity, suggesting that some other factor apart from the absolute level of illumination was involved. The study is often cited in the methods books as an example of poor design – there should have been a control group whose working conditions were not altered, so that meaningful comparisons could be made with productivity in the experimental group where lighting conditions *were* being changed. However, the Hawthorne effect is much more simply a demonstration of the central thesis of sociology: that people are social beings. The workers in the study were responding to the interest shown in them by the researchers. Such findings are witness to the falsity of 'scientism', which, as Capra (1983) says, has consistently undervalued intuition, emotion, feeling and direct individual experience as ways of knowing. The undervaluation of these ways of knowing in both the social and the natural sciences has gone hand-in-hand with the biomedical model of human beings as physical bodies subject to malfunctioning. Disease is the breakdown of the machine, the doctor's task is repair by physical or chemical means, and the theory underpinning this sees the body as cellular or molecular biology, not inhabiting the same frame as a psyche, an identity, a social being intimately connected to the social and material world. In aping the natural sciences, sociology thus committed itself to a biologically determinist model of behaviour – and has spent much of its (relatively short) life trying to come to terms with, or escape from, the inevitable problems this poses.

All of this amounts to at least part of the explanation as to why feminist sociologists in particular have often opted to use 'qualitative' methods in their work. As their name suggests, such methods allow for an exploration of the quality rather than the quantity of experiences; they allow for the study of meanings, and of processes, rather than the relationships between events. Most qualitative work employs small samples and in-depth tape-recorded interviewing. Embedded within that activity called women's studies, qualitative research methods thus also do seem to offer the potential for generating a sociology *for* women as endorsed by Finch and others. It is less clear how a sociology for women can be erected on the foundations of quantitative work.

Shouting 'Eureka'

As the end of one research contract came into sight, generating the need to get on with obtaining the next one, all these various strands of experience came together into a single fairly simple idea. Phrased as a question, this became 'Can social support in pregnancy improve the health of women and their babies?' The operationalization of the question in research terms was to prove complex, but its early formulation had the advantage of seeming both to build logically on my previous work and interests, and to take me forward into the future in a new and challenging way.

Intellectual reflexivity within any paradigm of knowledge is difficult. In the epigraph to this chapter, the image of the sociological researcher as passenger, imprinted like a photographic negative, offers itself both as descriptor and as object of criticism. On the one hand, the motives of those who ride in buses seem obvious and reasonable. On the other, it is only by getting off the bus that one may gain any clear evaluation of what riding in it was like.

One of the issues here is what kind of activity research itself 'is'. Published versions of research in both the social and the natural sciences are forms of reconstructed logic. They have, as Silverman (1985: 4) has said, 'a problematic relation to how the research was carried out and, more certainly, to how it was conceived – jumping out of the bath and shouting "Eureka" is not, after all, something to be emphasized in a sober scientific journal.' The notion of intellectual work as a simple unilinear process is part of the problem – part of the misleading ideology of the 'rational' scientist mode of knowledge (the right-hand side of table A again). Even more fundamentally, the problem is how to attempt to advance knowledge at the same time as being critical about the process and model of knowledge-construction itself. Thus it is difficult, if not impossible, to debate the determinants of reproductive health without using a terminology which carries its own limiting cultural baggage. The very title of the SSPO study appears to confirm the two-models divide of table A: social support *and* pregnancy outcome. The social, the qualitative, the hard-to-measure, on the one side; the biological, the quantitative, the easy-to-measure, on the other. Though this was not the only definition of pregnancy outcome used in the study, there was an emphasis on the biological in the use of birthweight as *the* outcome. 'Pregnancy outcome' is a bit like 'obstetrical product'; of course pregnancies have outcomes and obstetricians work to produce something, but is this how, conscious of our humanness, we wish to speak of the births of human beings and the labours of those (women) who give them life?

'Labour' describes what women do to give birth to children and what men and women do to make goods and services for use or exchange in home or marketplace. The double meaning produces a double irony:

> When anthropologists, armed with concepts of production and labour that they associate with work done primarily by men in factories and enterprises outside the home, try to describe preindustrial societies, they often completely overlook the labour that women do; when medical doctors describe the labour that women do in childbirth, their expectations centre on how labour of other kinds is organized in our society and how technology and machinery can be used to control those who labour. In both cases women lose, in the first by being overlooked, and in the second by having a complex process that interrelates physical, emotional and mental experience treated as if it could be broken down and managed like other forms of production. (Martin 1987: 66)

Reproduction, which is not a derivative of production, is increasingly subject to commodification. With the rise of the artificial reproduction industry, ova, semen and uteruses join babies on the commodity assembly line as products to be manipulated, bartered for, and sold as industrial materials (Rothman 1989). This industry is dominated and controlled by men (Corea 1985).

As authors such as Harding (1986), Hartsock (1984) and Rose (1986) have argued, the masculine domination of science and of society both result in, and are preceded by, profoundly gender-differentiated life experiences. Masculinity itself is in some sense attained by resistance to the enclosing structures of everyday domestic life: in reaching for the world 'outside' this, abstract conceptual experience is conceived as preferable to the demeaningly concrete (Hartsock 1984).

Sandra Harding has pointed out a further critical characterization of the scientific enterprise in modern society – that it is 'sacred':

> We are told that human understanding is decreased rather than increased by attempting to account for the nature and situation of scientific activity in the ways science recommends accounting for all other social activity. This belief makes science sacred. Perhaps it even removes scientists from the realm of the completely human.

It is thus 'taboo to suggest that natural science ... is ... a historically varying set of social practices ... that a *thoroughgoing* and *scientific* appreciation of sciences requires descriptions and explanations of the regularities and underlying causal tendencies of science's own social practices and beliefs' (Harding 1986: 38–9). The social and political construction of gender, the economic system, and the pursuit of understanding through science are all, therefore, linked. It can be argued that the social construction of science as an 'objective, value-neutral' activity acts effectively to legitimate patriarchal social relations, as in the contention that scientific inquiry can yield abstract and absolute truths about nature, thus making science 'the instrument for "man's" domination of the world' (Harding 1986).

If women are largely alienated from science thus defined, then this helps to explain the fondness of women social scientists for methods of studying the social world that are distant from the quantitative, mechanistic and manipulative model of how the natural sciences operate. Even this is not straightforward, however. Geneticist Barbara McClintock's account of how in her work on the cytogenetics of maize she came to see the Neurospora chromosomes provides an alternative version of scientific activity as it 'really' is which is at odds with the way it is said to be (Keller 1983). What is startling about McClintock's account is the importance of the capacity of union with what is to be known in facilitating the scientist's understanding of the inherent lawfulness of nature. The feeling of union is quite compatible with the viewpoint that nature *is* lawful. But empathy, rather than opposition, is more productive as an approach to law discovery. In other words, the union of social and natural is as integral to natural as it is to social science. All of which suggests that what is required as an endpoint as well as a method is an 'integrated understanding of the relationship between the biological and the social' (Rose et al. 1984: 10).

The problem, however, is how to arrive at this point without employing the dualistic language of table A. The account provided in this book is only a partial and personal attempt to arrive at the endpoint in a way that seeks above all to be *conscious* of the epistemological routes adopted and fixes thus uncovered. What I have chosen to do is to spell out in some detail each of the methodological steps in the process of doing the research, together with the theoretical and ideological assumptions on which these appear to be based. It is these that very often invite critiques of the kind referred to above. One result of my approach is that I may frequently appear not only to be pushing the bus uphill (downhill, with the brakes on?) and sitting in it at the same time, but also standing in the road simply staring blankly and uncomprehendingly at it.

The detailed story of the SSPO research is continued in chapter 4. The next two chapters explore the two central hypotheses of the study design: that social support is good for health and that only controlled evaluations can test such notions effectively. By taking a critical journey through the landscape of previous work, we map more precisely the itinerary and destination of the SSPO study.

2

'A Friend a Day Keeps the Doctor Away': Social Support and Health

Just as the *Penicillium* mould was once looked on as a bothersome bacteriostatic contaminant that spoiled culture growths, so the placebo effect has sometimes been considered an unwanted therapeutic contaminant that interfered with efforts to isolate specific remedies. (Adler and Hammett 1973: 595)

In a study of Nazi concentration camp survivors, the people who experienced most problems recovering from their ordeal were those who were moved from camp to camp during and after the war; by comparison, those survivors who had stayed in one camp fared better (Davidson 1979). In Alameda County, California, people who in 1965 belonged to a church or temple were two and a half times more likely to be alive nine years later than people without such an affiliation (Berkman and Syme 1979). A 1960s study of mice revealed that mice placed in a conflict situation were more likely to develop hypertension when with strange mice rather than with their litter mates (Henry et al. 1967). An investigation of the growth of barley seeds demonstrated that seeds watered from a beaker held for fifteen minutes in a healer's hand grew faster and taller and had a greater yield than seeds not so watered (Grad 1963). One hundred and eight people in Czechoslovakia suffering from a variety of psychological and physical disorders were given thirteen types of non-active (placebo) pills over two years; 51 per cent got better; twenty-five patients experienced side-effects, including somnolence, insomnia, palpitations, irritability, low blood pressure, headache, diarrhoea and collapse; such side-effects were more likely when the pills were reddish-grey, or greyish-green-yellow, whereas yellow-white or plain white capsules were least likely to evoke unpleasant reactions (Honzak et al. 1972).

Among the social origins of the Social Support and Pregnancy Outcome study, as we saw in chapter 1, was the idea that social support is good for health. What follows is not intended to be a comprehensive review. Such reviews exist (see e.g. Berkman 1984; Cohen and Syme 1985; Cohen and Wills 1985; Dean 1986; Gottlieb 1981a; Leavy 1983; Oakley 1985; Oakley 1988; Schaefer et al. 1981). Instead, this chapter is an attempt to draw together ideas, insights and problems from disparate areas of sociology, psychology, psychiatry, history, epidemiology and medicine to address the question: why, in the first place, should anyone suppose that social support can be helpful to childbearing women and their families?

The rising star of social support

The concept of 'social support' first rose to prominence in the 1970s. The American epidemiologist, Lisa Berkman, who has been responsible, together with colleagues, for some of the most revealing analyses in this field, puts it thus:

> From shopping bags in California bearing 'Friends make good medicine' to editorials in the *Journal of the American Medical Association*, 'A Friend, Not an Apple, a Day will Help Keep the Doctor Away', the message is that social support is both good preventive and curative medicine. Like chicken soup, its powers are believed to be pervasive, the reasons for its effects are unknown, and knowledge of its qualities is widespread and based on folk wisdom . . . From interactions among mice litter mates to collegiality among university graduates, evidence has been garnered to support the notion that social ties are related to good health and well-being. (Berkman 1984: 413).

Increase in research interest in social support was exponential: the number of articles in the Social Science Citation Index with the term 'social support' in the title rose from two in 1972 to over fifty in 1982 (House and Kahn 1985); in the two years from 1982 to 1984 the literature contained more citations on social support than in the whole of the previous decade (Wortman 1984). Of the forty-six studies included by Richard Leavy (1983) in his review of social support and psychological disorder, over 80 per cent were carried out after 1978.

This changing fashion amounts to what Badura (1985: 3) has termed a 'paradigm shift' in theories about health. Like most such shifts, this one is partly a question of reinventing the wheel. Scattered observations for hundreds of years have drawn attention to the importance in the genesis of illness of how people feel about their social environments (see e.g. Home 1794; Snow 1893). The healing support of friendship was commented on by Francis Bacon, among others, who said – meaning, presumably, to include both sexes – that 'this communicating of a man's self to his friend works two contrary effects; for it redoubleth joys, and cutteth griefs in half. For there is no man that imparteth his joys to his friend, but he joyeth the more, and no man that imparteth his griefs to his friend, but he grieveth the less' (Bacon, quoted in Henderson et al. 1981: 11). Bacon's understanding of friendship may have been limited by the cultural and intellectual habits of the time. But somewhat more surprising, in view of its name – the knowledge or wisdom (*logos*) of a friend (*socius*) – is the way in which sociology ignored until recently the field of friendship and of 'sociable' relationships. Although it is recognized as significant in everyday life, there has been little serious analysis of friendship as a form of personal relationship occurring in modern industrialized societies. Friendship has been treated as peripheral to the core economic and social relations of capitalism: 'It is seen as an extra, as something that adds a little flavour to social life, but which of itself is relatively unimportant in the nitty-gritty of economic and social organisation. In other words, in a somewhat unsociological fashion, friendship is taken to be essentially a personal matter, rather than one which has any social interest or consequence' (Allan 1989: 1–2). Although the community studies of the late 1950s and 1960s put interpersonal ties back on the ecological map by demonstrating that the social changes of increasing urbanization and industrialization had not banished a sense of community, the focus in these studies was not on the personal meanings of friendship; the individual was hidden behind the screen of the household and the family. The dominant traditions within sociology have not encouraged an interest in friendship, reflecting as they do narrowly economic or specifically gendered theories of the division of social and sociological labour. When the world is divided into the male-dominated public domain of work, and the female-dominated private domain of the family, the conceptual leap required to envisage friendship as bridging these categories has usually proved too much for the sociological imagination.

There are other reasons, too. While gender is the most significant social factor affecting friendship patterns (Bell 1981), the historical importance of friendships, particularly among women, has been veiled by a deep-seated cultural anxiety about the 'sexual' meaning of these (Raymond 1986). Friendship as one of four great forms of love (Lewis 1960) has been demoted by the primary twentieth-century definition of love as powered by the sexual impulse (Faderman 1981). As generic categories, love and feelings are poorly understood as sociological phenomena (Alberoni 1983; Bendelow 1992; Hochschild 1975). The reasons why these extraordinarily important areas of human life have not been part of scientific study are linked with the gendered nature both of life and of science: love, friendship and connections with others are women's matters, while science must ignore matters of the heart (Miller 1976; Rose 1986). A web of classist and sexist assumptions ties the sociological literature on family and community together, so that the working classes (especially the women) are seen to rely on kin for social contacts, while the middle classes (especially the men) are seen as transcending this primitive dependence and choosing with whom they associate (see Allan 1979; Oakley and Rajan 1991). Furthermore, the study of sociable relations has been dominated by quantification: contact rates are regarded as the prime measure of sociability, and taken as indicators of quality (Allan 1979: 10).

Conceptually, social support overlaps with friendship, and both with family, kin and neighbourhood relations. While interest in social support and sociable relations is now increasing in different fields, this is nowhere more so than in the study of health.

The weakness of the medical model

An important reason for the current 'fashion' in social support research is the increasing realization that conventional risk factors are able to explain only a small part of the picture of individual and group differences in health, death and disease. Because the exploration of health has traditionally been framed as the search for factors causing disease, the 'set' of this literature is not towards how to explain health by identifying 'benefit' factors, but rather towards how to understand death in terms of 'risk' factors. For example, as regards cardiovascular disease – a main and increasing cause of death in modern industrialized societies – research has shown that conventional medical risk factors such as high blood pressure, cholesterol levels and smoking are only able to explain about half of the disease that occurs. That is, these factors leave 40–50 per cent of the variance between individuals unexplained (Badura 1985). In one large German longitudinal study, 15 per cent of the heart disease patients were free of any of the standard risk factors (Badura 1985). In one of the best-known studies in this area, the UK Whitehall study of civil servants, the health of men in different 'grades' of the service was examined in relation to a range of risk factors (Marmot et al. 1984). While blood pressure predicted mortality *within* grades, men in lower grades with the *same* blood pressure as men in higher grades had higher mortality (Marmot 1987). A second major reason for the development of social support research has been evidence about the persistence (or re-emergence) of social class differences in illness and death. These first began to be noted when systematic statistics started to be collected in the late nineteenth century (see Farr 1885). The category of causes of death more common in social class V than in social class I is large, and includes bronchitis, pneumonia, most cancers, peptic ulcer, cerebrovascular disease, suicide and motor vehicle accidents. A few diseases, for example cancer of the colon, show no social class differences, and for a few others, for example, myeloid leukaemia, lymphosarcoma, Hodgkin's disease, melanoma and cancer of the testis, there is a reverse social class gradient (Madge and Marmot 1987). Though there are differences between countries, a similar pattern is to be found for the USA, France, Germany and Finland, and to a lesser extent in the Netherlands, Norway and Sweden.

In Britain and elsewhere, the state health and welfare provision set up after the Second World War was widely regarded as the solution to these inequalities in health. But by the 1960s the observation was being made that social class differences in mortality and morbidity had persisted despite this intended redistribution of life-chances. Social class differences had even emerged for some causes of death that had not previously been class-differentiated: working-class people were worse off in new ways (Fox 1988). Careful attempts to address the 'artefactual' explanation of this phenomenon – the argument that the less healthy move downwards in the social scale – succeeded in showing the persistence and widening of 'real' differentials over time; though the evidence considered, like much in this area, was limited to a consideration of *men's* experiences. As noted in chapter 1, the different meanings and patterning of work for women have made them marginal to a scheme of social classification premised on the notion that it is only men who 'work' (Goldblatt 1989). Domestic labour has not been considered an occupation relevant to health. Since women predominate in this sphere, the failure to consider how domestic work affects the worker is more serious for women, but it also applies to men. Thus in one example of a Swedish study of social influences on mortality, which examined the experiences of men in 1913 and 1923, the checklist of activities that formed part of the inquiry omitted all home-based forms of labour (Welin et al. 1985).

Social class differences in health and disease, as has so often been said, explain nothing in themselves. The material and psychological conditions of different forms of labour and different domestic circumstances are likely to be important, and have multiple ramifications. But it is possible, too, that different positions in the social structure lock into social connectedness in different ways. With the documentation of social inequalities in health outcomes came an intensified search for the ways in which people's relationships to the social structure may impinge on their health. While a large part of the research on medical risk factors and health outcomes has been confined to men and to heart disease, and has focused on mortality, a disproportionate share of the studies on social risk factors have been carried out on populations of women suffering from psychological problems or from female cancers. Gender-blindness is a feature of this research area, as it is of many others. This is despite the fact that there are gender differences in social connectedness, medical risks and health which may offer clues to the development of enhanced theoretical understandings of the whole area. For example, it is well known that marriage represents a different kind of social bond for men and for women (Madge and Marmot 1987; Bernard 1973). In the prospective community health study in Alameda County, California, significant differences in mortality rates by marital status were found for men but not for women (Berkman and Breslow 1983). In this study, four categories of social relationship formed what the researchers called a Social Network Index: (1) marital state, (2) friends and relations, (3) church membership, (4) group membership. The Social Network Index proved to be differently related to the main causes of death for men and for women. For ischaemic heart disease and 'other' causes of death (including respiratory and digestive diseases, accidents and suicide) the Social Network Index was a stronger discriminator for women, whereas for cerebrovascular and other circulatory disease, it discriminated better for men (for cancer the sexes were more or less the same) (Berkman and Syme 1979). Other studies have found long-term increased mortality following bereavement among widowers, but not among widows (Helsing et al. 1981; Susser 1981). It is a common finding that women report more supportive relationships than men at all stages of the life cycle (Leavy 1983), though they are also more likely than men to be critical of the level and quality of support. Taken in combination with these other findings, the fact that women also show higher levels of morbidity, particularly psychological morbidity, may contain some important pointers not only to the broad understanding of gender and health, but to an unravelling of the mysteries of social support.

A third important spur to the empirical investigation of the way in which social relationships impinge on health has been the social support deficits of medicine itself. Here the 'consumer dissatisfaction' literature has listed a litany of grievances, including

> objections to the impersonal manner in which patients or clients are treated at the hands of efficiency-minded professional practitioners; frustrations encountered in their attempts to find their way through a health care bureaucracy that has become so specialized as to mystify the average consumer, and so fragmented as to render most services either incomplete or redundant; criticism of a system of care that in its awe of high technology and sophisticated interventions, tends to downplay the patient's role in effecting change and to entirely overlook the role his or her family members and close friends can play in the course of treatment; and, finally, vexations in the face of a health care enterprise committed neither to the preventive tasks of identifying and neutralizing psychosocial stressors in the environment, nor to the work of promoting health through environmental action.
> (Gottlieb 1981c: 29)

What is social support?

As Madge and Marmot (1987: 93) have observed, 'There seems to be little controversy, either among the academic or the lay population, that something about social relationships can be good for health, although quite what is important remains unclear.' This question – what is social support – is clearly crucial, not only to the literature drawn on in this chapter, but to the Social Support and Pregnancy Outcome study itself. The question weaves its way in and out of the text of this book. So far as the technical literature is concerned, there are almost as many definitions as there are studies. Most researchers would agree with Richard Leavy (1983: 3) that 'While most of us have a feel for what support involves, a mere feel for a concept does little to provide a theoretical framework for research and intervention efforts.' Some researchers provide only the vaguest definitions of social support, while others, though precise, are circular or even counter-intuitive. The notion that social support consists of support that is social is one such offering (Lin et al. 1979). Another begs all the important and interesting questions by viewing social support as whatever makes people healthy (Beels 1981). Although we may be tempted to view social support as universally and intrinsically beneficial, such a definition not only makes hypothesis-testing research impossible, but also counters some of the evidence we already have that support both given and received may be experienced as more of a burden than a benefit, particularly in situations involving serious illness (see DiMatteo and Hays 1981). In certain common conditions, including cancer and miscarriage (see Oakley et al. 1990a), it is a commonplace that 'supportive' behaviours towards the 'ill' person are frequently perceived as unhelpful, though they are equally frequently understood to be offered with benign intent. Close friends are not always able to provide more useful support and help than more distant contacts, whose very unfamiliarity with the issues at stake can facilitate needed formation and advice (Wellman 1979). This observation is at the heart of the understanding of research as a social process. Without people's willingness to unburden themselves to researchers (whom they did not previously know), many of the studies referred to in this book would not have been possible, nor, indeed, would the SSPO study itself, building, as it did, self-consciously, on the insight that important social support may be derived from the process of 'being interviewed'.

There are now more than twenty instruments for assessing social support in population surveys (Marmot 1987). According to Leavy (1983: 16), none of these constitutes an 'assessment instrument which comprehensively measures the central components of social support with acceptable levels of reliability or validity'. In a review of the concept of social support as applied to pregnancy, Brown (1986: 4) notes:

> The domain assigned to social support varies from the expansive view that support is the overriding construct for the provision of social relationships, to the specifically focussed view that support is information, nurturance, empathy, encouragement, validating behaviour, constructive genuineness, sharedness and reciprocity, instrumental help, or recognition of competence. *The nature and specificity of each definition of social support depends on the study for which it was designed.* (italics added)

Some researchers have included in their definitions of social support the availability of material resources, such as income and housing, or have taken dissatisfaction with work or housing situations as indicators of low social support (see the discussion in Thoits 1982). But poverty is neither analytically nor experientially equivalent to impoverished social ties. Similarly with arguments such as that of Cobb (1976: 303), that any association between the extent to which pregnant women 'want' their babies and the risk of low birthweight is to be explained causally as a growth-retarding effect of the transmission of information from mother to fetus concerning 'wantedness': this is to conflate the cultural representation of motives for motherhood with the effects of stress on childbearing, rather than to understand how both are materially produced by the 'institution' of motherhood.

Conceptual confusion extends to the equation of social support with social class (see Oakley and Rajan 1991). Or social support may be viewed as coterminous with marriage, though, as Gottlieb observes, 'One need not to be a clinician to recognize that family members and friends do not always merit the appellation "support system", and the fact that this sort of labelling is widespread in the literature reveals something about the romanticism or myopia that has seeped into research on the topic of social support' (Gottlieb 1981c: 30). Pursuing such romantic assumptions to their logical conclusion, the position is easily reached that the very *existence* of a social relationship implies that support is derived from it, which is clearly not the case: 'The fact of the matter is that people must have connections with other people in order to receive social support, but social connectedness is not equivalent to, nor is it a guarantee of access to, social support' (Gottlieb 1981b: 206). This basic caveat is illustrated in Wellman's (1979) research on the intimate ties of Toronto's East Yorkers. Wellman found that, although most (61 per cent) people said they had at least five intimate ties, only 30 per cent of these 'intimates' were regarded as sources of help in emergencies, and only 22 per cent were considered to help with everyday needs. Further, and as Leavy (1983: 11) has said, 'Having support is one thing; being satisfied with it is another.'

Different aspects and types of social relationships must be distinguished from one another. This is particularly so as regards unravelling the links between social relationships and different health outcomes. The failure to distinguish accurately what is at issue may result in misleading conclusions being drawn about the significance of particular social ties. For example, Brown and Harris's (1978) path-breaking work on the health-protecting effects of an intimate relationship with a man for women at risk of developing depression might lead to generalizations about the health-promoting effects of heterosexual intimacy *per se*, were it not for other studies which indicate that the intimate in question may be either male or female, and that a crucial component of the relationship is instrumental rather than purely emotional help (see Miller and Ingham 1976; Paykel et al. 1980; Roy 1978; Slater and Depue 1981; Surtees 1980).

The task of researching social support requires definitions at both conceptual and theoretical levels and in deciding how the concept is to be 'operationalized', that is, measured. At the conceptual/theoretical level, probably the most often quoted definition is Cobb's, according to which social support is 'information leading the subject to believe that he [*sic*] is cared for and loved . . . esteemed and valued . . . [and] that he belongs to a network of communication and mutual obligation' (Cobb 1976: 300). It is remarkable that, as Leavy (1983) notes, only one study has collected information on how 'ordinary' people see social support. This study showed that what the researcher called 'emotionally sustaining behaviour' (which included listening, showing concern and conveying intimacy) was the most valued single feature of social support. Second in importance were 'problem-solving behaviours', for example material, including financial, help (Gottlieb 1978).

The distinction between emotional, informational and instrumental aspects of social bonds is commonly made, as by Schaefer and colleagues:

> *Emotional* support includes intimacy and attachment, reassurance, and being able to confide in and rely on another – all of which contribute to the feeling that one is loved or cared about, or even that one is a member of the group, not a stranger. *Tangible* support involves direct aid or services and can include loans, gifts of money or goods, and provision of services such as taking care of needy persons or doing a chore for them. *Informational* support includes giving information and advice which could help a person solve a problem and providing feedback about how a person is doing. (Schaefer et al. 1981: 385–6)

These distinctions are summed up in Kahn and Antonucci's (1980) phrase, the 'three A's – affect, affirmation and aid'.

No excursion into the social support literature gets very far without encountering the notion of social network. The basic idea is simple: social ties do not form isolated units but are interconnected, so that one person's friends and relatives are likely to know each other, and the extent of interconnectedness between network members then becomes potentially a feature of the social support available to any individual. Within the sociological study of relationships, the idea of social network gained particular currency with Elizabeth Bott's study of *Family and Social Network* in the late 1950s. Bott showed that the types of relationships married couples had with one another were linked with the types and extent of relationships beyond the immediate household. Marriages in which husband and wife tended to have a degree of separation between their roles were more likely than 'joint role relationships' to be linked with extended family ties.

Networks provide shared norms, values and ideologies, whereas individual relationships lack this collective consensual element. Network analysis is thus often hailed in the social support literature as providing a solution to the methodological problem that asking people about their social support at the same time as measuring their wellbeing runs the risk that those who feel well will rate their social support positively, whereas those who feel ill will rate the same amount of social support more negatively. Network analysis is viewed as providing a quantitative entrée to the field, a way of circumventing the potential 'bias' of subjective perceptions. However, the finding that social network size is less closely related to health outcomes than perceived social support, and that the relationship between network size and perceived support is due to overlap between the two measures (Schaefer et al. 1981), has posed something of a challenge to this quantitative solution. In practice, it has proved important to take into account other features of social networks aside from quantity, including density (the extent to which network members are in contact with one another), accessibility (including geographical proximity and material resources such as transport and telephones), stability over time and reciprocity.

But it has been argued that, as a measure of the sheer *quantity* of relationships an individual has, social networks show some positive relationship to *physical* health outcomes (Orth-Gomer and Unden 1987). Conversely, the *quality* of relationships is seen as more important to *psychological* wellbeing (Porritt 1979; Barrera 1981). Given the pervasiveness of the underlying dichotomous thinking, this neat representation *within* social support research of the cultural discourse set out in table A is perhaps not surprising.

Choice of strategies for measuring social support depends on many factors, including researchers' predilections as to the fruitfulness of different measures. An unusual assessment of social support is Norman Cousins's description of how he evaluated the effect of tackling a collagen disease with the dual strategy of laughter and large doses of vitamin C. The hiring of Marx brothers' films to make Cousins laugh rested on the scientifically untested premise that happiness has biochemical effects. He discovered 'that a few minutes of solid belly laughter would give me an hour or more of pain-free sleep'. Watching the Marx brothers resulted in lowered white-cell counts, despite the fact that 'At that time, of course, nothing was known about the ability of the brain to produce or activate secretions called endorphins that have painkilling capabilities' (Cousins 1989: 14). But Cousins's choice of treatment had the unanticipated side-effect of disturbing other hospital patients, who were denied the direct benefits of laughter therapy: the result was his premature discharge from hospital. There have been other cinematographical experiments. Lennart Levi and colleagues in Sweden showed four different films on successive evenings to 'twenty healthy female clerks' who were asked to do nothing other than watch the films and provide urine samples. The first film, a bland concoction of natural scenery made by Norwegian Railways, produced calm, relaxation and boredom, and a decline in adrenalin and noradrenalin outputs. The next evening Stanley Kubrick's *Paths of Glory* caused anger, excitement and increased adrenalin. *Charley's Aunt*, film number three, met with laughter and evoked a similar hormone response.

Finally, a film entitled *The Mark of Satan*, which provoked reactions of fear and excitement, caused both adrenalin and noradrenalin outputs to rise (Poteliakhoff and Carruthers 1981).

Pleasing the patient for a change

Cousins's use of vitamin C was based on a theory (and some supporting evidence – see Stone 1972) that the vitamin promotes physical health via identifiable biochemical pathways. In many medical studies, however, the administration of vitamin C has had another rationale: that of a placebo. Studies which pay some attention to what is called 'the placebo response' are also studies about social support and health. The reason they are not traditionally included under this heading has to do with the two models of table A: the fact that one way of improving people's health is to give them medicines which are supposedly chemically inert is taken as a gold standard against which chemically active drugs must be tested. Placebos are methodological controls, instruments of scientific inquiry like inter-views. Evidence that both interviews and placebos can make people feel better (or worse) is profoundly disturbing to the philosophy of the body–mind dichotomy.

The concept of a 'placebo' has a curious linguistic and epistemological history. The term comes from the Latin word meaning 'I shall please', and was originally used in the fourteenth century to describe the singing of vespers for the dead (which begin with the words 'Placebo Domino'). By Chaucer's day, as a result of the practice of singing vespers on behalf of strangers for pay, the word had acquired the negative meaning of servile flatterer (Brody 1977). From the early nineteenth century on, the word 'placebo' was used to refer to any medicine 'given more to please than to benefit the patient' (Gaddum 1954).

As Beecher (1955: 1602) has put it:

> Reasons for the use of the placebo can be indicated by summarizing . . . its common purposes: as a psychological instrument in the therapy of certain ailments arising out of mental illness, as a resource of the harassed doctor in dealing with the neurotic patient, to determine the true effect of drugs apart from suggestion in experimental work, as a device for eliminating bias not only on the part of the patient but also, when used as an unknown, of the observer, and, finally, as a tool of importance in the study of the mechanisms of drug action.

Placebos differ from standard medicines in that, while the health-promoting effects of the latter can be referred to a scientific explanation, those of placebos supposedly cannot. Although the beneficial effect of placebos on health may be expressed through physiological pathways, these are crucially *mysterious and unknown to physical science*. Given the historical basis of most medical practice, it is true that, as Adler and Hammett (1973: 595) have observed, 'the history of medicine up until the last 100 to 150 years has been the history of this pervasive placebo effect'. Doctors' attempts to cure illness have largely depended on the willingness of patients to *believe* in the medical ability to alleviate suffering. What this means, in turn, is that the history of medicine is the history of the importance to health of social support.

In a 1987 UK study of general practice consultations, researchers compared the effects of 'positive' consultations with and without treatment with those of 'negative' consultations with and without treatment. The 'patients' who took part in the study had symptoms, but no definite diagnosis has been made. 'Treatment' consisted of a diagnosis on the basis of the symptoms and a placebo medication. In 'positive' consultations the 'patients' who took part in the study had symptoms, but no definite diagnosis had been made. 'Treatment' consisted of a diagnosis on the basis of the symptoms and a placebo medication. In 'positive' consultations the consultations got better compared with 39 per cent of those who had 'negative' ones. Whether or not 'treatment' was given made no difference. These results confirmed the view that doctors themselves are powerful therapeutic agents and in this sense historically the most frequently used drugs for treating illness (Thomas 1987). This, of course, is the underlying proposal of psychotherapy: the therapist's aim of improving the patient's health can only be achieved by psychosocial means; no technical-medical procedures are involved. Here, also, recent work has confirmed the significance of social relationships. A study of people classed as having 'neurotic disorder' which compared drug (diazepam and dothiepin) and psychological treatments (cognitive and behaviour therapy and self-help treatment, and a 'placebo' drug) found that all groups did equally well or badly except for the diazepam group, which did somewhat worse than the others (Tyrer et al. 1988). An earlier study (Brill et al. 1964) comparing psychoanalytic therapy, psychoactive drugs and placebo pills with a control group of patients on the waiting list for treatment also concluded that there were no significant differences between the different forms of treatment, including placebo. Placebo pills were as good (or as bad) as psychoanalysis in making people better. While a meta-analysis of over 500 studies comparing some form of psychological therapy with a control treatment appeared to show a greater effectiveness overall for psychological therapy (Smith and Glass 1977), a re-analysis of the same data looking at the comparative effects of placebo and psychotherapy failed to find any superior benefit for psychotherapy. Treatments designed as placebo – ranging from chemically inert pills to listening to records, relaxation training, language classes and discussion groups oriented to 'irrelevant' topics – were as likely to be associated with improvement as professional psychotherapy (Prioleau et al. 1983). Commenting on these findings, Frank

(1983: 291) observed:

> With many patients the placebo may be as effective as psychotherapy because the placebo condition contains the necessary, and possibly the sufficient, ingredient for much of the beneficial effect of all forms of psychotherapy. This is a helping person who listens to the patient's complaints and offers a procedure to relieve them.

Or, as another commentator put it, 'The very word *psychotherapy* is misleading in its dualistic implications and opposition to the concept of *somatotherapy*' (Sebeok 1983: 300).

The use of placebo pills in studies of the effectiveness of psychotherapy highlights the major referent of the term in medical literature: the comparison in drug trials of supposedly 'active' drugs with the supposedly chemically inert placebo remedy. This use of placebos dates from the early 1980s, when concern over adequate testing of new drugs led to the design of so-called double-blind randomized controlled trials. (The term 'double blind' refers to the fact that neither researchers nor research participants are supposed to know the status of the different pills ingested by members of different treatment groups.) A particularly clear-cut demonstration of the need for this design is a case cited by Wolf (1959: 149–50). An asthmatic patient tried many drugs over many years until he found one that appeared to be effective. In order to test this, his doctor substituted a placebo, accomplishing the shift from placebo to drug several times to ensure a reliable result: each time, the drug proved effective and the placebo not. But when the pharmaceutical company supplying the drug was contacted for a new supply, it revealed that, in order to test the basis of the many positive reports of the new drug received, in this case a placebo had been made available instead.

As used in controlled clinical trials, placebos have been reported to be effective in a wide range of illness conditions, including headache, migraine, travel sickness, insomnia, psychoses, neurosis, cerebral infarction, multiple sclerosis, epilepsy, Parkinson's disease, alcoholism, asthma, hay fever, colds, coughs, angina pectoris, hypertension, arthritis, gastrointestinal disorders, constipation, warts, acne, skeletal disease, chronic urticaria and enuresis (Totman 1979). In fact they have been shown to influence virtually any condition or symptom upon which they have been tested (Brody 1977: 124). The literature of obstetrics and gynaecology is certainly replete with trials which show the advantages of placebo treatment in achieving benefits such as shorter labours (see e.g. Davies and Rose 1977; McAuley et al. 1982; Phillips et al. 1960), relief from pregnancy sickness (see e.g. FitzGerald 1955; King 1955) and treatment of pre-eclampsia (see e.g. Ferguson 1953). A review by Hemminki and Starfield (1978) of eighteen controlled clinical trials assessing the effectiveness of drugs used to prevent preterm birth found that, in the thirteen trials judged methodologically adequate, eleven found the placebo as effective (or ineffective) as the drug in postponing delivery. None of the trials found the drug more likely than the placebo to obtain a more satisfactory outcome for the baby. Although a problem with the review might have been the small size of the trials, similar findings have been reported in a later study (Goldstein et al. 1989).

Like 'active' drugs, placebos have been shown to be associated with a wide range of toxic side-effects, including palpitations, irritability, insomnia, headache, diarrhoea, collapse, rash and death (Brody 1977). Not only has the colour of placebo pills been shown to be important (Honzak et al. 1972), but placebos given in capsule form are apparently more powerful than those given in the form of pills, an injection works better than either, and an injection that stings works better than a painless one (Evans 1974). A study by Park and Covi (1965) drew attention to the importance of *belief* in the efficacy of treatment: in this study researchers gave sugar capsules to fifteen people with neurotic complaints, telling them that the capsules contained no medicine, but that they had helped other patients in the past, and that the doctors were convinced they were of benefit. Fourteen of the fifteen people took the capsules as recommended, and all but one (who was under particular stress, as her husband had tried to commit suicide) got better. When the patients were divided into three groups – those certain that the capsules contained nothing, those certain that they contained an active drug, and those not certain – it was clear that the two groups expressing certainty showed the most improvement.

Although the use of placebos in drug trials is based on the assumption that placebos represent pharmacologically inert substances, they have been shown to have biochemical effects. For example, their administration increases levels of endorphins (endogenous pain-relieving chemicals) circulating in the body (Levine et al. 1978). Such evidence, by placing 'inactive' drugs in the same category as 'active' ones, once more disturbs the whole philosophy of western medicine. It is, as Brody has argued, akin to Roentgen's discovery of X-rays, which was not believed by many physicists at the time, for the reason that extant systems of understanding could not accommodate the existence of rays from a cathode-ray tube capable of causing a plate to glow across a room.

'New' discoveries which fit standard knowledge paradigms are far more likely to be accepted than those which do not. One consequence of this is that discoveries that threaten the epistemological status quo may be adjusted to fit it. Thus a large body of work has pursued a quest for something called 'the placebo reactor' – a type of personality likely to respond positively to placebo theory (see e.g. Bourne 1971). The aim of this quest is to identify such people in order to exclude them from randomized controlled trials. One unanticipated problem here has been that results of trials comparing drugs and placebos has shown the importance of distinguishing between those who take the therapy as instructed and those who do not; 'compliers', whether to drug or placebo regimes, apparently have better outcomes than 'non-compliers' (Sackett 1989).

Another manifestation of the need to dismiss the placebo response as inconvenient nonsense is its identification as statistical regression. Statisticians have argued that a large part of the placebo response can be accounted for by the tendency for patients 'selected for abnormalcy' to improve because of the tendency towards statistical regression to the mean (McDonald et al. 1983). In other words, the chief interest of 'scientific' medicine has not been in exploring the placebo effect as evidence of the interconnectedness of mind and body, but in excluding it from its domain precisely *because* of its proven therapeutic effectiveness.

What health outcomes does social support influence?

The apparent importance of social support, whether expressed as 'placebo' therapy or more explicitly defined, extends to a wide range of physical and psychological health outcomes. Much of the early work was carried out in the mental health field. In his classic study of suicide, Emile Durkheim drew attention to the dependence of mental health on a sense of being integrated into the social fabric; as with much subsequent work, Durkheim's analysis of the importance of personal ties was restricted in the main to marriage (Durkheim 1952). Faris and Dunham's studies in the 1930s on mental disorder in Chicago identified socially isolated individuals living in the most materially disadvantaged sections of the city as most prone to schizophrenia (Faris and Dunham 1939). Following on from this work, enmeshment in social relationships has been shown to be associated with lower risks of distress and depression, both in general and in the presence of life stress (Bloom and Spiegel 1984; Brown and Harris 1978; Gore 1978; Holahan and Moos 1981).

In relation to physical survival, three prospective studies of community samples in the USA have shown that people with few social relationships have at least twice the risk of mortality of people with many social relationships. In the Alameda County study already referred to, 6928 adults in Alameda County, California, became part of a 'Human Population Laboratory Study' in 1965. Follow-up studies nine and twelve years later demonstrated that mortality from all causes was greater in people with low levels of social support. This relationship held independently of a large number of factors that might be expected to influence mortality, including initial physical health status, socio-economic status, smoking, alcohol use, level of physical activity, obesity, race, life satisfaction and use of preventive health services (Berkman and Syme 1979). The Tecumseh Community health study was carried out in Michigan by House and colleagues: 2754 men and women aged 35–69 were interviewed and medically examined in 1967. Four components of social integration and activities proved statistically significant for men's health after adjusting for age and other risk factors: marital status, and attendance at voluntary associations, spectator events and classes and lectures. Among women only church attendance was statistically significant (House et al. 1982). A third prospective community study conducted in North Carolina by Blazer (1982) on 331 men and women aged 65 or older found three measures of social support – 'roles and attachments available' (including spouse, siblings and children), frequency of interaction, and perceptions of social support – to be significant risk factors for mortality thirty months later. The item most predictive of death was perceived impaired social support, and the item least predictive of death was impaired frequency of interaction (Berkman 1984).

Social support and reproduction

Reproduction might appear to be the bodily condition most closely linked to social support, as an intimate relationship is normally required to initiate it. However, fathers' relations with mothers turn out to be part of the problem.

Until fairly recently, the bulk of the literature on pregnancy and support was heavily weighted by the 'maritalist' assumption of much social support research. Thus married mothers were assumed to be supported, whereas unmarried mothers were not. This assumption was then taken to explain the widespread and long-lived pattern of poorer pregnancy outcome in unwed mothers. Overwhelmingly preoccupied with the problem of extramarital conception, researchers viewed the question of the optimum conditions for having babies through the moral lens of a commitment to the legitimate family as the proper locus for reproduction. Just what it was about the marital relationship that was supposed to give pregnant women support (money? housing? moral support? affection? help with housework? access to a wider kin group? etc.) and just what 'support' might mean in this context were thus not framed as topics of inquiry.

Commenting on this literature in 1967, medical sociologist Raymond Illsley remarked on the almost total absence of 'systematic, well-designed studies', and warned against basing *any* social or biological interpretations on such a shaky foundation (Illsley 1967: 92). Twenty-five years later the legacy of this pro-maritalist view continues to inform research and policy (see Phoenix 1991), but in some respects the world has moved on. A number of studies have examined pregnancy outcomes in the light of the social support and other resources available to mothers, and within the framework of the ordinary and extraordinary stresses that accompany childbearing. One of the earliest of these studies was carried out on a sample of 170 army wives in the USA, who were followed by researchers through the deliveries of their babies at a military hospital. Two questionnaires given at registration for antenatal care and at 32 weeks of pregnancy collected information about 'psychosocial assets' and about life events. Neither of these on their own appeared to be related to pregnancy outcome, but, when taken together, psychosocial assets were found to have a buffering effect in the presence of stress. Women with a high level of stress who also had considerable psychosocial assets had a pregnancy complication rate of 33 per cent compared with one of 91 per cent among women with high stress but low psychosocial assets (Nuckolls et al. 1972). A later study along the same lines confirmed these findings (Wilcox 1981). There was, however, a major problem with the conceptualization of 'psychosocial assets', which were seen as a kind of non-biological rubbish bin containing not only the 'quality' of the marriage relationship, and relationships with other family members and friends, but something called 'ego strength' as well as feelings about the pregnancy.

A third study looked at the 'Nuckolls' hypothesis in a retrospective study of 166 mothers of preterm babies and 299 mothers of term babies (Berkowitz and Kasl 1983). Life events were linked with risk of preterm delivery. Mothers who had support from their partners had a slightly lower risk of giving birth early overall. A difference by ethnic group indicated the need to consider cultural norms about marriage and male–female relationships: for white women, partner support was associated with a lower risk of giving birth early, but for black women the opposite was the case. The retrospective 'bias' of this study – the possible reconstruction of the events of pregnancy in the light of pregnancy outcome – was tested in two studies by Richard Newton and colleagues in the UK. Both of these examined life events in relation to preterm/low-birthweight births, and found a significant relationship, whether the study design was retrospective or prospective (Newton et al. 1979; Newton and Hunt 1984).

Two further American studies which are often referred to are those of Norbeck and Tilden (1983) and Smilkstein and colleagues (1984). The first attempted a more rigorous test of hypotheses about the interactions between stress and support in relation to pregnancy complications. Support was subdivided into 'emotional' and 'tangible', and it was the latter form of support that appeared to be most closely related to poor pregnancy outcome. The second study focused on two concepts of risk – biomedical and psychosocial – and examined the capacity of each to predict pregnancy complications. Psychosocial risk, which included low family support and life events, proved more predictive of poor outcome either on its own or in combination with biomedical risk than the latter alone. 'Family support' can mean many things. One of the aspects that is most important is help with housework, which in a study of Ohio mothers proved more highly associated with birthweight than other dimensions of support, including quality of communication with partner and community involvement (Pascoe et al. 1987). In evaluating the importance of family support, marital status will not do as a proxy: a Canadian study showed unmarried women living with partners to be at lower risk of having small babies than married women living with their husbands (Doucet et al. 1989). Widening the net further than pregnancy complications, the social support resources available to, and used by, mothers have been linked with the informal learning opportunities provided to young children at home independently of family stress and the family's material circumstances (Pascoe et al. 1981; Pascoe and Earp 1984).

These studies were all observational ones; that is, the research charted the relationships between reproductive events and support and stress observable within the mothers' usual environments. The methodological challenge of such studies lies in untangling associated factors from 'causal' factors: it can be hard to say with any degree of confidence that social support is the crucial protective factor when it may be associated with other factors which are in themselves related to better outcomes for mother and child, such as higher income, better housing and more education. Refined statistical methods can go some of the way towards meeting this challenge, but intervention studies, in which an additional element of social support is introduced and its effects compared with what happens to people who do not have it, are the only reliable way to overcome it.

As observed earlier, contemporary interest in studying the importance of social support to health has been stimulated by a long history of complaints about the non-supportive nature of medical care. The major message of these complaints concerns the importance of continuous, personal care: the relevance to health (in all its aspects) of the feeling that there is someone who will listen to, and who knows and cares about, those health-related needs that stem from being the person who is living in the body which is the focus of the medical gaze. Indeed, the technical literature of social support has made it possible to incorporate women's 'demands' for more personal care within the scientific mode, in much the same way as their call for less dehumanizing and depersonalizing labour care was translated in the 1960s into the new technical language of maternal–infant bonding (Arney 1982).

How does social support work?

As Joan Bloom (1990: 635) has said in a recent review, 'Rather than continuing to accumulate additional studies that demonstrate the importance of social support for health, the challenge to the research community is to determine how social support contributes to health.' Four main hypotheses emerge from the literature:

1 Social support affects health directly.
2 Social support improves health by acting as a buffer to stress.
3 Social support makes stress less likely.
4 Social support facilitates recovery from illness or crisis.

Reviews of the evidence for and against both the buffering and the direct effects hypotheses indicate that both can be supported from existing work (Cohen and Wills 1985). A methodological problem is that, since the very occurrence of stress may mean changes in social support resources, the two terms may simply be opposite sides of the same coin. So far as the third and fourth hypotheses are concerned, these may well be connections underlying the social class inequalities in health (see Oakley et al. 1982 for a review), though the relationship between social class and social connections is a complex one (see Oakley and Rajan 1991).

In postulating bodily pathways for the translation of social support into improved health outcomes, most researchers step sideways into a different, though related, conceptual and empirical territory – that of stress research. The 'father' of stress research was epidemiologist John Cassel, whose original interest lay in charting the health-damaging consequences of materially deprived urban environments, and whose work gave rise to the observation that what protects against both physical and mental illness in such environments is social ties (Cassel 1976). Cassel's model of understanding was a medical one, drawing on animal and microbial research to postulate an impact of urban social disorganization on changes in people's biochemical 'host resistance' to disease. In this model, social relationships function both as pathogens and as factors capable of boosting immune resistance.

Some contemporary researchers regard the notion of stress as simply too vague to be helpful as a research tool. Others, however, have 'gone to the other extreme and made liberal use of standard psychosocial instruments that are blithely fed into multivariate analyses' resulting in 'causal inferences based on the size of the regression coefficient' (Marmot 1987: 9). From a sociological point of view, 'Stress has become as interesting an issue today as money, power, and sex' (Epstein 1985: 282) (though we lack the evidence to judge whether in fact the experience of stress is more prevalent today than it was in the past). The term 'stress' shares a linguistic origin with 'distress', and refers to 'the overpowering pressure of some adverse force or influence' (*Oxford English Dictionary*). Its use from the eighteenth century on increasingly displayed the semantic confusion of a double meaning: both the events/things/circumstances producing stress, and the individual's response to these 'external' stimuli. Modern methods of biochemical investigation have shown how hormonal and immune system functioning are both important in mediating between environmentally induced stress and health outcomes. There is good evidence that stress brings about changes in adrenalin, noradrenalin and cortisol production (Henry 1986) – hormones linked to a wide range of illnesses, including heart disease and cancer. The findings for human beings are supported by animal experiments which show the altering of neural, hormonal and immune systems by stressful circumstances leading to disease states (Ader et al. 1963; Calhoun 1962; Gross 1972; Ratcliffe 1962).

A main assumption, then, is that social support 'works' by reducing or blocking these physiological responses to stress. To this somewhat negative argument can be added more recent speculative (though intuitive) evidence that social relationships, particularly those involving physical touch, may act as boosters to the immune system independently of the presence or absence of particular stressors (Odent 1986). The notion that physical contact may be an important health-promoting component of social relationships has, interestingly, been almost totally ignored by researchers, except in the study of infants and their mothers, where it is theoretically subsumed within the concept of maternal–infant bonding (see Oakley 1986).

Since the 1970s, the idea that social support may be good for health because stress is bad has increasingly been encapsulated within the jargon of 'life events'. An early and often quoted study here is Meyer and Haggerty's (1962) subjection of the throats of Boston families to repeated swabs, resulting in the conclusion that family crises were four times as common in the two weeks preceding the appearance of streptococcal infections as in the two weeks following them. Like the investigation of social support, the notion of life events as potential illness-causing agents has been more thoroughly explored in relation to psychological than to physical health outcomes. Since the mid-1960s, literally hundreds of studies have studied the relevance of life events to health outcomes, many using the 'Schedule of Recent Experiences' developed by Holmes and Rahe (1967), though this has been subject to extensive criticism (see e.g. Brown and Harris 1978). A major methodological issue is the measurement of life events and their significance to health outcomes *independently* of the question of the meaning of particular events to particular people. As with social support and stress research, the central concept here, that of life event, has suffered from a unipolar interpretation: just as social support is seen as good, and stress as bad, so life events tend to be conceived of as negative happenings. Whereas most social support may be good, and most stress and life events bad, for health, it is easy to think of instances where the opposite may be the case. For example, as noted above, the 'social support' provided by marriage may be a mixed blessing. Similarly, marital breakdown can be a positive as well as a negative life event when it brings to an end a period of unconstructive turmoil, and allows people to rebuild their close relationships in a more comfortable way.

The research challenge

A certain hostility to the role of social factors in influencing patterns of health and illness is built into the development of modern medicine. In part this is because medicine has needed to define itself as a technical discipline distinct from the social, and doctors have wanted to carve out an identity for themselves in which they are able to offer more than an ordinary social understanding of human suffering (Stacey 1988). For the same reason, medicine has manifested a historical scepticism about the utility of social science to contribute anything to an understanding of why some people become ill and die while others remain well. The relevance of social science is at the margins of medicine, as in the common confusion among doctors between social *science*, on the one hand, and social *work* on the other (Oakley 1980; Stacey and Homans 1978). Although the emergence of 'social medicine' in the 1950s in Britain, the USA and elsewhere seems at first sight to reverse this scepticism and confusion, the vitality of social medicine itself proved limited by the tunnel vision of the social embedded in it (Oakley 1991a; Webster n.d.).

These considerations pose a critical challenge. For, if social support research truly represents a paradigm shift, then to what extent are our attempts to wrestle from the tangle of ideas that fall under the heading of social support some sensible, watertight, testable 'scientific' notion of what it is we want to study actually at odds with the essence of the new enterprise? How can we define and measure without falling into any of the old traps? As House and Kahn have said,

> The research appeal of social support . . . is based neither on the specificity of the concept, nor on the emergence of some uniquely successful empirical measure. Rather, like the related concept of stress, social support has attracted researchers and stimulated research across the biomedical, behavioural and social sciences because of its integrative promise and intuitive appeal. It suggests an underlying common element in seemingly diverse phenomena and it captures something that all of us have experienced. (House and Kahn 1985: 84)

Cohen and Syme, whose agnostic position on the evidence linking social support and health was cited earlier, argue that significant advances in this area will only occur through a focus on the *processes* linking support and wellbeing: 'It must be asked whether the effects of social support on health and well-being are mediated by behavioural change, physiological change, perceptual change, or some combination of these three' (Cohen and Syme 1985: 15). Moreover, and as Dean (1986) has pointed out, the relevance of research on social support and health to the activity of health promotion will remain uncertain until researchers take on board the task of exploring the links between social support, on the one hand, and self-care behaviour, including coping behaviour, on the other. How important are social relationships and the resources (or burdens) they have to offer in influencing people's ability to cope and their perceptions of their coping status? Understanding the pathways by which social support may affect health involves a consideration of coping, since the protective effect of social ties is assumed to include 'the facilitation of coping strategies and adaptive behaviours that mitigate adverse effects through stress reduction and the promotion of psychophysiological homeostasis' (Shonkoff 1984: 310). In certain areas, for example motherhood (Graham 1982) and lay perceptions of illness (Cornwell 1984), coping has indeed emerged as a critical concept.

As the study of social support and allied fields becomes more sophisticated, so more attention is coming to be paid to the question of *meaning*. What is important is not only the individual's social situation, but the meaning s/he attaches to it. An early example of the importance of meaning is to be found in the study of the effect of migration on health – a field explored principally because of its capacity to answer questions about the role of genetic influences. Migration from stable communities to more hostile and competitive environments increases blood pressure and the risk of cardiovascular disease, but studies of different migrant groups have showed the health impact of migration to be mediated by the *meanings* attached to migration. Thus, in a study of Chinese and Hungarian migrants to the USA, the Chinese, who went to the USA to study or gain professional experience but were then prevented by the communist accession to power from returning to China, were shown to be at significantly greater health risk than Hungarians, who had chosen the move to the USA as a response to insecurity, frustration and threat in their own country (Hinkle 1980).

In social support research it is important that researchers be sensitive not only to socially structured contexts that discriminate between the meaning of social support to individuals, but also to *individual* differences, and the importance of different life situations and circumstances. For example, low-density networks have been shown to be supportive for middle-aged American women returning to college (Hirsch 1980), whereas high-density networks are reported to work better for single parents relying on their families for help (McLanahan et al. 1981). Most importantly, in studying individual responses, we must also not be distracted from understanding the power of environmental influences on health. In a follow-up to the Alameda County study, Kaplan and colleagues showed that characteristics of area of residence suggesting poverty were able to predict mortality independently of *all* personal characteristics measured (Kaplan and Camacho 1983).

The poverty of social support in overcoming the health-damaging effects of material deprivation is an important point returned to later in this book. But the question of *how* social support works begs the more fundamental question of *whether* it works. Much research in this field has been retrospective, and inquiries into the significance of social support to health outcomes have been coloured by the tendency of outcomes to affect the reporting of past events and processes. In addition, much research has been correlational: that is, it has merely documented a relationship

between social support and health. Statistical methods are used to demonstrate the association of different indices of social support with improved
health outcomes. The leap from correlation to cause is more difficult. The
result is that, as Cohen and Syme (1985: 15) have baldly put it: 'It is not
known why social support is associated with health.'

To answer this question, two strategies are needed. One is a perspective
that integrates the traditional concerns of medical and social research.
While epidemiology can map the incidence and prevalence of health
outcomes, stress and social support in large numbers of people, more
detailed in-depth inquiries are required to illuminate the processes
involved at the individual level in mediating relationships between health
outcomes, on the one hand, and potential causal factors on the other. The
other requirement is controlled intervention studies designed to examine
the relationship between specific types of support and different ways of
evaluating health.

3

Sickness in Salonica and Other
Stories

The central question in the study of living things is how to decide whether
an observed event is to be attributed to the meaningless play of chance on
the one hand, or to causation ... on the other. (Silverman 1980: 128)

While serving as an army medical officer in the Second World War,
epidemiologist Archie Cochrane was captured in June 1941 and sent to a
prisoner-of-war camp in Salonica, Greece. Conditions in the camp were
appalling. Cochrane instituted a medical surveillance system, and found an
outbreak of leg oedema accompanied by jaundice, from which he himself
was one of the sufferers. In desperation, and vaguely remembering the
phrase 'wet beri-beri', he decided to see if he could show that the oedema
was due to a vitamin deficiency. Having managed to obtain some yeast on
the black market, he recruited twenty young prisoners, cleared two wards,
and numbered the twenty prisoners off: odd numbers to one ward, even
numbers to the other. The men in one ward got two spoonfuls of yeast
each every day, and the men in the other ward got one tablet of vitamin C.
The outcome of the experiment was assessed mainly by frequency of
urination, as there were no buckets available to measure volume. For the
first two days, there was no difference between the wards, but by the
fourth day the difference was conclusive. Cochrane conducted two simple
tests: he asked the members of each ward whether they felt better, worse
or the same – nine out of ten in the yeast ward said they felt better; and he
watched the men walking, deciding that oedema among members of the
yeast ward was less than among members of the vitamin C ward. He wrote
up the results of this experiment, presented them to the Germans, and
asked for more food and more yeast. The Germans produced more yeast,
which Cochrane gave to the men, and the oedema disappeared. Commenting on this, 'my first, worst, and most successful clinical trial', at a distance
of more than forty years, he observed:

On reflection, it was not a good trial. I was testing the wrong hypothesis. The
oedema was not wet beri-beri. Furthermore, the numbers were too small,

the time too short, and the outcome measurements poor. Yet the treatment worked. I still do not know why. I imagine that the simplest explanation is that the small amount of protein in the yeast raised the plasma proteins sufficiently to correct fluid balance.

There are two additional points worth making. Firstly, it could be argued that the trial was randomized and controlled, although this last was somewhat inadequate. In those early days, when the randomized controlled trial was little known in medicine, this was something of an achievement. At the same time I can take little credit as the design of the trial was largely fortuitous. Secondly, the German doctor's remark, when I asked for more help, was 'Ärzte sind überflüssig' ('doctors are superfluous'). This was probably correct, but it was amazing what a little bit of science and a little bit of luck achieved. (Cochrane 1984: 1727)

Intellectual knowledge is 'produced' within particular sociocultural contexts and by means of different methodological pathways. Though Cochrane achieved a successful randomized controlled trial in a prisoner-of-war camp, most of the studies discussed in the previous chapter used the less scientifically resilient approach of simply describing observations about social aspects of people's lives in relation to their health. The main drawback of this approach within the scientific paradigm of knowledge to which Cochrane's trial appeals is the difficulty of moving beyond the listing of associations and correlations to an understanding of causal relationships. Even when the potential bias of retrospective studies is overcome by following through a sample over time, this objection still stands. People who have lots of friends may have fewer serious illnesses than their relatively friendless peers, but is this because people in better health are better able to make friends, or is it because social bonds protect bodies from malfunctioning? Women who give birth to small babies are less likely than those who give birth to average-sized babies to be connected to a nexus of family and community support; but, once again, how is it possible to move from this correlational statement to the assertion that the possession of social ties *causes* women's bodies to grow babies more effectively than they would do in conditions of social isolation? Since this question was basic to the genesis of the SSPO study, it is important to preface the description of the study offered in chapters 4–10 by looking at how experimental, as distinct from observational, research methods may help to answer it.

Natural and unnatural experiments

For a number of years, it has been argued in some quarters that the only reliable way to answer such questions is to intervene in the 'natural' situation and study the effects of manipulating particular variables, as

Cochrane did with diet in the prisoner-of-war camp. From this point of view, the whole of medicine represents an intervention study, and so do other professionalized services, including those of education and social work. In each case, people's lives are changed by the addition of an intervention which rests on an assumption of beneficence. In each case, however, the problem is potentially the same as it was before: how do we 'know' that the intervention has 'in fact' done any good?

Intervention studies are variously named and variously designed, according to the different disciplines in which they are carried out. Sociologists use the term 'action research' for what social workers or psychologists call 'intervention research' and epidemiologists call 'randomized controlled trials' (RCTs). Although it is not strictly equivalent, because of the lack of a control group, 'action research' in social science spells out the twin goals of many RCTs in medicine: 'the improvement of services through increased knowledge and the development of knowledge through the study of innovatory practice' (Maughan and Rutter 1985: 26). The action-research model specifies that our attention be given not only to the evaluation of *outcomes* of different approaches but to the *processes* involved in securing those outcomes. In this it differs from most medical research practice, which tends to dismiss a focus on process through its 'scientific' disregard for the importance of social relations. But whether we call it action research or an RCT, and whether we are speaking about health, education or welfare services in either the formal or the voluntary sector, it is not only the effectiveness of innovatory practices that must be tested. *Accepted* practices must come under scrutiny as well. What is done by service providers in the name of promoting people's welfare may rest more on long-held beliefs about efficacy than on any other logic of effect.

Disciplinary differences in methodological nomenclature also point to a difference in the architecture of studies. The essential question here is not *what* is done to *whom*, but *how* the people to whom it is done are *chosen*, and how, by extension, the people are selected who are to serve the function of a 'control' group by *not* having anything done to them. (The French word for 'control' is *témoin*, meaning 'witness', which is perhaps more accurate, as well as being less unacceptably passive.) RCTs in the medical field are so called because they are trials of treatments using a control group chosen by random allocation – by the use of a table of random numbers. In action research in the social science field, the use of random allocation is rare. General awareness of the importance in social science research design of allocation method is low, as indicated by the large number of studies which simply do not say how the study population was divided into experimental and control groups (see Rapoport 1985). Interventions are described and their effects judged without reference to methodological issues needed to contextualize these evaluations (see e.g. Gottlieb 1981; Leavy 1983); alternatively, the advantages of randomized experimentation, while acknowledged, may be dismissed as contentious (see Hauser-Cram 1990).

As Silverman (1985) notes, the modern technical language of 'random allocation' or 'randomization' is predated by the older historical principle of limiting risk by lot: one consults the gods, or casts lots, or tosses a coin. The fictional advantages and disadvantages of using this method as a guide to life decisions have been outlined by Luke Rhinehart, novelist and bored New York psychiatrist, in *The Dice Man* (1972). Having tired of rational decision-making, and deciding instead to use the throw of the dice to determine his actions, Rhinehart quickly discovers that 'the dice can show almost as poor judgement as a human' (Rhinehart 1972: 75).

The method of the RCT comes originally from agriculture, where it was devised as a solution to the problem that very long series of observations involving impracticable amounts of research time were required to answer questions about different ways of treating the soil (Dawson 1986). The concept of random allocation of treatments to different plots of land was developed in the 1920s by R. A. Fisher, a biometrist working at the Agricultural Research Station in Harpenden, UK. Even further back, the method of experimentation as a strategy to increase understanding of the world was proposed by Francis Bacon under the heading of 'invented experiences'. Bacon's contemporary, Galileo, advocated, somewhat diffe-rently, the use of an experimental design to test postulated laws. However, the underlying quest was the same: the desire to distinguish things that happen by chance from things that happen because they are manifesta-tions of some underlying law or causal relationship.

As a research method applicable to human subjects, the RCT is generally said to have been invented in 1946 in the UK, when a new drug, streptomycin, was proposed as a cure for tuberculosis in human beings, having first proved efficacious for the same purpose in guinea pigs. Because supplies of the new drug were scarce, the Medical Research Council in Britain decided to administer it in the form of a controlled trial, giving it on the basis of selection according to a table of random numbers to some people with tuberculosis and not to others (Silverman 1980). D'Arcy Hart, who worked on the MRC streptomycin trial as director of the specially created Tuberculosis Research Unit, remembers coming to the use of random numbers from an earlier and largely forgotten trial using alternate numbers to assess the value of the antibiotic patulin in treating the common cold (D'Arcy Hart 1991). Two previous uncontrolled studies had given contradictory results. The MRC patulin trial sought volunteers with colds in eleven factories, three Post Office units and two public schools in 1944, and the resulting 1348 colds treated either with patulin or with a placebo solution (dripped uncomfortably down the nose via a teaspoon) showed the placebo solution to work best (Patulin Clinical Trials Committee 1944).

Behind this apocryphal story of the origins of the randomized control-led trial is a history of previous attempts to carry out unbiased compari-sons of the effectiveness of different medical treatments. The most famous of these is the mid-eighteenth-century 'trial' of the value of oranges and lemons in curing scurvy among sailors. Other early contenders include Queen Caroline's insistence that the value of smallpox inoculation be tested on prisoners in Newgate prison (who were rewarded with their lives for agreeing to take part), and in 'charity' children before being used in the royal nursery (Silverman 1985).

The RCT is essentially an experimental test ('trial') of a particular treatment/approach (or set of treatments/approaches) comparing two or more groups of subjects who are allocated to these groups at random, i.e. according to the play of chance. As a research technique, randomization offers three principal advantages. First, each study unit (plot of earth, person, institution, etc.) has an equal chance of being or not being in the experimental group. Estimates of chance variability are consequently much easier to come by. Second, assignment on the basis of a table of random numbers eradicates the potential for *bias*: researchers are unable to influence their results by choosing to load their experimental group with 'favourable' factors – 'good' seeds, middle-class women, well-resourced institutions. Third, the method allows the researchers evenly to distribute both those factors *known* to be associated with different outcomes and those which may be, but are *unknown*. An instructive example of the latter is a trial of a cholesterol-lowering drug versus placebo in the prevention of repeat myocardial infarction in men (Coronary Drug Project Research Group 1980). In this study, no overall benefit for the active drug was found. However, 20 per cent of those prescribed the drug had not actually taken it and mortality in this group was significantly higher, which might lead to the conclusion that the drug really did work. Researchers then went on to look at the group given placebo pills: 20 per cent of these had also not taken their pills and *their* mortality was also significantly higher than those who had. In fact the group that fared best of the four (drug-prescribed compliers/non-compliers and placebo-prescribed compliers/non-compliers) were men who took the placebo as prescribed. The *behavioural* fact of 'non-compliance' had an unanticipated importance greater than that of *physical* risk factors, and use of random allocation distributed the propensity to disobey doctors' orders equally between treatment groups. This allowed valid conclusions to be drawn about the 'real' value of the 'active' drug.

The main advantage of random allocation here is its *unpredictability*. The allocation method guides research participants into intervention and control groups unmediated by the consciousness of researchers. Almost every other method of deciding on the membership of intervention and control groups has been shown to load the dice against the arbitration of chance. For example, because it allows researchers to *predict* what will happen, allocating *alternate* research participants to experimental and control groups permits researchers to rearrange the order in which different research participants are presented for allocation to fit their own views of what will best suit individuals. Using hospital or other case-note number suffers from the same weakness; people whom the researchers feel will definitely benefit from the intervention may not be entered into the study if it is obvious they will become part of the control group, and may be entered only if they will receive the intervention. There are many examples of trials in which the choices of researchers affected the allocation of patients to experimental and control groups. The impact of researcher choice on group allocation matters because it affects the credibility of the research results: such experimental and control groups contain individuals allocated not by chance, but by choices reflecting factors known to be associated with different outcomes. William Silverman describes one study of the effect of artificial light on the occurrence of retrolental fibroplasia (oxygen-induced blindness in babies):

> Assignment to 'light' or 'no light' was made on the basis of blue and white marbles in a box. One day, I noted that our head nurse reached into the box for a marble and then replaced it because it wasn't the colour that corresponded to her belief about the best treatment for her babies. I became convinced that we had to shift to sealed envelopes, as used in the British streptomycin trial. When the first sealed envelope was drawn, the resident physician held it up to the light to see the assignment inside. I took the envelopes home and my wife[1] and I wrapped each assignment-sticker in black paper and resealed the envelopes. (Silverman 1980: 140)

Careful analysis of studies using different designs has shown the advantages offered by 'true' randomization. Those using historical controls find more significant differences between tested therapies than those using controls selected by random allocation (T. C. Chalmers 1983). In an analysis of 145 papers reporting trials of treatments for acute myocardial infarction, significant differences were reported in 58.1 per cent of the non-randomized studies but in only 16.6 per cent of those using random allocation. The randomized studies were divided into those in which the randomization was 'blinded' and those in which it was not. In the former case, assignment to experimental and control groups was prearranged at random and communicated to the researcher only after the patient had consented and been accepted into the study; common methods were the use of opaque envelopes or a telephone call to a statistical centre. In non-blind randomization, an open table of random numbers or date of birth or hospital case-note number was used, and the doctors could accept or reject a patient into the study after treatment assignment had been made. Differences were again found between the two methods. Statistically significant differences between experimental and control groups were reported for 8.8 per cent of the blinded randomized studies but for 24.4 per cent of the non-blinded ones (T. C. Chalmers et al. 1983).

Conclusions about the effectiveness of treatments based on an RCT rest upon two issues – an assessment of *significance* and a judgement about *causation*. Traditionally, tests of statistical significance are used to determine whether any observed difference between trial groups is due to sampling variability or is evidence of a 'real' difference. If a difference is 'significant' in this sense (see pp. 262–6 for a discussion of significance tests), then, as Schwartz and colleagues put it in their classic text *Clinical Trials*,

> a judgement of causation allows us to attribute it to the difference between [the] two treatments. This is only possible if the two groups are strictly comparable in all respects apart from the treatments given. Providing two such comparable groups is another statistical problem the correct solution of which is obtained by randomization. (Schwartz et al. 1980: 7)

The prerequisite for any RCT is *uncertainty* about the effects of a particular treatment. If something is known to work (and to be acceptable and without harmful effects) then there is no reason to put it to the test in the form of a trial. It is, however, this very issue of certainty/uncertainty that constitutes one of the central problems of the contemporary debate about RCTs. People can be certain that something (e.g. streptomycin, social support) is effective but have no 'real' basis for their certainty; conversely, unless they are able to admit uncertainty, 'real' knowledge can never be gained.

These advantages have led to a characterization of RCTs within medicine and health care research more generally as 'the most scientifically valid method' of evaluating different procedures or types of care (Bracken 1987: 1111). Over the last twenty years, the RCT has been promoted as the major evaluative tool within medicine. As one physician wrote in 1983,

Table 3.1 Randomized controlled trials in perinatal medicine as a proportion of all publications in selected obstetric, paediatric and anaesthetic journals, 1966–1988

Type of journal	1966–1970	1971–1975	1976–1980	1981–1986	1986–1988
Obstetric journals:					
Total no. of publications	5567	5778	6201	7351	4727
No. perinatal trials	95	95	187	210	143
Trial publication rate (%)	(1.7)	(1.6)	(3.0)	(2.9)	(3.0)
Paediatric journals:					
Total no. of publications	5627	8031	8713	9255	5502
No. perinatal trials	51	83	136	233	137
Trial publication rate (%)	(0.9)	(1.0)	(1.6)	(2.5)	(2.5)
Anaesthetic journals:					
Total no. of publications	2990	4283	4736	6469	4747
No. perinatal trials	15	32	38	113	137
Trial publication rate (%)	(0.5)	(0.8)	(0.8)	(1.8)	(2.9)

Source: Chalmers 1989: 14

During my professional lifetime the prospective randomized controlled trial has progressed from an interesting tool devised by workers of high and subtle intellect for use in extremely well-defined and limited circumstances largely outside the province of the ordinary clinician to a central concept . . . For those of Kuhnian mind, we have seen the throwing of a massive Gestalt switch. (Dudley 1983: 957)

While this may be so, clinicians remain resistant to the demotion of their claims to certainty required by the RCT. Table 3.1 is evidence of this, showing as it does only a creeping advance for trial publications as a proportion of all in leading medical journals. And, as noted above, the scientific rigour of the RCT has almost totally escaped the attention of 'social' scientists.

Controlled and uncontrolled experiments

Most health care and other interventions in human life have not been carried out using the design of the RCT. They have been mounted on the basis that faith will guide the observer towards how to judge the effectiveness of the particular intervention. A false legitimacy and credibility can thus be claimed for outcomes which are due to the operation of factors other than the experimental strategy itself. An example from the perinatal field will illustrate this. In a Californian study assessing a programme aimed at preventing preterm labour (Herron et al. 1982), women booking for pregnancy care were divided into high- and low-'risk' groups. The low-risk women had standard care, while those considered to be at high risk attended a special clinic every week in addition to their routine care. In the special clinic women were examined, 'educated' in the early detection of preterm labour symptoms, and encouraged to telephone staff if they thought anything was wrong; those who, despite these procedures, went in to preterm labour were treated with betamimetic drugs. In order to evaluate the results of the programme, a comparison was made of the preterm delivery rates in both risk groups (4 per cent for the high-risk and 0.9 per cent for the low-risk women respectively) with the rate in an affiliated institution over the same time period. The latter's rate had remained stable, whereas that in the research institution had fallen by two-thirds. From this it was concluded that the intensive care programme had been effective. But other possibilities could equally well have obtained: the populations of the two institutions may have been different, or factors leading to a fall in preterm delivery may have been operating in one institution but not in the other. The design of the intervention made it impossible to determine which of these interpretations most closely describes what had happened.

In the US particularly, a large amount of public money has been invested in these kinds of uncontrolled health and education intervention

programmes. Reviewing forty-nine studies of early-intervention programmes for preschool children, Dunst and Rheingrover (1981) found only *one*
that had used random assignment. Joel Fischer's (1973) review of social
casework identified seventy studies aimed at the evaluation of effectiveness, but only eleven studies met the minimum methodological criteria of
a randomly selected control group. Most education and social work
interventions, and a good many in the health field, have focused on the
provision of additional services for the socially disadvantaged, and/or for
black and other ethnic minorities. While the focus on social disadvantage
may make sense to policy-makers, there has been virtually no discussion of
the profound ethical implications of trying out uncontrolled interventions
on relatively powerless social groups. These programmes include the
infamous Head Start educational intervention (see Farran 1990; Zigler and
Weiss 1985, for discussions); the nationwide Improved Pregnancy Outcome programme (see Peoples et al. 1984); the Improved Child Health
Projects (see Strobino et al. 1986); the Special Supplementation Food
Program for Women, Infants and Children (see Kotelchuck et al. 1984;
Rush 1984); and the Maternity and Infant Care Projects (see Peoples and
Siegel 1983). Various combinations of education, counselling, advice,
clinical care and practical and other professional help have been provided
under these headings, but the design of such studies makes it impossible
to disentangle the potential impact of the different components of the
intervention in question.

Of the random-allocated interventions that have been carried out in the
general health field, almost without exception people assigned to receive
support have fared better mentally and physically than those in control
groups. It is striking that in some cases a limited intervention is associated
with significant health effects; for example, in a study of people with the
degenerative disease of osteoarthritis, bi-weekly telephone calls over six
months from interviewers collecting study data were associated with
improvements in functional status and reported social support resources
(Weinberger et al. 1986). In 1968 a Chicago doctor, John Carpenter, and
colleagues found that interviews with medical students conducted as part
of standard medical education could significantly decrease pregnancy and
labour anxiety and the use of pre-delivery medication. Moreover, there
was a 'dose' effect, with women who had talked to medical students on
more occasions using less medication than those who had had less contact.

Most randomly controlled interventions in health are more ambitious
than either the Weinberger or the Carpenter study. A Californian trial of
'psychosocial' intervention with eighty-six breast cancer patients involved
weekly supportive group therapy and self-hypnosis for pain over a year-
long period. The therapy groups, led by a psychiatrist, a social worker, and
a therapist who had herself had breast cancer, were intended to encourage
women to talk about how to cope with the disease. Those in the intervention group survived twice as long as those having routine care. Unfortun-

ately, and as is often the case with medical RCTs, no information was gathered about the women's quality of life (Spiegel et al. 1989). Whether or not such interventions are characteristic of professional, as distinct from lay, support resources is another important research question (see Lenrow and Burch 1981: 238).

In the breast cancer study, the social support provided by the *group* was regarded as of primary therapeutic importance. Other group-based health interventions single out as the therapeutic agent the *content* of the group's work rather than its social dynamics. Thus, trials of eight-week relaxation sessions in reducing coronary risk have shown this approach effectively to lower blood pressure and coronary heart disease symptoms not only immediately following the intervention but four years later. The research team attributed the improvement to the methods of stress management taught (which were combined with the use of health education materials) and not to the social support of the group situation (Patel et al. 1985).

In so far as they demonstrate the health-promoting importance of essentially *non-professional* activities, findings of controlled social support interventions may threaten professionals' claims to expertise. Fischer's review of social work interventions (Fischer 1973) found that only one of the eleven methodologically adequate studies showed any effect of social work intervention: in this study of 164 elderly persons who had difficulty caring for themselves, the input of intensive individualized services from experienced caseworkers over a one-year period resulted in significantly higher death and institutionalization rates in the experimental as compared with the control group (Blenker et al. 1971). Commenting on these findings, Blenker and colleagues suggest the possibility that the 'dosage' of social worker support may have been 'too strong, our intervention too overwhelming, our takeover too final', and that perhaps 'we are prone to introduce the greatest changes in lives least able to bear them' (Blenker et al. 1971: 499). Conversely, a Danish study of elderly people employed interviewers (not social workers) to carry out three-monthly home visits to elderly people living in their own homes, with the aim of assessing whether or not medical and/or social preventive intervention needs that were disclosed to, and met, via the co-ordination of the interviewers could influence admission rates to hospitals and nursing homes. A control group, not visited, was interviewed for outcome data at the end of the study. Significantly fewer intervention-group elderly people were admitted to hospital, moved into nursing homes, made emergency medical calls or died (Hendriksen et al. 1984). The threat that controlled studies may pose to ideologies of professional expertise also extends to education. In one US pre-school education experiment, for instance, the impact of a new curriculum on 2- to 3-year-olds which seemed to be significant was found, when compared with a control group, to be no more effective than that of teachers simply reacting to children's initiatives (Palmer 1973).

One study not included in Fischer's 1973 review was the Cambridge–

Somerville Youth Study. This project, designed in the US during the 1930s Depression, was aimed ambitiously at the prevention of delinquency. The study took 650 'difficult' and 'average' boys aged between 5 and 11 – 325 matched pairs of which one of each was entered by random allocation into the experimental group and one into a control group. The 325 boys in the experimental group were assigned social workers and the help of a project team, which included a psychologist, psychiatrists, educational tutors and medical doctors. The programme ran from 1939 to 1945, during which period 'treated' boys were visited at home on average twice a month. An initial evaluation in 1948 showed that slightly more boys from the treatment group had been brought to court for a slightly larger number of offences (Powers and Witmer 1951). In 1975 there was a follow-up study of the 506 men from the original population who could be located; 42 per cent of the treatment group and 32 per cent of the control group had experienced 'undesirable outcomes' defined as criminal conviction, death before 35, alcoholism, schizophrenia or manic depression. These differences were 'statistically' significant. A search for subsets in the treatment population who might have benefited from the programme revealed none; on the contrary, several seemed to have been particularly disadvantaged by it, including boys aged between 9 and 11 at the onset of 'treatment', those visited very frequently and those whose counsellors had focused on personal or family problems. One explanation of these findings was the imposition on the boys of inappropriately middle-class values; another was the encouragement of dependency, with withdrawal effects at the termination of the programme; yet a third is the possible stigmatization resulting from social work intervention. In interviews carried out with 343 survivors to provide further illumination, significantly more of the treatment group confessed to being dissatisfied with life, work and marriage (more had been divorced), leading to the suggestion that 'treatment laid the groundwork for subsequent disillusionment' (McCord 1981: 402).

Controlled evaluations of social work interventions remain few and far between, despite the fact that these 'should be seen as an important and constructive means of appraising traditional modes of practice and of obtaining greatest benefit from the potentially valuable resource that social work represents' (Nolan et al. 1987: 415). The authors of this statement were responsible for a controlled trial of social work in 345 chronically ill Canadian children, the results of which demonstrated no effect of social work support on the children's behaviour, functioning or self-esteem or on that of mothers or family coping processes, despite the fact that social work support increased the utilization of primary care and hospital services. Most of the parents did not judge the social work support helpful to the child. Significantly, perhaps, the social workers' own judgements of their effectiveness showed poor agreement with those of the families.

Caring for women: interventions in motherhood

The content, design, effectiveness and implications of controlled interventions in pregnancy have recently been reviewed in the weighty two-volume compendium *Effective Care in Pregnancy and Childbirth* edited by Iain Chalmers, Murray Enkin and Marc Keirse, using the comprehensive database of controlled trials in perinatal medicine held at the National Perinatal Epidemiology Unit in Oxford (Chalmers et al. 1989a). The *Effective Care* volumes provide a systematic, methodologically grounded guide to science in perinatal care – that is, to the exercise of distinguishing those clinical interventions that are 'really' effective, appropriate and safe from those that are merely believed or claimed to be so. Both sorts tend to shelter under the umbrella of routine care. So do various forms of 'social' care provided for childbearing women which may also act to improve health and wellbeing. These form the background for the study described in this book – the *raison d'être* for supposing that, even within the narrowed frame of reference of the quantitative medical model, providing 'the milk of human kindness' (an apposite metaphor in the reproductive field?) may advance the health of both women and their children.

Lay companions in Guatemala City and elsewhere

In 1980, Roberto Sosa, John Kennell and Marshall Klaus published a path-breaking study conducted in Guatemala, showing that the support of a lay companion in labour significantly decreased the incidence of medical problems and increased maternal wellbeing. Women arriving at the Social Security Hospital in Guatemala City who had no known medical complications and were having their first child were offered randomization by sealed envelopes either to receive routine care or to receive the support of an untrained woman companion throughout labour. Support consisted of 'physical contact (e.g. rubbing the mother's back and holding her hands), conversation, and the presence of a friendly companion' (Sosa et al. 1980: 597). The design of this study was not simple, since women who developed problems were removed from the study, and both groups had forty-five minutes' private skin-to-skin contact with their newborns after delivery to test another favoured hypothesis of the research team about the importance of post-birth mother–infant bonding. But 63 per cent of intervention-group women had no problems, compared with 21 per cent of control-group women, and there was a differential distribution of problems between the groups: for example, 27 per cent of the control-group women, but 19 per cent of the intervention-group women, experienced Caesarean sections. Post-birth, the supported mothers were also more awake and stroked, smiled at and talked to their babies more. Sosa and colleagues' view is that the powerfully health-promoting effects of human companionship may well underlie the findings of studies of other perinatal interventions. For example, a number of randomized controlled trials of electronic fetal heart-rate monitoring in labour have failed to demonstrate the quick fix of technological solutions (Grant 1989). But the individualized midwifery care and close physical contact received by mothers in the control groups of these studies may well have acted to reduce anxiety and improve outcome, so countering or masking any 'real' benefit of the technological aid (Killien and Shy 1989).

The Guatemala research team went on to carry out a second larger study in the same hospital (Klaus et al. 1986). In this, women were randomized either to receive standard care or lay support, again provided by local women with no obstetric training who gave both emotional and physical support. Table 3.2 shows the outcomes of the second study. They are similar in direction of effect to those of the first study and demonstrate 'the benefits associated with the introduction of support during labour in a population of poor women who routinely undergo labour alone in a crowded ward' (Klaus et al. 1986: 586). The research team speculated about the mechanisms by which social support can have these effects: the presence of a companion could directly influence the likelihood of obstetricians intervening; or lay support may reduce anxiety and therefore adrenalin production known to be a factor in the prolongation of labour. In an observation pertinent to our own SSPO study, they also conjecture that 'social support might reduce the number of infants admitted for intensive care' (Klaus et al. 1986: 587).

The Guatemalan studies used 'low-risk' women. Many social interventions have adopted the opposite strategy and tested the impact of support

Table 3.2 Perinatal problems in supported and unsupported women

Problem	Supported (N = 168) %	Unsupported (N = 249) %	Significance
No problems	73	41	
Total problems	27	59	p < 0.001
Caesarean section	7	17	p < 0.01
Meconium staining	13	18	
Asphyxia	2	3	
Oxytocin	2	13	p < 0.001
Analgesia	1	4	
Forceps	1	3	
Other	1	1	

Source: Klaus et al. 1986: 586

in women known or expected to have problems. In Birmingham, England, Judy Dance (1987) looked at the effect of 'linkworkers' on the care of Pakistani women who had already had one low-birthweight baby. Of fifty women in the study, twenty-five were randomized to have linkworker support; the linkworkers were women of childbearing age with some formal western education, and were fluent English-speakers who also spoke at least one of the local minority languages. They visited the intervention-group women three to five times during pregnancy to give information on health needs, facilities and services, and to advise, befriend and support. The effect of this scheme was to increase birthweight from 2748 g in the control group, to 2974 g in the intervention group, and to concentrate other positive experiences more in the intervention than in the control group, including fewer medical problems and more happiness in pregnancy, shorter labours, less analgesia and fewer babies with feeding problems (Dance 1987).

Talking to the patient

In the Guatemalan and Birmingham studies, part of the social interveners' role was 'talking to the patient'. Whatever the users of professional health care may want (and there is evidence that many *do* want to be talked to), the evolution of modern technological medicine has demoted the importance of talk within medical encounters (Reiser 1978). Whereas formerly doctors needed to talk to patients to obtain information about their condition, now laboratory tests and other technologies of information-gathering have replaced with more 'objective' data the doctor's reliance on the patient as a source of information. Conversation has consequently left the clinical domain and entered that of the social.

Carpenter and colleagues' study of the benefits of talking to medical students is one which underlines the importance of conversation to health (Carpenter et al. 1968). The health-promoting power of talk can also be demonstrated by comparing medical encounters with and without talking. Two studies of ultrasound examination, one British, one American, have done this. In the American study (Field et al. 1985) twenty pregnant women were assigned to a group in which no feedback was given about the process of the examination, and twenty women were allowed to see the ultrasound monitor and 'were given a running description of fetal anatomy, measurements, and movements'. Not only were the women in the latter group significantly less anxious, but they slept better and ate more in pregnancy, had fewer obstetric complications, and less irritable and larger babies. In the British study, talking to women about the ultrasound examinations resulted in short-term changes in health-related behaviour, including cigarette smoking, alcohol consumption and visiting the dentist (Reading et al. 1982).

As with the Guatemalan studies, the findings of the US study have led to the suggestion that the social support provided in the course of carrying out ultrasound may be the factor responsible for any improved outcomes attributed to ultrasound screening itself. In a recent Swedish controlled trial of one-stage ultrasound, the fact that the screening was done in 'a "comfortable" atmosphere' in which 'there was usually time for parents to take a good look at the fetus' was felt to be the most probable explanation for the higher mean birthweight and better perinatal health of screened babies (Waldenstrom et al. 1988: 588). However, the social support effects of ultrasound have also been subjected to a different interpretation: that of maternal–infant bonding. This interpretation is consistent with the general obstetrical response to evidence about consumer dissatisfaction, which has been to admit the legitimacy of mothers' complaints about depersonalized care in the form of a new technical language psychologizing the social (Arney 1982). As others have argued, the 'pseudoscience' of bonding theory is derived from a large number of small intervention studies evaluating the effects of increased postnatal contact between mothers and babies. Many of these studies are short on methodological rigour. Of the five 'best' trials identified in a review by Thomson and Kramer (1984), three reported a beneficial effect of extra early contact, while two demonstrated none.

As regards ultrasound and maternal–infant bonding, it is interesting that the evidence of behavioural effects on women is taken to constitute a case for routine ultrasound, despite lack of evidence of its clinical effectiveness (Shafi et al. 1988; on clinical effectiveness, see Neilson and Grant 1989). There are, of course, other ways of encouraging communication in maternity care aside from providing high-cost technology to talk about. One way is to transfer the responsibility for holding information about the progress of pregnancy from the care-givers to pregnant women themselves. Here two British studies, one in London, and one in rural Berkshire, have demonstrated the power of 'allowing' women to hold their own case-notes. In the rural study, case-note carrying resulted in women feeling that communication with doctors and midwives was easier; they also felt more in control (Elbourne et al. 1987). These findings were paralleled in the London study, which also reported a tendency towards fewer low-birthweight babies in the group of women holding their own case-notes (Lovell et al. 1986).

Education for childbirth or for women?

Ever since the 'founding father' of natural childbirth, Grantly Dick-Read, pioneered the value of psychological preparation for childbirth in the 1930s, antenatal education has had its proselytizers, its enthusiastic users, its sceptics and its critics. Controlled studies of antenatal education with adequate sample sizes are far fewer than reports of success based on observation. And as David Banta (1984: 6) has argued, 'the efficacy of an educational procedure is no more self-evident than is that of a medical procedure.'

While the results of different controlled studies in the area of antenatal education conflict, overall, as Penny Simkin and Murray Enkin (1989) demonstrate in their review, it is justifiable to claim that prepared women use less analgesic medication and feel less pain in labour. A study by Timm (1979) examined the hypothesis that this effect is due specifically to childbirth preparation, and not to some generalized social support. In a comparison of prenatal classes with knitting classes, knitting proved less effective than antenatal education in reducing labour medication. A crucial missing piece of information concerns whether or not the mothers assigned to the knitting group liked knitting: if they disliked it, it is hardly surprising that it did not relax them. Maternal preference emerged as critical in another study of the effect of music on fetal state in late pregnancy: fetuses moved more when their mothers liked the music being played than when they did not (a direct effect of fetal preference was ruled out by transmitting the music to mothers through earphones) (Zimmer et al. 1982).

The training of childbirth educators has been shown to be important, though in what are perhaps counter-intuitive ways. In a US study, teachers trained in communication skills were more likely to have pupils who reported significantly higher levels of labour pain than a comparison group with untrained teachers. The researchers interpreted this finding as evidence for the 'analgesic ideal' model of prepared childbirth: in emphasizing the goal of pain- and analgesia-free childbirth, childbirth educators may positively discourage open communication of pain experiences (Cogan and Winer 1982). There are likely to be different positive and negative effects from different methods of childbirth preparation, and the field is one particularly prone to different fashions. Murray Enkin and colleagues' own study of Leboyer delivery showed that the *expectation* of a gentle, noise-free, lamplit delivery with unhurried cord-cutting and paternal bathing of the infant was sufficient to produce shorter labours. Eight months on, although no 'objective' differences between infants delivered by Leboyer and routine methods could be detected, women who had experienced Leboyer deliveries were significantly more likely to *refer* their child's behaviour to the method of its birth (Nelson et al. 1980).

The father's role in natural childbirth practices is often regarded as pivotal. Indeed, paternal attendance at childbirth is one of the main ways in which institutionalized childbirth has responded to the consumer demand for more humane care. There does, however, remain a lack of clarity about what fathers should actually *do* at childbirth and, indeed, whether mothers want them there in the first place. Childbirth education has been generally criticized for its heterosexist bias (see e.g. Oakley 1981b); many practices and texts are suffused with the ideology of the happy nuclear family. One North American study even set out to use antenatal education to increase couples' intimacy; comparing standard Lamaze classes with Lamaze classes topped up with 'interpersonal need' exercises, it aimed to increase 'love scale scores'. The study failed in this objective, though the women in the intervention group did demonstrate more need for affection (Spence Cagle 1984). Like the higher pain levels admitted by the women in the Cogan and Winer study, this finding can be seen either as a beneficial or as a negative effect.

As with most of the studies discussed in this chapter, controlled trials of childbirth education vary in the type and range of outcomes they report. Most are restricted to the labour and delivery period. One of the earliest studies, however, set out to examine the effectiveness of preparation for parenthood in reducing unhappiness after childbirth (Gordon and Gordon 1960). Two strategies were compared: 'normal' antenatal education, and an enhanced programme of two extra forty-minute periods of instruction and discussion which emphasized the importance of new mothers exploiting the social support resources of their own family and neighbourhood networks, looking after themselves, and keeping up outside interests. The enhanced programme achieved significantly less post-delivery emotional upset (Gordon and Gordon 1960). Similar interventions introduced *after* birth have been shown to have positive social support effects. In New York State, Olds and colleagues employed public health nurses in a series of postnatal visits to educate women about parenthood, and encourage their use of both formal and informal social support resources. Visited women reported feeling more in control and having happier children, and their children had fewer physician-treated accidents and hospital emergency admissions (Olds et al. 1986). Group interventions have been tried, too, as in McGuire and Gottlieb's (1979) study of social support groups among new parents led by family physicians and their wives.[2] Compared with the results for couples receiving 'written educational materials only', the social support groups had an impact on couples' mobilization of the help of family and friends. The effectiveness of social support is likely to be dramatically demonstrated in particular circumstances, for example when babies die. An Oxford study of perinatal bereavement counselling found significantly reduced chances of psychiatric disorders among counselled women (Forrest et al. 1982).

Antenatal education can be supportive or didactic. As well as the substantial literature on education for childbirth, there is also one on the education of women according to professional definitions of healthy motherhood. As Judith Lumley and Jill Astbury put it (1989: 237), 'The most common form of remedy offered to pregnant women comes in the guise of "advice". However, this is no ordinary advice, there being no option of refusal.' A major focus of professional energy has been anti-smoking advice or cessation programmes. These have varied from giving personalized supportive counselling (see e.g. Sexton and Hebel 1984; Windsor et al. 1985), to employing 'shock' tactics such as demonstrating the level of carbon monoxide in the alveolar air of 'public prenatal patients' in North Carolina (Bauman et al. 1983), to telling women not to smoke 'for the sake of the baby' (Donovan 1977). The more socially supportive interventions that have included help on *how* to give up smoking have generally been the most effective, both in terms of reduced smoking and in terms of increased birthweight (other outcomes including women's experiences of motherhood have not been looked at) (see Lumley and Astbury (1989) for a discussion). Smoking during pregnancy is an area in which uncontrolled observations are particularly likely to suggest an impact of educational programmes. However, many women change their behaviour in pregnancy without any professional intervention of any kind: some 25 per cent, for example, will give up smoking. An uncontrolled anti-smoking health education intervention could lead to this 25 per cent cessation rate being judged a programme success (Banta 1984).

The popularity of anti-smoking interventions derives from health professionals' identification of maternal smoking as a factor underlying poor perinatal health and as one capable of change. A similar view holds for health service use. Based on the assumption that low rates of health service use in pregnancy and afterwards contribute to the chances of adverse health outcomes, mothers have been exhorted by means of various 'social' interventions to make more use of professional care. Once again, most of the target populations used in such studies have been socially disadvantaged. Programmes of pre- and postnatal home visits from child psychologists (Larson 1980), 'perinatal nurse practitioners' (Yanover et al. 1976) and public health nurses (Gutelius et al. 1977; Olds et al. 1986) have been hailed as effective ways to promote more appropriate health service use, as well as other outcomes including enhanced maternal child attachment and participatory fathers (Larson 1980; Yanover et al. 1976; Olds et al. 1986), and improved nutrition and child development (Gutelius et al. 1977). In the latter study, the intervention of public health nurses was said to be associated with a greater likelihood of mothers going back into education and of fathers not changing their jobs. Such associations highlight the need for an interpretation at the level of meaning to supplement the results of tests of 'statistical' significance. The need for more methodological sophistication is confirmed by another study carried out in North Carolina by Marie Lowe. The study aim was to induce greater 'compliance' with medical recommendations in a sample of 'Negro primigravidae' randomized to receive instructions from public health nurses or to receive routine care. The object of the instructional programme was to increase the keeping of clinic appointments and to change eating, smoking, drinking, medicine-taking, rest, exercise and personal hygiene habits. However, the only areas which showed change due to the programme were gardening work (more in the instructed group) and sleeping for eight hours a night (more in the control group). The investigator concluded that these somewhat curious findings 'suggest a need to examine critically the traditional practice of public health nursing' (Lowe 1970: 63).

What do women really want?

In answering the ill-formed question 'What do women want?' (see Riley 1977), much of the consumer satisfaction literature identifies continuity of care as the *sine qua non* of client-sensitive care. A major group of randomized controlled interventions confirms the relevance of this finding to maternal and infant health. This category of studies overlaps with those which compare the acceptability and effectiveness of midwife and obstetrician care, since the professional ideology of midwifery emphasizes caring for pregnant women on an individual basis as people enmeshed in social lives rather than merely vehicles for fetal growth, and midwives' focus on the presumed *normality* of childbirth also stresses the importance of *social care* as distinct from *clinical interventions*. Caroline Flint's 'Know Your Midwife' (KYM) scheme pioneered as a research study at St George's Hospital in London is the exemplar here (Flint and Poulengeris 1987). Comparing maternal and infant outcomes among 503 women randomized to receive care from a team of four midwives, with those in 498 women randomized to receive normal hospital care, Flint found significantly greater satisfaction, control and information among women in the KYM group, as well as lower antenatal hospital admission rates, more spontaneous labours, less analgesia and slightly bigger babies (see table 3.3). The St George's study echoed findings of earlier explorations of the health-promoting potential of midwife care. Lillian Runnerstrom in the US compared nurse-midwife care with care provided by obstetric residents for 4500 women with uncomplicated pregnancies. She found that nurse midwives, compared with doctors, more often used no or only inhalational analgesia, their care was associated with shorter labours, a lower operative-delivery rate, a lower LBW rate and fewer postnatal complications (Runnerstrom 1969).[3] A second American study carried out in the mid-1970s also concluded that mothers cared for by nurse midwives had more spontaneous deliveries (Slome et al. 1976).

   Controlled studies of (nurse-) midwife and obstetrician care are usually restricted to women defined as at low risk of developing problems, presumably because midwives are not seen as the appropriate people to provide care for high-risk women. Two French trials have examined the health-promoting potential of additional home visits by midwives for a different group of women: those with pregnancy complications. (Routine home visits by midwives are included in the normal maternity care system in France.) The first study demonstrated an adverse effect of home visits on women with medical risk, but a protective effect on those with 'social' risk (Spira et al. 1981). Doubts have been raised about whether the randomiz-

Table 3.3 Pregnancy outcomes in women receiving continuity of care (the Know Your Midwife scheme) and those receiving routine antenatal care

Outcome	Know Your Midwife (N = 503) %	Control (N = 498) %	Significance
Oxytocin	28	38	p < 0.01
Caesarean section	8	7	
Forceps/ventouse	12	16	p < 0.05
Analgesia[a]	49	62	p < 0.0001
Resuscitation[b]	20	27	p < 0.05
Birthweight:			
2500 g or less	7	8	
2501–3500 g	61	64	
3501–4500 g	32	27	
4501 g or more	<1	1	
Total	100	100	
Mean birthweight in grams (s.d.[b])	3284 (0.55)	3218 (0.55)	

[a]Excluding entonox.
[b]Excluding mucus extraction.
[c]Standard deviation.
Source: Flint and Poulengeris n.d.

ation 'worked' in this case, as the group of women visited at home had more medical risks than the group not visited (Lumley 1988). The second French study, set up (unusually) to look at the economic costs of service use and women's satisfaction (in that order), instead of the usual narrow range of obstetric outcomes, found that midwife home visits reduced outpatient clinic visits and substantially raised women's satisfaction (Blondel et al. n.d.).

Midwives are not only more likely to provide social care, they are more likely to be found doing this in community settings. In a Glasgow study comparing hospital antenatal and community clinic care, Reid and colleagues (1983) reported that women judged the community clinic more personal and friendly than the hospital clinic, experienced more continuity of care and were more satisfied overall. They were also more likely to have normal-weight babies, though this was not statistically significant. Against the advantages of community care was the stereotyping by clinic staff of patients attending these clinics as irresponsible, childish and unable to make 'sensible' health care decisions. One is reminded here of the lessons of the Cambridge–Somerville Youth Study.

Given that many social investigations in this field have explored the potential of social support to help socially disadvantaged women in particular, it is surprising that few have specifically aimed to provide material aid. In Gary, Indiana, between 1970 and 1974, an income maintenance experiment was carried out in a predominantly poor black area (Kehrer and Wohin 1979). Its object was not the promotion of healthy pregnancy *per se*, but rather to test the superiority of a negative income-tax procedure over traditional forms of public welfare. On the assumption that the incidence of LBW is affected by take-up of prenatal care and by diet,[4] it was hypothesized that the Gary experiment could have influenced birthweight by increasing the amount of money available for spending on medical care and on food. Birthweight data for 404 of the programme's participants (256 experimental and 148 control group) did not support this view: experimental-group babies had a mean birthweight 26 g lower than that of controls. However, subgroup analysis revealed statistically significant beneficial effects of the income maintenance programme for young smoking mothers and for smoking mothers aged 18 and older who had had a short interval between their pregnancies. The notion that any beneficial health effects of income maintenance had been secured via greater use of medical care was ruled out by the data on prenatal care in the two groups, but there was some evidence from nutritional data collected as part of the original experiment that the quality of diets of experimental-group families had improved.

In the Indiana study, it was not known whether women benefited directly from any improvement in household diet. The traditional assumption of household studies – that within households there is an equitable distribution of resources – has been shown to be a poor match with the empirical evidence (Brannen and Wilson 1987). Because of this, it has been difficult to judge the effectiveness of trials of dietary supplementation in pregnancy, and essential to consider all such studies as social interventions in which the concentration of research interest in experimental groups may well achieve a health-promoting 'placebo' effect which is then falsely attributed to the 'mechanical' effect of extra food. The evidence, as judged by birthweight, is that both natural and iatrogenic dietary restriction in pregnancy is health-damaging. Trials of dietary *advice* show higher rates of normal birthweight (Cameron and Graham 1944; Berry and Wiehl 1952); so do studies of dietary *supplementation* in which the research design makes it difficult to establish whether 'target' mothers took the supplementary food or gave it to other household members (see Rush 1989 for a discussion). In an interesting analysis of a dietary supplementation programme in San Francisco, Adams and colleagues compared the pregnancy results of three groups of women, one receiving a high-protein and one a low-protein supplement and the third a vitamin–mineral preparation. All three groups of women had LBW rates lower than would be expected in that population, suggesting a non-specific beneficial research effect (Adams et al. 1978). Trials in which supplementation is not under the participants' control have produced a complicated array of findings. Type of supplementation is crucial: the higher the protein density, the greater the chance that birthweight will be *decreased*. The size of the birthweight effect in trials of nutritional counselling and/or supplementation with lower-protein-density foods is in the range 30–50 g and is generally substantially lower than experimenters have hoped for (see Rush 1989 for a review).

Promises of Evian water

All the various groups of intervention studies drawn on this chapter provided fuel for the argument that giving people social support is likely to be good for their health. It was against this background that the SSPO study was planned. It is obvious that social interventions in health, although adding up to impressive evidence that social support *is* health-promoting, have varied ethically, methodologically, conceptually and in terms of the policy concerns they address. A major problem, particularly in the area of motherhood, is with the lack of consistency in the different outcome measures used. For example, while one study may use birthweight and make no reference to other labour and delivery variables, or to the quality of mothers' experiences, another will focus on the latter to the exclusion of the former. These problems of non-compatibility bedevil the newly fashionable exercise of meta-analysis – combining data from many smaller studies to increase the statistical power of the studies to answer questions about the effectiveness of particular interventions. Two meta-analyses have been carried out using many of the perinatal studies referred to in this chapter. One looked at psychological and behavioural effects (Elbourne et al. 1989); the other at effects on gestational age at delivery and birthweight (Elbourne and Oakley 1991). The former drew on fourteen trials of enhanced social and psychological support in pregnancy, concluding that supported women are less likely than controls to feel unhappy, nervous and worried during pregnancy, less likely to feel negatively about the forthcoming birth, to have difficulties communicating with staff, to feel in control during pregnancy, to attend antenatal classes, to be satisfied with antenatal care, to have a companion with them during labour and to report a worry-free labour; after delivery they are also less likely to be unhappy, fathers are more likely to be involved in infant care, and the women are more likely to be breastfeeding and to feel in control in the early weeks of motherhood. The second study examined the gestational age and birthweight impact of thirty-five social interventions in pregnancy, finding no statistical evidence that social support affected the preterm delivery rate or the rate of LBW or very-low-birthweight babies.

Interpretation of the importance of these 'meta-analytical' findings is returned to in chapter 11.

We were not alone in planning our SSPO study: at the same time as we were trying to get funding, there were others who were taking forward similar ideas. An important medium of communication was a conference held in Evian, France, in 1985, which reviewed the state of the art in the field of preterm birth prevention. Each of the studies discussed at the Evian conference was unique, but all shared the goal of trying to *prevent* LBW/preterm birth by a variety of social and medical means. Three studies in particular carried out in West Australia, South Carolina and South Manchester all helped to shape the London-based SSPO study (and in turn our study fed into the design and interpretation of theirs). In South Carolina, obstetrician Henry Heins had already embarked on this area of research out of a concern with the high level of perinatal mortality and low birthweight (the highest of all the US states) in South Carolina, a predominantly poor rural area. Clinicians there were especially concerned about the rate of childbearing in young women, and had set up a service to provide extra support for young mothers. Called the 'Resource Mothers Program', this service provided advisers from the local community who visited pregnant teenagers at home and helped in a variety of practical ways during pregnancy (Heins et al. 1987). The Resource Mothers, like the labour companions in Guatemala City, were local women, mothers themselves, judged to have 'personal warmth, successful parenting experience, knowledge of community resources [and] demonstrated leadership' (Heins et al. 1987: 1–2). They were given six weeks' training to acquaint them with local community resources, relevant medical knowledge and 'home visiting' skills and were paid a minimum wage of $8000 p.a. and expenses for their work, which included 24-hour-a-day availability to the women they were supporting. During monthly visits, the Resource Mothers were instructed to focus their intervention on 'the strength of each mother, the teen's family and friends', and to encourage use of the women's own social support networks. The aims of the study were to increase use of medical and social services, to 'improve maternal childbearing attitudes and parenting behaviour' and to promote women's confidence and control. It will be obvious that these goals are somewhat contradictory, combining as they do an awareness of women's pregnancy needs with the motive of a more overtly instructional programme designed to produce 'good' mothers. A main purpose of the Resource Mothers' home visits was to stress the unborn's dependence on the mother's healthy behaviour, in particular the importance of attending for regular prenatal checks, diet, reduction of alcohol, nicotine and caffeine intake, exercise and rest, and 'no drugs of any kind without permission'. The young mothers in the study were interrogated by the Resource Mothers as to their childrearing practices, and observed and rated feeding and 'diapering' their babies.

The Resource Mothers programme was an uncontrolled intervention, which made it difficult to judge whether it was successful or not. In order to evaluate it, Heins used a matched cohort design, taking 575 young women who had taken part in the programme and matching these with another 575 who had not. The matching extended to maternal age and obstetric history, year of delivery, county of residence and race and sex of child. Most of the young women were black (89 per cent) and single (93 per cent). On this basis Heins argued that the provision of Resource Mothers lowered the rate of very-low-birthweight babies and of neonatal and infant deaths.

To overcome the objection that, despite matching of cases and controls, whatever the Resource Mothers did could not be proved to have worked, Heins then set up an RCT of nurse-midwife prenatal care. In this trial, all women attending state-funded prenatal clinics in South Carolina were eligible provided they had previously had a low-birthweight baby or scored ten or more on a risk-scoring system composed of a mix of social and medical factors, and developed in previous work by French and US obstetricians (see Papiernik-Berkhauer 1980; Creasy et al. 1980; and pp. 268–70 for a discussion). A total of 1458 women were randomized by telephone either to the intervention group, which received nurse-midwifery prenatal care in a separate LBW prevention clinic, or to the control group receiving normal high-risk obstetric care. Funding for the trial also covered the payment of most of the women's medical expenses, irrespective of group allocation, provided gross family income was less than 150 per cent of a prevailing poverty guideline, and the women were less than 30 weeks pregnant at trial entry. In the intervention group, women were seen every one to two weeks throughout pregnancy by a nurse midwife, and were referred to obstetricians only if medical complications arose. An important part of the care was teaching women to recognize early warning signs of preterm labour; they were also examined internally at each visit to assess the condition of the cervix. Control-group women receiving standard high-risk care were seen less often, with less of an emphasis on their social circumstances, and were not taught to recognize impending preterm labour or given routine internal examinations. The results of the study in terms of birthweight groups are shown in table 3.4. It was concluded that the study had been 'unable to detect any evidence of an important reduction in the incidence of either LBW or preterm birth'; but the research team argued that the results could usefully be interpreted to conclude that nurse-midwife care was as effective as that provided by obstetricians for women judged to be at risk of having LBW babies (Heins et al. 1990).

A second study whose design and rationale paralleled those of the SSPO study was carried out in Western Australia. Its prime movers were Fiona Stanley and Bob Bryce, medically trained epidemiologists. Their intention was to test the power to reduce the incidence of preterm labour

Table 3.4 Birthweight outcomes in the South Carolina social support trial

Birthweight group	Intervention (N = 667) %	Control (N = 679) %
Less than 1500 g	4	4
1500–2499 g	15	16
2500 g or more	81	80
Total	100	100

Source: Heins et al. 1990

of 'socio-medical support' provided by midwives (see Stanley and Bryce 1986). Women attending public hospital antenatal clinics or the offices of obstetricians or GPs were offered enrolment if they spoke English, were less than 25 weeks pregnant and had any one or more of previous preterm birth, previous LBW babies, previous perinatal deaths, three or more previous spontaneous first-trimester abortions, one or more previous spontaneous second-trimester abortions or an antepartum haemorrhage in a previous pregnancy. The basis on which enrolment was offered was explained as allocation either to a programme of home visits designed to provide a listening ear for the women's problems or to interviews with a researcher inquiring into women's pregnancy feelings. Women in the control group received standard obstetric care in addition to research visits, and women in the intervention group received the offer of midwife visits plus the research interviews.

The research midwives made home visits and telephone calls and aimed to increase 'expressive support by providing sympathy, empathy, understanding, acceptance and affection'. A total of 1970 women were enrolled in the trial, 983 of whom were allocated to be offered the intervention. The project achieved a statistically non-significant decrease in the incidence of preterm birth, from 15 per cent in the control to 13 per cent in the intervention group (see table 3.5). Adjusting for the potential confounding variables of obstetric history, social class, smoking, age, private versus public antenatal care, race and multiple pregnancy, the results showed a statistically significant effect of the programme. Analysis of subgroups showed that women who benefited most were socially supported and middle class. This was different from the subgroup analysis in the Heins study, which showed maximum effect in black women with high-risk scores.

A third controlled intervention with a similar rationale to the SSPO study was carried out by Brenda Spencer in South Manchester (Spencer and Morris 1986; Spencer et al. 1989). The Manchester team used 'Family Workers' to provide their intervention, modelled on the French *travailleuses familiales* system. The Manchester Family Workers were funded by

Table 3.5 The Western Australia trial of antenatal social support: pregnancy outcomes

Outcome	Programme (N = 981) %	Control (N = 986) %
Live and stillbirths less than 2500 g	12	13
Births at less than 37 weeks gestation	13	15
Mean birthweight (g)	(3140)	(3120)

Source: Bryce et al. 1991

the Manpower Services Commission, which provided employment for certain categories of unemployed people. Like the Resource Mothers and the Guatemalan labour companions, they were women with no professional training in the health or social services, but 'carefully selected on other criteria, related to personality and general life experience'. They had to show ability to empathize and be non-judgemental in relation to their clients' attitudes and behaviours. Their role was seen as one of primary prevention through the medium of home visits and practically oriented help including the facilitation of access to services, the provision of information about financial benefits, improved housing and the principles of healthy nutrition. As with the Heins and Stanley trials, a list of risk criteria were used to identify the research population, including both social (class, 'marital' status, employment) and medical (previous LBW and perinatal death, spontaneous abortions, short interpregnancy interval). Women had to be less than 24 weeks pregnant. Once identified, they were randomized, and those allocated to the intervention group were sent a letter offering the help of a Family Worker; 41 per cent accepted. Acceptors were more likely to be middle class, employed and married and to have had a previous LBW and/or perinatal death. Birthweight outcomes at the end of the study showed either no difference or a small (statistically 'non-

Table 3.6 The South Manchester Family Worker project: pregnancy outcomes

Outcome	Experimental (N = 602) %	Control (N = 581) %
Live and stillbirths less than 2500 g	9	9
Births at less than 37 weeks gestation	10	9
Mean birthweight (g)	(3180)	(3215)

Source: Spencer et al. 1989

significant') positive effect of the Family Worker help: the figures are given in table 3.6. The design of this trial, as noted in chapter 6, had significant implications for the analysis of data. Randomization was carried out before women were asked if they wished to take part (those allocated to the control group were not told about the study), and a significant proportion of experimental-group women – nearly 60 per cent – refused the offer of Family Worker help. However, following the practice of analysing trials on an 'intention to treat' basis, the figures shown in table 3.6 include in the experimental group the women who did not receive the intervention.

Consenting adults?

A subject of considerable importance in the design of randomized controlled interventions is the extent to which, and the way in which, people who take part in research are asked for their consent on the basis of information about the aims and content of the research. Chapter 6 considers some of the ways in which the issue of women's consent was raised in the course of our study. In general terms, the question of consent problematizes the division between quantitative and qualitative methodology in critical ways: whereas the laboratory-science model of controlled experimental research presupposes no social consciousness on the part of those who take part in research, the social model of research requires that research participants be informed and consenting, and, indeed, that researchers take on board research participants' consciousness of their role as a variable of potential 'confounding' importance to interpretation of the study findings. To seek consent is to intervene. In studies of social support particularly, the intervention of asking for consent must be viewed as liable to blur the division between intervention and control groups in ways that can significantly alter research findings.

Little information is given in the published papers referred to in this chapter concerning the consent process, especially in the earlier studies. Until the late 1950s there was almost no discussion, in either Europe or North America, of informed consent in medical or health research. The term itself seems to have been created in legal circles in 1957, and this legal base has been a continuing important pressure on doctors and medical researchers to consider the issue of what patients should know. Consent to participate in research is not yet, however, the rule in medical research. Faulder (1985) estimates that as many as 10 per cent of British patients may be included in RCTs of one kind or another, and are likely to be in varying states of ignorance about their status as research subjects. An example highlighted in the British press recently is that of Evelyn Thomas, an Open University lecturer who spent four years establishing that she had been entered without her knowledge into two trials of breast cancer treatments. For both these trials, ethics committee approval had been given *but did not require informed consent*. Evelyn Thomas points out that her opposition to what happened was not based on hostility to the importance of RCTs: 'As a scientist who has herself carried out physiological research on human subjects, obviously I approve of scientific methods in medicine. But RCTs must only be used with the informed consent of participating patients' (Thomas 1988).

In the USA, written signed consent came into fashion in the 1960s, although as protection more for the doctor than for the patient, given the different organizational base of the US health care system, and its more obvious domination by the practice and threat of litigation. In Britain, the current legal position is that, in seeking informed consent, doctors are not obliged fully to disclose all the risks of any procedure, particularly when disclosure is thought by the doctor likely to cause the patient undue anxiety and/or persuade her/him not to accept treatment medically deemed to be beneficial (Brahams 1983). The essential conflict is between what Fader and Beauchamp (1986: 171) term the 'principle of consent', on the one hand, and a 'methodology of deception', on the other. Following the 'methodology of deception' principle enables researchers to adhere more strictly to the quantitative laboratory-science model of research than they would otherwise be able to do. It is important to note that informed consent is an issue in the ordinary practice setting, as well as in research. In a recent study in Birmingham of patient consent to vaginal examinations by medical students in a hospital with a high proportion of Asian and West Indian patients, although it was hospital practice to solicit verbal consent for medical students' vaginal examinations in the clinic setting, patients were not asked for consent regarding, nor indeed informed about, the very common practice of students carrying out such examinations on anaesthetized patients. A questionnaire among hospital patients showed that 100 per cent believed their consent should be sought in such situations. Some would feel 'physically assaulted' if this were not done (Bibby et al. 1988).

It has been customary to design RCTs in a number of ways. The differences between the designs centre on two issues: (1) the relationship between randomization, consent and data collection and (2) whether or not the trial analysis is done on an 'intention to treat' basis (so that data are collected on all randomly allocated subjects) or only on the basis of those who *were* treated. Figure 3.1 shows three variations on the possible combinations of these practices. In design A, which has been in common use, informed consent is sought from the experimental group only after randomization. But data are collected on all randomized subjects, whether or not their consent to take part in the research was requested and obtained, so that the subgroups of subjects randomized to the experimental and control groups who do not give their consent none the less

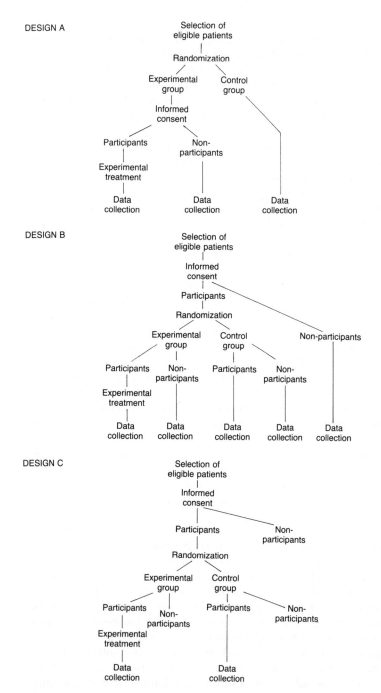

DESIGN A

Selection of eligible patients

Randomization

Experimental group — Control group

Informed consent

Participants — Non-participants

Experimental treatment

Data collection — Data collection — Data collection

DESIGN B

Selection of eligible patients

Informed consent

Participants

Randomization — Non-participants

Experimental group — Control group

Participants — Non-participants — Participants — Non-participants

Experimental treatment

Data collection — Data collection — Data collection — Data collection — Data collection

DESIGN C

Selection of eligible patients

Informed consent

Participants — Non-participants

Randomization

Experimental group — Control group

Participants — Non-participants — Participants — Non-participants

Experimental treatment

Data collection — Data collection

Figure 3.1 Different designs for randomized controlled trials

involuntarily contribute data. In design B, consent is solicited before randomization, but, because data collection and analysis proceed on the 'intention to treat' principle, once again data on all patients are collected, whether or not they regard themselves as participating in the research; data are also collected on those who did not consent to take part in the trial. This seems to be the most frequently used RCT design at the moment in UK medical research. In design C, like design B, consent is sought before randomization. But, by contrast with design B, only those who agree have information collected on them; those who refuse either initially or subsequently are excluded from data collection and analysis.

Since there is no national register of RCTs, it is hard to know the distribution of different designs. The Stanley and Spencer social support studies used design A, in which only the experimental-group women were informed that they had been randomized and asked for their consent. In the Heins study, no informed consent was asked for or given following a decision of the Institutional Review Board of the Medical University of South Carolina, which declared such a procedure unnecessary 'because there was no unusual or hazardous risk involved in prenatal care given in either group' (Heins et al. 1990: 343). For our own SSPO study, we chose to use design C. The reasons why we chose to use it can be deduced from the arguments advanced in favour of the other methods, particularly design A, which is defended on the grounds that giving people information about the possible side-effects of different treatments may be hazardous to their health (Loftus and Fries 1979). In another version of this response, the danger that the stress of receiving information may affect health directly results in the conclusion not that *all* patients in a trial should be equally informed, irrespective of group allocation, but rather that *no* patient should be informed at all (Papaioannou 1982; see Oakley 1989 for a discussion).

How researchers treat the issue of consent is important for ethical, methodological and theoretical reasons. The ethical debate is taken up later in this book. As regards methodology, in the light of the evidence discussed in this and the previous chapter, it is clearly crucial for intervention studies to include an informed control group, if for no other purpose than to act as a control for the social support input of whatever is being done to the intervention group. Controlled trials of dietary advice, for example, cannot hope to distinguish the impact of dietary advice from the enhanced support that intervention-group members may feel as a result of the researchers' interest in them, unless there is a comparison group in whom the researchers are also interested but for whom they are not providing the particular dietary intervention under test. Secondly, trials using design A are stuck with the problem that people allocated to receive an intervention who refuse consent must be included in the analysis with those who did receive it. In the Spencer trial, for example, some 60 per cent of women randomized to receive the intervention were in this position.

Conclusion

Social interventions in motherhood, childhood and family life derive from policy concerns about the extent to which people are receiving the help they need to achieve health and wellbeing in societies known to be socially inequitable. Such interventions also result from the interests of academic researchers in understanding the relative inputs to health and wellbeing of formal and informal support, and of childhood and adult socialization. A major problem in understanding social interventions lies with the challenge these may pose to commonsense understandings of how health is best promoted: it may seem self-evident that additional feeding of pregnant women will benefit their infants, that hormonal supplementation will increase the chances of successful pregnancy, that new educational curricula will improve children's learning, that additional stimulation in infancy will have long-term cognitive effects, that social work services to socially disadvantaged children will help prevent delinquency; yet, in all these cases, comparison of how 'treated' groups fare with those untreated contrasts common sense with the findings of systematic evaluation.

Without such bases for comparative evaluation, it can be difficult to make sense of research findings. Discussing the long-term evaluation of the Cambridge–Somerville Youth Study, Joan McCord comments:

> Had there been no control group, evaluation of the program might have led to radically different conclusions. Client evaluation seems to have been favourable ... Two thirds of the men responded that the program had been helpful ... The men mentioned that the program had kept them off the streets, taught them to be more understanding, showed them that there were people around who cared. (McCord 1982: 403–4)

However, because the study design included a control group, these favourable comments were countered by statistical evidence of negative effects. Were the apparent negative effects of the Cambridge–Somerville social work experiment due to the particular input of social workers, to characteristics of the populations enrolled in the study or to the psychologically powerful and plausible view that social interventions create dependency and an illusory promise of a just and hospitable society? What do we make of such findings, compared, say, with those of the Perry pre-school programme which used a pre-school service plus teachers' home visits with disadvantaged black children and found less criminal conviction, use of welfare services and teenage pregnancy, and more high school graduation and employment, sixteen years later (Berrueta-Clement et al. 1984)?

In what way are teachers different from social workers? To what extent are changes across the decades from the 1930s to the 1980s in the social and political climate of service provision and poverty crucially responsible for the different impact of apparently similar interventions?

These kinds of important questions provide the framework for any intervention study. The findings of the SSPO study discussed later in this book must be contextualized in the same way. Although the study was set up deliberately to test the hypothesis that it is the *general* social support effect of many health care interventions that 'works', there are none the less important questions to be answered about the content, process and implications of the research midwives' work in our study. We used both quantitative and qualitative methods to overcome the objection that the divide between quantitatively guided outcome evaluation and qualitatively directed studies which explore processes is inimical to the development of a rounded understanding of why things happen as they do (Zigler and Weiss 1985: 83). But the use and integration of a combined methodology itself poses problems. We can easily be returned to the notion that the line fault in our consciousness is that of dualistic thinking, and it is this that creates the illusion of two worlds to be bridged.

4

Eve in the Garden of Health Research

> The lack of independence of social science research from current beliefs
> and valuations in the surrounding society is illustrated dramatically by the
> fact that it rarely blazes the way towards new perspectives. (Myrdal 1969:
> 47)

The lives of most social researchers are dominated by the recurrent need
to produce research proposals. This is particularly so for contract researchers – people who must raise their own salaries in addition to the direct
costs of the research. Between 1976 and 1984 contract research employment in English universities increased by 76 per cent. In 1982, when the
first proposals for the study described in this book were being written,
contract researchers made up a quarter of the UK academic workforce.
Half of those surveyed in a 1984 study had no job to go to at the end of
their current contract, and the majority were on contracts of less than three
years (Advisory Board for the Research Councils 1989). As a report on the
terms and conditions of social research funding in Britain put it in 1980:

> Research workers, like anyone else, need to live, enjoy at least the possibility
> of security of employment without frequent moves, and over time look for
> career advancement in terms of responsibilities and rewards. Competent
> researchers will have a professional approach to their work, which depends
> on the possibility of commitment to research and accumulation of skills and
> experience. The general pattern of research funding does little to support
> research careers in this sense. It is evident that single-project grants, without
> continuity of institutional base, do not promote security, and this is a
> characteristic mode of research funding. (Social Research Association 1980:
> 26)

In addition to their limited-contract employment, all researchers operate
within what Basil Bernstein (1984) has called a 'culture of impermanence'.
This imposes isolation from other researchers and academic staff, and a
unique rhythm, sequence and deadlines resulting from the funding process.

For contract researchers, a research proposal is essentially a job application: failure of the proposal to secure funding means unemployment. For
researchers whose contracts do not require the continual re-financing of
their own jobs, the research proposal plays an important role as professional justification: the measure of a 'good' researcher is the number of

research proposals successfully funded; or, to put it another way, the 'failure' to raise money is an easy invitation to professional criticism. It could, of course, equally be argued (but rarely is) that imaginative and innovative researchers are particularly likely to write proposals which are not funded, since current funding structures operate in such a way as to inhibit the recognition of innovation (see Horrobin 1978).

A research proposal is a curious document. Its status is not that of a publication nor even of a public text; if unfunded, it is likely to languish in a filing cabinet, to be consigned to the wastepaper basket, or otherwise forgotten. On the other hand, if a research proposal is successful, its status immediately changes; it becomes the blueprint for a subsequent exercise whose scale may range from small to enormous, and which may involve just the researcher, or alternatively a large team of people and organizations.

But both successful and unsuccessful research proposals must begin by negotiating the same series of processes. They must be formulated as plans in the researcher's head, and be written down in appropriate technical language. They must be read and commented on by peers and superiors, some of whose reactions, mediated by institutional power relations, lead to changes in the aims and design of the research. Every research proposal must have a financial budget. These may be produced initially by researchers working on their own, or by researchers and administrators together, labouring in a kind of internecine struggle in which the researcher's ideals are pitted against the administrator's notion of what the institution can support and demand. Few research grants are made directly to an individual. One institution – the funding body – offers research money to another institution – the grant-administering body – in the name of the labours of the researcher(s) with whom the proposal originated. A major factor in the expense of research is thus that the costs of the institution itself have to be met. The current pricing policy of higher education institutions in the UK can mean the inflation of research budgets by a sum of 140 per cent or more of payroll costs to service the institution itself. From 1992 the system of dual funding in the UK, whereby research-council-funded work is also resourced through the University Funding Council, will cease, and universities will be expected to charge the full costs of research, including those of housing it. The financing of research therefore involves more than contract researchers' need for employment and the budgeting of direct research costs; it is also crucially about the maintenance of the institutional culture which controls and appropriates the social and intellectual property of research.

This chapter is called 'Eve in the Garden of Health Research' after an account I gave at a World Health Organization meeting in 1983 of my first attempt to obtaining funding for the Social Support and Pregnancy Outcome project. The original paper discussed the gendered division of labour in health care lying behind the different models of explanation for health and illness and the different approaches to research described in chapter 1. My metaphor – or one of them – was of being lost in a rural maze of bureaucratic and other rules and regulations concerning what was regarded as 'fundable' and what not. It was hardly a Garden of Eden, but I slowly began to understand that my proposed research committed the original sin of deviating from social science funders' notions of what real research ought to look like.

'A few technical points . . .'

My early notes for the study show me grappling with the articulation (usual at this stage of the research process) of what exactly was the problem I wanted to study. 'Why is the idea attractive?' I asked myself, and answered: (1) because of the opportunity to study the relationships between social factors and pregnancy outcome 'via an easily available biological indicator' (birthweight); (2) because it 'makes possible an examination of the hypothesis that medical care is itself a cause of stress'; and (3) because 'the proportion of small babies has remained relatively stable and . . . it may be a contribution to the social class difference in mortality.' I was locked more firmly then in the right-hand side of table A than I am now. The initial plan was to interview four or five times in pregnancy about fifty women with a history of LBW and about twenty without. The focus would be on stress and life events, but the social circumstances of 'high- and low-risk' mothers would also be documented. In addition, there would be a control group who would not be part of the study but would provide some measure of any 'Hawthorne effect'.

At some point between these early notes and the first full draft of a research proposal, I moved to the proposition that the appropriate design for what I wanted to study was that of a randomized controlled trial. This methodology, together with its scientific and ethical implications, was discussed in chapter 3 and is explored further in chapter 6. At least two interpretations are possible of why I came to see this approach as the one to adopt in the Social Support and Pregnancy study. According to the first interpretation, I had been indoctrinated by the ethos of a unit – the Oxford National Perinatal Epidemiology Unit – that was soon to become famous for its advocacy of RCTs in answering questions about the effectiveness and safety of different medical perinatal procedures. The second interpretation is that the elegantly simple method of the RCT, together with its logically necessary constituent of some sort of action or intervention 'package' intended to change something in order better to arrive at an understanding of it, did indeed have an unexplored applicability to topics of sociological inquiry. A third possibility has suggested itself with the wisdom of hindsight: that in order to work towards a synthesis of the two models of knowledge presented in table A one must have experience of both. The SSPO study was to be my induction into quantitative research.

In November 1981 I wrote to Raymond Illsley, then director of the Medical Research Council's Medical Sociology Unit in Aberdeen, long-time researcher of social aspects of reproduction, and chair of the Social Affairs Committee of the Social Science Research Council, asking him to comment on the outline of my project on 'Social factors and pregnancy outcome'. The proposal now was to identify a sample of 200 pregnant women, with, as before, a history of LBW, and randomly allocate them either to receive a programme of supportive social science interviewing or to serve as a control group who would not be offered any extra attention during pregnancy. Both groups would be interviewed postnatally. The aim of the pregnancy interviews with the intervention women would be to provide social support, but also to collect a wide range of social data in such areas as nutrition, smoking, work and so forth. The combination of two aims was to avoid putting all one's eggs in the same basket; should the social support intervention not 'work', the data collected during it could be used epidemiologically to explore some of the connections between social variables during pregnancy and the fates of mother and child. Both biological and social outcome measures were proposed, including the babies' birthweights and the mothers' physical and mental health following delivery.

Raymond Illsley commented on my outline proposal in a letter in early December 1981. He said:

> I agree that an approach of the kind you suggest would be valuable. Since our early in-depth studies of first pregnancies in the 1950s there has been no serious attempt to chart the events of pregnancy in a comprehensive fashion taking into account the various parameters of behaviour, nutritional, income and expenditure and psychological influences.

He went on to comment:

> My major reservation applies to the size of the sample. However valuable your descriptive account of the experience of pregnancy, given your initial hypotheses and the design of the study, its potential value will be judged upon (1) its ability to demonstrate an intervention effect; (2) its ability to interpret the meaning of any intervention effect. I do not believe that this can be done using only 100 index and 100 control cases.

Further, Illsley observed:

> Birthweight is doubtless influenced by many factors of which social support is only one. The room for intervention effects is restricted by the effects of other concurrent influences.

As to funding:

> My impression is that the study fits awkwardly (like many good ideas) between MRC and SSRC. My first resort would be DHSS, who are likely to be both informed and sympathetic.

At Illsley's suggestion I contacted the secretary of the new Social Affairs Committee (the SSRC was currently going through a period of reorganization), who advised against the DHSS, which she thought was short of money at the time. As the proposal was likely to be fairly expensive, we discussed going for a pilot study first, but she did not recommend this, in view of the probable difficulty of arranging for a continuation of the grant.

The proposal was redrafted following Illsley's comments, in particular by doubling the proposed sample size. In order to calculate the number of women who would need to be included in the study, the research proposal followed convention among 'triallers', and settled on one 'outcome' of pregnancy to use in this calculation (see Schwarz et al. 1980). Because of the importance of birthweight in the intellectual genesis of the study, this seemed the obvious candidate. In our calculations there was a considerable premium in keeping sample numbers as low as possible. This was because a larger study would mean including more women in the intervention group, and employing more people to provide the intervention, and thus a costlier study. Also, as the collection of labour-intensive quantitative data was planned, a larger study would make the integration of qualitative and quantitative methods more difficult.

We decided not to use simply the proportion of low- to normal-birthweight babies in our calculations, since, in order to show a statistically significant difference between the proportions of women in experimental and control groups who 'repeated' a low-birthweight delivery, a substantially sized sample would be needed. On the assumption (based on previous work) that about 30 per cent of women would have another LBW baby, to show a statistically significant decrease of 25 per cent (from 30 per cent to 22.5 per cent) in this rate in the experimental group would require more than 1000 women in total. A more modest alternative was to compare the *mean birthweight* of babies born to women in the intervention group with that of their counterparts in the control group. This would allow a considerably smaller sample, though only if the size of the desired 'birthweight effect' was itself sufficiently large. A 'birthweight effect' of 40 g would require 1200 women. So we shifted our sights to 140 g, on three grounds: (1) the cost considerations; (2) the fact that clinicians would not be impressed by a 40 g effect of a social support intervention, whereas they might be by a 140 g effect; (3) the knowledge that 140 g was the direction of the 'smoking effect' on birthweight, which attracted the attention of many health professionals and policy-makers. A figure of this order would require a sample of about 400 women (divided between intervention and control groups), which seemed about right in view of the other aims of the study.

The design of the revised proposal, prefaced by a fairly extensive review of the social factors and pregnancy literature, was sent out in January 1982 to the eighteen members of the NPEU's Advisory Committee, twelve of whom replied. In addition, I sent the proposal for comment to a number of other people in this country and abroad, including paediatricians, epidemiologists and social scientists. In the process of designing what one hopes will be fundable research, such consultation is normal: if expert opinion is sampled in advance, the final proposal may be improved and so less likely to falter on the rock of objections put by referees.

The discussion below of the comments received in this process is included because they throw a good deal of light on the context within which the research came eventually to be done, and which, in important ways, limits the kind of research it is *possible* to do. These issues are returned to in chapter 11.

Two of the three social scientists consulted felt positive about the study, though each raised important limitations, from a social science point of view, of the proposal as it stood: the fact that low birthweight 'is many things', so that its use to define 'risk' mixes different groups, at least some of which will not prove to be 'at risk' at all; the need to understand the *processes* that link social factors and the fate of pregnancy; social variation in medical definitions and terminologies themselves (for example, of respiratory distress syndrome, which was then to be an outcome of the study); possible undercosting of the study in terms of the amount of time the intervention would require. The third social scientist, well known for his work on the aetiology of psychiatric disorder, was sceptical about the notion of an *intervention* study, and wrote to advise that in his view it was essential to carry out an epidemiological-type inquiry first, in order to try to establish just what is the role of psychosocial factors in pregnancy outcome.

A long letter from a representative of one of the maternity services user-organizations raised a different, but very valid, point about the content of the proposed social support. Its author commented:

> What your paper does not tell me is what kind of social support would be offered to the women you describe as socially disadvantaged. Would it be **actual** food, advice on diet, help with household chores, care of a child or children (occasional), shopping, transport, or what? An improved diet might be achieved not by nutritional supplements but by better choice of more wholesome food (perhaps more 'whole' foods, more fruit and vegetables), perhaps a money supplement to pay for a better diet. Most young women accustomed to convenience food, supermarket shopping and the taste of tinned, packeted, pre-prepared and flavoured food may think the preparation of fresh food at home impossibly time-consuming, or not particularly nice. Would help with basic cooking during pregnancy be an idea? ... I would be disappointed if the results were inconclusive because, apart from conversation, not enough actual help had been given to reduce stress, or to change a woman's life or health in any way.
>
> I was reminded of a film about a Health Visitor calling on a young

pregnant woman, in a substandard home full of problems, and coping with a toddler as well, I couldn't help wishing that the HV would talk to her *while* helping with the washing-up, nappy-washing, floor-cleaning, or something practical, instead of just sitting around chatting and making an extra tea-cup to wash! I do not mean to be critical of interviewers, but that is how I think stress might be increased.

The more medically oriented comments ranged from the highly technical to the pessimistically practical. One over-committed medical statistician began his letter:

Your draft proposal was put on one side until I had a nice quiet train journey ... I have read this with interest, though wonder whether you will be producing a somewhat shorter version before submission – I say this because many referees are extremely busy, not necessarily motivated to read lengthy material, and require it to be presented to them in a way that it is easy to absorb.

Concerning the calculation of sample size in relation to outcomes hypothesized to be influenced by social support, an American paediatrician suggested:

Why not be more explicit here: the primary outcome measure (140 g increase in mean birthweight) is under *test*; the secondary outcome measures are not under test (since the impact cannot be specified, and the size of the study calculated on the basis of the primary outcome places a ceiling on the magnitude of difference which can be detected in these secondary outcomes). The differences observed will provide the basis for number-specific predictions which can be tested by *further* trials.

Viewing the proposed study within the context of complaints made by women about maternity care, an Australian epidemiologist underlined the importance of considering medical care itself as a source of stress in pregnancy. She noted:

I've come across several women in the past month who didn't come for any antenatal care in the present pregnancy – one because she did last time and still had a stillbirth; the others because they kept being admitted for suspected fetal growth retardation last time (causing enormous family problems each time) – and gave birth to infants of normal weight!

In a similarly realistic vein, a British community physician observed that 'It seems a most important proposal and I very much hope it can be funded. My experience of medical bodies makes me pessimistic, but perhaps the SSRC might be more hopeful.'

Other comments on the proposal design included the view that, since information about pregnancy would only be obtained post-delivery from the control group, such information would be 'soft'. This commentator remarked: 'I would take the gamble of antenatal collection in group 2 [the control group] – it would work *against* the hypothesis because any positive outcome would be stronger!' On the nutrition section of the proposal, he argued – interestingly, in view of the study's central hypothesis concerning the role of stress in pregnancy complications – that 'Nutrition may itself lead to biochemical and psychological CNS change and hence affect "stress" – rather than nutrition affecting gestation directly.' And on the issue of who should give the intervention he observed, 'But if you did use "specially trained" HV you could then potentially translate any positive aspects of study into the normal health service ... perhaps could do this *as well* as a parallel experiment. I – control, II – social scientist, III – HV.' A general practitioner echoed the above view of the value of health visitors as givers of social support, going on to remark:

> I suppose what I am saying is that you have selected a particular and fairly restricted form of supportive intervention which by itself is never likely to be undertaken except in an experimental framework. Do you see this as part of a series of similar studies taking different aspects of supportive care in order to identify which is most useful or productive?

Finally, I quote from a letter sent in response to the proposal by David Rush, a paediatric epidemiologist who has carried out much important work in the area of nutrition and birthweight. Some of his reactions were to prove predictive of what actually happened when we did the study, as we shall see later. David Rush observed in his letter:

> You are exploring the ecological relationship of adverse perinatal outcome and increased social stress, both more likely among women of lower social status. To move from this ecological relationship to an intervention study offering social support seems to me to omit an important interim step, which is to demonstrate that, *within* social class strata, the presumed factor, stress (which might account for the differences *across* social class), actually can be shown to account for different outcome ... Our work with the 1958 and 1970 birth cohorts does show that large parts of social class differences can be accounted for by differences in smoking ... We do not know that stress is directly associated with adverse perinatal outcome, and we do not know that social support, in the form being given, is an effective response to stress. A positive answer to the experiment would answer both questions, since both elements would have to be in place. A negative outcome would be indeterminant, another reason for pursuing an analytic study, either in conjunction with, or prior to, an experimental intervention. Might you discuss directly with some potential subjects what *their* perceived needs are for social support, particularly in Class V? Respondents may be quite articulate about what elements of their lives are more stressful, and what help would be most welcome. My guess is that an interview might be lower on the list than

concrete things such as baby minding, help in the house, and ways to overcome some of the very real limitations of bringing up young children in poverty ... One of the trials I had always hoped to be able to do was of money. It would be of great interest to try to determine how much of the stress of low income could be alleviated by a monetary grant. Do you think a control group which might receive an extra pregnancy benefit might be possible?...

A few technical points: ... I am afraid I must be most sceptical about your expectations of making a 140 gram change in birthweight. No intervention I know of has had that much of an effect. I think it is much more likely that 30, 40, or 50 grams is closer to the mark.

By this time, discussions about the revised proposal had been held with staff at the SSRC and with the Department of Health, who had decided to support the proposal to the extent of committing themselves to half its cost; the review process was, however, to be left to the SSRC. After final

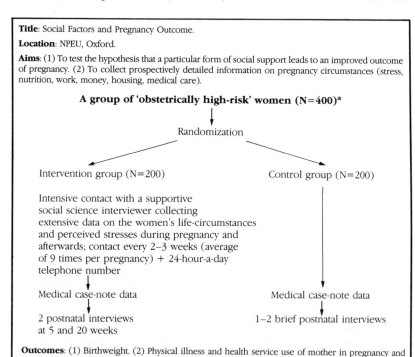

Title: Social Factors and Pregnancy Outcome.

Location: NPEU, Oxford.

Aims: (1) To test the hypothesis that a particular form of social support leads to an improved outcome of pregnancy. (2) To collect prospectively detailed information on pregnancy circumstances (stress, nutrition, work, money, housing, medical care).

A group of 'obstetrically high-risk' women (N=400)[a]

Randomization

Intervention group (N=200)   Control group (N=200)

Intensive contact with a supportive social science interviewer collecting extensive data on the women's life-circumstances and perceived stresses during pregnancy and afterwards; contact every 2–3 weeks (average of 9 times per pregnancy) + 24-hour-a-day telephone number

Medical case-note data   Medical case-note data

2 postnatal interviews   1–2 brief postnatal interviews
at 5 and 20 weeks

Outcomes: (1) Birthweight. (2) Physical illness and health service use of mother in pregnancy and postnatally. (3) Labour duration, analgesia, obstetric intervention. (4) Infant neonatal condition, feeding, weight gain, illness and health service use in first six weeks. (5) Mother–baby relationship. (6) Maternal 'adjustment' and psychiatric state postnatally. (7) Maternal attitudes to obstetric care.

Staff and cost: £201,196 over 5 years; AO for 5 years; 4 interviewers for 2 years; computer programmer for 4 years; 50 per cent secretary for 5 years.

[a]Women with a previous LBW delivery unassociated with major congenital malformation, multiple pregnancy or elective delivery and not belonging to an ethnic minority population, booking before 24 weeks.

Figure 4.1   Design 1 (1981–1984)

revisions, the study proposal was submitted to the SSRC at the end of April 1982, for a decision in November. Its design is shown in figure 4.1.

The SSRC wrote to me saying that it had been decided to hold a site visit for the application 'as is usual with applications of this scale'. The object was for SSRC representatives to discuss the proposed research with the applicant; and for the applicant to answer any points made anonymously by referees and then to revise the application before its final consideration by the whole committee. I would be sent an abstract of referees' comments in good time before the site visit, which was scheduled for 7 October 1982. 'Site visit' did, however, turn out to be something of a misnomer, since we were all asked to go to the SSRC office in Temple Avenue in London, instead of their coming to see us in Oxford from where the research would be co-ordinated.

'The problem with the research design'

A telephone call made in early September to pursue the abstract of referees' comments elicited the information that, even if the study was funded, it could not start in March 1983 as planned, because there was no money available. 'Nothing before June', I wrote despondently in my file, noting that this would leave me salary-less for three months. The abstract of comments, which arrived three weeks before the site visit, arranged the comments of the SSRC referees under three headings: 'Research design'; 'Definition of variables'; 'Methodology'. Under the first heading came the following remark:

> The problem with the research design is that this particular combination of an essentially quantitative question about reproduction, 'what is the impact of extra hand holding during pregnancy on final birthweight', and essentially theoretical concerns about the sociology of confinement, 'in what ways does social class operate through pregnancy', leads to inappropriate research designs for both.

I was mystified by this one. But my notes show that I prepared to defend myself at the site visit thus:

> it seems to me that *both* questions ideally demand *larger* sample numbers than I have proposed ... I don't see one objective – the intervention – as quantitative and the other – data-collection on social factors – as theoretical. Both appear to me to demand a *quantitative* approach and to raise important questions about the factors mediating between the environment on the one hand and health and illness on the other, and about the appropriateness (or otherwise) of current patterns of clinical care during pregnancy to this interaction.

The next point was that antenatal care varies between hospitals, and Oxford (which I was not proposing to use in any case) was untypical, because it 'has half the national average of perinatal deaths'. To this I responded somewhat sharply by reminding the SSRC that, since randomization would be carried out *within* each centre, any differences in antenatal care routines *between* centres should not bias the results. Additionally,

> The point about Oxford having a lower than average PMR and a lower incidence of LBW is true, but again this misses the crucial point, which is that the recurrence rate of LBW is the same in Oxford as elsewhere. Since the incidence is lower, one would expect a smaller number of cases over a specified period of time meeting the criterion for the trial (a previous LBW delivery), but, once included, one would not expect there to be anything untypical about these cases as opposed to those entered from other centres.

Referees' comments moved on to the unrepresentativeness of the sample: as the women belonged to a high-risk group, the special medical care they would receive would surely invalidate the results of the intervention study. I repeated the argument of the proposal that the sample was intended to be representative only of women with a history of LBW delivery, and that the reason for choosing a 'high-risk' sample was to maximize the chances of showing an effect of the proposed intervention:

> The grounds for choosing ... this group [are that it] contributes heavily to the group of babies with the greatest chance of dying in the perinatal period. There are no theoretical grounds for supposing that if the intervention works in this group it will not work in the pregnant population as a whole ... I think it's worth remembering that even after having two LBW babies a woman has a 70 per cent chance of producing a normal-weight baby ...
>
> On the matter of exceptional attitudes and exceptional treatment ... some hospitals would give extra care to women with this kind of obstetric history, while others may not; however, this doesn't really matter from the viewpoint of the research design, since random allocation should achieve an equal distribution between experimental and control groups of whatever type of care is practised in any particular centre.

The SSRC referees also offered the opinion that factors contributing to birthweight such as maternal height and length of gestation needed to be held equal in the two groups. Again, I reminded the SSRC of the principles of a randomized controlled design: that the use of random numbers to decide which women were offered the intervention and which were not should secure the same distribution of the short and the tall (and the in-between) in the two groups. Indeed, this was a main reason for adopting such an approach.

Moving on to questions raised about sampling, I found myself again confronted with the objection that 'a random sample would not be able to yield details of causes and effects. One possibility might be a matched-pairs design of 200 subjects to control for some of the unwanted variables.' I held my breath and refrained from pointing out that no sample ever in itself yielded 'causes and effects' and reiterated the by now tedious point that use of random allocation does away with the need to control for 'unwanted' variables – even supposing one has any way of knowing in advance what these might be.

When it came to the section of comments under the heading 'Definition of variables', the referees appeared to be confused by my notion of 'socially supportive interviewing'. Their remarks indicated that they saw interviewing as interviewing and social support as something quite different. They were also concerned about the policy implications: if the intervention proved successful, how could/should antenatal services be reorganized? I replied to the effect that the model of interviewing as merely data collection was based on a fundamental misunderstanding of this aspect of research – on a refusal to see it as a *social* relationship. To the latter point I responded by commenting that this was essentially a trial of a non-clinical form of antenatal care in an era when most medical routines for pregnancy care were moving in the direction of *more* clinical care and more technology – despite the fact that these had not been shown to be effective, either in general or in terms of caring for women with poor obstetric histories. The first objective, therefore, was to see if the alternative approach of non-clinical, *social* care worked; then to identify why it did, and what should be done about it. These aims could not necessarily all be achieved within the limits of a single study.

The SSRC referees raised a number of minor points under the 'Methodology' heading, including the need for liaison with health service personnel (to 'increase access, and credibility of the interpretation of case-notes and findings'(?)) and the worry about the assessors of change being also the agents of that looked-for change. To this I responded by agreeing and by reporting an estimate secured from Social and Community Planning Research for a 'blind' evaluation of intervention and control women, which would cost the SSRC an extra £10,000–11,000.

My responses to the abstract were conveyed round a large table at Temple Avenue to a company of SSRC representatives/delegates, and with the support of three colleagues from the NPEU and of Margaret Stacey from Warwick University, representing sociology. The atmosphere was tense. Within a short time of our arrival, and before our 'external' representative, Meg Stacey, had found us, the SSRC announced the bad news that they had decided to turn down the project in its present form. The good news (which seemed small recompense at the time) was that they would probably be prepared to fund me for a short time to work on an alternative proposal.

Getting at the oyster

Because the SSRC had decided to reject the proposal, the Department of Health was no longer willing to offer any financial support for it. On 22

October 1982 I had a conversation with the new secretary of the Social Affairs Committee about the nature of the committee's notion of short-term funding for me. She suggested I ask for eighteen months, and had done a preliminary costing which fitted the budget in under a £25,000 ceiling. Would I do a revised costing for the 12 November meeting of the committee? On 29 October I also discussed the situation with Raymond Illsley, who said that the central objection of the 'site-visiting' party had been that I needed to specify what social support was, before undertaking an intervention study to test its effectiveness. The concern was expressed that a trial on two important topics – birthweight and social support – might be of little value when there was no evidence that the kind of support being suggested would in practice be supportive. Illsley suggested that I put in a revised application for two years' personal support for myself, and not much else, in order to work on this task, as well as carrying out a literature review which would (among other things) tackle the comment made by one of the SSRC's referees that the terms 'social class' and 'social support' needed to be disentangled. On 1 November I sent the revised proposal to the SSRC. I also wrote to request a letter explaining their reasons for turning down the original application. There was no reply to this letter, so I wrote the following January, and received a reply from another new staff member (the third) saying that he had looked through the file and found 'a synopsis of referees' comments' (the same as had been dispatched before the site visit) which he enclosed, hoping this 'will be of some use'.

The SSRC eventually agreed to fund me for eighteen months, from 1 July 1983 to 31 December 1984, 'to define and operationalize the concept of "social support", to study the literature, and to carry out the necessary pilot work'.

On 18 May 1983 I was sent a circular letter from the SSRC concerning publicity for the small grant they had now made. Initial publicity would be left to me and the institution (Oxford University) administering the grant. But, if there was to be a press release, the SSRC wanted to agree the wording first. Furthermore, would I send them a statement about the project for the next issue of the annual 'Research Supported by the SSRC'? They would like 200 words, 'explaining it in simple terms':

> I emphasize this since it is important that the abstract should be understand-able to social scientists in disciplines other than your own, and to the intelligent layman. (This last point has been emphasized by Lord Rothschild, who was asked to review our work recently. A copy of his relevant recom-mendation is attached for your information. On his authority therefore, I must urge you to suppress unnecessary jargon and neologisms in your abstract.)
>
> Finally, may I remind you that it is a condition of grant that you mention the SSRC's support in any article, book, broadcast or press release. You will appreciate that it is particularly important at present that the value of such research should be publicly recognised.

The attached recommendation described the most serious weakness of the SSRC as its failure to make known to the general public – 'the man in the street' – its own work and that of the social scientists it finances. 'The efforts of the SSRC in this respect are primitive and unprofessional.' Lord Rothschild took particular objection to the 'succulent bivalve' syndrome ('succulent bivalve' = oyster),[1] and made a number of suggestions about how the SSRC's own language might be improved, including by purchasing four copies of Sir Ernest Gowers's *Plain Words*.

My own attempt at conveying the message of the research to the man in the street went as follows:

Social Factors and Pregnancy Outcome
Social class differences in the birthweight and survival of babies are a persisting feature of the health care scene in Britain. It is not clear why this is so, despite the fact that the phenomenon has been noted ever since national birth and death statistics began to be collected a century ago. Improved standards and techniques of medical care have not much affected the social class differences, and one reason is that forms of pregnancy care offered to date have not succeeded in lowering one major contributor to the difference – the proportion of low-birthweight babies born.

This study will examine the various explanations and evidence put forward as to why membership of different social groups should be associated with different chances of reproductive 'success'. In particular, it will look at the evidence as to the impact of social networks and supportive relationships (or lack of these) on the health of pregnant women and their babies. Studies describing various kinds of interventions (such as dietary advice and health education) carried out with the goal of improving the chances of successful pregnancy will be analysed. The aim is to design a project in which social support is provided to women at high risk of giving birth to low-birthweight babies, and the effect of this assessed by comparison with a similar group not receiving the social support.

'A Change in Structure for Changing Circumstance'?

Some of the lessons of all this are obvious. On a practical level, high staff turnover within an organization such as the SSRC is an effective barrier to communication both internally and externally. It hardly needs to be said that the fiasco of 'site visits' should not be engaged in when a decision has already been taken not to go ahead with a piece of research. In circumstances where informal decisions are made for shared funding between research councils and government departments, the refereeing process should not be unilateral. And so on. But the SSRC was having a difficult time of its own, and so was social science, and so were the universities. The present tense would do almost as well for all of these statements. 'We have been cursed to live in interesting times' is how Colin Bell (1984: 14) puts it.

Bell (1984) and others have told the story of what was happening to the SSRC around the time it was asked to make a decision about the 'Social Factors and Pregnancy Outcome' proposal. It is clear from these accounts that the timing of the proposal was hardly propitious. Successive cuts to the SSRC's budget had been announced, and successively smaller proportions of its expenditure had been channelled in the direction of sociological research. By 1976, 91 per cent of the SSRC's expenditure on new research programmes went to work on economic forecasting, organizational decision-making and management, educational management and performance and the analysis of public sector policy (Bell 1984: 20). In the summer of 1981 the University Grants Committee decreed a reduction in social science places in universities; the heyday of British sociology was over, with contraction substituted for the expansionary wave of the 1960s, when twenty-five new chairs in sociology were established in the space of seven years (University Grants Committee 1989). Also in the summer of 1981, the internal restructuring of the SSRC was announced, resulting in the abolition of the old Sociology and Social Administration Committee, and the re-forming of the old committee structure into a smaller set of multidisciplinary committees. All this was deemed 'A Change in Structure for Changing Circumstances' (See Social Science Research Council 1981). At the end of the year, the external survey of the SSRC's structure and activities under the aegis of Lord Rothschild was initiated. The aim of both these moves was supposedly to increase the relevance of social science research to policy, and to discourage theoretical or fundamental research whose policy implications, especially in economic terms, might be either non-existent or unclear.

My own meeting with Raymond Illsley at the end of October to discuss the outcome of the 'site visit' took place two days before a candlelit[2] meeting of the Sociology and Social Administration Committee members at the National Liberal Club in London to discuss and protest about the restructuring proposals. Lord Rothschild's report, which surprised many people by recommending salvage of the SSRC, though not without change, was published the month the money for the pilot study was granted. Despite the defences of Rothschild, which recommended that the SSRC's budget be maintained in real terms for three years, Keith Joseph cut £6 million from it in October 1982. The name change to the *Economic* and Social Research Council was agreed the following year, taking effect on the first working day of 1984. Douglas Hague, Chairman of Council from October 1983, insisted that it would have preferred to be known as the Social and Economic Research Council, but, as this would have resulted in the same acronym as the Science and Engineering Research Council, the idea had to be dropped. Hague maintained that the change of name 'does not mean the ESRC proposes to increase its support for research in economics at the expense of any other group of researchers. The fact that funds for research will be short in 1984/5 will clearly mean very keen competition for research funds, but a balanced research programme remains an important objective' (Economic and Social Research Council 1984: 3). Such contextual dislocations explain some of the vagaries of treatment my research proposal received, and some of the internal re-adjustments may (as Bell contends) add up to manoeuvres which did succeed in ensuring survival of the SSRC through subsequent financial and political attacks. But what is more difficult to explain is why a project that was not discipline-bound but firmly problem-oriented was not deemed to be 'fundable' research.[3] Although funds for sociological research had been cut, the SSRC was actually giving money back to the Treasury because not enough applications were rated sufficiently highly to be regarded as fundable.[4] A crucial element here was the 'peer review process' – the way in which the views solicited by the SSRC of members of the social science community operated to make certain kinds of research less fundable than others. Where a research protocol introduces a paradigm of research previously little recognized in that disciplinary domain in which it is proposed to work, the peer review process may well inhibit funding. Of some relevance here is the fact that the internal organization of the SSRC had become very unwieldy, bureaucratic and conservative (and remains so despite several reorganizations since); as Ditton and Williams (1981) observe, these features are precisely those that inhibit the recognition and funding of innovatory research.

Some years after all this, in 1986, I received a request from the Evaluation and Dissemination Sub-Committee of the Social Affairs Committee of the ESRC to complete a questionnaire on the results of ESRC/SSRC-funded research. The questionnaire enquired about publication and other dissemination, and about others' uses of one's research, ending with a section headed 'Reflections on research dissemination' in which I took the opportunity to write the following observations:

> My major comment about the ESRC's role in this research goes as follows: I submitted a sizeable application to the ESRC in 1981 (with appropriate encouragement) only to meet with the response of a very badly organized site visit which resulted in pilot funding for one and a half years. This left me with no job for some months, which was inconvenient, to put it mildly. (I have three dependent children.) More seriously, the site visit team did not appear to understand the proposed research design. I should add that the main project is now funded by the DHSS after a prolonged struggle – for three years, with a team of six. I am glad that the DHSS was able to provide the money, but sad (as a sociologist) that the ESRC did not have the imagination to see how important the project was. This highlights one significant drawback of current modes of evaluation, which is that there tends to be a conservative emphasis within them. Innovative (or discipline-bridging) proposals tend not to get funded.

As an editorial in *The Times Higher Education Supplement* put it in 1982, 'Bashing the Social Science Research Council is an easy game, but thinking up a better organization for postgraduate study and research in the social sciences is a serious and difficult task' (Editorial 1982). Or, as Margaret Stacey phrased it in a submission to Lord Rothschild's review, if the SSRC or a similar body did not exist, it would have to be invented (Stacey 1982). The basic (and still unmet) challenge is one of designing such an organization so it can successfully act as the bastion of defence for a broadly based social science, without at the same time being blinded either by narrow-minded professional imperialism or by short-term political constraints to the need for imaginative fundamental research. The general background for this is Britain's poor record of research investment: alone of the major OECD countries it did not increase its expenditure on research and development over the period 1981–6, and a major reason for lagging behind other countries was the greater share of the R and D budget in the UK devoted to defence spending (Association of University Teachers 1989; Smith 1988; Ince 1986). The implications of this resource distribution may be far-reaching, and include some of the public health issues discussed in chapter 1 as the rationale for the Social Support and Pregnancy Outcome project. It has, for example, been shown that there is a direct and inverse relationship between the proportion of countries' GNPs allocated to arms expenditure on the one hand, and infant mortality rates on the other (Woolhandler and Himmelstein 1985). What is bad for research may be bad for health, not because research is necessarily health-promoting (even for researchers), but because the same impetus that leads governments to formulate research *policies* and to invest in *high-quality research* is also likely to generate a commitment to practices which protect the nation's health.

5

A Bite of the Apple

We recommend that the Department of Health co-ordinate a programme of systematic social and medical research aimed at establishing the reasons for, and reducing the incidence of, low birthweight. (Social Services Committee 1988–9: ix)

For some issues open-ended interview techniques are essential. We have to listen to what people say and allow them to define the problem in their own terms. (Richards 1983: 165)

When she entered the pilot study for the Social Support and Pregnancy Outcome project, Tracey Arkwright[1] was a 20-year-old unemployed telex operator living with her 19-year-old husband in a council flat on a treeless, graffiti-strewn East London estate. Steve Arkwright had worked as a labourer, but was currently without a job. The previous year their first child, a boy, had been born early, weighing 992 g, and had died after two days. Tracey described what happened:

Six and a half months I was, and I'd been doing some things up here [in the flat ready to move in]. I think that's why I had him, and then I went home and had some pains, then about 2 o'clock in the morning they got stronger and I had the baby at 6 the next morning . . .

That night, about 4 in the morning, my husband phoned the hospital up, because the baby'd lost some oxygen in his brain, you know what I mean, and he was just getting worse, and then on the Friday they were telling me what was wrong with him and on the Saturday he died . . .

It could have been anything, you know, maybe I done things, it could have been that . . . Painting, as I wanted the place decorated before he was born . . .

He said, like, the doctor who delivered him, said it's because you smoked that he come out early. I don't believe that really. I don't think it brings on the birth. It might make the baby small, but I don't think it brings it on. That's what he said, anyway . . .

I never liked him because when I was having the baby, and when I was in theatre, he said when you get the next feeling you want to push, tell me. There was about twenty people there, and I don't know, I used to be embarrassed before about those things, but I shouted out, what is this, a puppet show? Because there was all these doctors in there, I had my legs strapped up, and I had the contraction, and I said I'm ready now, I started shouting at him. Then when the baby come out, they all rushed off, I didn't know what was happening, they said to me he has a fifty-fifty chance of living. That all he said. He got a fifty-fifty chance of living. I was so mixed up, they showed me the baby and I said take him away. I thought it would be like . . . because it was early, I didn't know what to expect, and then when I went up to the hospital to see him, that's when I got the greatest shock of my life . . . I can't remember, but it was his dad that made me touch him, he said to me, go on touch him, you love him, he's your baby, he'll know that you're there if you touch him, so I did. You know what I mean, and I kept on touching him, it was nice.

I went up there after, to talk about how he died and that, and it was everything that was wrong with him . . . if he had lived, he might have been brain-damaged, his kidneys, everything you could think of, when the doctor told me, I just walked out, I wasn't ready . . .

I got a photo of him if you want to see him . . .

[Before the funeral] we brought the baby home, we kept him round me mum's house for the weekend, it was nice, you know. A lot of people were frightened to see and that. I liked it. I used to go and speak to him. I used to sit down there with him . . .

My mum turned religious after he died. When he died she went to church, and now she goes all the time . . . She had a baby when she was – I mean she has got six girls, so you can understand why I wanted a boy, she had a little boy when she was younger and he died, and it just brings it back, but I mean she loved my baby a lot . . . I got it out of her a little bit . . . then the tears started to come down her face and then I started crying . . .

I didn't hardly cry, like at the funeral, the priest said, why don't she cry, why don't she let it out, but I just didn't, my mum thought I didn't care . . .

I cry now, sometimes I get into a depression and that, not since I've been pregnant but before, it used to last for maybe a couple of days. I talk about him, people say to me, like a nurse up there said to me, is this your first? I say no, it's my second, I don't ever deny it, like some people would, I couldn't, I talk about him openly . . .

I do think that God took him for a reason. You know what I mean. I suppose with my mum, she has put a lot of it into my head, but it's a nice thing to believe that he is in heaven. It's nice to believe that he's not just dead . . .

We weren't married when I was pregnant with the first baby . . . I've never been on the pill in my life, 'cause I've only ever been with my husband, as soon as I went with him, I didn't come on . . . I went for a pregnancy test and I found that I wasn't pregnant and I got upset, even though we weren't married, I wanted to have one, but then I went for another pregnancy test and I was pregnant, then we got married. But we have always been together, I've been with him for about six years, on and off, you know . . .

My husband went into prison . . . just after the baby died. I was to go on the pill, I didn't though, but I never got pregnant, then he come out, it took me quite a while . . . He was in prison for thieving, to pay the cost of the funeral. You know, the hospital said they could bury him, but I wouldn't have that . . .

[With this pregnancy] I haven't really thought whether it would happen again, I don't want to think about that, you know what I mean. Because the hospital said when I get near to the time that they will take me in, so I won't think about that, like what happened before, I suppose it could, I don't know.

It is not unusual for interviewers to carry in their head memories of particular interviews which stand as vignettes for the whole of that particular research enterprise. The interview with Tracey, in which memorably she both wept and smoked[2] over an album of photographs of her dead baby, trapped and wired but much loved in an incubator, is one of those. The poignancy of her situation deepened as we went on: waiting to be rehoused away from the inhospitable and now unbearably memory-laden estate ('What do you have to do to make them understand? Commit suicide or something?'); a violent husband ('he uses me as a punch-bag'); little prospect of secure employment for either of them; inadequate income; and problems in the present pregnancy. Tracey was admitted to hospital twice for a total of five weeks, but, despite efforts to stop her labour, she gave birth at 33 weeks to a boy weighing 4 lbs 3 oz (1900 g). When I last saw her a month after the birth, Sam was well and due home in a few days, and Tracey had begun to worry about how she could possibly manage to look after him adequately away from all the machines and equipment which had been so necessary to his survival in the hospital.

Tracey's story, though individual, shares themes with many others that I heard during the pilot study, and which later took shape as systematic patterns during the main project itself. Among these themes are: the unresolved anguish of having a small, sick baby in the past, and the consequent increased anxiety in the next pregnancy; inability to get enough of the right kind of information from medical and midwifery staff; problems of insensitive care; physical and/or emotional and/or financial difficulties with partners; trouble with other relatives; and, last but not least, the task of becoming and being a mother in conditions of poverty. In this chapter, I look at the way in which these themes emerged in the pilot study, and at other 'results' of this stage of the research.

Operationalizing the concept

The task assigned by the SSRC, 'operationalizing the concept of social support', was made more difficult by the financial hiatus their decision created: I was first to be unemployed for three months. Such episodes, which are common in the lives of contract researchers, do nothing to aid the development of a sound research base. In the event, the Department of Health stepped in and paid me to conduct a literature review. However, the challenge of doing what the SSRC had asked me to do remained. How do you define and operationalize something in the context of pregnancy as a process which lasts nine months, when you only have eighteen months in total? Most important of all, the pilot study was not resourced to explore the method proposed for the main study: a controlled evaluation of the effects of a social support intervention.

While it was obvious that I had in some sense to 'pilot' my rejected proposal, how to do it was therefore less clear. Social support could not be defined without exploring women's own definitions of what this was, which would mean interviewing. The interviewing, however, could not constitute the evaluated intervention in the sense in which this had been a central element in the rejected proposal. I therefore decided to interview a small number of women through pregnancy, trying to make the 'interviewing' process as congenial (supportive) to them as possible, and offering them my phone number on a 24-hour basis. I would at least then be taking further the idea that interviewing might be transformed into a form of social support. During the interviews I would concentrate on three particular themes: social support in relation to a previous experience of having a small baby; the woman's own current social relationships and networks, and the extent to which these were perceived as supportive; and her self-perceived support needs during the current pregnancy.

One feature of social research is the reconstruction in public documents of the *ad hoc* nature of the research process. Thus, in the end-of-grant report for the pilot study, all these deliberations appear as a set of (relatively) clearly defined objectives. Reiterating the impossibility of the task assigned to me ('Some important questions about the feasibility of the projected RCT of a social support intervention cannot be answered in advance by a pilot study that does not use the same methodology'), I speculated that it might none the less be possible, through a small pilot study, to 'illuminate some aspects of the social and personal process of post-LBW pregnancy', and that, in addition, this could throw some light on the following five issues:

1 Methods of sample selection: what is the best way of securing a sample of women who have previously delivered a low-birthweight infant?
2 What are some of the practical problems involved in attempting to provide a social support intervention?
3 How is this intervention perceived by the women to whom it is offered, and (how) do their perceptions reflect the different degrees of social support already existing in their lives?
4 What are some of the key parameters of the experiences of the women in this group with respect to delivering a low-birthweight infant and undergoing a subsequent pregnancy with its obstetric characterization as 'high risk'?
5 To what extent do there seem to be differences in social support or stress during pregnancy between women who 'repeat' LBW and those who do not?

The design of the 'pilot' study is shown in figure 5.1. In addition to the library research, I planned to interview about twenty women three times each, twice in pregnancy and once postnatally. Semi-structured interview schedules were written for each interview, covering background social and medical information, and moving on to an account of the current

Title: Social Factors and Pregnancy Outcome: 'Pilot' Study.

Location: NPEU, Oxford.

Aims: (1) To establish appropriate methodological procedures for selecting a high-risk sample and providing a social support intervention in pregnancy. (2) To collect data on the experiences of women following a LBW delivery and on their perceptions of a social support intervention. (3) To examine the relationship between the extent of social support/stress in pregnancy and whether or not women 'repeat' LBW. (4) To carry out a literature survey in the field of social interventions in pregnancy care.

A group of 'obstetrically-high risk' women (N=20)[a]

↓

2 'supportive' interviews in pregnancy + 24-hour-a-day telephone number

↓

Medical case-note data

↓

1 postnatal interview at 6 weeks

Outcomes: (1) Methodological. (2) Women's perceptions of the intervention. (3) The incidence of repeat LBW in relation to stress/social support factors. (4) A report of the literature survey.

Staff and costs: £25,660 over 18 months; AO plus research expenses.

[a]Women with a previous LBW delivery, fluent English-speakers and booking before 24 weeks.

Figure 5.1   Design 2 (1983–1985)

pregnancy – what had happened so far, what the women expected/feared would happen, how they felt about it physically and emotionally.

Questions about life events were included, using a predetermined list of events as developed by Cochrane and Robertson (1973), and amended by Richard Newton in his two studies on the relationship between stress in pregnancy and preterm delivery and low birthweight (Newton et al. 1979; Newton and Hunt 1984). Because of the importance of exploring the women's own social support resources, a long schedule of questions about social interaction developed by Scott Henderson and colleagues in the USA was also included (Henderson et al. 1981). The interviews were to be tape-recorded and transcribed.

In order to obtain the sample of women with a history of LBW delivery, I needed to negotiate access to a hospital. I tried one large London teaching hospital first, writing to a friend on the staff, and after some delay securing an interview with a consultant, to whom I sent a copy of my research proposal. I had heard from someone else that this particular man, who is quite well known in the childbirth education field, had made various public statements hostile to my work. When I went to see him in October 1983, he immediately began with a conversation which appeared to be about what he thought I had once said about epidurals in a study of mine he had never read. It was relatively easy to refer him to what I had actually said, which was quite different. On a second tack, he voiced the opinion that no non-medical person can evaluate what doctors do. I perhaps somewhat unwisely said that that was fine, but in that case doctors needed to evaluate themselves, and there was as yet not a great deal of evidence they were willing to do this. We proceeded along these lines for a while. When we came to the social support study, he said that in his view it was a 'colossal' waste of money and had nothing to do with social support. He went on to say he was not worried about what *I* might do, given access to 'his' patients; he was only worried about what my 'minions' would do. I replied that there were no minions in this study (lack of money again). We next discussed the matter of 'consent'. How would the women I wanted to interview be told about the study? It should, of course, be done in such a way that they did not feel coerced. I explained that it is normal for social scientists to go to considerable lengths to explain to would-be participants what studies are about, and to stress both the aspect of confidentiality and of freedom to say yes or no. The consultant was unhappy with this, and argued that the midwives in the hospital booking clinics should both find the women for me and tell the women about the study. I had to agree to this, saying I would produce a form of words for the midwives to read. I made a private note to the effect that this could not be the method chosen for the main study (it is quite interesting that through all this I never gave up the notion that there *would* be a main study). Finally the consultant gave me a form to fill in for the ethics committee.

After completing this, I went to China for three weeks as a delegate to a World Health Organization conference on perinatal care. When I returned, in November, permission had apparently been obtained from the ethics committee (see pp. 128–30 on the practices of ethics committees). I wrote two paragraphs for the antenatal clinic midwives: one outlining the selection criteria, the other describing the study so that they could describe it to the women. I suggested they use the following words:

> We have a small research project going on in this hospital which is looking at women's experiences of pregnancy following the birth of a small baby in the last pregnancy. The research is being done by Dr Ann Oakley,[3] who works in a medical research unit in Oxford. Dr Oakley has asked me to invite you to take part in this research. If you agree, this would mean that Dr Oakley would get in touch with you in your home twice in pregnancy and once after the birth of your baby. She would be grateful for your help with this research, but of course your medical care with us will be exactly the same whether or not you choose to take part.

Like many processes of social research, finding women to take part in the study proved more difficult and time-consuming than textbook descriptions suggest. Names came in slowly. I arranged to telephone the sister in charge of the antenatal clinic every Friday afternoon; often she would have no name for me, or only one. I had no way of knowing how assiduously the clinic midwives were looking for women who would fit the study criteria (pinned to the staff notice board) – nor, of course, whether or not they were using the form of words I had suggested. It became clear that another hospital was needed if the research was to be completed on time. A friendly consultant at another teaching hospital obliged; I sent him a note about the study and the same proposed paragraph for the midwives as I had sent to the first hospital. I was not, this time, asked to complete an ethics committee form. Again I telephoned once a week to find out if anyone had agreed.

Armed with a short list of names, I then telephoned and drove round London, eventually obtaining fifteen participants for my pilot study. I stopped at fifteen, rather than proceeding to twenty, as time was running out. Fourteen women were interviewed twice in pregnancy and once after the end of the pregnancy. Another woman miscarried between her saying she would take part and my arriving to see her. I did not know this until I got there, so I continued with a form of the interview rather than tell her that because she was no longer pregnant I was no longer interested in talking to her. Alice was a student from Zimbabwe taking a degree in applied social science and doing agency nursing to support herself; her earlier LBW baby – whose exact weight she could not remember, but the hospital had noted it as 5 lb (2268 g) – was a healthy 8-year-old living with her parents in Zimbabwe. During this pregnancy she had had no antenatal care – but the war was on, most of the hospitals were closed, and there was no transport available. The baby had not had any problems or any special medical care after his birth. Despite this she had blamed herself, she, the daughter of a minister, for 'having premarital sex ... I just thought, I managed not to have any sexual relationships before I was 25 and when I was just, you know, relenting, then you think, oh, God is punishing me for that.' Alice's next baby had died at about 10 weeks, and, when she went to book in at the hospital a week after this, the doctor performing the ultrasound scan asked her to come back a week later, when he told her the baby was dead and that he had suspected this the first time. She had been bleeding, and then went into hospital. Afterwards she expressed great sadness that the baby had been lost, and that the hospital had not been able to explain why – a common theme in the 'effort after meaning' experienced by many women after miscarriage (Oakley et al. 1990a).

The fourteen women left in the sample had a total of twenty previous births between them, seventeen of which were technically low birthweight, and nine of which were preterm as well. Four of the babies had died. Twelve of the women had at least one child currently living with them; aside from Tracey Arkwright, another woman, Carol Briffit, was in a childless situation, as her first child had been adopted by her (infertile) sister and her second had died. Eight women had one child living with them, three had two, and one (an orthodox Jew) had seven. This was one of the ways in which my small sample contained within it a great diversity of experience. Others concerned ethnicity, employment, class and the role of men. Eleven women were white British, one was black (Afro-Caribbean), and two were East African Asians. Four of the fourteen were employed during the pregnancy, two full-time, two part-time. With respect to the knotty question of social class, on the basis of the mother's present or previous occupation there was a class split of nine middle class and five working class, while on the basis of the occupation of the baby's father the sample was evenly divided, seven middle and seven working class. Nine women were married and living with their husbands (though not always in harmony); one was married but living in a women's refuge during the research; two were unmarried but cohabiting; one was divorced and cohabiting some of the time; and one was divorced and not cohabiting with the father of her expected baby, who lived round the corner with his wife and four other children.

Irrespectively of what the midwives in the hospital clinics had told them, I emphasized to all the women before interviewing them that this study was a prelude to a larger study that would look at the role of extra social support in pregnancy in helping women who had previously had a small baby. I said that I wanted to talk to them about their experiences of this, and about their needs and circumstances during the present pregnancy, and that I would be visiting twice during pregnancy and once after the delivery, and telephoning in-between these times to see how they were feeling. In addition, I gave them my phone numbers at work and at home and explained that an important part of the study was to provide a 24-hour-a-day telephone number for mothers to discuss anything that was worrying them.

The first pilot interview was done in December 1983 and the last in January 1985 (after the funding had finished). The first pregnancy interview was carried out on average at 17 weeks and lasted 1.3 hours; the second, at 27 weeks, lasted 1.2 hours; and the third was done at 6 weeks post-delivery and was the longest of the three – 1.6 hours. These averages concealed a large amount of variation, and several interviews lasted more than three hours. I left a stamped addressed postcard with the women at the second pregnancy interview for them to fill in and send me when the baby had been born, so that I would know when to contact them afterwards. All these cards were returned. The average number of times the women telephoned me in pregnancy was two, and only two of the calls came after 10 o'clock at night or before 8 o'clock in the morning. The exception was a mother who had asked me if I would be present at the birth (see p. 106). In view of some researchers' expectations that working-class women will not make use of the telephone for such purposes, it was interesting that there was no class difference in calls made. I took detailed notes on all the telephone conversations, many of which were focused on a particular issue on which the woman wanted help, advice or information.

In trying to make sense both of these aspects of interviewing women and of all they told me, I focused the analysis on three questions. The first question was: how did the pilot contribute to the design of the main study? For example, how did the women react to the experience of being visited by someone who was both 'interviewing', in the sense of collecting information, and offering a listening ear? How did this extra set of social encounters relate to the social networks and relationships in which they were 'naturally' involved? What kinds of approaches and questions proved fruitful in talking to the women? How did the process of acquiring names from antenatal clinics work? Were there any problems from the point of view of hospital or other medical staff in conducting this type of study? The second question addressed, albeit in a limited way, the hypotheses that would be taken up in the main study: namely, what are the links between stress and social support in pregnancy (whether researcher-provided or of the 'natural' sort), on the one hand, and what are the links between these and the outcome of pregnancy in terms of the baby's survival and health and the mother's health and satisfaction, on the other? Thirdly, and much the most fruitful area to be explored in a small pilot study of this kind, was the question of the key issues for women experiencing pregnancies after having a low-birthweight baby in the past.

Three concepts proved critical in the data analysis. These concepts were risk, social support and antenatal 'care'. In each case what emerged was a *problematization* of the concept by the women in the interviews. What was risk, and who defined who was at risk in what ways? Is social support the same thing as social relationships or not? How much of antenatal care is genuinely caring? Though these issues were particularly salient to women with a background of having LBW babies, they are of much more general relevance. Indeed, their emergence in a study which is not representative of the general population is one example of the theoretical understandings to be gained by studying the 'deviant' case (see e.g. Voysey 1975).

Risks of antenatal 'care'?

The extent to which the women viewed themselves as at risk could not be predicted simply from their obstetric histories. For example, one woman with two previous LBW children saw herself as perfectly normal and problem-free in the current pregnancy, resenting the hospital's attempt to provide intensive monitoring of her pregnancy. Another woman with only one previous LBW child regarded the next pregnancy as beset with all kinds of dangers and potential complications, and was much more accepting of her medical care – though conscious also of its stress-creating potential. A number of different meanings of the term 'risk' were highlighted in the women's accounts: specifically, the risk of embarking on a next pregnancy carrying the burden of anxiety derived from a past experience, the risk of being viewed as 'at risk' by health professionals when this is at odds with one's own experience, the risk of having a child to bring up who is handicapped or disabled in some way, and 'subjectively' experienced risk which is not taken seriously by health professionals. These points are illustrated below in three brief case-studies. (The discussion of what 'risk' in this context means is continued in chapter 10.)

Judith Clarke: 'living with George'

Judith Clarke's previous child, a boy, had been born at 27 weeks weighing 960 g and had suffered severe and permanent hearing damage because of oxygen treatment. Now aged 3, George had a number of behaviour problems and developmental delays owing to his hearing impairment, and required a lot of support and specialist help. Judith was naturally concerned that her experience with George would repeat itself, as she did not feel she could cope with the burden of caring for *two* handicapped children. Her recall of what had happened with George had remained vivid:

> I was spotting through most of the pregnancy. Because of this my family doctor put me on certificates so that I didn't go to work, I was supposed to rest. During this time I went to the local hospital . . .
>
> My doctor had written in a letter that I was bleeding quite heavily at the time I went to the hospital for my appointment, but they still insisted on doing an internal, which I have since found out is very dangerous when you're in that sort of situation . . . I was 11 weeks, which is a very dodgy time, because of the changeover of the egg to the placenta. The doctor I found was very bombastic, no other word for it , obviously I was very concerned, being my first pregnancy, about what was happening. I obviously had questions, which weren't answered, and I was just told, oh you're being silly, which isn't much help . . .
>
> The treatment I found was absolutely appalling . . . On the Friday three days before George was born I went to the hospital. I had lost weight, I obviously wasn't in very good condition, and the doctor examined me and he said, oh everything is fine, but on the Tuesday I had a few pains which I thought was constipation, not really knowing anything about giving birth.

She went into hospital two days later:

> They said, oh no, you're not in labour, then a doctor examined me and he said I was but I wouldn't have it. By the time they got me into a hospital gown and on to a machine it was 8 o'clock . . . I just said to the young girl who was there, there wasn't even proper staff there, I said this baby is going to be born, do you want to take the responsibility of it being born here? She said, you're just being silly, there aren't any signs on the machine . . . she said, oh well, I'll get a nurse to come, so the nurse came and said, yes, the head is engaged all right, they whipped me down to the delivery room and twenty minutes later George was born. The time he was born I could have sold tickets, there were three doctors and three sisters there, but unfortunately the help came far to late. If they had done their job properly, they might have been able to stop him being born.

The baby was transferred during the night to another hospital with specialist neonatal facilities. Judith was told the next morning she would not be accompanying him. She was then later urgently summoned to an ambulance 'full of old ladies':

> The lady driver looked at me and said, are you going to make it, and I said I'm going to make it if I have to walk there. Obviously I wanted to be with my child . . .
>
> I didn't hold him, I didn't even touch him till he was a month old . . . I had my first cuddle on the 2nd of May and he was born 2nd April . . . but I sort of just knew he wasn't going to die.

He did, however, have many health problems:

> The doctors thought he was Down syndrome and they wanted to do a marrow test on him at Great Ormond Street, they told my husband before me, and my husband said, what do you think the chances are, and they said, well, about 90 per cent . . . he had all the classic symptoms, high forehead, high activity of the eyes, gap in his toes, one line across the palm of his hand . . .
>
> It was the same instinctive thing that I knew he didn't have it when they said to me his hearing might be damaged – I said yes . . .
>
> He had chronic lung disease, when he was born his feet were out, so they thought he might have club foot. He was on the respirator for two weeks, he was in hospital for nearly four months . . . he was jaundiced, on the second day he had to have a complete blood exchange. I've got a book here, with it all written down. They did mention his sight but that's fine. He had lesions in his eye but they're OK now.

When she brought George home,

> We still didn't know about his legs, about his walking, or whether he was brain-damaged, because they said they wouldn't be able to be definite until he got older . . . we had to take him back every two or three months to the clinic and it was only as time went by – it seemed to me that there was a great big list of possibilities that could be wrong – it was only as time went by that they ticked most of them off.

Judith talked about the immediate difficulties after George was born – 'I was three months at home without him and it sounds terrible, but it was as though it was just a bad dream that never happened, you know, I didn't have a child' – and about the profound threat to self-confidence:

> The main thing that comes over . . . is that you're not a proper woman because you haven't carried a baby full term, I don't know if anybody has ever said that before to you but that's the feeling that I had, I felt very inadequate, that I couldn't carry a child, and this time I hope I can, just to see what a normal pregnancy is like. Because everyone says that being pregnant is the most wonderful experience for a woman.

Unhappily, in the next pregnancy Judith went on to have another early delivery at 24 weeks of a 580 g baby that could not be resuscitated. Tests showed a virus infection. When talking about this to me, she said:

> I know stress plays a big role at times, but it just seems to me sometimes that really when I'm pregnant my whole body seems to be rejecting the baby. But how medically that could be I don't know. You know if you have a bug or something you know your system is fighting it but you can't actually feel the right cells attacking but you know they're doing it, it's like that. That's the easiest way I can explain it.

Judith had, however, been unable to get any of the doctors involved in her care to take seriously her explanation of what had happened to her in these two pregnancies. Her narrative makes clear that inattention to women's own assessments of events during pregnancy and labour can add an extra, needless element of anxiety: it is a 'risk' in its own right from the 'patient's' point of view.

Jean Weybridge: 'I think I'm going to be a good study for you'

In contrast to Judith Clarke, Jean Weybridge's previous experience was of having a low-birthweight baby who, though requiring some weeks of intensive care, survived without any obvious health problems. Of the fourteen women for whom I attempted to provide support in pregnancy, Jean was one of two who made the most intensive use of the support service on offer, telephoning me on ten separate occasions. Her first phone call, nine days after I first saw her, was concerned, in order, with the following themes:

1 Her 2-year-old son, James (the LBW 'survivor'), was 'playing up' at bedtime, refusing food and having temper tantrums: 'He's getting on top of me,' Jean said.
2 Her feeling of being very stressed in general: is this bad for the baby?
3 Concern about the next hospital antenatal visit; she has no one to leave her son with and is worried he will be disruptive in the antenatal clinic.
4 The fact that she forgot to mention in the interview that James had had a hernia operation the previous summer.
5 She is worried about the possible recurrence of a rash she'd had in the previous pregnancy.
6 James fell out of his cot the other night.

A week later she telephoned with a worry about the ultrasound scan result from the hospital visit. According to her dates, she was then 14 weeks pregnant, but the ultrasound technician had made her 15 weeks and

2 days. What did this mean? She was to have another scan in a week. James had been back to the children's clinic and 'they were very happy with him – his weight and height are at the tenth centile.' She had got used to the evening and other problems – 'I know it's just a phase' – and was giving James some Phenergan to help him sleep. She had had a headache last week and had taken some paracetamol, hoping this would not harm the baby.

The third phone call, three weeks later, was chiefly occupied with an account of an episode of cystitis, the reporting of the baby's first movements (accompanied by a concern that James's movements had been felt earlier in pregnancy than this), and a disturbing argument with her husband two weeks previously. He had rung the doorbell instead of using his key, waking James, who had just gone to sleep. 'My heart was really banging. I thought: how's the baby taking this?' She also wanted to know whether they should abstain from sex because of the cystitis.

The next time she rang it was to report an argument with a doctor at the antenatal clinic. She remarked, 'I think I'm going to be a good study for you!' The doctor had studied the scan results and said something about the baby starting out on the middle line but having now dropped below this. Jean had immediately become very upset and had asked him what he was trying to say. In the end he had gone to fetch the consultant, who 'was very pleasant but treated me like an idiot. She said come back in two weeks.' Call number five reported a more satisfactory encounter with a doctor who decided the previous doctor had made a mistake with the ultrasound dating and had consequently underestimated the growth of the baby. She did another scan, and told Jean there were 'no structural abnormalities' and that she was quite happy with all the measurements. 'She told me not to come back for a month. She said go away and enjoy this pregnancy. That was so encouraging, I thought that was so nice.' Jean made her next phone call from the hospital. She had solved the problem of making the lengthy trips from home to hospital and back, since James had broken his leg and she was now living in the hospital with him: 'The only thing to be said for it is that it's handy for the antenatal clinic!'

As the pregnancy progressed, the dispute between the ultrasound scans and Jean's own dates intensified: this was the main topic of the next three calls. Jean was particularly unhappy because the hospital planned to induce her 'at term', and the two-week discrepancy in dates between ultrasound and her own reckoning meant that the baby might only be 38 weeks at this point. By 30 weeks she had had six scans, the last of which coincided with an article in one of the Sunday papers about the possible dangers of ultrasound in pregnancy. She also became very concerned about the effects on her of repeated trips to the hospital (now James's leg had mended, he no longer provided a reason for her to live in the hospital):

All this rushing around is very stressful. I've been now two days running. It's exhausting, there's no doubt about it. And each time I've got to get James looked after. Last time we took minicabs. I went once with him on the Underground – it really was awful, lifting him up and down escalators with buggies and all that . . . My husband feels it's almost detrimental, my dragging myself to the hospital for all these scans. Last week I had to take James and we had a two-hour wait, which is not unusual, but with a very small toddler it's not easy. He was very good, but by the time we got home we were both completely exhausted and he was very fractious.

By this point some of Jean's anxiety was focused on the impending labour. James had been born by Caesarean section: 'I'm more nervous about going into labour and doing the whole thing naturally than having a Caesarean, because it's an unknown quantity. I mean, I know it's better doing it naturally but I'm really in quite a state about it.' For the remainder of the pregnancy, she asked me to telephone her weekly.

Quite early on, Jean had asked me whether I would come to the hospital with her for the birth. Although this was not part of the social support I had planned to offer, I agreed. Jean phoned me at 3 a.m. one morning close to the expected delivery date to say that she and her husband were about to go into hospital. Her husband telephoned from there one and three-quarter hours later to report that Jean was 3 cm dilated. I arrived at 5.30. Jean was in bed, and seemed comfortable. Her husband was asleep in a chair. Jean said, 'He's only sleeping because he know's I've got you to talk to.' She concentrated on her breathing exercises, and examination showed that her cervix had dilated to 7 cm by 8.30. The contractions were quite powerful, and Jean was finding them difficult to handle, but was doing so with support and encouragement from myself and the midwives, and without any analgesia.

Unfortunately, though I had said I would be there, I had to leave the hospital at 9.45 a.m. to attend as external examiner a PhD examination in central London. The examination was straightforward, the candidate got her PhD, and I was back in the hospital at 12.30. By then Jean had had an epidural injection. 'They seemed to get so much stronger after you left,' she said of the contractions, 'and I couldn't handle them.' She was now drowsy, sleeping intermittently, and her husband was going in and out of the room making telephone calls. Jean said, 'He came up trumps while you were away – I got upset, and he got me under control.'

Between 12.30 and 7.15, Jean had three 'top-ups' of her epidural. She then had a 'trial of forceps', which did not succeed in delivering the baby. In the end she went to the operating theatre for an epidural Caesarean. By the end of the labour she had experienced all of the following: gas and air, epidural analgesia, electronic fetal heart-rate monitoring, forceps and a Caesarean section. The staff would not allow me to be present for the final delivery, so I waited for the news and then went home. Jean telephoned me a couple of days later to tell me that the baby, a girl, was 'beautiful, she's got blonde hair like a little doll, and she's a good feeder. Did they tell you the weight? 6lb 10oz!'

As the study by Marshall Klaus and his co-workers quoted in chapter 3 found, the continuous presence of a companion can significantly reduce the incidence of labour complications (Klaus et al. 1986). To generalize from the above experience, it could be said that such companions need to be free of other duties such as PhD examinations if the hypothesis that this form of care is effective is properly to be tested. On the other hand, in the real world, there is no such thing as 100 per cent support. My notes, taken during Jean's labour, indicate that I was aware of particular functions of my role as an 'extra' in the labour room:

Occasional support for J when no one else around. Even with 2 midwives, staff nurse and husband, still some times when support needed.

Adviser to husband on interventions. Wouldn't agree to anything without consulting me, viz., breaking waters, clip on fetal head, internal monitor, forceps delivery.

Husband panicked when fetal heart dipped, and I calmed him down.

J very worried re delivery. Wanted a normal delivery but frightened; asked if forceps would stretch her for ever. Long discussion a.m. about episiotomy and who should sew.

After the last home interview, carried out when the new baby was a few weeks old, I asked my standard question about how Jean had felt about taking part in the research. Jean told me:

I found it a fantastic back-up that I could pick up the phone if I needed to speak to you. I mean, whatever it was, you had the contact right through. That was wonderful because I said to my husband, if there is anything, I'll speak to Ann about it, I'll mention that to her next time I see her. It was very reassuring. This is what you don't have at the hospital – you're not going every week to start with, and you have niggling worries here and there, and you don't know who to contact, and when they see you, unless you write down everything you want to ask, you've been waiting for hours, you're tired, they're tired, they've seen lots of women and it somehow all goes by the board, and when you really most need it, there's no one you can speak to.

Her husband offered the comment:

I don't know whether we've been any use to you, but you've been a tremendous benefit really. I can see the relationship that Jean has with you, and she really regards you as a friend whom she can contact, and it's really been very reassuring to have you along at the birth. I mean I was – Jean will probably tell you – I was very much in favour of your being around at that time because I saw that it was good for Jean to have somebody to talk to, rationally and logically and removed from the intimate circle.

Jean: 'I was just trying this afternoon to think what else could you use me for, what other research could you do after this so that I could still see you from time to time!' Husband: 'Marriage guidance?' Jean: 'Would you be interested in a third pregnancy?' Husband: 'We could arrange it!'

There is clearly a danger in drawing general inferences from particular case-studies of this kind. Although it could be argued that my 'support' of Jean through an anxiety-laden pregnancy was successful – both in preceding the birth of a healthy, normal-weight child, and in terms of the attitudes of Jean and her husband to my presence – it is, of course, impossible to know whether this was in any way the crucial factor. Indeed, the impossibility of reaching any such conclusion with a research design involving an observational study of a small sample of women was the very reason why I had planned the research differently – as an intervention study which would be carried out in such a way that more confidence could be attached to the comparison of 'outcomes' for women offered support and for those receiving antenatal-care-as-usual. It is too easy to be self-congratulatory about 'interviewing' which seems to have gone well, although what I was providing in this case was, and was intended to be, somewhat more than the 'ordinary' interviewing experience. When my experience with the Weybridges is contrasted with the quite different and unhappy conclusion of Judith Clarke's pregnancy, it can be seen that whatever socially supportive interviewing can do must be pitted against significant biological and other odds. None the less, every woman in the pilot sample spoke, at some point in the stories they told, both of the risk attached to their having given birth to one LBW child, and of the demoralizing effect of antenatal care experienced as less than 'caring'. There was no doubt that my help was more appreciated when women lacked other sources of social support.

'This is what you don't have . . .'

The extent to which a women has support available and is able to make use of it cannot be judged simply from the number of social relationships in which she is involved. Joy Richardson, in the final case-study from the pilot sample drawn on in this chapter, illustrates this important point particularly clearly.

Joy comes from a highly orthodox Jewish family living in North London. Her husband is engaged in religious studies: they live in a small house with their seven children aged from 2 to 14. Joy also had a miscarriage between the first two children. It was her sixth child, a girl, who had been the LBW baby:

The funny thing was, there was a sort of discrepancy whether she was early or not. I knew when I became pregnant, or I thought I did, and when I went for my first booking at the hospital I was about 17 weeks. They examined me and said, that's amazing, you're very small for 17 weeks. You're really 12 weeks. You've made a mistake, or it was a false period and you're . . . Well, that's never happened to me. I thought that's very strange. Because I thought I was pregnant all that time. You certainly get a feeling. Especially after six other pregnancies!

The baby was born at term weighing 2lb 12oz (1247 g):

I had the feeling all through the pregnancy that the baby wasn't growing, because I didn't look the same as I did during normal pregnancy, and it just looked as if it wasn't the same amount of anything, same amount of water, same amount of baby, same amount of anything. And I think towards the end I had various things which were worrying, like I had some high blood pressure, I had a bit of protein in the urine, I had a lot of headaches, I wasn't feeling right. And I had a number of scans through pregnancy because of this worrying about the size, and whenever I had a scan nobody ever told me anything, nobody explained, nobody said . . .

I was worried, but everybody kept saying, there's nothing to worry about, we can hear the heartbeat, and I was feeling that the kicks weren't strong, it just wasn't feeling right, when I was six months or seven months or eight months or whatever it was, it just didn't feel like a strong baby. And then, in the last month, I started getting really worried because the kicking was tailing off, it was less than it used to be, it was as if the baby was lacking in strength, giving up. I was getting very, very worried. And finally, I think in that last month, I had another scan, and during the scan you could tell from the face of the person who was doing the scan, that they felt that the baby was not quite right.

My next appointment was in a week. They wouldn't tell me, they said, well, you'll find out at your next appointment how the baby's growing, we're not allowed to tell you. And I thought that was awful, and I had never yet once seen the consultant, the person that I was under, you know how you're under somebody, but at your antenatals you see either a registrar or another doctor . . . And I really wanted to see the consultant, because I felt that perhaps he would know a bit more about it, so I rang up to try and get a private appointment to see him, and the next appointment I could get was only after my next antenatal, so I phoned up the antenatal nurse and said I would like to make sure that at the next antenatal I see the consultant, so she said, OK, you'll see the consultant. And it was during that week that I had the baby, so I never saw him, in fact.

And how I had the baby was very traumatic. Because it was over the weekend, I was at home, I think it was on the Friday before this weekend, I felt that my blood pressure was very high then, I felt as if the kicking of the baby had stopped, I just didn't feel anything at all. So I took myself off to the doctor and I said I'm very worried, can you have a listen? So he listened, and he said, well, the baby's heart is beating away. Everything is all right, but your blood pressure's a bit high. Go home and stay in bed for the weekend. I had this clonking headache. I wasn't feeling very happy about it, so I went to bed, tried to stay in bed, the house was very busy and very noisy, and although I was quietly in bed I was, you know, very het up and not feeling good at all. And I think by Saturday evening I decided that I would have the baby Sunday morning, I decided I was going to go into hospital. I sort of farmed out the children, I phoned up some friends and asked them if they would have them, and I think I went in on Saturday evening or Sunday.

I said to them, I don't feel right, I've got this bad headache, and my blood pressure's up and the kicking feels very weak or not at all ... Also I felt contractions, mild contractions. And I felt that they were real contractions, you know how you have contractions during the last month? Well, it wasn't like that, they were very large contractions. Regular. They said, we'll keep you in here, and I stayed there and then on Monday, I think, they examined me with a machine which shows whether the contractions are proper ones or not ... and by some miracle during the time I was on the machine the contractions weren't there. They thought I was mad. I said to them, the contractions have stopped now I'm on that machine. They did, I just didn't feel the same when I was on the machine. They said no, it's all right, it's only practising.

And I came off the machine and I went back to bed and I carried on having these contractions. I was sure of it. They just ignored me and that was it, they were practice contractions, nothing to worry about. I said, what would you have done if you felt they were real contractions? They said, well, we would have given you something to stop it, because the baby is too early ... So later I said to myself that was a miracle that they thought that they were Braxton Hicks contractions because in fact I think the baby really had to be born then. It was about on its last legs.

I stayed in bed all that day, and in the evening I remember the nurse came over and I said I've got a very bad headache and I can't get to sleep, I've got contractions every twenty minutes. So she said, oh it's all right, just take two Panadol and go to sleep. So she gave me this Panadol, and I can't remember if I took them or not, because I thought I was in labour. And I think I finally fell asleep, and then I just woke up at 1 o'clock, about 1 o'clock, or something like that. And I was still having these contractions, and I had a show, and I called somebody in and said I've had a show. I'm having contractions every five minutes. I think they were getting faster and faster, and they were very very mild, you know, they weren't severe at all; I could have just stayed in bed and not bothered anybody.

Then she called the doctor, and they said, right, you know, get her into the delivery room, and I had the baby very, very quickly. The doctor just said to me as the baby was going to be born she was going to use forceps because it was very, very small, to protect it ... I heard her say, go and call a paediatrician. Then the baby was born. I didn't see it. The paed. just wrapped the baby up and disappeared. And no one said anything. And it was just very traumatic. I suppose they didn't know what to say to me, how the baby was or anything. But you know it was such a different experience to having a baby normally and seeing the baby afterwards. I had one other one – the one that's four now didn't cry straight away, there was a bit of a hassle, some trouble with that one, but otherwise apart from that there hasn't been anything.

Joy's account of this birth resonates with many others recorded in this study and elsewhere in which the narrative stream is channelled through a feeling of isolation and fighting to be taken seriously. In her case the problem was compounded by an extended family that had become quite hostile to her ever-increasing household. Each time she gets pregnant, the family says:

> Can you afford it, will you be able to cope, that sort of thing. Therefore I'm reticent about telling them, I put it off. There are two reasons. Number 1, there's a Jewish rule that . . . when you're pregnant you don't talk about it for at least a few months until you're showing, and people notice . . . that's basically to avoid what we call the evil eye, that if something good happens, you don't go around talking about it in case you reverse it. The second reason I don't tell them is that they won't take it very well . . .
>
> When I was expecting the little baby, at that time somebody in my family heard, and she said to me, this was my grandmother, she looked terribly worried, and she said, where are you going to put it? Now that played on my mind very, very much, and when the baby ended up in an incubator, I felt doubly bad. I never forgot that. I don't know if I've held it against her, but it's played on my mind a lot . . .
>
> I can understand their fear and their worries and apprehension, it's not that they don't like children – they're worried on my behalf. We're not totally self-supporting, and therefore to them I suppose it seems terribly wrong that we should have more . . .
>
> I mean I've chatted to my mother about it, during the last pregnancy, and she said, you're not going to have any more, are you, and I said to her, look . . . to us children are important, you know we make a lot of sacrifices in other things, we don't have luxuries, we don't go on holiday, we don't have a television, we don't spend money like my mother – she goes gallivanting on holiday twelve times a year or whatever – to us the children are important, we feel that we're putting ourselves out for that, and if I want to have another child, because that to me is my treasure, then who are you to say to me, you know, you've got enough, you shouldn't want to have any more, you should be satisfied? Why should I be satisfied? If a millionaire wants to have more money, I'm entitled to have more children.

I asked Joy about the people who were most important to her in terms of friendship and support:

> Well, I've got very different relationships with my brother, my older brother – I've also got a younger half-brother because my mother remarried. But I'd say my older brother and my mother and my grandmother, those are the main relationships. Probably one or two friends who have similar lives to me. One of them lives close to here, but I don't see that much of her . . . she's

a lot busier than I am, we were a lot closer in the past, we've become less close as she's got more involved in her work . . .

My mother I'd speak to more or less every day, the same with my grandmother . . . My mother might pop in and visit me during the week . . . And my grandmother . . . comes here about once a week, that way she can see all of the children and I don't have to take all of them to her. We've got a difficult relationship with my stepfather because he's never got on well with my husband . . .

My grandmother generally phones me twice a day. It used to be once a day, now she'll generally phone twice, just for a quick exchange, hallo, how are you? How are the children, are they all in school, if not what's wrong? etc. OK, speak to you tonight. The same again after they've come home from school . . .

My mother gets round to it once a day, maybe at 10 o'clock at night she'll ring me up, hallo, you've forgotten about me! Other than that, I might not speak to many people . . . a lot of my friendships are a product of circumstances, we're working together in the same group, and then we're close, but other than that we're not. I have a circle of people that I know, not necessarily intimate friends, but I am in contact with. I wouldn't say I had a lot of close friends . . . I think I'd like to have more friends . . . I'd say I've got a lot of acquaintances . . . I've also got a couple of ladies who've helped me a lot through a period about fifteen years ago when I was becoming more orthodox, who are also part of this same particular [religious] circle, slightly older than me . . . who I relate to well, more in a mother-figure sense. Not so much friends as advisers.

When I asked Joy about her needs in the present pregnancy, she talked in terms of the need for relief from a somewhat gruelling domestic routine:

I'd like to be able to get to bed a lot earlier, I'd like to get into the routine of not being so tired . . . My oldest daughter will often go to bed about 10.30, much too late . . . and the next one down is beginning to get a bit like that. I really have to work very hard on him to go to bed about 9.30, and her to go to bed at 10.30. There's very little time without them in the evening . . .

What I tend to do is to resurface over the weekend. Saturday I can sleep later in the morning and then go back to bed a little during the day . . . if I don't have to do something, or watch somebody. By the time Saturday evening comes I feel much better. Then Sundays are always very hectic . . . I'm off to teach [Hebrew] in the morning, and then I come back and start making lunch. In the afternoon I have all the family over, get people ready, then bed and sandwiches routine. I make sandwiches for four of the children, two of them have dinner at school, and then I make my husband a salad which I usually do in the morning after I see the children off . . .

Every evening I cook a meal. My husband comes in about 6.30, by which time I generally have tried to give the first shift their supper. I have to do it in two shifts because we can't all sit round the kitchen table. It's easier to get the younger ones fed first and try to get two into bed before giving the second lot supper, and then the rest can be slowly shepherded upstairs. I'll pop up later and tell them all to be quiet and go to sleep, that sort of thing.

That's why I like to go out. Perhaps once a week I'll have one of my meetings to go to. I don't get out a lot with my husband, we don't have much of a social life together ... the kind of life we lead, the men of our circle generally have their own things to do during the evening. They will either go out to learn something in a group of other people, or they will go out to teach. We might have one evening when we're both at home.

And apart from needing to go to bed earlier?

I think I'd like to feel things are all right with the pregnancy ... I'd like to be reassured ... the fact that you go to these hospitals and you don't see the same person each time, you see a different doctor probably every time you go, you more or less have to put over to them what you think ought to be in your notes, you have to try and make sure they're on the wavelength of checking the right things.

A number of things are striking about this narrative. First, and most obviously, there is the question of Joy's domestic workload, most of which is shouldered alone. Secondly, although she lives in what anyone would describe as a tightly knit family and community, centred on the synagogue of orthodox Judaism, the mutual obligations this imposes are a source of both stress and support to her. Thirdly, as regards her experience of pregnancy, there is the tension between her knowledge of her body and the 'care' of experts: this becomes a 'problem in itself'. But what fortunately did not prove to be a problem in this pregnancy was the birth and health of the baby, a boy, born on time and weighing 3317 g.

In conclusion then ...?

I found it difficult to know what conclusions to draw from all of this for the purpose of reporting to the ESRC on their investment in the study. As regards the aims of the study listed above, it was clear that dependence on already overworked essential clinic staff to find the women who would take part in the study was not the best arrangement. With regard to the practical problems of providing such support, the main difficulty was that I had too much else to do to be available to the women as much as I, and they, would have liked. I myself ended up relying on a complex system of help, with friends, family and colleagues taking and passing on phone messages from the women, some of whom were telephoned by me from distant places such as Helsinki and Amsterdam where I was attending international meetings – though, thanks to the magic of direct dialling, this was not (I hope) obvious.

The main themes emerging from the interviews have already been covered in this chapter. Before ending with some comments about how the women themselves regarded the intervention, it is worth discussing the extent to which the pilot study threw any light on the complex relationships between social support, stress and low birthweight.

Social support, stress and low birthweight

Most of the women in the pilot study led chronically stressful lives in which events such as partners' unemployment, the imprisonment or severe illness of a friend, and their own complicated pregnancies added extra layers of stress and difficulty. Three of the women lived with or were married to men who were physically violent towards them; four had no regular source of income on which to support themselves and their children; six had partners who were unemployed; two became homeless during the pregnancy; and two took drug overdoses. In their own accounts of what had happened, and their own search for meaning, all the women made connections between stress and the risk to their own and their babies' health. Stress could be acute or chronic, involving life events and/ or constant difficulty. Contacts with medical services were typically described as adding to, rather than reducing, stress. Along with poor diet, smoking and biology – being small oneself or coming from a family prone to LBW – stress was identified by the women as a cause of LBW. The findings with respect to smoking, a renowned case of mismatch between the perspectives of health care users and providers, echoed those of other studies (see e.g. Graham 1976; below, pp. 320–5). Nine of the fourteen women smoked. All knew of the medical argument that smoking contributes to LBW, but all weighed this 'knowledge' against the competing 'knowledge' of the perceived stress-reducing effects of cigarette smoking, and/or of the experiences of women who have smoked but nevertheless had large babies.

Since the pilot study was not conducted as a controlled intervention, the exercise of adding up the birthweights of the women's babies was of only limited value. Median birthweight achieved in this pregnancy by the thirteen women with singleton pregnancies (one had twins) was 2792 g, which is considerably lower than the national figure, and evidence of this being an 'at risk' group. The expected birthweight increase between one pregnancy and the next is in general about 150 g (Bakketeig et al. 1979); the women in the pilot study achieved an average increase of 635 g (median 411 g) (t-test $p < 0.05$). The expected number of women 'repeating' a technically LBW (2500 g) baby in this sample would be 3.8; four women actually had babies weighing less than 2500 g.

Because of the small size of the sample, it is important not to attach too much importance to the findings for birthweight alone. Two conclusions can reasonably be drawn: (1) the pilot study provided no evidence for this type of social support intervention having any negative effect; (2) although the proportion of women having another LBW baby was about what would be expected, this is quite compatible with a fairly notable impact of the intervention on average/median birthweight.

No clear associations emerged between achieved birthweight in the index pregnancies and aspects of the women's own social networks/ relationships and life stress. Again the sample was too small to make searching for these in a statistical sense a meaningful exercise. All the women were asked at the time of the last home contact how they felt about the 'unnatural' social support of their involvement in the research, and all made positive comments. A highly positive perception of the research was associated with a higher median birthweight than that occurring with a less positive perception (1306 g versus 208 g). Although the social support may have aided fetal growth, this interpretation cannot, of course, be disentangled from the likelihood that having a healthy baby encourages the viewing of pregnancy events through rose-coloured spectacles.

How have you felt about this research?

Jean Weybridge's answer to this question has already been quoted. The other thirteen women commented thus:

> I've enjoyed it, it's been all right. I feel that I have talked to you . . . It's been something to look forward to.

> To be quite honest with you, I've had so many people asking me questions, it's just like second nature . . . If it's going to help someone in the future if you can find out new information, then I'm glad to have helped.

> I think it's been nice. It's nice to chat to someone who isn't involved. You can say anything. I mean, you don't know me!

> I suppose I'm always grateful for something that slows me down a bit.

> What's it for, anyway?

> I was a bit wary at first . . . I thought, what would you be like, and would you disappear and I'd never see you any more? But when you first came down and started talking to me . . . I started feeling a bit better.

> It's really good I think, because it helps, even if it doesn't help me, it helps someone else.

> To be honest, it's nice. To be able to talk for a length of time.

> It's better than the other research that's going on – that's just lists of questions.

> I've felt all right. I don't mind.

Absolutely delighted. And I've been ever so grateful for all your advice –
well, you haven't given me advice, but you have given me a listening ear! . . . I
feel confidential with you, which is most important.

I felt I didn't have to sit down and worry about the one I lost . . . when you
came down and I spoke to you about it and I got it out of my system.

I was a bit wary at first when I was down the hospital and they rushed me
into saying something I'd rather have thought about . . . But when you came
down and talked to me, I knew I could talk to you and it weren't going to be
just a list you were going to file away.

This last observation raises the moral dilemma of what research is
conducted for, and what happens to the results of research. Even before
that, there are critical moral questions about how the results of research
are themselves produced out of the 'raw' data. As we shall see in subsequent chapters, these issues are no less pressing (though they have
traditionally been less visible) for quantitative than for qualitative research.

6

Who's Afraid of the Randomized
Controlled Trial?

A first step, therefore, in extending the feminist critique to the foundations of scientific thought is to reconceptualize objectivity as a dialectical process so as to allow for the possibility of distinguishing the objective effort from the objectivist illusion. (Keller 1989: 179).

During 1984, when I had continued to discuss mounting a randomized controlled study of social support and pregnancy, one prominent member of the NPEU's advisory board, a paediatrician, had expressed the view that I would never get funding for it: 'This is nothing to do with whether the study itself is good or bad. The truth is that because of the hybrid nature you will never find a grant-giving body fully capable of understanding the thrust of the proposal.' When the ESRC's period of funding for the 'Social Factors and Pregnancy Outcome' project came to an end in December 1984, the last baby in the study sample had only just been born, two of the postnatal interviews remained to be done, and the study as a whole still had to be analysed and written up in the form of a final report. In January 1985 I moved from Oxford to a permanent university-funded research post at the Thomas Coram Research Unit (TCRU) in London. This provided a welcome relief from the uncertainties and repetitive deadlines of a contract researcher's 'career', but did not solve the problem of securing funding for the main SSPO study.

The 'hybrid' nature of the study was a main cause of the difficulty. But the social support study had followed me to my new place of work, whether I liked it or not. Aside from the unfinished business of the interviewing, data analysis and writing up, the women continued to ring me up. One, Andrea Field, telephoned in January reporting a series of bizarre occurrences mixed with reports of harmful feelings towards her new baby. It eventually transpired that she had just been diagnosed as suffering from paranoid schizophrenia, in the aftermath of a highly stressful pregnancy in which her baby's father had maintained a dramatic and ambivalent double life as husband and father in one family and visiting father-to-be in Andrea's own.

'The field is an important one'

At TCRU my funding discussions were now with the Department of Health, who provided core funding for the unit. A turning-point came with the suggestion in January 1985, when the Research Management Division at the Department of Health had its own budget cut, that the attractiveness of the proposal to funders might be increased by introducing into it an element of economic cost-benefit analysis. Incorporated into the next version of the proposal was thus an economic cost-benefit analysis of the savings to the National Health Service that would accrue as a result of the research accomplishing even a minor shift in the birthweight distribution. Neonatal intensive care is an expensive technology, and birthweight predicts the cost (Guillemin and Holmstrom 1986). In 1983 a place in an intensive care unit cost £297 a day in the UK. The cost per survivor for very-low-birthweight (<1500 g) babies was £4490 (Sandhu et al. 1986). This fell to around £2500 for infants above 1500 g and rose to £10,000 for those below 1000 g (Newns et al. 1984). In North America costs are even higher – $59,500 in Canada in 1978 for babies under 1500 g and $102,500 for those under 1000 g (Boyle et al. 1983). On the basis of such studies, our calculation proposed that a target increase of 150 g in mean birthweight would reduce the costs of intensive care for babies who needed it by about £1000 per child. The Australian study set up in parallel to ours calculated that a 25 per cent reduction in the incidence of preterm birth would save $1.5 million annually in intensive care costs and result in the births of twelve fewer handicapped children per year (Stanley n.d.).

At a meeting with Department of Health customers two new outline proposals were discussed. One was for the RCT, and one was for an alternative observational study. The conclusions of this meeting were set down in a letter from the Department of Health liaison officer in the following terms:

> The field in which Ann Oakley wishes to carry out research is an important one, singled out by the Social Services Committee as deserving high priority (1980 Report on Perinatal Mortality paragraph 457 (a)) ... we should try to get something worthwhile from Mrs Oakley's[1] ideas ... If Mrs Oakley wants our support what she has to do is to construct from the best of her two proposals a project which more clearly:
>
> i. suggests an intervention package likely to be meaningful to Social Class IV and V mothers
> ii. shows how unplanned-for forms of social support will be given weight; and
> iii. shows how a random sample will be selected, given the known problems about access ...

In . . . summary . . . there is Departmental support for proposal 1 provided that the modifications suggested are taken on board and some indication is given of what the SSRC pilot study has shown.

A formal protocol was submitted to the Department of Health and a new set of referees' comments solicited and passed on to me in September 1985. Like the earlier generation of SSRC comments, these contained inconsistencies and contradictions as well as some helpful observations. For example, a 'Professor of Obstetrics and Gynaecology' confessed to being

> quite impressed by this application. There is certainly plenty of evidence that a whole range of pregnancy complications, such as low birthweight at delivery, is associated with significant social deprivation and an increased incidence of 'life events'. To provide additional social support for such women seems a reasonable method of potentially improving outcome. There is certainly a need for some improvement, when the incidence of low birthweight has shown no change in the UK for around 40 years!
>
> While I personally suspect that the minimal social support to be provided is unlikely to counteract the deleterious effects of years of social deprivation, I would be strongly in favour of supporting this study, because I believe it will provide reliable answers about the potential value of social support in pregnancy. Convincing, positive findings would have an enormous impact on the provision of care for pregnant women . . . *I would consider the whole study very good value for the money requested.* (italics added)

A 'Professor of Medical Genetics' disagreed, remarking, perhaps not surprisingly:

> As this type of project is outside my field of expertise, I have some diffidence in giving an opinion. I suppose my main anxiety concerns the proposed 'social support intervention' and the general paucity of evidence that three home visits conducted by a midwife after 24 weeks' gestation are likely to make any impact on birthweight. Apart from encouragement not to smoke, to improve diet and seek expert help with problems, are there no more specific interventions? Surely the same advice is available from the GP and from the antenatal clinic. I would like to see the results of a review of the causes of LBW with some hypotheses about strategies for prevention before mounting such a programme . . . *Finally the study is a most expensive one and must be judged in competition with proposals which have a better chance of yielding useful information likely to have an impact on the incidence of low birthweight.* (italics added)

A 'Professor of Economics' voiced the 'niggling' epistemological question of 'what procedures will be undertaken to enable one to distinguish the effect of "social" intervention on LBW as distinct from "placebo" or "Hawthorne" effects?'; while a 'Professor of Child Health' cheerily observed:

> It will be wrong to view this as merely an enquiry to see whether chatting up pregnant women increases the birthweight of their babies by a moderate 150 g ... even attempting the exercise, I think will produce a lot of interesting information. I am fully in favour of expanding the role of midwives, or rather, as I suspect, re-enforcing their traditional role.

From the social science side, a 'Social Scientist' raised the important and predictive objection that 'It is the study midwives who will be responsible for entering patients into the trial; but I trust that the allocation into study and control groups will not be their responsibility – it would be so tempting for them to manipulate the ones they perceived as more needy into the study group'; while a 'Professor of Social Medicine' commented somewhat technically:

> The research design seeks additional statistical efficiency through defining a high-risk group. They propose recruiting pregnancies where the previous pregnancy was of LBW. It is estimated that 25% of recruited pregnancies will also have LBW. However, this introduces some new problems, for which I cannot see easy answers. First, the efficacy of the intervention procedure, if it is demonstrated, will only have limited application.
>
> Second, high risk of LBW is not synonymous with a high level of responsiveness to intervention. Much of the prediction may be through intractable items such as mother's height, rather than tractable items related to specific pregnancies. Third, it has been found in other studies, especially those related to health education related to smoking, that it is the para-0 women who are most responsive to intervention. Their effective exclusion from this study not only excludes a 'statistically efficient' component, but excludes a group to which consequent policy recommendations might most profitably be directed. (The possible effect of a previous LBW in counteracting complacency arising from a successful first pregnancy, with subsequent resistance to intervention, might partly counteract this effect; but it is extremely difficult to predict the outcome of this kind of selection in these terms.)

Finally a 'Professor of Sociology' rightly insisted that it was important

> that overt attention should be paid to the material circumstances of the mothers: Dr Oakley is aware of the social class correlates of LBW. Within that there is likely to be a clustering of LBW within multiple deprivations including social isolation and poverty. Referral to other agencies is to be part of the content of the intervention. I would hope the reason for referral, including material deprivation, will be recorded and also the midwives' and mothers' views as to how far the referral itself had a satisfactory outcome ... I would like to see some indication of the mother's material circumstances, relative affluence or poverty, recorded systematically.

The way in which such comments are obtained and used as the basis of funding decisions deserves attention, in the same way as the mechanism of peer review has been scrutinized (Peters and Ceci 1982). The general question in both instances is the same: are these the best means of securing sound, high-quality research?

Despite the problems identified by referees, the Department of Health agreed to fund the SSPO study for three years from September 1985 at a cost of £113,918. Because I had now left the NPEU, with its resource of medical and epidemiological expertise, the final protocol named a collaborator there, Dr Adrian Grant, who had extensive experience in the RCT field, and was willing to help at all stages of the study.

Getting started

The revised research design funded by the Department of Health is shown in figure 6.1. The plan now was to invite women with a history of LBW delivery to take part in the study, on the understanding that each woman would be randomly allocated either to the intervention group, which would be offered social support in addition to usual antenatal care, or to the control group, which would receive antenatal care as usual. In order to reach the necessary numbers, the study would need to be carried out in more than one centre. In each centre a research midwife would go through antenatal clinic notes and identify eligible women, explain the study to them, and then ring us in London for the allocation of women who agreed to take part. Intervention women would be offered a programme of at least three home visits in pregnancy, plus a 24-hour phone number. All the women in the study would be sent a postal questionnaire six weeks after delivery to explore their experiences of pregnancy and motherhood and taking part in the research. Hospital case-note information would also be drawn on, to build up a picture of how the women and babies in the two groups had fared in comparison with one another.

This design had changed, though not substantially, from the one submitted to the SSRC (figure 4.1). The two main changes were in the personnel of the social supporters – then social scientists, now midwives – and in the method of collecting data postnatally – then interviews, now a postal survey. The substitution of midwives for social scientists was largely a response to the Department of Health's concern with the policy implications of a successful intervention: should a social-scientist-provided intervention succeed in improving the health of mothers and babies, the policy implication – that social scientists be employed in antenatal clinics – although good for the job prospects of social scientists in our increasingly besieged climate, would be anomalous within the existing structure of the maternity services. From this point of view, midwives were an obvious and very satisfactory choice, given the traditional emphasis in midwifery on providing continuity of care in pregnancy. The use of a postal survey instead of in-depth interviews for obtaining postnatal information from

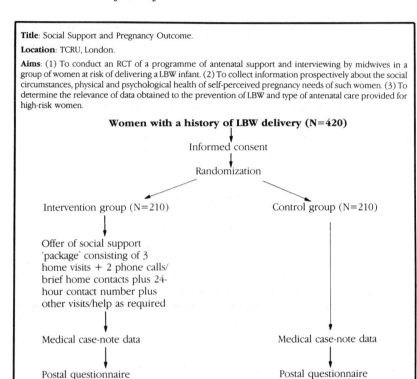

Title: Social Support and Pregnancy Outcome.

Location: TCRU, London.

Aims: (1) To conduct an RCT of a programme of antenatal support and interviewing by midwives in a group of women at risk of delivering a LBW infant. (2) To collect information prospectively about the social circumstances, physical and psychological health of self-perceived pregnancy needs of such women. (3) To determine the relevance of data obtained to the prevention of LBW and type of antenatal care provided for high-risk women.

Women with a history of LBW delivery (N=420)

Informed consent

Randomization

Intervention group (N=210)   Control group (N=210)

Offer of social support
'package' consisting of 3
home visits + 2 phone calls/
brief home contacts plus 24-
hour contact number plus
other visits/help as required

Medical case-note data   Medical case-note data

Postal questionnaire   Postal questionnaire
6 weeks after delivery[b]   6 weeks after delivery[b]

Outcomes: (1) Birthweight and gestational age. (2) Physical health of the mother in pregnancy and post-delivery. (3) Labour duration, analgesia and obstetric intervention. (4) Infant neonatal condition, feeding, infant weight gain, illness and health service use in first six weeks. (5) 'Psychosocial' health, including postpartum depression, maternal satisfaction with care, maternal-infant attachment, mother's confidence and control over life.

Staff and costs: £113,918 over 3 years; 4 part-time midwives for 2 years; research co-ordinator half-time for 2 years; fulltime secretary for 3 years.

[a]Excluding LBW deliveries associated with congenital malformation, multiple pregnancy or elective delivery; booking before 24 weeks, and fluent English-speakers.

[b]Later a one-year questionnaire was also carried out.

[c]Extended to 3 years, and then to 4 (plus part-time computer programmer) for analysis of one-year follow-up data.

Figure 6.1   Design 3 (1985–1988)

mothers was chosen because of the need to ensure 'blindness' in outcome evaluation. As some important outcome measures were to be based on mothers' reports, these needed to be obtained in such a way that any differences between intervention and control groups could not have been influenced by anyone 'loading' the intervention group with more favourable outcomes. Both the decision to use midwives and the choice of a postal survey made the study cheaper, not an unimportant consideration.[2]

The criteria for selecting the women who would take part in the study had been much discussed, and had settled into three considerations, which we hoped would be simple to apply in practice. The first – that women should in the past have given birth to at least one LBW baby unassociated with major congenital malformation or non-spontaneous delivery (induction of labour, Caesarean section) that was likely to have been the reason for the LBW – was to prove relatively easy to identify from the antenatal clinic booking notes the midwives used to select the sample. Similar studies to ours were using more complex lists of obstetric criteria (see pp. 67–70), with more or less the same result in terms of generating a 'high-risk' population. The second criterion was that the women should be less than 24 weeks pregnant at booking: this was to ensure sufficient time for the giving of the intervention, but was balanced against the known observation that women who book later than others have more than their fair share of social and obstetric problems (see Oakley 1984: 265–71). Our third stipulation – that fluency in English was needed – had been quite controversial, as the argument was put that ethnic-minority women (who would be more likely to have problems in speaking English) might be most in need of social support. Against this, it had also been pointed out that birthweight had a different 'meaning' in ethnic-minority populations – for example, a small baby of an Asian mother was less at risk of health problems. The deciding factor was, again, money: the Department of Health would not supplement the grant to cover the costs of providing social supporters fluent in the various minority languages.[3]

The Department's funding for the study covered six salaries – those of a research co-ordinator, an administrator/secretary and four midwives. All the posts except the administrator/secretary's were part-time, and only one (the administrator's) was for the duration of the study. Lyn Rajan, who was appointed research co-ordinator, came across the advertisement for the job almost by accident:

> I can still picture being handed the advert, carefully cut out of *The Guardian* by one of the other researchers in the Sociology Department at the University of Surrey. For some reason, despite carefully scanning the *Education Guardian* for the previous six months, I had missed it, but my colleague had picked it out as being 'just the thing' for me . . . I was desperately looking for a research post [as] my contract was due to expire in a few weeks . . . I had been employed . . . as a research assistant in the Sociology Department at Surrey for the previous three years. In 1980 I'd started the Surrey MSc course in Social Research, and it was while I was completing the dissertation that I was asked to help out with writing documentation for a series of A-level and undergraduate software packages using SPSS [the Statistical Package for the Social Sciences] with data from the General Household Survey. As this contract came to an end, I was asked if I would be interested in a year's full-time work on a national survey into computerization in Social Services Departments. A research assistant learns very quickly to grasp opportunities as they arise. Unemployment looms large on the horizon.
>
> The survey was to use a microcomputer for data analysis and the presentation of the final report. This was a very new concept at that time. Up

till then only mainframe computers had the capacity to handle large quantities of data. The skills that I acquired from this completely new way of working were to prove invaluable ...

This project came to an end and with some relief I decided ... that full-time work ... was too much when combined with looking after four young children ... But I had proved my usefulness at Surrey and for the next year or so as each two-month contract came to an end another lecturer would find the money to pay me for another couple of months on a different project. In this way I learnt, amongst other things, to be versatile and to live with insecurity ... But ... the time had come to move on. I completed the application form – I remember there was a section in it that asked why I wanted the job, and my replying that I couldn't have phrased the advert to describe a job that would have suited me better, a comment that seems a little naive in retrospect, but one that was in fact borne out in practice ...

I had long been a great admirer of Ann Oakley's work, ever since the day in 1977 when *Housewife* opened my eyes to the futility of the home-locked child-bound existence into which I had unthinkingly drifted ... after a nerve-racking interview ... I was given the job. Ann telephoned me herself to give me the good news: I remember I was hanging out the washing when the phone rang. I could hardly believe my luck. A two-year contract seemed like long-term security for someone used to two months at a time. This was later extended for another year, as more money was made available, and then for a further year so that we could follow up the women in the study.

I started work in mid-September, and our first tasks were to negotiate access to the hospitals chosen for the study, to appoint the research midwives, and to prepare the research instruments. It was an exciting time, especially when the first two midwives began to enrol women into the study and things really got under way.

Negotiating access

Access to the hospitals was to prove more troublesome than finding the research midwives. However, one was crucial to the other, since we could hardly advertise for the midwives until we knew which geographical areas were to be included in the study. The process of negotiating for access had begun the previous year, out of a concern that being able to demonstrate the acceptability of the study to enough hospital staff might be important to a successful funding decision. This is very much a chicken-and-egg affair: researchers may need to establish they have access before being funded to carry out a particular piece of work, but on the other hand no institution is likely to promise access for a study that may never happen.

All research is a compromise between the ideal and the practicable. Our decisions about which hospitals to approach for help with the SSPO study were based on a mix of considerations: hospital size; typicality or otherwise; the presence of clinicians and/or senior midwives known to be sympathetic to research. Size – number of deliveries per annum – was critical, as we needed to be sure of finding our sample of 420 'at-risk' women within a sufficiently short period (around a year) to enable us to complete the study on time. Numbers of deliveries could be obtained from hospitals, but, because we wanted only women with a history of LBW delivery, we needed to know the rate of LBW in each place, and this was only available for health authorities, not hospitals. We also needed an estimate of the proportion of deliveries to women who had already had a child; Hospital Inpatient Enquiry statistics gave a figure of 53 per cent for this. Finally, we had to guess at the proportion of 'eligible' women who would agree to take part in the study – for the purpose of the initial sums we put this figure at 70 per cent. (This proved to be a considerable underestimate; see pp. 227.

We began by approaching six hospitals – four in the South of England, and two in the Midlands. For one of the hospitals in the South, we decided to test the hypothesis that the health authority rate for LBW might be an underestimate of the hospital rate (as proportionately more mothers with complicated pregnancies would be referred to the hospital for delivery). The health authority figure was 5.7 per cent; Lyn Rajan undertook a painstaking analysis of 600 hospital cases, coming up with a figure of 7.1 per cent. On this basis we calculated that this hospital would provide us with seventy-six women over a year. Similar calculations were carried out for the other hospitals. The issue of whether a hospital was 'typical' or not was hard to solve, as on one level it seemed that every hospital would be different. Although teaching hospitals might be regarded as a priori untypical, yet they should offer the advantage of a concentration of referrals of 'high-risk' cases, and thus a better guarantee of our reaching our planned sample size more quickly. Co-operation from the hospitals was needed principally in order to allow us access to the names of women eligible to take part in the study. But each participating hospital would also need to provide some office accommodation and facilities for the research midwife working in that area.

Two of the hospitals we approached at first were ruled out rather quickly – one because too much research was already going on there, and one because there was a shortage of office accommodation. What happened in the other four in terms of negotiating the approval of staff and ethics committees for the projects is described below as a case-study in this unexplored aspect of the research process. The hospitals are referred to by number rather than name, as they are throughout the book.

Hospital 1

I wrote to one of the NPEU's advisers, who had commented on the first version of the RCT proposal, in December 1984, concerning access to a hospital in the Midlands in which he worked. His reply, two months later, bemoaned the fact that there were already some seventy research projects under way in the Obstetrics and Gynaecology Department. He would refer me to a colleague at another hospital not too far away if I would like. I waited to take up his offer until the Department of Health had agreed to fund the study, writing to the suggested consultant in August 1985, and receiving a prompt reply. This indicated some enthusiasm for the study, but a concern that all five obstetrics and gynaecology consultants needed to be enlisted in order for projected sample numbers to be reached on time. The contact consultant said later on the telephone that there should be no problem with the ethics committee, as this was chaired by his own anaesthetist, and could be convened and required to give a decision at 48–72 hours' notice.

In November I went to Hospital 1 for a meeting with obstetrical and midwifery staff in order to run through the details of the proposal. The worries voiced by staff included: (1) whether the sample as a whole would be big enough to answer the questions posed; (2) how the women with a history of LBW delivery would be identified, and whether the midwives in the antenatal clinic should be asked to do this for us; (3) the fact that the research midwives would need to be *practising* midwives (even though they would not be performing any clinical care during the study); (4) concern that the research midwife we decided to employ be acceptable to the hospital staff – and not one of their own midwives, who were in short supply; (5) lack of office space; and (6) the possibility that the study would lead to extra social work referrals. Talking through these points appeared to offer the staff some reassurance that the study would probably not be too intrusive on their work or time.

The proposal then went to a meeting of the Division of Obstetrics and Gynaecology in early November. It received support from those who attended, and the consultant undertook to convene a meeting of the ethics committee the following week. Some delay followed; a month later he rang to request that we fill in three sets of forms with which he promised to 'accost' his anaesthetist immediately. On 30 December 1985 he wrote to say that the proposal had been passed on 'chairman's prerogative' without a meeting of the ethics committee actually taking place.

Hospital 2

Adrian Grant at the NPEU approached this hospital in December 1984, and a month later the consultant whom he had contacted replied to the effect that the hospital would be interested in taking part. We did not pursue this until September 1985, once the funding decision had been made.

At the consultant's suggestion, a meeting took place in November with midwifery staff only, to discuss details of the proposal. The midwives' concerns here differed somewhat from those voiced in Hospital 1. They included: (1) the importance of liaising with community midwives, as a high proportion of the patients had 'shared' care; (2) the fact that the community midwives were likely to consider they were giving social support anyway; and (3) the need to stress to the consultants that the research midwives would not be directly advising any of the women in the intervention group.

The midwives who came to this meeting then told the consultant that they were happy for the study to go ahead. It was again not felt that a meeting of the ethics committee would be necessary. We received the go-ahead from the hospital shortly after this.

Hospital 3

Adrian Grant wrote to the Director of Nursing Services at this hospital in July 1985; a meeting was set up with the midwifery staff in August. The main issues raised were: (1) whether the study women would be told the research midwives were midwives; (2) whether extra referrals made because of the study would add unduly to the hospital/community midwives' caseloads; (3) the community midwives would want to know whenever 'their' patients contacted the research midwife; (4) the area already had a 'dial-a-midwife' service; (5) the area was too middle class; (6) how we would ensure 'blindness' – even if we asked the women in the study not to tell their midwives that they were in the intervention group, they would do so, and the midwives would then be very likely to alter their behaviour; (7) what kind of person we were going to employ as a research midwife, and what input the hospital would have into the selection process.

The Director of Nursing Services declared she would put the proposal through as a 'midwifery' project. She proposed to send a copy of the protocol to the chairman of the Division of Obstetrics and Gynaecology 'to get it through on the nod' and said she would have a word with the secretary of the ethics committee to establish what the procedure there should be. However, the secretary proved to be otherwise occupied, looking for another job, and there was a three-month delay before we received a letter from the chairman saying that it had been formally agreed to 'provide accommodation for your trial'. We were not informed as to the role of the ethics committee in reaching this agreement.

Hospital 4

Adrian Grant wrote to a consultant here in July 1985, following this with a detailed protocol in August. A meeting was set up in October to discuss it, and the plan was that it would go to the ethics committee meeting on 13 November, so that an advertisement for a research midwife could be placed in a local paper the following week. This would allow us to have someone in post and actively recruiting by the planned starting date of January 1986. The anxieties articulated by clinicians at the October meet-

ing were interesting. The first concerned the confidentiality of some of the
questions we planned to ask in the home interviews, and of the data the
research midwife would be handling (to which a lockable filing cabinet
was an easy answer). Secondly, there was concern about space. The
midwife, once appointed, would need to have a 'home' in the hospital, and
somewhere quiet to talk to the women who might take part in the study.
The consultant agreed to provide a desk and filing cabinet space in his
own room in the antenatal clinic for this purpose. Only three of the five
consultants had said they would support the study: what about the other
two? We decided that there would probably be enough entrants for the
study on this limited basis.

Quite unexpectedly, the ethics committee then turned down the proposal. The grounds on which they did so were based on objections
by medical members of the committee, and communicated to us by
telephone:

1   The committee is concerned at the length of the questionnaire[4] from
    the point of view of its reliability, reproducibility and content.
2   There were several comments concerning the personal nature of some
    of the questions posed and it was felt they could be taken by some
    patients as offensive. These related particularly to questions of social
    and marital status as well as income.
3   We were concerned at the effect of the intervention by midwives on
    patient care . . .
4   The use of a tape recorder was clearly controversial, and required
    further thought.
5   It was noted that there was little emphasis on diet in the study which it
    was felt could be of some relevance.

Objection to the 'personal' nature of some of the interview questions took
no account of the clearly stated reasons for asking these questions,[5] and
seemed odd from a group of professionals known not infrequently to err
in the direction of offending patient privacy themselves (see e.g. Bibby et
al. 1988). The third point, concerning the possible impact of the intervention on patient care, seemed to indicate some feeling of threat. The
reference to diet suggested that the consultants' understandings of social
support were framed in the old-style health education model in which the
aim of any social intervention could only be to instruct mothers in the
science of proper motherhood. Finally, the observations about the use of
tape recorders and the 'reliability and reproducibility' of the interviews
appeared to be made in ignorance of the conventions of social science
research. After further discussions with the 'friendly' consultant, who
advised on strategic responses to these issues, the proposal was passed by
the ethics committee in mid-January.

Are ethics committees ethical?

A few general points are raised by these experiences. First of all, it is undoubtedly the case that ethical guidelines for research are important in any and every field. Researchers may behave unethically for all sorts of reasons, and may often do so without any definite intention in that direction. If they are confident of the ethical soundness of their own plans, they may feel this abrogates the need to be pushed through the delaying and potentially obstructive 'sieve' of an ethics committee; but this certainty is, of course, one of the main reasons why the safeguard of ethics committees is needed. In the case of the SSPO study, while we benefited from the irregular means deployed to pass our proposal through the ethics committee barrier, it is clearly the case that these committees ought to have paid more scrupulous and systematic attention to their business and to have been more representative of both patient, and research communities.

The literature on 'informed consent' places a certain reliance on the work of ethics committees.[6] For example, it is often argued that the task of arbitrating the value of particular research studies is better left to ethics committees than to the judgement of would-be participants, because 'Only such committees have the experience, skill, information, and emotional detachment to judge the merits of a research protocol; the individual patient has none.' Moreover, 'As a rule, patients will consent to randomization on the basis of skeleton information only, if they know that a committee of professional and other interested people has on their behalf studied and approved the scientific merits and ethical aspects of the trial. Most patients will not need, want, or ask for more' (Papaioannou 1982: 828).

However, as our experience in the SSPO study showed, reliance on the efficacy or ethical behaviour of ethics committees is dangerously ill informed. In Britain, no law requires the submission of research proposals to such bodies. There are no statutory or other regulations governing the membership of ethics committees or the practices followed in them, which are widely variable (British Medical Association, 1981).[7] There is a good deal of evidence that, as a mechanism of social control over research, the reviewing process carried out by hospital or area ethics committees is inadequate. A recent review of the performance of twenty-three UK ethics committees found long delays in processing applications (mean 11.5 weeks with a range from 3 to 32 weeks), and great variation in their size, membership, meeting habits and functioning (Ginzler et al. 1990). A second, larger, study of 254 committees reported a range in size from one member to seventy-three, with half of all committees having only one lay member and one in ten having none (Neuberger 1991). Studies in the US (where such committees are known as Institutional Review Boards) have revealed substantial inconsistencies in ethical and technical matters between and even within boards when presented with the same research proposal. Some of these inconsistencies flow from the influence of board members' personal socio-political values (Ceci et al. 1985; see Benson 1989 for a review). In her account of her experience as a lay member of the General Medical Council, Jean Robinson points out that in any case no professional sanctions are applied to doctors who carry out research on patients without the approval of ethics committees. When the GMC was informed of some medical research on Asian women in a London ante-natal clinic which had not been cleared by the relevant ethics committee, their reply was that the matter was not sufficiently serious to justify the holding of a formal inquiry; in other words, 'doctors can research on patients in Britain without the local ethics committee's knowledge or approval, *without fear of being struck off the register*' (Robinson 1988: 29).

Existing official guidelines on the ethical aspects of biomedical research do, as Herxheimer has shown, serve in the main to consider the ethics of research from the viewpoint of the research community. The fact is that patients 'are still mostly passive participants in trials, unwitting beneficiaries of the results [and] ignorant victims of the mistakes,' as 'clinical trials are planned, conducted, regulated, and used largely by medical and paramedical scientists in academic institutions, industry, and government, with virtually no input from ordinary people' (Herxheimer 1988: 1128). Because ethics committees' main role relates to biomedical research, they may perform particularly badly for social research, as Dance (1987) found when requesting approval for her study of linkworkers and pregnancy outcome in Pakistani women. Social interventions are theoretically risky, just as medical interventions are. Alternatively, the role of such committees as 'censors of research' may come into play when research methods, designs or topics do not seem to fit the standard medical format. This is a particular problem for multidisciplinary research (Hemminki and Kojo-Austin 1989).

A sense of humour needed

The advertisements for the part-time research midwives for the SSPO study placed in four local papers, said that job applicants needed to have 'a midwifery qualification and an interest in research', and that they would be involved in 'home visiting and interviewing of high-risk women'. A job description was dispatched to all who enquired about the posts. This stated:

> The job of the research midwife is essentially concerned with the provision of social support to a group of women at risk of delivering LBW babies. Each of the 4 part-time research midwives will be responsible for identifying in each centre women who are eligible to enter the study, informing them

about the study and asking their consent to be included in it, and then carrying out a number of home visits and other contacts with the women allocated to receive the social support intervention. (The allocation to 'intervention' and 'control' groups will be done by the research midwives telephoning the Thomas Coram Unit.)

The research midwives involved in this study will not be providing any clinical care, since the women in the study will be receiving the usual hospital antenatal care.

The research midwives' task will be twofold: (1) to discuss with the women any anxieties or problems they encounter during pregnancy, and (2) to collect some information from the women about their social circumstances, health and self-perceived needs. The social support intervention will consist of a 'minimum package' of three home visits by the research midwives during pregnancy, two telephone calls (a brief visit for women without telephones), one (brief) postnatal visit and the provision by the midwives to the women of a 24-hour contact telephone number.

The average 'case load' per midwife will be about fifty women over a period of some one and three-quarter years. Each midwife will be provided with a base in the hospital and with the necessary research materials (including a tape recorder and a radiopager). Aside from seeing the women in the intervention group, the research midwives will need to attend some meetings in London. Travel costs (both to and from London and for local travel) are covered by the study's budget.

Six completed applications came in for each post, and four midwives per post were interviewed by selection committees, which included representatives of the hospitals where the midwives would be based. The selection process emphasized, as well as the formal qualifications needed, an interest in, and commitment to, the aims of the study, openness to a different model of health education from the one dominant in midwifery training, and, last but not least, a sense of humour.

The four successful candidates were quite different from one another in style and personality. All, however, happened to be mothers. This was, of course, not quite accidental, as the combination of motherhood and full-time midwifery is particularly onerous and leads many midwives with young children to find other occupations. One of the four midwives we proposed to employ was a part-time senior midwife aged 32 with two children, who had trained as a midwife fairly recently, after she had become a mother herself. She continued to work part-time at the hospital during the course of the study, a situation which posed some interesting dilemmas (see p. 180). A second, aged 30, had been qualified as a midwife for seven years but was currently doing part-time agency nursing, and looking after her 2-year-old son. The third, the youngest at 26 when the study started, had been a midwife for four years but was also now occupied with motherhood. The fourth, at 38 the most senior, qualified as a midwife fifteen years previously, and was doing part-time night work as a staff midwife in one of the hospitals taking part in the study. (She gave this up when she started work for us.)

Two of the midwives started work in January and two in March 1986. During two separate 'induction' days held in London, the study and the midwives' role were explained and discussed fully. Each had been sent a package of material to read which included a copy of the full protocol for the study, extracts from two 'methods' pieces on interviewing, a paper on RCTs, some background literature on social support and health, and on smoking, diet, alcohol, sex and stress in relation to pregnancy outcome, material on poverty and financial benefits, a chapter on women's experiences on antenatal care, one of women, health and the family, and some basic statistical/demographic material on LBW and on families and motherhood.

The professional training of midwives emphasizes the role of the midwife as provider of client-sensitive care and as guardian of the concept of normal pregnancy. But it also embodies another somewhat different notion, that of the midwife as moral educator, leading childbearing women into medically acceptable ways of behaving (see e.g. Myles 1981). This was one of several ideas it was necessary to discuss with the research midwives before they started work on the study. The definition of social support that we wanted to operationalize centred on *listening* to women, on *talking* to women about their pregnancy needs and circumstances, and *giving information only when required*. A fourth component was carrying out *referrals* to other agencies, such as social services or the hospital clinic, when appropriate. In all of these, the midwives' personal relationships with the women, their ability to develop rapport and react sensitively to the women's expressed needs and problems, were crucially important. We were also clear that social support was not clinical care, health education, or a device for raising the uptake of medical or other services.

Although all the research midwives were sympathetic to the notion that any advice or information offered the women in the study should not be gratuitous, but a response to the women's own expressed needs, this went against the grain of midwifery training, particularly as regards topics such as smoking in pregnancy. This proved a major discussion point throughout the study (p. 175). Since the midwives would probably be asked for information by women in the intervention group, or the subject would come up indirectly, and it was important to attempt some standardization of the information each gave, we had written guidelines covering topics such as diet, smoking, alcohol, exercise, financial benefits, and so forth (see appendix I). Somewhat contradictorily also, the midwives were being asked to provide social support as well as collect information. For the three home visits with the intervention women, we had written semi-structured interview schedules. These covered areas such as social background and experiences of medical care. The interview schedules had two functions, the first of which was to provide a basis for the interaction between the midwives and the study women. Turning up on someone's doorstep and saying, 'I'm here to give you social support', had been found to be something of a conversation-stopper in the Western Australian study of social support that was further advanced than ours (F. J. Stanley, personal communication). The second function of the interviews was to flesh out the study with some in-depth qualitative data. Though these data were important, we stressed that the provision of social support was the prior aim, so that the interview schedules should only be used when the women and the midwives were happy about this. A parallel tension was the need to provide good-quality social support at the same time as maximizing the numbers to be included in the study. The sample size of 420 had been increased to 440, to be on the safe side. Recruitment was planned to take a year. In each centre the target number reflected the size of the population and the amount of the midwife's time that would be available: in two of the centres the midwives were to work half-time, in one two-fifths and in the other three-fifths time.

An even greater contradiction was built into our study design: the goal of providing social support for some women while withholding it from others, in the interests of testing the idea that social support 'works' in improving the health of mothers and babies. This is the point at which the two different models of knowledge production discussed in chapters 1–3 meet, and collide. The philosophical resolution of the problem is one challenge (see chapter 12). A more immediate problem was the moral dilemmas the research midwives felt to be posed by the study design. We were asking them, on the one hand, to believe that social support does work – their enthusiasm for the notion had, after all, been a qualification for the job in the first place. But we were also requiring the suspension of belief that is necessary for a randomized controlled trial: asking the question 'Does social support benefit pregnant women or not?' with the implicit counterpart to this; 'Does social support harm pregnant women or not?' We had also to take into account the midwives' feelings – as traditional advocates of pregnant women's own standpoints – that the trial might be something women themselves might not want, and that the exercise of singling out a particular group of women for study – those with a history of having LBW babies – might be adding to, rather than subtracting from, their problems.

Midwifery education does not contain much of an exposure to research methodology, and the professional opportunities for midwives to engage in evaluation studies are very limited. The ethical and methodological issues in the SSPO study were not only discussion points during the induction days but themes that recurred throughout the study. It seemed important to be open to them – and to encourage debate. As the primary movers in the research, we did, however, stress two points in particular. First, we emphasized the desirability of explaining fully to the women who were asked to take part precisely what the study was about; to this end, we wrote guidelines for 'informed consent' (see appendix I) for the midwives to use. Secondly, we emphasized the need to be as scrupulous as possible about the randomization process, in view of the very human tendency to want to influence this. Randomization was to be done in the following way. The midwives would telephone the study secretary in London and give the names of the women who had agreed to take part. The study secretary[8] had sheets of allocations derived from a table of random numbers, and she would enter each name in the order given, and then inform the midwives, who would inform the women, as to allocation status.

From the point of view of openness to discussing these critical issues in the study design, the monthly meetings in London, to which the midwives all came, were absolutely critical. Research is a lonely business. Each of the research midwives in the SSPO study worked on her own in a particular area, so that the only opportunity to meet and discuss with each other and us the nature of the experience of giving support was during these meetings. They fulfilled other necessary functions, too, and the midwives staggered away from them with bags of equipment and documents. Some of the documents were to be read, others were to be completed. A recurrent complaint from the midwives was about the volume of paperwork they were asked to complete – only to return it each time at the next meeting and collect a new load!

The 'housework' of the RCT

The first woman was entered into the study and randomly allocated on 21 January 1986. Almost immediately her research midwife was involved in giving support in a crisis situation. Cherry Dodd, a part-time shop assistant married to a self-employed painter and decorator, had a major asthma attack when 18 weeks pregnant, and went into hospital to be treated with steroids and a respirator. She asked for the research midwife to be contacted, as she was worried about the possible effect of the treatment on the baby and had a general 'phobia' of hospitals.

The research midwife went to see her, and said she would find out about the possible effect of the asthma medication on the baby; subsequent medical enquiries produced the opinion that the lack of oxygen would theoretically prove more of a risk than the steroids. The hospital doctor asked the research midwife for advice about discharge, and the midwife, after talking to Cherry, suggested she be sent home as soon as possible. Dependence on the research midwife as a mediator between herself and the hospital seemed to have been established, since Cherry phoned her a couple of months later in tears to say that the hospital had told her she needed complete bed-rest but had not explained how she was to achieve this with a toddler to look after. The research midwife spent a couple of hours with her drinking coffee, and felt she had been of some help. Cherry's difficult pregnancy had a successful outcome, and a healthy baby boy was born a week before term weighing 2740 g. Cheryl wrote on her postnatal questionnaire that the research midwife 'was able to reassure, especially after hospital visits. Acted as an "interpreter" between hospital and myself. Her advice was very useful.'

As our research midwives made their visits to the four antenatal clinics and scanned the notes for potential recruits to the study, they came back to us with a number of queries about how the 'eligibility' criteria were to be interpreted. Although we had deliberately kept these simple – (1) booking before 24 weeks; (2) fluent in English; (3) at least one previous singleton baby weighing less than 2500 g (unassociated with major congenital malformation or with elective delivery that might have been responsible for the LBW) – not surprisingly, the last of these criteria required some elaboration. Some of the midwives' queries were:

> RMW1:[9] recruiting a lady who has been told the baby she's expecting has a hernia on the umbilicus. RMW1 thinks maybe it will be an exomphalos – congenital umbilical hernia. Now 24 weeks, scan says 24, doctor says 26. Should she be included? [Answer: no, on grounds of late gestation.]

> RMW2: one lady found but baby was 2530 g at 39 weeks. [Answer: exclude – previous baby more than 2500 g.]

> RMW2: lady had Caesarean at 36 weeks for APH [a haemorrhage starting before labour] but baby – 1920 g – was growth-retarded all along. [Answer: include.]

> RMW3: One lady turned out to be staff nurse at the hospital. Any difficulties about this? [Answer: no.]

> RMW3: should this lady be included? 1st pregnancy: 23 wks, 2lb. 2nd pregnancy: 34 wks, 6lb. Had stitch for incompetent cervix. [Answer: yes.]

Recruitment was faster in three of the centres than the fourth, and in two there were more women eligible for recruitment than the midwives could see. To cope with this, we developed a system whereby the midwives rang us with a list of eligible names and we halved the number by random selection (so they would not be tempted to choose the women they thought they might like to have in the study).

All the midwives' enquiries were placed in a large lever-arch file kept in Sandra Stone's room. As the study progressed, this file came to be known as 'Sandra's problem file'. In it every telephone conversation with the four midwives concerning the study women and any action we at our end took in relation to the midwives' queries were recorded. The 'problem file' material complemented other data that were being collected and processed at the same time. While the computer-held quantitative data are able to tell us how many contacts each woman had with her research midwife, and which broad categories any problems discussed fell into, the 'problem file' fleshes out this information with more intimate and human details.[10]

Which women to include in the study was only the first problem. After that it was necessary for the midwives to do their best to ensure that all the women allocated to the intervention group were offered the 'minimum package' of three visits plus two phone calls. The midwives were also asked to restrict their contacts with the control-group women to a minimum, so as to minimize the chances of control-group women feeling supported. On the assumption that the midwives' support would have an effect, such contact with the control group would tend to narrow any outcome differences between the two groups, and reduce the chances of the study finding that social support was health-promoting. The requirement to offer the intervention to women allocated to the intervention group and withhold it from those allocated to the control group proved difficult. For a start, contacting some of the women allocated to be offered the intervention was not easy:

15.5.86. RMW1 called. She has been to visit this lady and done 1st interview. Made 2 subsequent appointments for 2nd interview but lady wasn't there for either. RMW1 put note through door to make 3rd appointment – RMW1 thinks the lady may be trying to back out of continuing.
16.5.86. RMW1 waited outside the house for half an hour – someone put the milk bottles out – RMW1 went in and saw her!

1.4.86. RMW3 phoned to check that SW was expecting her. Spoke to mother – didn't seem to know if she was expected. Said SW may be there later.
10 p.m. Called to see her, spoke to unidentified woman, SW had arrived, heard the RMW was visiting and 'ran off to her sister's house'.
RMW3 wrote to SW restating why she wanted to see her, inviting her to phone, and saying she might pop in to her B and B accommodation.
April Popped into B and B – no answer, but obviously someone at home. Repeated next week.

This woman was never available to see the research midwife, so no intervention was given.[11] A boy weighing 2780 g was born in August. He died of septicaemia aged 4 months.

In another case resulting in no intervention, the midwife went to considerable lengths to enlist participation:

9.4.86. RMW1 originally approached this lady in the clinic and she agreed to being included – asked lots of questions and said she would co-operate. RMW1 then had her allocated and sent letter to fix first interview. No response so telephoned last Friday to arrange for 1st interview and she said her husband didn't want her in the study. RMW1 gave her her home telephone number and asked her to ring when it was convenient. Didn't hear, so sent a letter today (9.4.86) to ask her to contact her, giving phone number and explaining about being on 24-hour call. Also said she would like to explain the study to the husband. Lady said, 'He could get nasty.' Problem: how far does RMW1 go to pursue this lady, already randomized into intervention group? 1st pregnancy – baby 1.9 died; 2nd pregnancy – baby 5.8 is OK. Husband doesn't see why his wife should be involved. Variously described as self-employed builder and long-distance lorry driver. Lady going into hospital for a stitch in about 2 weeks. Sandra suggested waiting to see if any response to the letter. If not, since the lady has already been allocated, perhaps RMW1 could see her while in hospital for the stitch? However, would have to be careful not to make the situation worse if the husband was around and if he is still very against it – could cause difficulties for her.

The midwife's notes, appended to these, said:

10.4.86. Notes checked [in antenatal clinic], not there.
16.4.86. Had threatened abortion last weekend. Going to Women's Hospital 24.4.86.
17.6.86. Saw in ANC. All well. Had scan.
15.7.86. Saw in ANC. Very pleased all well. Another 13/52 to go.
10.9.86. Saw in ANC – didn't speak though.
    No intervention actually taken place as far as interviews concerned.

Even when one or more home visits had taken place, this was no guarantee of continued contact, which could be jeopardized for reasons quite extrinsic to the study:

24.7.86. RMW4 phoned. Went again today, door open. Little girl playing nearby. RMW4 asked the little girl if her mum was in and asked her to ask her if she could speak to her. The message came back via the little girl that 'Mum doesn't want to see you any more.' RMW4 spoke to the lady through a crack in the door, and said, 'It's OK if you don't want to see me, but couldn't you come out and speak to me about it? I will accept your decision.' Message came back via the child again, 'I don't want to speak to you.' RMW4 wrote quick note to say she wouldn't call again, but it would be appreciated if she would fill in postnatal later on. Note came back with child, unopened. RMW4 asked child if mum was all right – she said, 'The baby is making her back hurt.' RMW4 asked if her dad was in – child said he'd gone to Grandma's. RMW4 suspects he may have left the family for good.
    11.9.86. GP trying to refer lady to consultant – 'defaulted 3 times'.

Repeated difficulty in securing interviews is a common experience in social science research, especially when socially disadvantaged samples are involved (for an example, see Phoenix 1991). Most importantly, this cannot be taken as meaning that the research participant has changed his/ her mind: some people's lives are not geared to the making and keeping of appointments.

The parallel but opposite problem – of women allocated to the control group who would rather not have been – was also material for the problem file. Although it had not been part of the original study design, and partly in response to our initial discussions about informed consent, the midwives gave all the women approached about the study a letter to take home with their telephone numbers on it. Women subsequently allocated to the control group thus knew how to get hold of them. As noted above, the midwives were asked to keep any such contacts as minimal as possible, and report to us all the instances in which it happened. The file includes:

RMW4: 40 yrs old. Son nearly 20. Bleeding and worried.

RMW4: In tears on the phone on Good Friday, wanted to talk to RMW4. Only 2 miles away so went to see her. Stayed about an hour reassuring her. No further contact.

RMW1: control lady went up to RMW1 in the clinic, told her she had changed her address, and then said, 'I have got a problem, the doctor has said the head is engaged, does that mean I'll go into labour?' RMW1 just said it probably only means things are moving along OK. No further communication.

RMW1: This lady telephoned RMW1. Told RMW1 she felt dizzy and asked what to do. RMW1 said to contact her GP. No further advice given. Minimal contact.

Control lady telephoned RMW3 and they spoke on the telephone for 30 mins. RMW3 had looked for her notes but couldn't find them – wanted to see if she had miscarried or delivered. Notes had been taken because private patient for antenatal care. Talked about her worries – had suture as a private patient because consultant had said it was the only way to ensure having a competent doctor do it! Consultant couldn't guarantee it would be one of his team otherwise.

Control lady. RMW2 said she was absolutely desperate to be intervention and was so upset when phoned because of her social circumstances that when she asked RMW2 if she knew the address of any mother and toddler groups, NCT groups, anything, because she's just moved into the area, she gave her a couple of phone numbers before she'd even got her allocated. She was heartbroken.

Some evidence of a 'deprivation' response was also gleaned from a few of the women who took part, in the questionnaires they filled in after delivery. One woman in the control group even went so far as to say she felt special as a result of taking part in the research; it was 'like belonging to an elite group' (see pp. 289–91).

A perhaps more perplexing situation that occurred at the beginning of the study was one in which a woman allocated to the intervention group complained and said she would rather have been in the control group: 'RMW1 spoke to her for two and a half hours and thought the lady had "thawed". 1 baby died at 2 days, 2 others weighed 5.6 and 4.13.' She went on to deliver a baby boy weighing 2890 g with a heart murmur and a 'clicky hip' who none the less did well; and the research midwife noted that her home interviews had all been very long, as 'she wouldn't stop talking'. Her initial reluctance to take part in the intervention appeared to be mostly nervousness. This experience was paralleled by others, in which women allocated to receive the intervention told the research midwives that they were well supported already, and then proceeded to make good use of their services.

Two women entered the study twice. In both instances the research midwives were asked to explain carefully to the women concerned that they had no guarantee of ending up in whichever group they might have wanted to be. In the event, Melanie Donald, who was allocated originally to the control group and had a termination for spina bifida, was re-entered into the control group in her next pregnancy, giving birth this time to a healthy son. Susan Roberts, who had been in the intervention group and had a baby girl who died at 23 weeks, was subsequently allocated to the control group. This baby was born at 29 weeks, weighing 1340 g, and was very sick, spending eight weeks in special care for respiratory problems. At one year there were still problems with his health. The research team also discussed another woman who was eligible for re-allocation as she had become pregnant again following the death of her first baby. Sarah Loder's postnatal observations about the research were positive, despite the fact that her baby had died: 'I was very pleased to have the research midwife come and visit me as well as being able to telephone her when I wanted to.' In view of the relationship they had built up, the research midwife said she would feel she would have to offer her support whatever the alloca-tion this time. We therefore decided not to re-allocate her. Although in her next pregnancy she was no longer part of the research project, the research midwife, who maintained contact with her throughout, was very pleased to report that she had a baby who did well, despite being induced a month early and spending some time in special care.

As noted earlier, the implementation of random allocation did not cease to be a subject of discussion as the study progressed. The midwives stated the view that random allocation was a problem, because its use to determine which women received additional social support meant that the women themselves could not choose their fates; it also meant that, in agreeing to participate in the study, they were agreeing to only a 50 per

cent chance of receiving additional social support. One midwife wrote, in a questionnaire we gave them half-way through the study, about the conflict between random allocation and the principles of her midwifery training:

> It's very strange in that, if this was practice and not research, you would evaluate each woman and decide if she needed the extra care for various reasons ... It's hard if you recruit someone who obviously has major problems and is desperate for extra help, and then she becomes control. I can feel guilty at showing her that extra care is available, and then not offering it to her – even more so if she eventually has a poor outcome to her pregnancy. Conversely, if she becomes intervention and has obvious major problems, I may wilt a little at finding the extra time and stamina to help her!
>
> It can be a shame if, at first interview, you feel that a woman has no problems, is well informed and supported, and yet you know you will keep on visiting, when you could spend that time with someone who would benefit more. But it's often not until you visit two or three times that problems become apparent.

And the following dialogue occurred during one of our meetings:

> RMW1: I think sometimes, after the first interview, I wouldn't mind writing down which group I thought they needed to be in. I mean, you see them the first time, and their history's nothing, but when you talk to them, you know how awful it is.
>
> RMW2: And it may not be anything to do with their obstetric history.
>
> RMW1: Very often it isn't. I went to a lady[12] the other day. On the first visit, everything seemed fine. We were talking away and I got to the section on major worries. She said, well, yes, I suppose I have, and it turned out that her older son and her husband, who was not his father, had never got on, which could have had a bearing on the pregnancy in which she'd had a small baby. He'd been in trouble with the police, writing cheques, and so had her son; she brought out all these problems existing in her family since she'd remarried, and she said she can see such a difference in her life now. But I mean that sort of thing doesn't come out at first, does it?

In other words, random numbers have the edge over human intuition because human beings are not always right in the judgements they make. It is also relevant to note, as we did in our discussions during the study, that the professional ideology of midwifery, along with that of other health professionals, has been shown to lead to discriminatory stereotyping of women, based on such characteristics as working-class or ethnic-minority status (see e.g. Graham and Oakley 1981; Macintyre 1976).

The midwives in the SSPO study tried various ploys to control the randomization process. At times some of them were quite sure that they had spotted an order in the randomizations enabling them to predict allocations in advance, and therefore to enter women in the order in which they thought would best suit the women's needs for support. Their 'controlling' strategies also included good-humouredly trying to persuade the study secretary to tell them in which order to enter different women (they were quick to realize that the secretary would have the pre-set allocation order in front of her when they telephoned). As well as the factor of women's own needs for social support, the four midwives openly confessed concern about distances they had to travel to carry out the home visits, and about other aspects of their work conditions, such as having to visit possibly dangerous ill-lit estates late in the evening. They understandably hoped their intervention-group women would live close to home in places which were comfortable and safe to visit.

Whose problem?

The 'problem file' contains a number of episodes in which the problem was not the 'correctness' of the allocation but the attitudes of other professionals to the study. We had anticipated some of these in our discussions about the study with staff in the four centres, and the four midwives had been carefully chosen to be as 'acceptable' as possible in their four locales. None the less, some of their colleagues did complain, usually because they felt threatened in some way by the study:

> RMW1 telephoned PR this morning to try to recruit her. The lady said she would think about it, and RMW1 said she would call back in due course for her answer. After RMW1 put the telephone down, she had a call from a GP – wouldn't give his name, nor the name of his patient – saying that he doesn't know anything about the study and 'what do you think you are doing?' RMW1 says it must be PR as she hadn't telephoned any other ladies that morning. RMW1 gave the GP the name/phone number of Mr D at the hospital and offered AO's number here which was declined. RMW1 says he was angry because the lady had told him that she was being asked not to discuss the study with other health professionals.

> RMW1 in a twitch! This lady is diabetic, she saw the diabetic clinic consultant yesterday who asked her to go for another appointment today. She said she couldn't 'because I'm seeing the midwife'. 'What midwife?' he asked. She briefly explained about RMW1 and said how pleased she was to have the support, and the consultant said, 'Well, I don't think it's a very good idea if it interferes with the care we are giving you.'

> RMW4: LM delivered baby on 28.2.87. When RMW4 went to see her in hospital, she was met by the sister, who said: 'I've got a confession to make – I know one of your ladies.' After speaking to LM, RMW4 thinks that the sister deliberately got talking to her and asked her about the study by implying that she already knew she was involved. RMW4 asked the sister what had

happened and she confirmed and apologized! RMW4 has worked with this sister and doesn't like her.

> RMW3 was asked to take part in a nursing research meeting. This was chaired by a health visitor, who asked RMW3 whether she thought any of the ladies RMW3 was seeing were also her 'patients'. RMW3 mentioned FL, who is no longer part of the study, and the lady 'went up the wall' [RMW3's phrase]. Suddenly said the research was unethical and she was very angry indeed that one of her patients was involved. RMW3 said all the obvious things – that the research didn't alter the care given, etc., but the lady was furious.

Although we had used the 'proper' channels to negotiate the siting of the study in the four hospitals, in two of them the research midwives had continual difficulties in carrying out their work. In each hospital we had asked for a desk, and had ourselves provided a lockable filing cabinet. Access to a telephone was necessary (in one hospital the study paid to have a special line installed); apart from that the only requirements were access to the case-notes, and somewhere reasonably private to discuss the study with the women who might take part. The fact that these modest requirements proved to be a source of repeated tension indicates some hostility to the research from hospital staff. For example, six months into the study one midwife went to the hospital one morning, to be met by the senior midwife,

> who told her she had to clear her office immediately – in an hour, and move everything, including filing cabinets. Asked where she could get a porter, she was told there weren't any available. She asked to have use of a trolley and was told that she couldn't use one because they belonged to the porters.
> The nurses on the ward were also very angry – they had to move the whole ward without help of the porters. The midwife got in touch with her husband and he went and spent the lunch time with her (an hour and a half) moving everything. New office OK, though no natural light. No phone available.

The study survived these teething problems, and the first baby was born in May 1986, after only 23½ weeks of pregnancy. He weighed 794 g. His mother was in the intervention group, which seemed an ominous portent for the success of the study in the terms in which we had originally conceived it. William spent many weeks in special care with a long list of problems – bilateral intraventricular haemorrhage, pneumonia, jaundice, hyperglycaemia, anaemia and pulmonary oedema. But the bad omen turned out not to be quite so bad after all, since William survived this ordeal, and in the one-year follow-up questionnaire[13] his mother described him as 'generally very healthy' and developing normally, allowing for his extreme prematurity. This was her first live child, following two miscarriages at 20 weeks, a little girl born at 28 weeks who died at 3 days, and another born at 25 weeks who died aged 4 months.

7

'One of Mummy's Ladies'

I'm not sure what if anything I can do to help her . . . When I recruited her
on the phone she was so nervous that all she said was just one word, yes
. . . The whole time I was there I didn't get anything spontaneous out of
her, but on the doorstep when I said goodbye she suddenly started talking
to me. (Research midwife, SSPO study)

There is a notable absence in the methods literature of descriptions of the
social processes involved in carrying out randomized controlled trials. In
part, this is because social scientists have not much used this research
design; in part, it is because those who used it tend to approach it from a
background which sees research as a mechanical process in which social
values and processes are not implicated. In any description of the processes of carrying out our study, the role of the research midwives is pivotal.
They occupied a peculiar, and particular, position within the research
design: neither researchers nor researched, they were also both of these at
the same time. Like the pregnant women who took part in the study, they
did not set the research agenda or write the research protocol. They were
asked to fit in with guidelines set by other people as to what the research
was about, and how it was to be done. Unlike the study women, they were
not themselves, as individuals, directly the subjects of data collection. And
yet they also played the role of researchers, by going into women's homes
with the technology of tape recorders and interview schedules, and by
collecting and recording data. Most crucially, the research midwives' own
perceptions and experiences as 'social supporters' constituted a major part
of the mechanism of effects the study was testing: the 'success' or otherwise of the study as a randomized controlled trial of social support in
pregnancy was to be judged on the basis of the ways in which they
interacted with the intervention-group women.

The title of this chapter comes from a remark made by one of the
research midwives' children on answering the telephone one day to one
of the study women: 'It's one of Mummy's ladies.' The chapter explores the
role of the research midwives in the study – what they did, said and felt;
how they were perceived by the study women; the impact of the study on
their lives. It draws on a range of material, including the 'problem-file', the

computer-held database relating to the intervention, the women's post-natal questionnaires, interviews with the midwives and questionnaires completed by them, and taped discussions at the monthly study meetings.

As we have already seen, the midwives' role in the study was made up of conflicting elements. In the first place, the injunction to provide social support seemed to them at times at odds with adhering to the methodology of a randomized controlled trial. Secondly, the midwives found that providing social support in practice had to contend with a burden of social disadvantage and difficulty in the lives of the study women which was likely to overwhelm any chance of the social support intervention having any beneficial impact. Thirdly, in attempting to provide support in such circumstances, the midwives sometimes found themselves up against gaps and deficiencies in the health and welfare services which they were powerless to change. Fourthly, there was the problem of their own task in all of this, a problem which could be reduced to the question: who supports the supporters?

The meaning of social support

In our early discussions with funding bodies and others, the question of what was meant by social support was often posed. Some people (including the ESRC) argued that we needed to define the exact meaning of the term before carrying out the study. The position we took, and from which the study was launched, was a different one. We took as our baseline a clear, negative definition of social support: social support was *not* clinical care; it was *not* anti-smoking advice, marital counselling or a strategy to encourage women to make more use of the antenatal services. Thus the research midwives were asked *not* to do any of these things. What they *were* asked to do was to *listen* to what the women had to say and to be responsive to any self-defined needs and perspectives. Social support was defined as the provision of a non-judgemental listening ear, discussing with women their pregnancy needs, giving information when asked to, and carrying our referrals when appropriate to other health and welfare professionals and voluntary and statutory agencies.

Providing this kind of support within the structure of a controlled experimental study gave rise to a critical tension: between the goal of attempting to *standardize* the ways in which the four midwives interacted with the women in their care, on the one hand, and the need to respond *individually* to women's needs, on the other. As noted earlier, the midwives were asked to provide a 'minimum support package' for all the women in the intervention group. But they were also asked to give as much extra support as the women wanted and their own caseloads would permit. The 'minimum package' of contact was defined as three home visits at 14, 20 and 28 weeks of pregnancy, plus two telephone calls or brief home visits between these times; radio-pagers were provided so the midwives could be contacted by the study women 24 hours a day.

Greater clarity about the meaning of social support aside from our 'negative' definition could be gained only by the careful documentation of whatever it was the research midwives did under this heading. At the end of the study we needed to be able to say what they had done – and we needed to be able to say this whether the social support intervention had 'worked' or not. Since we did not see our study as the definitive study of social support in pregnancy, but rather as a contribution to a field of research and knowledge, the ability to describe what we had done was important to the goal of pointing out future directions for research – what others might do to complement what we had done, just as what we had decided to do had been in part determined by existing work.

What did the midwives do?

Of the 255 women allocated to be offered the social support intervention, 238 were seen at home for the first interview, 235 for the second, and 224 for the third.[1] The mean time in pregnancy for each of these contacts was somewhat later than planned, mostly because initial booking times were later than expected. At each contact most of the women were not referred elsewhere by the research midwives, and did not request any 'lifestyle' information. Detailed information on this is given in figure 9.1, table 2 (p. 237).

During the study, the research midwives somewhat altered their behaviour towards the women they were supporting. The data sheets they filled in recorded their definitions of the nature of that particular contact (to give advice, support, carry out referrals, etc.). We looked at the amount of advice they gave in the early, compared with the later, part of the study; in two of the centres, the average number of times advice was given increased slightly and in the other two it decreased slightly. The pattern for the giving of support/reassurance followed the same trend, with the two centres in which advice-giving increased also tending to provide more support/reassurance at the end of the study. There were clear differences in the social class composition of the four centres, with women in centres 1 and 4 being generally more disadvantaged than those in centres 2 and 3 (table 7.1). Working-class women[2] in general received more advice and more support/reassurance, but less of the research midwives' time. Looking at the four centres separately, three of the four gave advice more frequently to working-class women, and the one which showed a reverse pattern was the centre with the smallest overall numbers and the largest middle-class population. For support/reassurance, three centres gave more to working-class mothers, and in the fourth there was no difference by class. Average total amounts of time spent with intervention-group mothers did vary by class, with working-class mothers receiving 12 per cent less of the midwives' time overall – 6 hours for middle-class and 5.3 hours for working-class women. Most of this difference obtained, not in relation to the minimum package, but in relation to extra time given, where the difference was 33 per cent – 93 minutes for middle-class versus 62 minutes for working-class women.

Our broad definition of social support, though more general than the social support definitions operationalized in other studies, for example the Manchester Family Worker study (Spencer et al. 1989), none the less allowed the research midwives to participate in a wide range of very different kinds of activities under the general heading of giving social support. These included: obtaining money from the social services to enable a woman to attend the antenatal clinic for a spina bifida test; taking a woman to visit her husband in prison; writing letters to housing departments and contacting health visitors about bad housing conditions; helping a woman to obtain a visa for her mother to come from Iran; providing secondhand baby clothes and other equipment; taking animals to the vet; helping a woman to obtain a heating allowance; obtaining information about financial benefits for disabled people; taking mothers and/or babies to hospital; contacting voluntary organizations to provide counselling for bereaved parents; sorting out eligibility for maternity pay/ benefit; writing to a mail order company about debts; explaining how to use head-lice shampoo; discussing with hospital staff realistic dietary guidelines for a woman with gestational diabetes; ensuring that necessary medical information about a back injury (a contra-indication for epidural analgesia) was included on medical notes; accompanying a woman for an ultrasound scan; obtaining information about the effects on the baby of maternal facial radiotherapy in pregnancy; arranging home tutoring for an

Table 7.1 Sample characteristics by centre

	Centre			
	1	2	3	4
	(N = 75)	(N = 33)	(N = 57)	(N = 83)
Characteristic	%	%	%	%
Smokers	42	41	30	43
Working class	73	49	51	79
Unmarried	26	8	9	20
Three or more previous births	22	13	13	15
More than one previous preterm birth	35	26	26	30

illiterate woman; and obtaining information about a rare medical condition and its effects on pregnancy. In some of these situations the research midwife needed to solicit help from others in meeting the mother's need, and in most cases the specific need to which the midwife was responding was only one of a nexus of socially determined needs arising out of material disadvantage and life stress. The following examples give a flavour of some of the work that went on:

Nancy Kennedy
This lady had a stillbirth in 1973. Macerated, with gross abnormalities. She wants a copy of the stillbirth certificate. Goes to friend's baby's grave on anniversary of death, because she doesn't know where her baby is. Five pregnancies since 1973: two miscarriages, one termination and two children. No proper help to get over stillbirth. Can RMW find out where baby's grave is? ('Problem file')

Sheila Scutt
This lady's husband rang me up and said what should they do if she had a bleed? I said you should ring the hospital and tell them it's the afterbirth, and as soon as they know that they'll send the flying squad out. He said what will that mean? I said it'll mean that a doctor and a midwife will come to the home in an ambulance, so if she's very poorly they can start to treat her then. So he wrote down what to say. He said shall I drive her in? Oh crikey, driving her in, haemorrhaging all over the place! (RMW4, monthly meeting)

Claudia Sandberg
She's the girl whose husband left her, because he said it wasn't his baby ... her father was in an accident as well, and was in intensive care. She rang me up one night, said she thought she was in prem. labour, could I go into hospital with her, so I did. And she wasn't. (RMW4, monthly meeting)

Carol Slater
I did an interesting thing this week, I had twins. I took Carol to a twins club. You know, my lady who's expecting twins. I took her to this twins club that we finally got into contact with. And of course all these other mothers either had twins or were having twins and they said what have you got? I said I'm a friend of Carol's. I don't know whether it will have helped, but she didn't want them to pick her up because they didn't know her. I've told her to keep the contact up because she lives quite a long way out, so she ought to be able to do that now. (RMW1, monthly meeting)

In some households the research midwives were able to gain an entrée where other 'officials' had not been acceptable. The common suspicion of social workers, health visitors and other representatives of the official services (see e.g. Mayall and Foster 1989) apparently did not extend to the research midwives. They were also entrusted with information that was not made available to those involved in the women's routine care, for example details of obstetric history, living arrangements, social circumstances and smoking behaviour. The midwives felt this was because they did not present themselves as having any kind of official authority over the women they were visiting, but instead were there in a general 'befriending' role. As one midwife said of Jill Pope and her family, who had multiple problems:

> They're anti everybody, but not me. She's terribly interested in research. As soon as I said research, she said, oh, come in. She said she told me about this Visa card [debt] because I'm not *from* anywhere. That's not the first time I've been told that. It's like husbands having jobs that social security don't know about, and all this sort of thing. (RMW1)

Jill Pope's situation as a blind mother of four with a disabled husband was especially problematic. The 'problem file' reads:

> 4.11.86. RMW1 telephoned. This lady has acute financial problems. Receives £86.20 (husband's disability allowance), £14.20 (child benefit times 2). Has to pay £11.15 (housing); has also run up debts of £1000 on Visa card and £30 monthly on mail order. Called Disability Alliance for information. Disability Rights handbook ordered for midwives' meeting next week.

> 3.12.86. RMW1 couldn't do proper interview but has written notes on the schedule. Ongoing financial problems. If husband could claim mobility allowance, they would get more benefit. But same doctor does the assessment (already done twice) so they don't think any good would come of asking him to do it again. RMW1 says husband not at all well. Under a psychiatrist, but doesn't seem to be helping. Gets invalidity allowance, £100 per week only. In permanent pain since car accident in which 2 people were killed. Perhaps he was partly to blame because he didn't claim compensation??? Doesn't like the health visitor or social workers because they pry. Jill is worried that husband won't be able to cope when she goes into labour . . . they don't get on with their respective families. 16 yr old daughter walked out when the mother was first pregnant, mother thinks she knows where she's gone. Older son has also gone. Two children are 5–6 and baby of about two and a half. Lots of hassles with neighbours about dogs – they don't seem to get on with anyone. Tried to get help from CAB but no use. Maybe RMW1 could approach CAB? Ask RNIB for help? Needs help during the day and at night when baby first goes home.

> [RMW1's writing] 14.1.87. Jill rang me at 12.19–12.41 p.m. Now changed surgeries. Wanted me to write a letter to help her move house. Husband's psychiatrist said he will do and GP also says he will . . . Not sure of main reason for wanting to move but aggravation from children next door is one. Apparently they had agreed an exchange and it turned out to be a friend – they were told she didn't want their carpets and they should get rid of them, and at the last minute they pulled out, now they have no carpets and everything is packed up. Jill is very depressed and so is her husband. He

disappeared in car the other day and acted as though drunk (though taking his tablets). Youngest daughter has been diagnosed as having glaucoma (as has Jill).

[Still in RMW1's writing] 7.7.87. Jill rang me at 01.30 sounding quite desperate. The baby (now 16 weeks) has been unwell for several days with a cold. Last week her GP came out and was very offhand, she has no confidence in him. His temperature was 102. She wanted me to go and sit with the other children while she and husband went to casualty with him. I suggested I took her and the baby and her husband stayed with the sleeping children.
    02.00 got to casualty.
    03.00 transferred to Children's Hospital.
    04.00 Admitted to Children's Hospital. He had a temperature of 39.6 on admission, raised blood count, and they were going to do a lumbar puncture.

[Still in RMW1's writing] Re Jill Pope 8.7.87. Telephone call 10.45–11.30 p.m. We had arranged to phone and I'm afraid I forgot, so Jill rang me. She sounded very depressed and unhappy. She hopes to collect the baby tomorrow. Her husband was very upset seeing him in hospital. The car had just failed its MOT and would cost £200 to repair, so the day after the baby went into hospital they bought a secondhand Datsun for £350 – have managed to raise half and hope sister will help with the rest. Just got a £25 grant from some association for redecorating. Rates increased by 65p since baby's arrival – didn't get the expected rebate. Daughter (oldest) is living with grandmother and claiming allowances etc. and hasn't told DHSS that she's with a relative, has also just spent 4 weeks in Hungary. Jill sounded very bitter about that, and said she can't even afford a day at the sea. We also talked about her trying to change doctors.

A very different scenario was provided by Veronica Bawden, who was still mourning a previous baby, and in this pregnancy had a lot of problems because of a rare medical condition. According to the 'problem file':

When RMW3 telephoned to tell her she was intervention group, Veronica cried with relief – spent 25 minutes on the phone! Lots of problems. Wants information on Stillbirth and Neonatal Death Association – had stillbirth 2 years ago and spoke about it for the first time to RMW3 now. Desperate for someone to talk to who has had a stillbirth and then had a child. RMW3 suggested putting her in touch with another of her ladies who had this situation – I said let me try to get information from the Association first. Found details of local group, names, etc., and telephoned RMW3. She's giving information to Veronica tomorrow, 5.1.86.

RMW3 called 6.11.86. Needs information about Cushing's syndrome[3] and effect on pregnancy . . . This lady was originally told she had Cushing's syndrome, but is now being told she has low blood pressure – 90/50 . . .

> This is her 2nd pregnancy, first was a stillbirth . . . Veronica wanted to talk so much that . . . the first interview . . . took 3 hours and even then RMW3 didn't finish it! She told RMW3 she'd never been able to speak to anyone about the stillbirth before . . . RMW3 desperately needs information to give to Veronica.

Veronica's medical history was complicated. As a teenager, she had apparently been obese, but a diagnosis of Cushing's syndrome had been made when her weight did not reduce during hospitalization on a low-calorie diet. This diagnosis had later been rescinded on the grounds that Veronica was hypotensive not hypertensive. She did, however, have a raised blood cortisol level in addition to other problems, including manic-depressive tendencies and amenorrhoea. Subsequently, Veronica had consulted a herbalist, who thought she was allergic to carbohydrates and had put her on a diet excluding these, also excluding milk and cheese, and had added a herbal preparation to help her general condition and increase her fertility. This had resulted in a dramatic weight loss of 8 stone, though tests showed her blood cortisol level continued to be raised. The previous stillbirth had happened at 36 weeks with a placental abruption.

Veronica's questions about her condition were detailed, and reflected both a lack of information from doctors and her anxiety about the fate of the present pregnancy. The questions as written out by her research midwife were:

1 Should she be under a medical consultant's care?
2 Should the pregnancy be monitored by a combined medical/obstetric team (at present GP only until 36 weeks)?
3 Could these problems have caused the stillbirth, and, if so, what is the chance of a repeat?
4 What effect on the fetus will a constantly low blood pressure have?
5 If these problems stem from the pituitary (and maybe the herbal preparation she's taking is helping this?) could there be any effect on Veronica's ability to breastfeed?
6 If cortisol has anti-insulin, diabetogenic properties, could she have developed an allergy to carbohydrates because the percentage of circulating carbohydrate is raised and becomes antigenic?
7 If so, could a low-carbohydrate diet mean that things will revert to normal?
8 What long-term effects will a diet like this have on her and baby?
9 She says her calcium level is low – what will the effects be?
10 If the adrenal cortex regulates the body's balance of carbohydrate, salt, carbon dioxide and minerals, could this mean that the cortisol and carbohydrate problem are linked? If so, how?

The process of information-getting involved our contacting a number of medical people in Oxford and was quite complex, as Cushing's syndrome is rare in pregnancy (there are only about 100 cases ever reported). The research midwife fed the information obtained back to Veronica, who maintained a pattern of regular contacts with her throughout the pregnancy as witnessed by successive entries in the 'problem file':

9.3.87. Blood pressure rising, extra visits to GP/midwife. Very anxious . . . Very worried, wants a section to avoid another disaster. Now 32/34 weeks. Uptight about labour – no information or booklets so RMW3 took books and Veronica is reading them. Going for a scan. Consultant has said that if her blood pressure goes up he will see her. RMW3 encouraged her to go and see him . . .

26.3.87. RMW3 telephoned. Veronica on the phone to her nearly every evening – so far 20 phone calls and 6 visits! Approaching the time when she lost the last baby.

9.4.87. Reported by RMW3 – Veronica not doing very well. Complains of abdominal pains. About 35 weeks now. RMW3 said if you're worried enough to phone me you should go to hospital or call GP. Her original GP has left – so Veronica turned up at the Maternity Unit with friend. Boyfriend thinks she is making a fuss – because of her anxiety the hospital kept her in for 3 days. Boyfriend being unsupportive, seems to think she is continually making a fuss about everything. Within 24 hours of being sent home she had slipped in the bath and was readmitted in case the baby had been hurt. Kept in for a further 24 hours. The registrar tried to discharge her this week – she burst into tears, feels she is safer in hospital. So long as they don't need the bed they've said they'll keep her there. To have a section at 38 weeks – no trial of labour. Ward sister has said to her accept you are OK at the moment, but abnormal anxiety. Won't get baby clothes out of the loft, nothing ready for the baby in case something happens. Sister/midwife hinted at problems between Veronica and boyfriend. RMW3 thinks he's had enough of her demanding attention all the time. Visits her when he can but only goes in for a few minutes 2/3 times a week.

Veronica delivered a healthy boy at 36 weeks who weighed 3180 g. In her postnatal questionnaire, she described herself as depressed during pregnancy because of worry about the baby, and said she was very anxious still ('I worry when I have to go to bed and that I can't check the baby so often as I do during the day'). She found the research midwife 'extremely helpful about everything', especially in making her feel more confident. This observation was repeated in the one-year questionnaire, which also confirmed the continuation of worries about the baby, now focused on the possibility of his choking and the consequent need to 'watch him all the time'.

There were a number of occasions on which the research midwives said or wrote that they felt totally helpless, including occasions with Jill Pope, and also Tamsin Rogers, a woman with much pregnancy anxiety and a number of stressful life events to contend with, including her mother's nervous breakdown. The research midwife brought this situation to a midwives' meeting and said she felt she was not being very helpful, and that Tamsin needed more support than she was able to give. We suggested that she might need to refer her to other agencies, such as a social worker. Partly because of the problems many of the other women had encountered with the social work service, the midwife was reluctant to do this, and in the end she coped without making a referral. Tamsin gave birth to a baby weighing 1942 g at 32–3 weeks, which did not encourage the research midwife to feel she had done well in this case.

The most difficult situations were those in which medical and social problems combined to suggest to the midwives that social support could be of little use. The discussion on 13 October 1986 of Mavis Martin's case, which illustrates this, also conveys something of the atmosphere of the meetings themselves:

> RMW4: She was one – when I got that run[4] of when I knew who was going to be intervention and who was going to be control – she was one who I thought was going to need the intervention. She certainly needs a lot of social support! She's got three children and she was booked for the GP unit. She's had all sorts of problems during the pregnancy. It wasn't planned and her other three were perfectly normal – no problems. This one, she's been ill from the word go. The GP's not doing anything about it. She's now been diagnosed as placenta praevia. She's been transferred to the consultant unit, and they admitted her about a fortnight ago. She went in one morning and discharged herself in the afternoon because there was no one to have the children for her. Her parents and his parents work and his job is on the line anyway because the firm needs to make somebody redundant, so any excuse for having time off means it'll be him. So she discharged herself and she's refusing to go back in. And I feel absolutely devastated when I see her because there's nothing I can do for her – not a thing. She needs somebody to have the children so she can go into hospital for the rest. She's bleeding – she's not bleeding heavily. She's 33 wks. She was 31 wks when all this blew up.
>
> AO: Do the hospital know about the childcare problem?
>
> RMW4: Yes, and they offered her foster parents. Of course they don't want that. No family wants it really, do they? You can't blame them. I can't blame her for discharging herself.
>
> RMW3: No, you have to look after the kids you've got, don't you? Am I right in thinking there's no money available?
>
> RMW4: No spare money, no. They're on a low income, but at the moment they're just below the FIS line. She's getting her free milk and vitamins . . . The other thing she's worried about is that she wants to be sterilized. She went up to the consultant unit – I said if you're having a section, that's the ideal opportunity. They won't do it because they say she's too young. And yet it's an unplanned pregnancy. She rang me up, and said, 'Can I insist on it?' I said don't give up trying. Whenever I go she says, 'Thanks very much for calling', and all this, and I just feel as though I've done absolutely nothing. The last time she rang she said, 'Can you come and see me now?'

I said yes, I can come, but I'll have to bring my little boy with me. He was fine. He just loved all these children around. And she's taking quiet life tablets at night at my suggestion, because she was getting so uptight about everything.

AO: What are those?

ALL IN UNISON: We don't know about those!

SS: I think we should buy them in bulk.

LR: Can you give them to all your family as well?

RMW3: Yes, even the dog!

RMW4: Another of my ladies, her husband said, 'You know these tablets, can I take them as well?'

A fourth situation the midwife found especially difficult concerned a woman who at first seemed unwilling to talk at all – one of the midwife's comments about her heads this chapter:

Maria Otter. 13.10.86. RMW3 says she doesn't know if she can help this lady. She was recruited on the telephone when the lady didn't say anything at all except 'yes'.

Did 1st interview. In a state of total anxiety. RMW3 thinks it was made worse by her being there. One previous baby now nearly 7 – 2460 g. Has taken her six and a half years to get up the courage to have another baby. Hospital phobic. Last pregnancy – said on notes had no pain, didn't know she was in labour. Told RMW3 she *did* know, but didn't tell her husband because she was so scared. Went in fully dilated. So anxious she wouldn't even look RMW3 in the face whilst talking. RMW3 put on tape recorder which made it worse – said she wished she hadn't used it. However, when she was leaving Maria spent 10 – 15 minutes on the doorstep chatting about all sorts of unimportant things. Maybe she does need someone to talk to?

4.6.87. RMW3 reported, went to get notes, but they weren't there. Asked if anyone knew anything and was asked, 'Do you think the situation is odd?' Little girl has psychological problems – very aggressive and not communicating. In therapy now, goes to special school. Husband – breakdown? Keeping baby in SCBU – it is well, but they are terrified to let it home. Older child not 'mothered', they say, could happen to this baby also.

Differences between the midwives

The qualitative data show considerable variation between the four research midwives in their attitudes to their role in the study. There was also variation in the amount of time they spent providing social support, and in the number of contacts they had with the women in the intervention group. Table 7.2 gives some information on this, taken from the data sheets completed by the midwives following each contact with the mothers in their sample. The first line of the table gives the average of the

Table 7.2 The social support intervention: timing and number of contacts by centre

Timing and no. of contacts	Centre			
	1 (N = 75)	2 (N = 33)	3 (N = 57)	4 (N = 83)
Total amount of time (hrs)	5.6	5.0	6.6	4.2
'Minimum package':				
Visit 1 (hrs)	1.8	1.6	1.8	1.3
Visit 2 (hrs)	1.5	1.5	1.5	1.1
Visit 3 (hrs)	1.6	1.3	1.5	1.1
Phone call 1 (mins)	12	9	7	9
Phone call 2 (mins)	10	12	9	10
Total time of 'minimum package' (hrs)	4.8	4.5	4.7	3.6
No. of home contacts (mean)	3.8	3.2	4.6	4.0
No. of phone contacts (mean)	3.5	3.3	6.8	3.6
No. of midwife-initiated contacts[a] (mean)	2.1	1.4	4.3	3.6
No. of woman-initiated contacts[a] (mean)	0.8	0.5	2.2	0.7

[a]Visits and phone calls

total amount of time spent by the midwives per intervention-group woman, including all visits and telephone calls, a total which ranges from 4.2 to 6.6 hours. The total time spent in providing the 'minimum package' of three home visits and two phone calls/brief home visits shows less variation, though the total for centre 4 (which had the highest caseload) is rather less than for the other three. There was a general tendency for the length of the visits to decrease from the first to the third.[5] Telephone calls tended to get longer. Mean numbers of home contacts range from 3.2 to 4.6 and of phone contacts from 3.3 to 6.8, depending on centre. The number of midwife-initiated contacts varied threefold: from a mean of 1.4 in centre 2 to a mean of 4.3 in centre 3. Woman-initiated contacts followed the same pattern. For all these contact variables, centre 2 had the lowest and centre 3 the highest means.

Table 7.3 is also based on the data sheets filled in by the research midwives. Since the midwives varied in the extent to which they took the

Table 7.3 Nature of the intervention by centre

	Centre			
	1 *(N = 75)*	*2* *(N = 33)*	*3* *(N = 57)*	*4* *(N = 83)*
Intervention	%	%	%	%
Total advice given more than 8 times (average = 8)	17	3	53	64
'Someone to talk to'/reassurance given more than 5 times (average = 5)	23	0	48	61
Advised to see GP/obstetrician/ midwife more (average = 2)	47	55	55	64
Advised to see health visitor/ other health professional more than 2 times (average = 2)	15	3	10	15
Information/advice on pregnancy given more than 2 times (average = 2)	47	52	79	64
Advised on benefits, housing, etc., more than 3 times (average = 3)	41	15	29	74
Advised on smoking	5	12	31	4
Advised on diet	13	6	52	22

exercise of filling in these data sheets seriously, the data in the table need to be regarded as subject to the proviso that they represent differences in the recording of aspects of the intervention which may or may not reflect differences in the way the intervention was in fact provided. There are clear differences between centres. It is interesting that the centres ranking highest on advice scores also ranked highest on the 'someone to talk to'/ reassurance given aspect, on referrals to GP, obstetrician or midwife, and on general advice relating to pregnancy. There would thus seem to be a tendency towards a lack of differentiation between advice, listening/ reassurance and referrals, with those midwives making more of one type of intervention making more of others as well (or at least recording it in this fashion on the data sheets).

During the monthly meetings, the midwives discussed the different ways in which they were interpreting the social support intervention in practice. They were invited to comment on this in the questionnaires we asked them to complete and in interviews at the end of the study:

I know my interviews are generally shorter than those of the other midwives. I wonder if this is because I haven't got the right approach, which means the ladies feel less able to 'open up'? (RMW4)

RMW3 always seemed to have so many problems, it made me wonder if I'd missed them or I hadn't brought them up when I should have done. Or perhaps I don't see them in the same light. Or maybe my mums are coping better. I know I spend a lot longer with my ladies than RMW4 does but then RMW4's got a lot more ladies! (RMW1)

I wonder if my outlook, lifestyle , is a little less conventional than the others and this could colour my reactions, approaches to situations? (RMW3)

I feel we were very different. Our characters are different, and the way we handled the women – the character of our caseloads was different, so that even though we were reacting differently, it was to different things ... I would say I'm very bad at paperwork. I know I am. Often when I'd had a conversation with someone, I'd say, oh God, I haven't written that down. I know it had to be done, but it was a chore. (RMW2)

Just like Dynasty?

The extent of social disadvantage and life stress among the study women which contributed to the midwives' workload can be documented quantitatively. Some indices are shown in table 7.4. A third of the women were living in poverty; nearly two out of five lived in rented housing or with relatives, and one-fifth in circumstances they described as 'crowded'; a quarter lacked a telephone; and one in five had partners who were unemployed. Two out of five women reported three or more life events in pregnancy, and around a third said they did not have enough control over their lives. The research midwives were asked to assess the extent to which the women they were supporting were under stress and in need of social support: according to table 7.5, rather more than two out of five were felt by the midwives to be experiencing high levels of stress; and evaluation of the women's social support needs went hand-in-hand with the assessment of stress levels.

Although many of the problems confronting the midwives stemmed directly from material disadvantage, others flowed from problems in social relations. Family and friends can be sources of support, but they can also *require* support. This entry from the 'problem file' sums up a recurrent theme:

21.8.86. Betty Trimmer, RMW3 just been to see this lady. When she was asked about her family, she said, 'Sit down and have a cup of tea, it's just like *Dynasty*.'

Her parents are divorced.
Husband's parents also divorced.
Her father married his mother.
Her mother married his father.
Her uncle married his auntie.
None of them get on. RMW3 expects lots of problems. Betty said she was
worried about her dog and the effect on her pregnancy.

Table 7.4 Social disadvantage and life stress among the SSPO study women

Disadvantage and stress	% of women (N = 467)
Income less than 140% of supplementary benefit level	31
Rented housing/living with relatives	38
Crowded housing	17
No telephone	24
Unemployed partner	19
Three or more life events in pregnancy	40
Not enough control over life	32

Table 7.5 Midwives' assessments of intervention women's stress and social support
needs

Stress and support needs	% of women
Stress	
First visit (N = 238):	
High stress	44
Low stress	56
Total	100
Third visit (N = 224):	
High stress	41
Low stress	59
Total	100
Support needs	
First visit (N = 238):	
High needs	42
Low needs	58
Total	100
Third visit (N = 224):	
High needs	44
Low needs	56
Total	100

Whatever effects these were, they were not manifested quantitatively in pregnancy 'outcome': Betty gave birth to a girl weighing 3350 g (7lb 6oz).

The three case-studies that follow from the problem file highlight other kinds of difficulties.

Tricia Marks

Problems: money, debts, unemployment, bad relationship with partner, illiteracy, suspected child sexual abuse, lack of family support.

This lady called RMW4 last week when RMW1 was on holiday. RMW1 called to see her today, and spent one and a half hours with her. The problem when she called was that they had no money or food, and had to sell the washing machine and a unit in the sitting room. Husband is getting a giro for £89.90 per fortnight, but they have enormous debts and are out of their depth. Threatened with a court order by mail order company. Offered to pay £5 now but owe a lot more. Husband has a record of non-payment of fines previously. Have sex problems – last week had a big bust-up. Reluctant to ask for help – I suggested CAB but RMW1 says they're not keen. In the last 10 days he's been offered a job cleaning 4 hours per evening, 13 hours per week. Not very well paid – Rolls Royce, £1.50 per hour – but RMW1 told him to take job and hope for a promotion.

4.6.87. RMW1 reported. Tricia isn't married. When RMW1 saw her to do 2nd interview, she said partner had a sex problem and thinks he's having another relationship ... she's worried about relationship of partner and 6-year-old daughter. Now 21 weeks pregnant. Both unemployed. Debts of about £700 or £800. They asked RMW1 to write a letter to mail order company to explain circumstances and to ask if they could pay back at very low rate. RMW1 did this. RMW1 thinks not very educated; Mick can't read. Problems stem from money difficulties. Mick said: 'I need someone to tell me what to do' (re financial problems).

11.7.87. Update from RMW1; she thinks if she approaches social services they could end up worse off financially ... Daughter, 6, by another man. Previously, if there had been a problem, she would have gone to grand-mother, but grandmother's now returned to Jamaica. Nowhere else for the child to go.

When speaking to RMW1, Mick said he was going to do the garden, and said 'This is where the greenhouse is going, and this is where the fishpond will be ...' RMW1 thinks this is very unrealistic as they are so short of money. Debts in his name. Bought wedding rings, but had to sell them. First said they were married, but now not ... Previous baby Marlon died, their child, stillbirth weighing 2lb 8 oz. RMW1 has never seen the 6-yr-old, she's always at school. Mother said she would never leave the child alone with partner. RMW1 said she'd make appointment with CAB and take them, but go first herself to explain. Tricia still suspicious he's seeing someone else. Another girl in the locality has a baby by him. Tricia thinks still seeing her. RMW1 says she feels apprehensive when he's there and won't go in unless Tricia's there also. Also odd that Tricia has had two 'falls' this pregnancy.

11.7.87. RMW1 went back to see Tricia last night and stayed for another one and a half hours. RMW1 says definitely sounds like sex problems with Mick and his 'other woman'. Tricia thinks he's seeing other women when he tells her he's doing overtime. Mick says he isn't being paid for the extra work he's doing, but Tricia doesn't think he's doing any extra. At the moment they have no money for food because they have spent money got through Giro last Thursday. Told RMW1 that last week she paid £31 on a TV debt they had. Daughter has head-lice – Tricia couldn't understand the instructions on the bottle of special shampoo. RMW1 explained it all.

20.8.87. Spoke to RMW1 – been to see Tricia last Tuesday (she is about 36 weeks by now). Went to the new address which was on the hospital files, but no one there. Deserted house, no furniture, etc. Went to old address – also deserted. RMW1 doesn't have a telephone number for Tricia so not very optimistic.

3.9.87. RMW1 phoned. Went into hospital yesterday and found Tricia had been in for 5 days. RMW1 went to ward to see her but found she'd discharged herself. Went to house at 7.30 p.m. – husband there who said Tricia in hospital. RMW1 told him she'd discharged herself and he 'went off the deep end' because he didn't know. Apparently she'd been collected by a social worker from the hospital and they went to pick up Tricia's daughter who'd been in care for 5 days. Husband told RMW1 not to go back. Tricia has lost 5 kilos and should have stayed in hospital but refuses. Husband unstable. Tricia hinted at sexual abuse with daughter. He says he'll leave her if anything happens to this baby. Relationship very shaky.

6.10.87. RMW1 notified me that Tricia had a baby girl on 28 September weighing 2720 g. On the hospital notes her name had been changed from Marks to Miller. RMW1 thinks this may mean Mick has left her.

Simone Churchill

Problems: bad housing, redundancy, male violence, money.

July 1986. RMW3 went to visit. Was shown damp flat including bedlinen which was mouldy. RMW3 suggested calling in Environmental Health Officer. When he arrived, Simone's husband attacked him and tried to strangle him. Also they have large ferocious alsatian – RMW3 very nervous. EHO said damp was caused by condensation – it was this comment that provoked husband to attack him.

10.7.86. RMW3 reported above information at TCRU meeting. Flat in very bad area. Always tried to visit in mornings. Always feels anxious. Husband has violent temper – recently broke down door to neighbour's flat. When EHO called the husband said he would kill him if he returned.

22.7.86. RMW3 has referred this lady to social services. RMW3 says they have enormous problems. No heating, damp flat, husband been made redundant – broke the home up after an argument with someone. Simone walked into town with three little girls to get money from social services to feed the children. Waiting in social services office for 7 hours with the children before they gave her money – she eventually put them on the counter and threatened to leave them there if something wasn't done.

29.8.86. RMW3 phoned. Simone's flat was featured on BBC News last night because it was so damp. As a result, she has been promised another flat next year instead of 1988!!! RMW3 asked me if there was any chance of getting some baby clothes. I said I would see what I could do.

11.9.86. Gave RMW3 a large selection of baby clothes for Simone.

16.9.86. RMW3 telephoned. She had been to see Simone yesterday and given her the baby clothes and cot linen, etc. Said she was 'over the moon'; also said to RMW3, 'Someone does care about me after all.' Absolutely thrilled. Also told RMW3 her husband had been involved in a big fight – had gone home covered in blood, got into the bath to clean up and had crashed out in the water and Simone had to drag him out before he drowned!

17.11.86. RMW3 saw Simone postnatally – delivered boy 3.11.86 weighing 3530 g. Absolutely delighted. She has been given semi-detached house with a garden. Postnatal contact about 15 minutes.

13.4.87. RMW3 telephoned about Simone Churchill. Simone had a baby boy on 3 November. Already had 3 little girls and desperately wanted a boy. She was living in a very damp, cold flat and had been agitating to be rehoused before the baby was born. The matter attracted some local papers and there was lots of publicity . . . Since baby was born at the beginning of November, the council have repeatedly put off the time for the move – always saying the house wasn't ready for her, they were still decorating, etc.
    Last week the little boy was found dead in his cot – post-mortem said he died of pneumonia. He had been in and out of hospital with chest infections etc. All the local councillors now blaming each other for the baby's death – front-page news in local papers.
    RMW3 is going to contact Simone by letter, asking her to contact her if she wants/needs to, and reminding her of telephone number etc. May well contact RMW3 because she didn't get on very well with the health visitor. Health visitor has been very hostile to RMW3. Said she thought AO should redo the research and we should make sure that the health visitors knew about it and which patients are connected with it – RMW3 said she couldn't stop her talking about it. Feels very threatened by the research . . .
    RMW3 thought maybe AO could also send brief note saying how sorry we are. RMW3 was very surprised when I said we had already had the postnatal questionnaire back – she was doubtful it would be returned because Simone had so many problems etc. – but she did return it, which RMW3 thinks is very significant – i.e. she appreciated all the help we gave her.

Clipped to these notes are copies of the item in the local newspaper headed 'Damp Flat Killed Baby'. Apparently other families had been moved after inspection by environmental health officers from the block of flats in which the Churchills lived, which was scheduled for demolition in 1986. The paper quoted Simone as saying, 'I have been to the council and told them it was their flat that killed my baby.'

Mary Smart

Problems: twin pregnancy, bad housing, money, drugs, drinking, criminal records, violence, dispute about child custody and access from previous marriage, rejection of child/ren, children in care, bad relationship with partner, bad relationship with mother, abused as child, lack of family support.

7.5.87. Having been allocated, she then said she was expecting twins! RMW3 went to do 1st interview – lives in grotty conditions, dogs fighting, etc. Before the interview RMW3 had to clear up a lot of blood from the kitchen – the meat!

Separated from husband, living with another man. Unsure of dates. Small for dates, looks small. Children at the moment at home. When separated, husband got court order for children and refused her access to them; court said they would be in moral/physical danger from her. Bit of a criminal record – has meddled with heroin – at the moment on a probation order and has to go to group therapy. At the time when husband and parents got control of children, was drinking heavily and she and boyfriend went on burglary binge. Also been involved with other drugs. Rejected second girl because wanted boy. Taken into special care. Mary was beaten by her father and taken into care. The two boys have also been in care.

In the past has been charged with GBH and ABH . . . Brother in Dartmoor for 3 yrs for malicious wounding. Now children back and partner has good job, not involved in crime any more. Partner has record also. Social services querying whether they should have these children. Husband involved with drugs previously . . .

When RMW3 was there, the social worker turned up because of the probation order. RMW3 said to Mary, 'Would you like me to leave?' . . . No, so RMW3 stayed. Social worker went in and RMW3 explained who she was. (Said I would send the social worker information about the project.) Also RMW3 said to social worker – let me know if you think I might jeopardize the situation or if you want to communicate with me . . . ring me and I will go and see her: most important thing is long-term relationship with Mary.

Not finished 1st interview.

Worried may take twins anyway. Or may miscarry because of looking after the children she already has.

[Undated] RMW3 said she had done 2nd interview this week but could not record because the lady insisted she would not talk with the recorder on. Involved in lots of criminal activities – i.e. running a mail order book in

someone else's name because she has been banned from having one herself.
Also involved in cannabis.

4.6.87. This lady has a probation officer, a family aid assistant, and also a
social worker. Smoking cannabis quite heavily. Very uptight because she
could lose other children when the twins arrive. Still refusing to go out,
keeps going into labour if she tries to do anything. Two boys at different
schools so she is running between the two. Very much wants to look after
the children she has, knows the twins are a poor risk . . . Thinks if the boys go
into care she may never get them back. Won't go into hospital for this reason.
RMW3 says she can understand why. RMW3 says this lady really cares for the
two boys and they respond very well to her and want to be with their
mother.

Was taking fertility drug – even though not married – and was expecting
triplets, though lost one!

Telephone call from RMW3 last Friday, 26 June. She went to see Mary this
morning who burst into tears. When RMW3 asked her what was the matter,
the following story came out: yesterday she went into her boys' bedroom
(they are 4 yrs and 7 yrs) where they were playing with 4-yr-old nephew.
None of them had any clothes on. When she asked what they were doing,
they said, 'playing rude games'.

Apparently the 4-yr-old had gone to the park, gone into some bushes, and
seen a couple having sex – but apparently oral and/or anal sex. The boys had
been 'exploring' each other with fingers and tongues. The boys said they
were copying what the 4-yr-old had seen. The 7-yr-old said he didn't do
anything, he just watched the others. RMW3 doesn't think the 4-yr-old had
been interfered with – they saw it as a game, though they did realize they
were doing something they shouldn't have been.

Mary was very upset – the nephew's mother got angry (though it was her
son who had seen the incident and was doing the copying), and said she
wouldn't be taking her children there any more. Mary is terrified that if she
reports the matter she will have the boys taken into care again, less worried
about the twins – says she is worried about the 2 she already has, not about
the 2 she might have. Has labour pains most days. Hospital say she should go
in for a rest, but she can't. The social services have said if the boys miss
school they will take them away again – therefore Mary has to walk a mile
each way to school.

Various facts: Mary's boyfriend is having a relationship with someone else
– Mary knows about it. Another problem is that an ex-boyfriend of hers
keeps going to the house – he is violent and Mary is upset because the
present boyfriend doesn't stand up to him.

RMW3 says she will contact Homestart, a voluntary organization of 'older'
women who have had children themselves who go into a home at a time of
crisis to look after children, etc. RMW3 thinks it would be good if they could
organize something like that for when Mary has to go into hospital to have
her twins.'

Mary had her twins on 3 July: a girl weighing 860 g who died aged one day
and a girl weighing 850 g who died aged two days.

15.7.87. [AO's writing] RMW3 rang re Mary Smart to say she's having a lot of contact because of Mary's problems. *Outline of story so far.* Picked up by police after row with boyfriend. (Mother phoned the police.) Wandering confused and bleeding heavily so police took her to hospital. She is wanted by the police because she went to her boyfriend's other girlfriend's place of work and beat her up.

Now in hospital. RMW3 went to see her there – she'd been waiting one and a half hours for a scan with a very full bladder (they'd forgotten her). Will need a D and C.

RMW3 says she's very bitter. Everyone says she should be over it by now (two weeks later). She's seen no one – no counsellor. Boyfriend has said since she's not pregnant any more she can go on giving him meals but he's going to go on seeing the other woman. Mother says she needs to see a psychiatrist. (RMW3 says is this because mother wants to keep the 2 boys?) Father won't speak to her. DHSS can't decide whether they'll give her the money for the funeral (£180). Babies are still in hospital mortuary . . . Ward clerk is the one who phoned RMW3 to tell her what was going on. She'd been warned to look out for Mary in case she wandered in to steal some other babies.

[RMW3's writing] Extra postnatal contact. I saw Mary for 40 minutes on 14.7.87 when informed of her admission to hospital . . . Still very upset . . . will contact her again later this week.

15–21.7.87. Several calls when door not answered.

22.7.87. 30 minutes' visit. Twelve midday, still in bed. Remains upset. Won't see medical social worker for bereavement counselling. Doesn't know if she wants another baby. Not sure if/when she wants her boys back because she feels trapped and needs to walk away at times. Relationship with boyfriend worsening. Funerals tomorrow, DHSS paying. Still bleeding. Won't go to hospital for postnatal. Psychiatrist says she's OK.

About her stay in the hospital, Mary wrote in her postnatal questionnaire: 'From start to finish it was a nightmare. Most of the doctors aren't fit to look after pigs, let alone women and babies.' In answer to the question why babies are born small, she replied: 'Because doctors would rather drink coffee and touch up the nurses than look after the patients.' And her suggestions about how the medical care of women with a history of LBW delivery might be improved included: 'More caring doctors and nurses and no waiting to see a doctor for three and a quarter hours while in labour.' These comments were made against a background which Mary described as offering her very little support either in pregnancy or since the twins' birth. She saw the research midwife as the most helpful person: 'I thought she was really nice, more of a friend, which I needed', but also noted that sometimes she felt she could have benefited from more of the midwife's time. The last comment on her questionnaire, most poignantly, was: 'I'm sorry if half of what I say doesn't make sense I still feel very bitter and I can't spell.'

A welfare state?

A study of this kind is informative not only about the limits of interventions such as social support in difficult lives, but of the ways in which the services routinely provided for promoting the health and welfare of individuals and families in difficulty actually work – or not. This was another major topic in the research midwives' experiences. During the negotiation with the four centres for the research, the need not to tread on the toes of those already providing antenatal care (whether in hospital or in the community) had been apparent. Each of the four midwives was dependent on the goodwill of staff locally towards the research, and their experiences were very different, from a very sympathetic attitude in one of the centres, to outright hostility and non-co-operation in another.

> I seemed to get a feeling that the senior medical staff had okayed it and not really consulted the ground roots first. (RMW1)

> I have been very pleased at how helpful people have been and at the interest shown in the work that we are doing. I have never been made to feel in the way or a nuisance. (RMW2)[6]

One reason why staff may have felt threatened is that in the course of the study the research midwives learnt a good deal about the kind of antenatal care normally provided. Here the midwives' lessons included: lack of communication between different branches of the services, the difficulty women experienced getting adequate information and/or having their own preferences for care respected, and the refusal of staff to recognize women's domestic and other responsibilities and to treat them as individuals in their own right. Examples from the monthly meetings include lack of information, and help for women with heightened anxiety because of past difficulties or present stress:

> RMW2: She's a lady who had ten years of infertility, got pregnant, had a stillbirth and then got pregnant again and obviously was very concerned about the baby ... She phoned me up and said she'd been having this pain when she walked, or she couldn't walk because of this pain, when she sat down the pain went away. So I told her to phone her GP immediately to see what he suggested and I said I'd phone her back this afternoon to see what he said. So I phoned her back and she said, 'He told me to take a couple of Panadol, and as I'm seeing Mr Cross in a couple of days' time to wait and see what he has to say' ... But the GP gave her the impression that it's that woman again. She said to me, 'They think I'm just panicking about every-

thing', which she's got every right to do in my opinion. I feel now with hindsight I should have said to her, phone the midwife, and I *know* they would have said come in, and they would have checked her over and she would have seen a doctor . . . Apparently she said to her husband, 'Well at least RMW2 asked me questions and I was able to talk to her about it, whereas with the GP it was just "take two Panadol", he didn't even ask if the baby was moving.' (Wanda Radcliffe)

A woman who had a stillbirth and was still seeing the research midwife got extra help from the services as a result:

RMW3: Because of the intervention she's been having postnatal help. Because I knew her social worker and I happened to say, had she been seen, how was she getting on? Just for my own interest. And she said, my God, what's happened, has she lost the baby? What's happened is that the system has broken down. They're meant to have every stillbirth referred straight back to the social work department so they get at least one visit from somebody in the social work department to make sure they've got some counselling help or whatever. And this system had broken down, and people on the wards weren't being referred back. And of course, once they'd said that, they asked me for her name and address, and she has had the postnatal counselling and support, but she should have had it anyway. (Sarah Loder)

Many stories, such as this one about Tania McPherson, concerned the manner in which medical care was delivered:

RMW3: This lady has a sister who had a stillbirth, her daughter has convulsions, and her husband's in intensive care . . . The same poor lady had the most horrific antenatal experience the other day too. She went in for a routine hospital antenatal and the houseman decided to listen to the baby with an ordinary stethoscope – remember her sister's baby's just been born dead – and he said to her, 'Oh, I can't hear the baby's heart with a stethoscope, you'll have to go upstairs and be monitored.' She went upstairs and this same chap put the things on and after a while he said, 'Something's wrong with that trace, something's wrong with that baby.' She was climbing the wall. And then an experienced midwife put them on properly. He sat there and he walked up and said to her, 'That's OK then', and walked off. Luckily she got hold of him and said, 'Come back here and explain to me what's going on' (she was a nurse). And he said, 'Well, it's all right now.' He didn't want to explain but she made him. In the end he said, 'Well, I don't think the monitor was on target.'

RMW1: They don't *think*, any of them. They've no idea of the distress and upset they cause!

In the following examples from the 'problem file', questions are raised about the 'ethical' nature of the research exercise itself.

Jenny Pilkington

[AO's writing] RMW3 called me with a 'crisis' she wants to talk through with someone. An intervention lady, now 32 weeks, with oedema of fingers and toes and face (and eyelids heavy + pulsing and throbbing). Previous pregnancy, pre-eclampsia at 32 weeks and induction at 34 weeks, live, very small baby. This lady talked to her earlier in the day about her symptoms. RMW3 advised her to phone her GP. She eventually talked to her GP who told her she was making a fuss and he'd think about giving her an appointment if she still had the symptoms on Friday. She told RMW3, who suggested she ring the GP unit. She did, and they referred her to a satellite GP unit where they said they'd send a district midwife out. Then someone (?Director of Midwifery) rang the lady to say she was making a fuss and she'd get a midwife visit in the morning, not before. RMW3 worried: what should she do? We agreed she would phone Jenny at 7 p.m., an hour after her husband was due home. Perhaps he will decide to take her into hospital (she lives 'out in the sticks'). If not, then RMW3 should ring hospital to tell them what's going on. I said I would carry the can if there were any problems as a result of this.

7.30 p.m. RMW3 phoned to say she had been to hospital and talked to midwife on duty who'd said that the district midwife who'd refused to go out was on a disciplinary charge for not visiting a PPH two weeks ago. The midwife on duty was then phoned by Jenny and she told her to go in – so she's now on her way to be admitted.

RMW3 phoned the next day to say Jenny was seen that evening and the hospital said she had pre-eclampsia which had indeed come on suddenly. They sent her home to rest and to be admitted again if symptoms persisted. Jenny told RMW3 that she's glad she *is* ill because now she doesn't feel she's just making a fuss for nothing.

Jenny was admitted to hospital twice, once for oedema and once to be induced. She gave birth to a healthy normal-weight girl.

Lorraine Martin

Baby due end of November. Husband works in Libya. Won't be home for the birth. Two children already – 6 yrs and 2 yrs. RMW2 did first visit at Lorraine's sister's house because she was told the house was in such a mess. Very old house, needs everything doing to it. Have applied for grants which are taking a long time to come through, but no shortage of money. 2nd visit at the house. No water in the bathroom, small hot-water heater in kitchen. Tarpaulin roof. Very cold. Downstairs loo blocked. Upstairs loo can only be used by flushing with a bucket of water. Children have to be taken to the sister for a bath. Depressed because the grants are taking so long. Husband was due back, so RMW2 thought problems would be sorted out.

Last Monday did 3rd visit. Showed RMW2 the three bedrooms, which have been decorated and which are very nice. Husband when he was home knocked out the downstairs loo and then discovered that it would have been quite easy to repair! Still no water in the bathroom. RMW2 asked her how long she would be in hospital after the delivery – was told Lorraine's mother would be 'popping in'. No one in the house in the evenings/nights. 2 early births previously at 37 and 36 weeks. RMW2 asked her if she'd seen the community midwife, because she was so worried about this lady. Lorraine said she knew the community midwife from previously (someone called Deborah) and she'd told Deborah that she was OK and didn't need a visit because everything was all right. (Deborah knew her when she was living somewhere else and had a very nice house, etc.) Therefore the community midwife did not do the statutory home visit. *But she has filled in the appropriate form to say that she has!* When RMW2 went back to the hospital she saw Deborah and was tempted to say something but felt she couldn't because of the confidentiality involved. Lorraine has an appointment at the clinic this week and RMW2 has advised her to tell them about the problems. RMW2 is very worried that if her waters go she won't have anyone to contact quickly. RMW2 says she will have to take the children with her to the hospital in an emergency and then ask the police to contact the mother (who is living in a mobile home without a telephone) to fetch the children. RMW2 says she wants to get someone involved, but doesn't know who. Also worried about getting the community midwife into trouble, although 'she deserves it'. Can't involve social worker because no financial difficulties. Environmental Health Officer contacted by Lorraine but not interested – again probably because financial position OK. RMW2 says she will go to ward and ask if they can keep Lorraine longer than normal (assuming children OK with mother).

5.11.86. [AO's writing] Advised RMW2 to mention the problem of Lorraine being alone at night to community midwife who can then try to persuade Lorraine to stay in hospital (RMW2: 'I would feel awful if she had a haemorrhage and I'd known about it').

Lorraine's baby was born at term, a reasonable weight. Her comments on the postnatal questionnaire showed she appreciated the research midwife's help, 'Although she always managed to call when I was eating or sleeping ... I'm glad I've made another friend.'

Dale Neff

RMW3: this lady has a lot of problems. History: 1 child, now 3½, boy, very bright. Also one daughter who died at 4½ months – cot death. She's worried about whether smoking cannabis will affect the baby. Attending Marriage Guidance, doesn't know if she will stay with her husband. Husband gambles and drinks. She was previously philosophy student at university, he is floor layer. She has sleep problems, recurring nightmare, wakes sobbing: she and son are in danger, and the husband just looks at them and laughs and goes away.

9.4.87. Phoned RMW3 re constipation problems. Very upset with GP, vulval oedema, doctor wouldn't visit.

4.6.87. Went to GP, who said baby was small, insisted on her having scan, and going into hospital for a rest. No one for other child to go to, so she said no: doctor got cross and shouted at her. She is refusing to see him again.

Lily Graham

RMW3: female baby, 1800 g, on 15.1.87. Husband phoned RMW3 in distraught state saying his wife was bleeding heavily, he'd phoned the hospital, who had told him to contact their GP. But he was unable to locate him. RMW3 told him to phone 999 for an ambulance – she heard it arrive because she lives nearby. Placental abruption – did a Caesarean immediately. RMW3 delighted she was home to tell him what to do. Suppose she hadn't been?

Roberta Archer

Baby due on 29th. Telephoned RMW2 today [22 May 1987] about Roberta Archer.

She phoned RMW2 yesterday saying she was losing 'water' – this was about 6.45 p.m. Didn't know whether her waters had broken or not. RMW3 told her to check with the hospital, but she is under her GP, not the hospital consultant. GP wouldn't come up to see her but told the hospital to stick her in the antenatal ward until the morning. RMW2 said in these circumstances they usually do various tests, but nothing was done because she is under the GP – very political situation . . . Roberta went home this morning and GP said he would see her there. Roberta phoned RMW2 to say she was still losing and still very anxious and the GP still hadn't turned up. RMW2 told her to ring the surgery in case the doctor had gone to see her in the hospital.

Last year Roberta had a miscarriage, and she says the doctor was less than diligent on that occasion and is frightened that his lack of interest will continue. Blames him for what happened.

Then Roberta's husband phoned RMW2 again about 2 p.m. today to say he didn't know what to do because Roberta was in a state, baby kicking violently, some tightening, etc., and still losing. RMW2 told him to leave it with her, and she'd see what she could do. RMW2 phoned the labour ward and asked what Roberta could do. They agreed to phone the GP's surgery and try to get him to go and see her . . . RMW2 said, 'There I go, interfering again . . .'

4.6.87. RMW2 reported Roberta had called her and said she had a leak at about 2.30 . . . Eventually the GP turned up and did an internal, and said her waters had gone and he would transfer her to consultant care. She told RMW2, she didn't know if she was on her head or her heels, one doctor did a specimen and said her waters had gone and he'd have to start her off and do CTG, then he came back and said he'd leave her for an hour then do another test to see if the waters had broken. Later he did a specimen which he said was positive. Midwife then went in and said they'd decided to leave her overnight. Another doctor said waters hadn't gone, if they had there would have been a gush and you'd know immediately. Roberta said, is this nonsense? RMW2 said yes.

Phoned RMW2 on Tuesday and said she'd gone in early hours of Sunday, waters *had* gone, first doctor apologized . . . Home now and all OK . . . (male, 7lb 5oz).

Samantha Varney

RMW1 called to see Samantha Varney, who said, 'I think I have a drink problem.' She drinks two and a half pints of lager every Thursday when she plays darts. Tape didn't work during this interview. Smoking, she says, has gone down. She had asked about having a section previously, and RMW1 sent all the information on that. Query whether husband may be drinking heavily? Also if Samantha is drinking more than she says? Sent alcohol guidelines[7] and details of fetal alcohol syndrome to RMW1.

8.1.87. RMW1 gave Samantha guidelines, she said, 'Now I have got the guidelines, I don't worry about it any more.' (Quick visit between 1st and 2nd interviews.)

Midwives' meeting 9.2.87. Samantha had a stillbirth at 32 weeks. RMW1 said 'trace' was very bad, couldn't understand why they hadn't done a section. Samantha is blaming the hospital. Refused to have anything to do with the baby – and so did husband. Funeral last Thursday. Husband said after that he didn't want to think about it any more. RMW1 contacted the local SANDS people, they're sending someone to see Samantha today. Samantha refused to see the social worker and the chaplain – would only see RMW1. Consultant (Mr Tinkler) told her to make sure she went to see him 'next time'. Baby weighed 4lb 2oz. Refused post-mortem, but has got photo. Maybe refused because of her drink problem – frightened in case post-mortem showed it up?

AO suggested that RMW1 attends the hospital mortality inquiry meeting – doesn't have to say which baby she's interested in finding out about.

First baby was delivered under same consultant – Samantha had a bad time and the hospital pulled her through, so unlikely she will create a fuss now. Mr Box on call the night she went in but saw her only once. Mr Tinkler called in the last hour. Should have been seen by more senior person earlier on.

8.3.87. RMW1 reported, went to the perinatal meeting. Mr Box attended. No comment made about RMW1 being there. Four cases discussed. 1st case was Varney baby. It was clear from the discussion that the 2 consultants didn't see eye to eye. One would have done a section quickly but not the other one. In hindsight he said he was wrong and he should have done a section and the baby would have survived. Could have prevented the baby's death, he admitted. Might have been a concealed APH but a section would have saved the baby anyway . . . Asked the GP who was present how the mother was coping.

26.3.87. RMW1 spoke to Samantha – told RMW1 she had a postnatal questionnaire from London and had filled it in with some 'nasty' comments. Has decided to go to a solicitor . . . Very bitter, but has been all along. Asks, 'Why didn't they do a section?' RMW1 saw husband who 'looks dreadful' – says it's really affecting Samantha now.

[RMW1's writing] Re lady Samantha Varney. I spent one and three-quarter hours with her on 22.4.87. She is very bitter, has been to a solicitor and wants to continue to prevent a similar thing happening to anyone else.

She definitely blames the doctors on duty that night – says her antenatal care was excellent and also postnatal care – but doesn't know whether that's due to the hospital trying to 'cover up'. Definitely feels they should have done a LSCS earlier – says she was quite prepared for that, feels that the doctors involved didn't know what they were doing. One member of staff said that the baby's heartbeat was low and a cause for concern.

A solicitor has told her that the hospital won't want to let the notes go if they think it means trouble, and it could be a long-drawn-out battle. She knows it won't bring Samantha back but feels she's got to do it for her. She says she doesn't know, but, if something had been done earlier, Susie might have still been here – she's also wondering if she should have held the baby or seen her, she says she didn't want to, but now she doesn't know. Says she'll continue however long it takes – husband agrees, also brother, but in-laws think she's left it too long and is doing it out of spite.

7.5.87. Reported by RMW1: grabbed Samantha's case-notes when she saw them lying around.

Went in on the 26th at 3.15 a.m.
Saw doctor
Dipped to 90
Observe
5.15 trace dipping, 2 cm dilated
Cross matched
6.00 CTG after 30 mins down to 90
3 cm
6.50 dipped to 70
7.00 worried about dip
7.30 fetal blood sample, epidural, head too high
8.15 elective section + 5 mins no fetal heart.

32 weeks, 4.2 g

Samantha determined to sue. Too many people involved, should have had a section as soon as she went in. RMW1 has not told Samantha she's seen the notes.

14.11.87. Samantha Varney rang me 10.43–10.53 a.m. Worried that her son may have German measles and she may be 2 months pregnant. Advised her to contact GP. She rang me back to say GP says not to worry – she had a previous antibody test and it's no cause for concern. Her husband is serving a 6-month prison sentence for dealing in videos and TVs. Has now moved from old address. She says if she definitely is pregnant she won't smoke or drink this pregnancy. She does feel guilty about her last pregnancy.

Samantha's comments on the postnatal questionnaire were very critical of her hospital care: 'Before the birth, I felt as if I was completely on my own, no questions were answered, and I feel very bitter towards the hospital. They made me feel as though I was a burden after my daughter died … The actual labour, I'm sorry to put this on paper, but I feel that if more had been done at this stage my daughter may have been alive today.' She noted that, apart from her husband, the research midwife had been the most helpful person during the pregnancy and its aftermath.

Alice Glaston

27.5.86. RMW3 telephoned re Alice Glaston. Young girl of 20 with many problems. Living in B and B. She has seen her today for 3rd interview and is worried there may be even more problems than at first anticipated – ?baby battering, ?criminal activities.

History is that Alice has been beaten up by her boyfriend – they split up but are back together now. Violent history – court supervision order. They are now living together in B and B. £300 has gone missing from Alice's social security. Boyfriend says it was 'lost'. RMW3 thinks he may have taken it. However, she also thinks this has become a sort of 'acceptable' lifestyle for Alice. Alice asked RMW3 to arrange for her to have a social worker. Got one.

Worse problem: RMW3 asked re drinking, Alice laughed. Then said her little boy didn't look well – he had fallen off a chair upstairs. RMW3 anxious, says she has a feeling all is not well. Child is very quiet – doesn't look well, doesn't respond, although always been 'bouncy' before – now quiet and withdrawn. Alice referred to the fall several times, and said she hadn't seen what happened but 'it must have happened while he was upstairs'. Alice also mentioned that they were having sex problems.

27.5.86. AO talked to RMW3. RMW3 has told emergency social worker today re suspected battering, and will tell Alice's social worker tomorrow. AO said she would speak to social worker and emphasize need for confidentiality. Boyfriend beat Alice in early pregnancy, resulting in symptoms of threatened miscarriage, and bed-rest. He's now under a court supervision order. Has problems with police. Alice originally asked RMW3 to arrange social worker. Social worker phoned Alice and boyfriend and asked them to go and see her. Not very sensitive. RMW3 doesn't think social worker is very good, and Alice doesn't get on with her very well. Now 32 weeks. Had first baby at 37 weeks. Weight gain poor.

28.5.86. RMW3 called. Phoned emergency social worker and has been
speaking to Alice's own social worker's head of department. They have
decided that somehow Timothy must be examined ... decided to have the
health visitor call round to see him to do a routine developmental check.
She will go in and do check today. If he doesn't look well she will ask for him
to be stripped ... Has been told not to involve RMW3 – must try to maintain
relationship between Alice and RMW3 for the future.

29.5.86. Spoke to RMW3. Health visitor saw Timothy yesterday and managed
to look under his clothes while playing with him on the floor. No sign of
physical injury. Some possibility the child may be ESN and therefore
sometimes appear 'glazed'. Health visitor has been concerned about whole
family for some time – been considering bringing in social services. Alice
has no idea RMW3 was involved.
    Another problem – where is Timothy going when Alice is in hospital for
Caesarean? Health visitor offered foster home because boyfriend not trusted
(money still 'lost'). Health visitor trying to get Alice to make satisfactory
arrangements for Timothy.

10.7.86. Since Alice has been in hospital she has changed dramatically –
brighter, eyes changed. Several staff have noticed the difference and commented that she must have been on something before – ?drugs. Timothy has
whooping cough, and has been passed on to neighbour while Alice is in
hospital. Health visitor saying that neighbour isn't suitable to look after him.
Delivered 17.7.86, female, 3090 g.

In the case of Jenny Pilkington, a delay in diagnosing pre-eclampsia
could have been fatal. In that of Lorraine Martin, the community midwife
failed to carry out a statutory home visit, so that the hazards of an
unsatisfactory home situation did not come to light. In the case of Dale
Neff, the GP's behaviour was not based on a realistic appraisal of pregnant
women's responsibilities to their existing children, and jeopardized the
care the mother was willing to receive from him in the future. In Lily
Graham's case, inadequate advice from the hospital could have caused the
death of a baby. Roberta Archer's case illustrates the tendency of health
professionals to give contradictory information and advice, as well as
demonstrating the confusion and anxiety that may result when maternity
care is shared between GP and hospital. Samantha Varney's situation is also
an example of an unmet need for information in particularly tragic
circumstances. The exclusion of parents from perinatal mortality inquiries
has been raised by other work (Gilligan 1980). Within the context of a
research study, this example provokes an ethical question, too, about the
researcher's responsibility: to meet the mother's need for information, or
to preserve the confidentiality of the hospital medical information? The
final situation, that of Alice Glaston, also raises ethical issues concerning
the responsibility of research, involving as it does the judgement that a
child might have been at risk. In all seven cases, the definition of the

research midwife's role as restricted to research prohibited her from actively intervening to criticize the standard of care provision. But in all seven cases the fact that the research midwife *did* know what was going on, and *did* take action, may well have altered the outcome of the situation.

Who supports the supporters?

Finally in this chapter, we look at the midwives' experiences of their role and the personal costs of being involved in the study.

Selling the research

Because there was often inadequate information on the booking notes, the research midwives sometimes had to wait until after the women had been seen at the clinic to establish their 'eligibility'. As some women would then not be due to return to the hospital clinic until 36 weeks of pregnancy, the research midwives had no opportunity to recruit them there, and had to do so by telephone, or by visits to the women's homes. The following conversation took place at one of the monthly meetings:

> RMW1: I hate doing it on the phone. They're very suspicious.
> RMW2: Yes, they are.
> RMW4: I haven't found that, but I don't feel it's fair to ask them to take part on the phone. I mean, they don't know you.
> RMW1: That's right, and you get so many weird people trying to sell things.
> RMW3: Which is basically what you're doing, isn't it?
> RMW4: Yes, you are. You're trying to sell them the research.
> RMW3: It takes me four and a half minutes to do a recruitment. My husband says I don't give them time to say no.
> RMW1: It takes me half an hour.
> RMW3: Not on the phone!
> RMW1: It does!
> RMW3: I'm dreadful. I go far too fast, and they say yes to get rid of me!

At another meeting:

> RMW1: I think they feel pressured.
> RMW3: Especially if you say you're a midwife – they're not used to saying no to health professionals.

The questionnaires the midwives filled in observed:

> Recruiting over the phone is impersonal, doesn't really give the lady a chance to ask questions or retain the information … Can't gauge her reaction by facial expression, either. (RMW1)

Sometimes when I recruit at their home, I find they are concerned as to how I have got their name, address, etc., and also (despite the ID card[8]) how official I am. (RMW4)

I love the idea of recruiting women at clinic, but find it very time-consuming, so have done, at most, 6 women this way. I prefer the telephone to a visit at home. For speed, and to maintain distance between myself and those who are eventually 'control'. (RMW3)

The fourth midwife found herself wondering how *she* would react if approached in this way:

I prefer to recruit at the clinic because I feel the women see me in what they might class the 'right setting' for a midwife, even though I am not in uniform. Also I find it far nicer – on the whole easier if speaking face to face. Having said that, I have been amazed at how receptive ladies have been to my recruiting them over the phone, the information they are very free to provide about themselves often without my asking. I often have wondered how I would react to a total stranger claiming to be a midwife telephoning completely out of the blue, who obviously has information about me. (RMW2)

The research midwives took the view that some of the control women were effectively receiving social support during the recruitment process, despite their efforts to minimize contact:

RMW1: It must affect them, if you see them at home . . . You can't just walk in and out again. They say, oh, are you a midwife? What about this? I try and give a very broad opinion. I say if you're in the intervention group we can talk about that.

RMW3: I say I'm sure that's something your district midwife would love to talk to you about. I think the district midwives will kill me!

One woman allocated to the control group was visited at home by the research midwife for recruitment. The following conversation, which took place at one of the monthly meetings, is interesting because it also shows the value of the midwives being able collectively to discuss and resolve difficult issues:

RMW1: . . . quite honestly I chewed it over all last weekend and I thought something ought to be done. I've never *seen* social conditions like that at all. There must have been eight or nine pints of milk floating around. Three on the doorstep. Some half used, some whole. I walked through one room, no carpet, and the floor had piles of clothes in one corner, piles in the other corner. She'd got a jumper on inside out, perhaps it's neither here nor there . . . She took me through to a room at the back. There was another pile of clothes in the corner, no carpet, a mug tipped over, a birdcage without a bird in with droppings in it. The floor was filthy. I had to sit down, but I perched on the edge. There was a fire that had two of the radiants broken. It reminded me of Trafalgar Square – pigeon droppings all over the floor ... She told me she can't read, this is an unwanted pregnancy, her husband's not talking to her and she was raped anyway (by her husband). The child she had in 1977 has abnormalities and they haven't talked since then. And then they had one in 1983 (without talking!). I wondered if I should do anything ...

RMW4: You can't, she's in the control group.

AO: Well, no, but if you feel you have a moral responsibility ...

RMW1: That's it. My poor husband and I chewed it over all weekend ...

AO: What are you worried about?

RMW1: The home conditions. They're positively unhealthy.

RMW4: But some homes are like that. That family'll be immune to those conditions. I mean, this home I go to, the carpet is black, the whole home is absolutely filthy ... if the children are well cared for it isn't up to anybody, is it?

Sticking to social support

During the midwives' induction days we emphasized the need for them to provide generalized social support without behaving in ways that might be dictated by their midwifery training. Responding to pregnancy smoking was an example of this. Two in five women in the SSPO study smoked during pregnancy, and standard health education practice followed by most health professionals is to advise against maternal smoking. The research midwives were asked not to do this, but only to provide information about pregnancy smoking and how to give up if asked about this by the women they were seeing. As the study progressed, all the midwives discussed how they had come to see anti-smoking advice as inappropriate, given the context of women's smoking in which the use of cigarettes to cope with stress is a prominent strategy (see Graham 1987; Oakley 1989).

The midwives did not, however, feel quite the same about the injunction that they were not to provide any clinical care:

RMW3: I wonder how different our reassurance or intervention would be if we had a sphygmometer and a pinard ... the number of women I've had who've been worried about their blood pressure and the baby's heart ...

RMW1: Oh yes, I've had a quite a few who've said if only I didn't have to sit in the clinic and I knew you were going to come and take my blood pressure. I say I don't think there is any way I can, I say I'm not clinically involved this time. It's talking ... But yes, I wish I'd got one. Particularly a sphyg, to be quite honest.

RMW3: With me it'd be the other one. I had one day when three women phoned me up and said they were worried the baby wasn't moving and couldn't I come and listen to them or what should they do? I thought it'd be so reassuring. But I'm sure the local midwives would have a dickey!

Breaking the relationship

The SSPO study was designed to test the effectiveness of a *pregnancy* intervention in improving maternal and infant health. Because of this, the research midwives were asked to provide support in pregnancy only, and not to carry over this support into the postnatal period. This proved extremely difficult in practice. Not only did the women the research midwives had been supporting want to see them afterwards, but the midwives themselves also felt they did not want abruptly to break the relationship that had been established:

> RMW1: I usually go and see my ladies and say how are you, it's a super baby, thank you for helping with the study ... I think it's quite important. You can't just let them deliver, you've got to have some contact.
>
> RMW2: I *want* to have some contact.
>
> RMW1: Oh, I do.
>
> RMW2: Sometimes I think I want to see them, but do they want to see me?
>
> RMW1: Oh, you can tell. Sometimes they want to sit and natter, and sometimes it's just yes, I'm fine, thank you, and they don't want to talk.
>
> RMW3: I've had a lot of them say, oh, do come and see me when I'm home with the baby.
>
> RMW1: I try to see them on the postnatal ward because then it is a quickie; if I go home and see them then I'm stuck for at least half an hour. It sounds awful to say it but at that time I don't feel I should be spending that amount of time. It's not that I don't *want* to be there ...

Sometimes it proved impossible to avoid a prolonged postnatal contact, albeit of an unorthodox kind:

> I was trying to be really good and avoid postnatal contact with my ladies. You remember my lovely lady Claudia, who's in a block of flats that's going to be knocked down? Because of damp. We've given her a lot of baby clothes. Just before this baby was born I'd been promised by our local NCT all their nearly new NCT stuff that they didn't sell for babies and I went and picked up four dustbin bags full of baby clothes. You've never seen such a mess in your whole life! Anyway, blow me down, she went and delivered before I could get them to her. I visited her in hospital and she was really pleased. She said, 'Have you got the stuff yet?' And I said, 'Yes, I'll get it to you.' I thought, well, I don't really want to go and do a home visit on her. So I said to my husband, 'Right, could you please, if you're going out that way, could you please just drop that bag through the door and say it's from me?' ... It took him two hours to get out of the house. Her husband decided he needed some support, thank you. He was there for two hours talking about the effect of the baby on the family, how he could cope as a dad. Made him coffee. And Claudia was saying, when's RMW3 going to come and see me again, I want to

show her the baby. I thought you'd better know she'd had some postnatal contact. (RMW3)

This midwife's comment flags the role of the women's partners in the research, which was significant in various ways. For example:

I had one lady, it took me two weeks to recruit her. I went to see her and she was out so I left a letter. Her husband rang me up to ask a little more because she had had a stillbirth, and it was only in February and her LMP was May so there wasn't that much time – because *he'd* found that when she talked about it, it made her depressed and therefore it made it difficult at home. Which was quite a reasonable response from him; he was concerned that I was going to make her more depressed. So we had quite a chat and he said he'd talk to her and get back in touch with me. He didn't, so I rang back a week later. He said she was quite willing to take part if it was only a postal questionnaire. So I had to explain that I couldn't promise that but I told him the first time and I said it again that I was quite willing to go and explain it to them. So I did that. And she was quite happy to take part. And she ended up as intervention. When I went back to do the interview, it transpired that his attitude is that when something like this happens the best thing to do is forget about it. And she feels that it's better for her to talk about it. So she is talking about it but not to him. She's talking to her mother and to friends and she can quite happily talk to me. (RMW4)

Or:

RMW2: I've got one husband whose wife won't express an opinion when he's in the room.
RMW1: Oh, that's quite common!
RMW2: I think she's scared of him. On the tape you can hear him shouting at the child. Asked in his presence if she has any problems with the child, she says, oh no, and the husband says, of course she's perfectly normal. And when he went out of the room she launched into a great tirade about how worried she is that the child doesn't eat anything. But I can't get rid of him . . . he's a very aggressive man. I left out one or two questions, you know, have you got any problems with your partner? I'm not going to ask that. He'll probably clock me one.

When we came to look in the analysis at the relationship between the social support provided by the research midwives and the women's own sources of support, we found that the male partners of the intervention-group women had become notably more 'helpful' around the house (table 7.6, over). This is in line with the findings of other intervention studies (see Elbourne et al. 1989). It was interpreted by the research midwives in two ways: either the women had felt enabled as a result of the midwives' support to ask for more help; or the men thought the midwives were

Table 7.6 Help with housework and childcare given by male partners of SSPO women

Type of help	Intervention (N = 237) %	Control (N = 230) %	Significance
In pregnancy:			
Helped often/quite often with shopping	81	70	p < 0.01
Helped often/quite often with other children	81	72	p < 0.05
After the birth:			
Helped often/quite often with shopping	81	74	p < 0.06
Helped often/quite often with other children	84	78	p < 0.05

watching them, and that they had better be on their 'best behaviour'. These explanations could be complementary, of course.

Terminating their relationships with the study women was even more problematic for the midwives when the outcome of the pregnancy was not a healthy baby. Sarah Loder haemorrhaged and reached hospital too late for a Caesarean to save the baby:

She phoned me up again last week. She said, oh I've had a reminder (for the postnatal questionnaire), but there's one or two things I really haven't sorted out what you want. They were all things not asking for an opinion, but she said she hadn't understood what we wanted from the question. And so I told her one or two very straightforward bits. I knew it wasn't that, and it took me another 25 minutes to get off the phone. What really came out in the conversation was how bad she felt that I didn't go and see her when the baby died and how she really needed me to go out there and she was desperate for me to talk to her, and nobody else understood because I'd seen her through the pregnancy, and how she'd felt she'd been under quite a lot of extra pressure because I wasn't there. And I . . . felt bad. I had a long chat with her about the effect of the stillbirth. I said, are you going to finish the questionnaire now? Oh yes, she said, I just didn't understand these bits. I think she was just hanging on to it as an excuse to phone me again. I said, look, if you feel really bad, give me a ring, I don't mind chatting with you. I said, if you feel that awful I'll try and pop out and see you. I think probably now I've said that she won't need it. But she was desperate, it was very sad . . . She obviously wanted postnatal help. I know it's not what we're here to do, but in a way I wonder if she felt worse because she'd had the intervention and then nothing, rather than if we hadn't done anything to her. (RMW2)

Job satisfaction versus role overload?

All the midwives commented on the practical problems of giving support to women who were living highly stressed lives in socially disadvantaged areas that could be dangerous to visit:

> I've tried to find her in six times. The first time I left a card saying when I'd come, and she rang back and said it's not convenient, so we arranged that I'd see her on the 18th. She wasn't in, so I left her another letter, and she did ring me and we made an appointment, so I went down ten minutes early thinking, ahah, and I sat there for ten minutes and nearly got done by a dog. (RMW1)

> I've got one lady with a very poor obstetric history. She lives on an awful estate and I don't like visiting. She's got four kids under five, a fifth on the way, and the husband says it's not his. He's beaten her up and walked out on her. He's told all his family and friends she's had an affair with someone. And they're coming down at intervals and attacking her, the woman, the children, with physical violence, and they're having to call the police, and she told me all this as the darkness was gathering and the kids were all crowding around and I felt *terribly* unsafe . . . I don't know what we can do because she doesn't want me to go during the day because she feels she can only talk to me when the children are asleep, and anyway you can't get a word in edgeways when they're up. (RMW3)

Another negative side to the research resulted from the fact that the midwives were employed part-time, yet were involved in a task capable of expanding to fill all the time (and more) available. Although they recognized that being on call 24 hours a day, and arranging for 'cover' during holiday periods, etc., was an important part of the intervention so far as the women were concerned, this could mean that they were rarely able to feel 'off duty': 'Being on constant call has meant that, although I'm only "working" two days a week, I feel the research is always at the forefront of my mind' (RMW2). But the fact that the women were able to telephone round the clock did not necessarily mean that they did so:

> It's very valuable, it is often mentioned in conversation, in terms of a 'safety valve' – it may not be needed, but they're glad it's there. Although they like the idea of the pager, they seem to avoid using it if they can, but again say they're reassured by the ease of access it gives them. So far my calls have ranged from 07.30 through to 01.45 . . . In general being on call has not been a problem in itself . . . [but] I remember thinking over the Christmas-time that I mustn't drink too much in case I didn't make sense if anyone called! (RMW3)

One of the research midwives was also working part-time as a labour-ward staff midwife during the study. Though it was clearly possible that she might be involved in giving clinical care to some of 'her' ladies, we did not feel her working as a staff midwife should have precluded her from becoming involved in the study, as it made for especially good contacts within the hospital. We did discuss with her what would happen if she found herself delivering any of the study women, and suggested that she avoid it if at all possible, and, if not, then she should write careful notes about the extent of the contact that had taken place. Two instances occurred:

> Janet Wilson (control). I had contact with Janet when she was admitted to the delivery suite, but, as she was for an emergency LSCS, contact was minimal, as all I did really was to prepare her for theatre. She did remember my name, so I took this opportunity of reminding her that a postnatal question-naire would be forthcoming shortly! I did scrub for the LSCS but as Janet had a GA I don't feel this is particularly relevant.

> [AO's writing] Helen Manners (intervention). RMW2 phoned to say 'I've got a confession to make – I delivered one of my ladies.' Says she couldn't resist the temptation. I said, 'I'm surprised you're resisted it for so long.' RMW2 says it was a very good experience for both of them – short labour, no drugs, etc. Helen said, 'I enjoyed it.' Baby 6lb 12oz.

The mixture of costs and benefits came out clearly in answer to a question about how the research had affected the research midwives' personal lives: 'It has made it easier for me to work while I have a young child. [But] it has been very difficult to give the social support at times of crisis at home, as I felt very guilty giving such personal help to "outsiders", even if I knew I had done all I could at home' (RMW4). For another midwife, the research meant that:

1   Husband has to go to work on the bus so I can have the car.
2   Don't have many evenings in – apart from family social life and activities. I find the best time to check notes and write case-histories at the hospital is evenings.
3   Clothes – different for work and home depending on who one is going to see – always wore uniform before.
4   Days were disjointed – to begin with I found it difficult to adjust to being out for two hours a.m. and two p.m. trying to fit in housework, shopping, etc . . . .
5   Made me more aware of how fortunate I am.
6   More money – increased seniority.
7   Learnt a lot about what is available locally. (RMW1)

All four research midwives agreed that their job satisfaction was poten-tially very high. But the degree to which this promise was realized depended on the extent to which it appeared that their support resulted in better outcomes for the women and their babies. Replies to the question 'How would you rate your level of satisfaction' included:

> Very good. I love it. It does vary, because some days are busy and bad and others are great. On the whole, more up days than down. However, my husband says I come home frustrated because I've been unable to help. (RMW1)

> This does vary. Obviously, if I've been of particular help to a lady with a problem during the pregnancy, then yes, there is a sense of achievement. But basically, to build up a good rapport with a woman, gain her trust and to support her through the pregnancy in whatever way she needs and at the end of the time to have a live healthy baby (of increased birthweight of course!), then that is sufficient job satisfaction for me. (RMW2)

We asked the midwives to write down the high and low points of the job. High points were:

> Meeting the women. (RMW2)

> Achieving a type of care not usually possible. Having a chance of acting on your own initiative. (RMW3)

> Bigger baby than *all* the others. Where there are previous prems, and this pregnancy has gone full-term ... Full-term normal delivery and quick discharge. Really getting to know people and families – when they say how good it's been and call me friend or 'mate' and when they've had a lot of problems and involvement and the outcome is very good. (RMW1)

> When a lady has a successful outcome to her pregnancy, especially if it is her first living baby. When a lady actually tells me I have helped. (RMW4)

And the low points:

> The paperwork. Aggravation over payment of expenses. (RMW4)[9]

> Saying goodbye. When we have a disaster or a baby that's not as big as before. (RMW1)

> Breaking off contact with the women immediately after delivery. (RMW2)

Although the four midwives shared the perception of the study as at least partly designed to raise birthweight, as they worked they developed a broader view of it, seeing it in the context of constraints and opportunities to improve on the qualities of women's experiences in other ways:

> AO: Are there any women you think of as outstanding 'successes'?

RMW1: Yes, an early one, Georgia Ketton. She'd had two small babies, and the consultant told her there was no way she was going to get through this pregnancy without the same sort of thing happening. And he had to induce her and the baby weighed 6½lb.

Kate Jones was another one. The young girl of whom the health visitor said she's bound to have another prem baby, and she went to 39 weeks and had a 6½lb baby. And a recent one, Bonny Howarth, she's come out with a 6½lb baby and kept out of hospital.

All right, the babies aren't huge. But Bonny was told she was going to have a small baby, and worried, and she didn't. So it definitely worked.

RMW3: I stopped measuring success as the baby, it's more their attitudes . . . As long as the baby's healthy, I haven't looked at the weight. If I managed to help them get more information, so they can find out more about benefits, or have home help, or helped through a rocky patch by giving them someone to talk to if they had marital problems – I feel far more satisfied with that aspect of the intervention.

Working as research midwives, and particularly on a study which had such obvious relevance to the routine provision of midwifery care, the midwives were conscious that the research might have an impact on their conceptions of what midwives could and should do, on their own future career plans, and on their ideas about how the routine services might be improved so as to provide more support for childbearing women. The following conversation took place at a meeting fairly late in the progress of the study:

RMW1: It's been a tremendous eyeopener.

RMW2: It's made me question the basis of a lot of clinical decision-making. I think we're inclined to forget the woman as a person.

RMW3: Especially when they tell a woman she's got to come into hospital for rest and they don't think of everything else at home.

RMW2: They think about this bump but they forget that there's a head up there and feet down the bottom.

RMW3: Let alone little appendages like children!

RMW1: And I don't think they realize the effect they have on women.

One midwife said the research had 'unsettled' her and made her unsure of the direction in which she wanted to go:

Where I had, and I hate to admit it, black and white areas, I have learnt there are a lot of grey ones. The study has taught me a lot about pregnancy, women's needs, lack of services available, lack of information imparted, lack of time available for these women, and having learnt these things I feel I want to make other personnel aware of them and maybe in some small way improve the care these women receive. (RMW2)

I would find it hard to practise as a midwife in a hospital where you have little say over how the women were cared for. (RMW3)

As to how the services might be improved, and midwives could become more effective, it would help 'To be more aware of social problems (i.e. housing, financial, family commitments). Midwives in hospital should make more time available to discuss these matters with the women, and act accordingly in their advice and care' (RMW4). A second wrote that 'Relationships are very important. Midwives need more time. They have contact with people at one of the most emotional times in their lives, so perhaps fewer ladies, more midwives and reduced caseloads' (RMW1). During her interview, she said:

> I think having done the research I'm much more aware of what the mothers actually go through before they come in and have their baby . . . Because you have the contact with the home and the family [as a research midwife] – I mean you're a guest in their home but you can't fail to pick up what's going on in the home. I think they give more because you're in their home and they're confident and happy in their own surroundings. When they come into hospital, they're in a totally alien environment. (RMW1)

Communication was regarded as critical:

> For some of the women I was the only midwife they were seeing, so I was answering basic questions like minor disorders of pregnancy and what they should do about them – not that I minded, but I didn't think that was what I was there for . . . More community staff are needed. Maybe this is where we need to centre a lot of the care – out in the community. I feel midwives should go and see the women . . . In an ideal world one midwife looks after you in pregnancy and delivers your baby. (RMW2)

The other side of this coin is strengthening the position of midwives:

> I'm sure my suggestions would be financially unviable! But provide more continuity of care; work in groups sharing the care of a group of women, with one of you always on call. Make care more flexible – especially the postnatal cut-off. Provide a drop-in centre for women, with pre-conceptional through to postnatal advice, information, exercise classes, etc. Give mid-wives their own clients so that women don't see their care as a back-up or poor alternative to GPs. Finally (tongue in cheek), get all midwives to have a baby themselves. (RMW3)

This last, not entirely facetious, comment highlights the importance of personal experience – in more ways than one, as the same midwife thoughtfully reflected in her interview:

> I didn't see the deficiencies before. When you're at the NHS end, you think the system's working, you think you're doing the best you can, but you don't get the women's opinions. You don't find out how long they are actually sitting in the clinic, how many doctors they see in the course of their

antenatal care, how often they don't get things explained to them. If you tell them things in the course of your ordinary work as a midwife, very rarely do they say they don't understand. It's made me realize how often people *think* they've explained something which they [the women] don't understand and they don't have anyone to come back and ask so they just go away and worry ... It never occurred to me how much it affects the women. They come to the hospital to see a doctor – the magic consultant – and they don't see him, but it never occurred to me how much it affected them seeing a different person each time. And that's why they don't ask questions. The inconsistencies, the advice that's different every time. It didn't occur to me how often the people working in the same team would tell someone something completely different. The other thing that's struck me is how often people are given advice they can't follow. To actually go home and rest, but there's nobody who's said ... does your husband realize he's got to do the housekeeping for you? – and very often we blithely say, go home and do this, and when they come back they're told off for not having followed that advice ... and there's no practical way that they can. (RMW3)

One aspect of personal experience all the midwives felt was relevant to their provision of the social support intervention was the fact that they were mothers.[10]

RMW3: ... I changed through having a child as well as through the research. I didn't realize what it's like. Several of these women have said to me they only want to be delivered by women who've had children themselves.

RMW1: Oh, that comes across, especially with health visitors and social workers. Especially with health visitors. Seventeen- and eighteen-year-old girls going in and telling them what to do with their babies when they don't know anything and it's the practical knowledge you need.

RMW3: Health visitors only need to do twelve weeks' obstetrics. Some women have said to me, she's not a midwife, she's not a children's nurse, she's not a mother – she should really be asking me what to do!

RMW2: I find a lot of women know. They say, oh, you've had children yourself, haven't you? They tell *me*.

RMW3: Quite a lot have asked me. Otherwise I'll say something and they'll say, oh yes, you've had children, haven't you? Sometimes you don't even have to say something. Perhaps they've had a baby with colic and you say, oh yes, and they know you're not just talking from professional knowledge. It's something you've been through ... *I think they know as much about you as you do about them by the end of the research.*

Conclusion

Different kinds of lessons can be derived from the experiences of the research midwives in the SSPO study. One set of lessons concerns the doing of research in the maternity services. This is an activity which requires delicate steering through the politics of the structure within which care is provided, including the control over obstetric work defined and exercised by medical and midwifery hierarchies (Garcia et al. 1988). Another moral is about the nature of the midwives' work in the study: their comments reflect both an appreciation of the autonomy the job offered them, and a dislike of the need to submit their work to the arbitration of pre-set rules. The clearest examples of this were in relation to the procedure for random allocation, and the termination of the social support when the babies were born. Because of the experimental design of the study, and the timing of the 'informed consent' procedure, the research midwives were also led to reflect – more, perhaps, than researchers in many other kinds of research – about the ways in which taking part in research may subtly and not so subtly influence the lives of those who agree to do so. Their reflections on the extent to which the study's design meant that women allocated to the control group may have both felt in receipt of support initially and then deprived of it are particularly interesting from the viewpoint of assessing the 'success' of the study. As noted earlier by designing the study in this way, so as to inform the control group for ethical reasons, we may well have minimized differences between intervention and control groups, and thus reduced our chances of establishing a 'statistically significant' impact of social support. (Conversely, of course, a 'deprivation' response on the part of some control group women may have worsened outcome and increased intervention – control group differences.)

Through the medium of the midwives' experiences, the SSPO study throws a good deal of light on the way in which the maternity services currently operate in the four areas where the study was done. Much of this is no surprise to anyone who is acquainted with the 'consumer satisfaction' literature. As the research midwives reported, the maternity services may too often consist of different professionals giving conflicting information and advice, the results of which can increase women's stress. This is particularly the case for a group already exposed to stress, as many of the women in the SSPO study were by virtue of their obstetric histories and current social and medical circumstances. In these respects, the findings of the SSPO study simply confirm other studies – both descriptive surveys of childbearing women's attitudes, and other intervention studies such as the trial of the 'Know Your Midwife' scheme which show the contribution that continuity of care can make to the health of women and babies (Flint and Poulengeris 1987). In addition, our study shows how the research role of generalized social supporter can be preferred by women to the scrutiny of social workers and health visitors, who are often seen as surveilling and monitoring, rather than as helping mothers in their childcare work.

The research midwives said their eyes had been opened through the research – to what it is really like trying to have a baby in conditions of poverty; to how it really feels waiting in line in an antenatal clinic, attempting unsuccessfully to obtain consistent information about one's care, and being treated to unrealistic admonitions about how to behave in pregnancy, as though pregnant women have nothing else to do apart from attend antenatal clinics and listen to health professionals. Visiting the women's homes was seen as particularly crucial to this altered vision. It is a well-known observation that institutional structures and systems can often be subversive of the goals they were set up to meet. As one of the research midwives in the SSPO study put it, 'What I was doing as research was only what I was trained to do.'

8

Four Women

In the social division of labour the work of articulating the local and
particular existence of actors to the abstracted conceptual mode of ruling
is done typically by women. (Smith 1987: 81)

One basic dilemma of social research concerns the aggregation of data.
Combining information from different sources and different individuals is
necessary in order to arrive at a composite picture; indeed, this is the
essence of the 'quantitative' method. But, in the process of doing this, the
uniqueness of individual standpoints – the core of the 'qualitative' method
– is sacrificed. People become numbers. The consequences of this process
for the women who took part in the SSPO study are outlined in chapter 9,
which reproduces the paper reporting the main quantitative findings
published in the *British Journal of Obstetrics and Gynaecology* in 1990.
Accompanying this paper in chapter 9 is a text exploring the notion of
'hard' data which is so often held up as a distinguishing mark of the
quantitative method. But the contrast between differently textured data –
the 'hard' data of one method, the 'soft' data of the other – is linked with
other issues, including that of the use of statistical tests. What is 'significant'
according to statistical tests may be a product – an artefact – of the
aggregative method. It may be a 'chance' finding, of no significance in
terms of the personal meaning of everyday life. People themselves may
speak of connections between aspects of their lives which are not revealed
by tests of statistical significance. In this sense, 'qualitative' material is able
to uncover the nature of social processes – why and how variables are
linked the way they 'are'. It may also, of course, suggest ideas to be
explored by manipulating and testing quantitative data – ideas which
spring from the sociological imagination rather than from the preformed
templates of the statistical method.

One necessity in dissolving the dichotomy between quantitative and
qualitative research methods is to reframe the relationship between
aggregated data and individual standpoints as *dialectical*. The two stand in
relation to one another as equal participants in a conversation; now one
speaks, then another. Each listens, and responds to the other's point of

view. Positions shift, as what is heard results in changes of viewpoint. What is being said at the end of the conversation is different from what was said at the beginning.

The material in this chapter represents one side of the conversation, complementing the position represented in chapter 9, and the experiences of the research midwives described in the previous chapter. The chapter contains four case-studies, selected from a possible total of 509, according to the following criteria: (1) there should be one from each of the four geographical areas included in the study; (2) they should be selected from the intervention group, in order to give a fuller picture of just what 'giving social support' means; and (3) they should exemplify and expand on a number of critical themes both within the study and outside it, that is, from within the frame of reference within which the SSPO study was, itself, 'conceived'. These themes concern the social and medical construction of women's reproductive bodies and social selves. Particular issues relate to the appropriation of women's domestic labour by the privatized family, the material (under)resourcing of women as mothers, the commodification of the female body and of reproduction by the medical system, and the ownership of expert knowledge about reproduction and motherhood. It is not women in patriarchal culture who 'know' about motherhood, but health professionals, who in line with their instructed positions construe women as ignorant and culpably resistant to the (supposed) benefits of professionalized medical knowledge.

The four women whose voices are heard in this chapter are Joy Digby, Jenny Frame, Carol Slater and Penny Tanner. Three of them live in poverty, and for these women one of the most painful tasks of motherhood is to provide materially for their children within a framework that makes adequate provision impossible. The fourth woman, Penny Tanner, is comfortably off in a material sense, but she is handicapped by a sense of low emotional wellbeing, is unhappy about feeling confined to the home, and about her feelings of guilt in relation to this. Two of the women became mothers very young. One – Carol Slater – has an unusual list of different reproductive losses. These different biographies are inserted into a frame which exposes the raw nature of maternal caring in a culture which sets up people other than mothers as arbiters of 'standards' of mothering work.

Most of the material used in the case-studies is taken from the tape-recorded interactions between the study women and the research midwives. Other sources of data are also drawn on, including the midwives' notes, the 'problem file' kept in London, transcripts of meetings, and the women's self-completed six-week and one-year questionnaires.

'They just won't let me have the chance'

Name: Joy Digby.

Age: 24.

Occupation: Has never been in paid employment.

Living arrangements: Husband, Jim (a steel fixer), and one son aged
9, Robin.

Material circumstances: Caravan, 32 ft by 10 ft, on caravan site. One
room, with kitchen and bathroom facilities. Telephone. Husband
has car, Joy can't drive. Weekly household income £106–25.

Mothering history: Son born LBW when Joy was 15. Concealed
pregnancy. Two miscarriages at 8 weeks, one year and five years
ago.

This pregnancy: Son born at 37 weeks weighing 3100 g. Some
problems after birth with feeding, hypoglycaemia, jaundice,
hypothermia.

The research midwife visited Joy in her caravan, which was damp, and cold
in winter: the family is waiting to be rehoused. The first home visit began
with a conversation about what had happened when Joy had had her first
child. Joy had conceived at the age of 15 while still at school, and had
concealed the pregnancy, later lying about the dates so her family would
not know whose baby it was: the baby's father had been in and out of
prison. Her parents' initial reaction on finding out about the pregnancy
had been to throw her out of the family home, though they took her back
later. Joy says she was crying through most of the pregnancy, and that may
have been what caused her son to be born early. She did not tell the baby's
father about the baby until after Robin was born: 'I wouldn't let him have
anything to do with it, he's a troublemaker, he's no good. I'd be terrified if
he got – you know, if he ever managed to take him or anything happened
to me and he got custody.' She said that what she had needed during that
pregnancy and birth was 'Somebody to explain things. Nobody ever has
the time to explain . . . Nobody told me why he was born early, nobody
explained whether it was my fault, their fault, or anything, you know I
didn't know whether it was because I'd got so big I couldn't stretch any
more, I just couldn't understand why he was born.' After the baby was
born, 'My mum and dad took over, they wanted to adopt him. They told me
that they could give him a better life than I could, they told me I wasn't
bringing him up right and that I couldn't look after him.' The midwife
asked: 'Do you think it would have helped if you had had a boyfriend who
was more responsible and sort of helping you and supporting you?

J: No, 'cos I felt wonderful that I had – I could give him all my love, I didn't
have to worry about giving anybody else any . . .

RMW3: What about your friends, what did they think about it?

J: Some of them were very embarrassed, you know, they wouldn't walk along the road with me, their parents had told them that, you know, Robin was a bastard, that was the actual word ... and they didn't want their children going round with somebody that's got one, you know ...

There was three of the girls that had had abortions by the time they were 15 ... nobody else had to know about it ... whereas everybody knew that I had had a baby, because, well, I showed him off ... I loved him.

Joy lived with her parents for the first two years. She had a 'nervous breakdown' when Robin was 2:

J: I belted him, that's why I got a social worker ... I slapped him so hard, I knocked him from one side of the room to the other.

RMW3: You were just so tired?

J: I just couldn't stand no more, I was being told, you know, you mustn't smack him, you mustn't touch him, you mustn't do this, you mustn't take him out in the rain, you mustn't take him unless you have got – it was horrible. I don't think anybody that is that age should stay at home when they have had a baby.

RMW3: Oh, I know, it's very hard, isn't it ...

J: They got my grandparents to have the baby for two weeks and they put me on Valium, which really hurt me because I didn't have him, and I felt they were taking over even more (*laughs*). But the Valium, I couldn't care less. Which didn't do a lot of good, because as soon as I come off that I wanted more of them.

When Robin was 4, Joy and he moved into a bedsit: 'I just couldn't stand it no more, I used to go crying to the council, you know, please help me. I used to cry to everybody and they had just had enough of me. They put me in a bedsit in the end.'

As a baby, Robin had been in special care for three or four weeks, with breathing and feeding problems. The research midwife asked how he was now:

J: I think that – I'm convinced that – they put a thing on his head to monitor his heart and I'm convinced it's done something to him.

RMW3: Really, why?

J: He's partly dyslexic, only they won't actually state that he's dyslexic, apparently they can't determine it exactly at that age ... it could be a reading problem. And the fact that he writes everything backwards and forwards, and he reads it, and puts it down and he thinks he's copied it exact I'm sure. You know, he could draw a car, a couple of cars, and it comes out really well. He'll spell to you verbally and it's lovely and he writes it down and it's terrible (*laughs*).

RMW3: Oh, gosh.

J: And he's partly deaf ... I'm sure that's something to do with being born early ... I have asked and asked but nobody has ever told me whether it is or not.

RMW3: I can't think of any reason why it should be to do with the electrodes and things they put on, but . . .

J: I didn't even know what they were for . . . I thought they were breaking my waters, and the next thing I knew was that he was born with this suction thing on his head . . . he's got a scar there now . . . I don't know what it was, it was to do with the heartbeat, I'm sure.

RMW3: It probably was, they do, they put a little wire on there, just so they can hear how he's doing, you know, to make sure his heart is beating OK.

They moved on to discuss the present pregnancy, which was planned:

> We talked about it before we got married, I told him that there's no way I was just staying with Robin, and there was no way that if he started treating this baby wonderfully and Robin funny, that's it, he's out (*laughs*). I love him, but I mean there's no way I could ever love anybody, you know, family or anybody, the way I love Robin.

The research midwife asked about her medical care so far during this pregnancy:

> (*laughs*) Well it's bloody awful, isn't it? I mean they told me I wasn't pregnant . . . I went to the doctor's . . . I thought I was pregnant . . . 'cos I'd been being sick . . . and I had a spot of blood in my pants . . . and he said, oh, I can't see you're pregnant, your womb is closed, you know, he gave me an internal, and he gave me some cough syrup and that was it . . . And I carried on being sick . . . he was horrible, the doctor, really.

The hospital didn't fare much better:

J: I mean I want to know whether my baby is healthy, everybody does, don't they? . . . He had a go at me for not knowing about the stitches and that. That curled me up, oh, I loved that . . .

RMW3: What was that about, the stitches?

J: He asked me how many stitches I had with Robin, and I said – I told him I'd been torn and that, because – they cut me into one, I don't know what the technical medical terms is, I just know they cut the two parts into one passageway to pass the baby through.

RMW3: And then had to stitch you up?

J: But I don't know, I suppose I must have had internal stitches as well as external, mustn't I?

RMW3: Probably.

J: But I don't know, I fell asleep, the man was quite happily there whistling away while he stitched me up, he was singing Christmas carols. I ask you, in April (*laughs*), and he got all this green on, and I felt like a Christmas tree, you know, I just needed a star on each leg (*laughs*). I just fell asleep while he was doing that, they took my baby away so I never had nothing to stay awake for.

RMW3: And he had a go at you because you didn't know how many stitches you had?

J: I don't know whether he was having a go, or whether he was just abrupt, or – he just seemed so nasty.

Joy feels healthy in this pregnancy, though very tired. Owing to lack of space in the caravan, she has to sleep on a single bed with her husband. Talking of sleeping:

RMW3: Do you find that now you're pregnant you and your husband have problems with sex, like?

J: He does, I don't (*laughs*).

RMW3: You have gone off the idea, have you?

J: Oh, I don't mind it, you know (*laughs*). I don't mind, that's part of marriage, isn't it?

RMW3: He's not very happy at the minute?

J: Oh, he's totally turned off.

RMW3: Really:

J: He is totally. He wants it, but he thinks my body is totally obnoxious (*laughs*).

RMW3: Really, because you're pregnant?

J: Mm. He still loves me, he loves the baby. He won't put his hand on it. I have actually felt the baby moving about, you know. You see, it's very strange, it's not very often and it's not very much but it's – you get, it's like a tiny ripple, isn't it?
He's terrified (*laughs*). I think it's going to be terrible, he's going to be scared to death to touch it.

RMW3: He's not used to babies?

J: No.

RMW3: You'll have a lot of looking after with him as well as the baby.

J: He thinks the nipples and things like that, he thinks they're disgusting, because they're about three times the size of normal, and you know the little spots around it, they have come up, so he thinks they're totally revolting . . .

RMW3: Oh gosh, how do you feel about that?

J: Oh, I went mad at first. I don't know, it can change your entire nature doesn't it, being pregnant. I was two ways, I would cry or I would shout and scream . . . It was funny, it was the day after you had phoned me to ask if everything was all right – no the day – yes, you asked if everything was all right and I said, yes, fine and that, and the very next day I kicked him out (*laughs*). So he went for about three or four hours . . . it hurt, oh it really did, it still hurts a bit now – now that he doesn't . . .

RMW3: That he doesn't want you at the minute?

J: Well, he wants me but . . .

RMW3: But not the way you are.

J: Yes. It really hurts, because I mean I love it, I love being able to feel the baby and it's nice . . .

RMW3: It's strange, isn't it? It's probably because he's scared of everything, he doesn't understand.

J: I don't know. Sometimes I feel he's worried about hurting me.

Joy's other worries about her husband concern his friends, and the possibility of his becoming involved in drug-taking:

> I mean he's only 21 and he's very mature . . . but people offer him things . . . I would go mad if he did . . . if I found out about it. But I'm pretty sure that he has. And I don't like it . . . I have seen people do it and you know, I have actually seen people go round shaking because they need a fix, and I hate it, I really hate it.

Aside from that, there is the problem of housing, and of the need for companionship:

> RMW3: Thinking of this pregnancy, can you think of anything else you'd like – any kind of care or support that you're not having that you would like this time round?
> J: I'd love it if people had more time for you.
> RMW3: Yes, time to sort of sit and chat, well, like this . . .
> J: I wouldn't mind if it was only for ten or fifteen minutes, but just somebody that had the time to talk. Not just weight, books, belly (*laughs*).
> RMW3: What about your family . . .?
> J: I just – I feel that I should be making a home and a nursery and I want somewhere to do it in, I want everything to be perfect, I want to be able to get everything, I couldn't possibly put a cot in here, you know, and I want to start, you know, home building. Do you know what I mean?
> RMW3: Yes.
> J: I want everything to be right, and I know we've got the money and we can do it, and they just won't let me have the chance, you know, it's like somebody is actually stopping me.
> RMW3: And what about actually looking after the housework and the washing and things, do you find that . . .
> J: I would love it if somebody gave me a hand (*laughs*). I'm just so tired that – I mean it would be nice if – my little Robin helps me lovely, but I would love it if somebody just came round and did that, you know, I'll sit here and talk to you while you get it done, you know.

The research midwife reported on this visit to the study secretary in London, who wrote in her 'problem file':

> RMW3 visited this lady who lives in a mobile home in wood. Probs: only has one bed, husband sleeping on the floor. Carries hot ashes around because they only have coal fire . . . Husband v. immature . . . Threw husband out once, and also turned on an ex-boyfriend and threatened him with a knife. Can be aggressive. Query re husband: drugs problem? Also probs re money – going on drugs?

By the time of the second interview, the research midwife's notes record a urinary infection and Jim's involvement in a road traffic accident. The relationship between Joy and Jim is worse:

Poor relationship with husband at present. She feels he's immature and uncaring. Says she wishes she'd not married him. Recently had a fight (physical) and he walked out – came back later. Not the first time she's hit him (tried to phone me when that occurred). He recently had a RTA [road traffic accident] – says he's got loss of memory of the event – she feels he knows it was his fault and is pretending not to remember. She says he's having less contact with his friends who take drugs illegally, but he threatens to have 'other women' when they fight. Most of her friends refuse to come and visit if he's here. Joy's worried that his 15-year-old brother is involved in either drugs or drinking – he's also stealing. Tells me that her father (a Romany) used to beat her and her mother, and she was often left alone in the house or locked in a car outside a pub in the evenings ... Severe financial problems, just not eligible for benefits. Have promised her some maternity clothes.

The family have also been promised a house before the baby arrives, and are applying for Family Income Supplement – the research midwife is to provide forms.

The second interview is in December, and there are icycles on the curtains inside the caravan. Jim is still uncomfortable with the reality of pregnancy:

He just can't stand the idea of it, it's something moving in there, he says it's like – you know, it's not, it doesn't feel right feeling something moving under somebody's skin, he says it feels horrible, it gives him the creeps ... I think he's been watching too many horror films. And waiting for the aliens to burst out (*laughs*).

The research midwife asks Joy if she's going to any antenatal classes, and Joy says no, the only ones in her area are at the GP's surgery, 'but the [women] all come from large houses and they drive me barmy'. They discuss Joy's health, and her encounters at the hospital:

J: The midwife's said my weight's up to me, as long as you think you can get rid of it afterwards and you're healthy with it, she doesn't – she says it's OK. But the doctor said about it ...
RMW3: Oh, I think he must have read your card wrong, I don't think you've done too badly at all.
J: He's the one that keeps on about things ...
RMW3: No, that's right, he's in a different world, isn't he, that one. Oh dear.
J: He's quite a nice doctor. He had a little girl that died of – what was it? – meningitis.
RMW3: Did he?
J: A long time ago, you know. He's quite a nice doctor because he understands other people's worry about their children.
RMW3: Oh, that's quite nice, isn't it?
J: But you know, he's not too – I don't like him as a grown-up doctor, I like him for the children.

RMW3: Yes, it's funny, you often get them like that, you find GPs – you find you like them for your children, but not for yourself.

The interview has become a conversation, interspersed with points at which the research midwife remembers to refer to the interview schedule and ask a question. For example:

RMW3: Do you think you've been more irritable than usual recently?

J: Probably (*laughs*).

RMW3: It's difficult not to be when you're feeling tired, isn't it?

J: You get to the state with it – one minute you think everything – sort of more things than usual – will go washing over you, and you don't mind, and the next minute you're snapping at all the little things.

RMW3: That's right, it's so hard.

J: I think I'm just a horrible person.

RMW3: No, you're not. You're a normal nice person. Now, what about the medical care you've had so far? How often have you been to the hospital now – is it just the once?

J: Twice, if you count the scan. They're really rude there when they give you a scan.

RMW3: Really?

J: I kept trying to find out what was happening, you know, I saw the baby's head and I was so excited, it does sound silly, doesn't it, but . . .

RMW3: Oh no.

J: Well, you know, it's like having the baby for the first time, you feel all this love and that, and you ask them things and that, and they're so rude and blunt, you know (*laughs*). And you say is there just the one there? Of course there is, and you think, oh God.

RMW3: Well, there's no need for that, is there?

J: And the heart, and the things like that. I asked what it was, it was kidneys, isn't it, down here, that show up? And I asked what it was in there and she sort of – she seemed like I should know.

RMW3: Silly woman.

J: You know, I kept asking, it is normal, isn't it? There is – everything's there? And she was, you know, she was really out of patience, she wasn't –

RMW3: Was she a little on the heavy side with short hair?

J: With short dark hair, yes.

RMW3: That's the only one round there who's like that, unfortunately.

J: She got this screen about half a mile off my tummy and just pinched it, it was freezing, it was horrible, and you are all sort of – I mean you haven't had a wee all morning (*laughs*).

About antenatal care in general:

J: I think it would be nice if they had a little bit more time . . . it doesn't help you, you get your coat off, sort of jump on the scales, jump on a bed, pull your sleeve up, you know it is, all the time you are . . .

RMW3: Yes.

J: You know, you've got questions lined up and you don't have time to ask them.

The research midwife discusses the general level of help and support Joy has:

RMW3: What about the other sort of – I know you're getting help from people like social services and that sort of thing, could you do with more help from them, or . . .

J: Well, they don't really do anything. I've decided to give up on them. I have tried but – you know, they made me feel ten times worse when I came out than when I went in, so I won't bother again.

RMW3: Especially as it's so important to you to get your housing right, isn't it? To get that sorted out.

J: I ended up crying in there, and she looked at me as though I was mad, you know. I didn't mean to, it was just the way – you sound so silly, don't you? . . . I think some people just don't understand, you know, they haven't got children.

RMW3: No, that's right, it's different, isn't it?

J: It's a shame you can't have a thing that – all women should have at least one baby (*laughs*).

By the third interview, the research midwife's notes record other difficulties to do with life in the caravan (fumes from the fire), and with Joy's young brother-in-law and Jim's friends, who are using the car without permission. She observes that Joy and Jim's friends are mostly 'bikers', and that Joy is very philosophical about one dying recently – this 'often happens' from accidents on bikes or from drugs. She notes that Joy 'Can't forgive her parents for trying to insist on adopting Robin'.

Despite all this, Joy is enjoying the pregnancy: 'I love laying there – you know I lay down in the afternoon and read a book or something, and I love laying there feeling it kicking, you know I love it.' Housing remains a problem. For example:

J: I think in a house at least you've got room to breathe. This place, it's dirty.

RMW3: Well, you're doing all you can, aren't you?

J: I used to bring my bowl in here and wash all this out every morning and do the fireplace because it looks all dirty, doesn't it, you know, it looks all sort of dusty and ashy, but I can't do it now, it gets too much, if I do it every day it gets so wearing.

RMW3: Whereas, if you were in a house, you could shut the door and not look at it, couldn't you?

J: Yes, you're stuck. It would be so nice to just get out and stay out for the day, I hate being here . . . I went and sat out on the step the other day, they all thought I was barmy, I sat there having a cup of tea (*laughs*).

RMW3: Oh, I don't blame you.

J: Well, I'd had enough of being in here. Can you imagine being here all day:

RMW3: It would drive me round the bend.

J: I've been here for seven years.

But it is difficult for Jim to visit the council to put pressure on them to provide rehousing, 'because he works from – usually he starts fairly early in the morning, and doesn't finish sometimes till 7, 8 o'clock ... I'm trying to get Jim's dad to go down there again, because he's something to do with the council. I told you, didn't I?'

RMW3: That's right, to see if he can do anything.

J: Well, I think he can frighten them into giving us somewhere ... His mum went down there yesterday.

RMW3: Really?

J: 'You've forgotten to sign your card sent in to be stamped, which should have been done the first of last month.' I had forgot about it, I was so worried about a house I forgot all about this card, so Jim's mum gone in there. That's it, she says, they can't find you a house but they can look at your bloody books to find you haven't – you know they were going to throw us off the council list after ten days!

RMW3: How ridiculous!

J: I mean we really do need to be taken off the list, don't we?

RMW3: It's so silly, isn't it?

J: I definitely think we'll still be here when the baby's born.

RMW3: Really?

J: The doctors say it's no good them writing any more because they – you know, they've tried it for different people before and nothing happens. They're all willing to write letters but if it's no good it's no good them writing, is it? It's a waste of their time.

RMW3: What about your health visitor, is she any good?

J: I told you what she said, didn't I?

RMW3: Yes, that's right, she's not going to be any good at all, is she? I'd forgotten about her.

J: Yes, it was so cold in the war they had to put hoods on them, you could do that in here, your husband *will* be able to sleep with you after the baby's born, won't he?

RMW3: It must be pretty difficult both of you sleeping in a single bed when you're not pregnant, never mind the baby.

J: Oh, it isn't very easy ...

RMW3: Do you feel you're under any [other] stress at all at the moment?

J: Apart from the housing, you get it worse from other people, you know, the housing people, they make you feel you're doing something that you're not meant to be doing, and that doctor, he really upset me, I was upset for a long time.

RMW3: Your GP?

J: That really upset me, I mean I was really shocked – as soon as he said that, that was it, I really thought I was going to have the baby and that it was going to die and – do you know what I mean, I told you what he said, didn't I?

RMW3: About the baby being small?

J: I was going to phone you up, and you phoned me, can you remember?

RMW3: Was that when the baby was small?

J: He told me that if it was born it would die, it stood no chance.

RMW3: Because he also said to you ...

J: All I asked was – what sort of size, you know, meaning – and he sort of said of about that size, but it wouldn't you know, and how many chances of living and how long it would be before it stood a chance of really living – I don't want to know the percentages and that, all I wanted to know was whether it was small, medium or . . . I just wanted to know – just roughly for the time I am to – well, it's of interest, isn't it, it's your body and you're carrying the baby and you made it, and you want to know a little about it, you know . . . I was crying for the week, you know, it just really sort of dragged me down.

RMW3: I am surprised.

J: And Mum – she said, 'The old sod', you know, she really got on her high horse about it . . . I don't want to know about infant mortality and . . .

RMW3: No, that's right. And if you're perfectly calm before, it's enough to put your blood pressure up.

J: I mean, I like reading books that are slightly on the medical side but not – I mean I wouldn't buy a medical journal simply because they tell you the bad mostly, I mean who wants to read about the bad bits, I want to read about the good bits (*laughs*).

Joy is frightened of having a Caesarean this time 'because my pelvis wasn't really very big last time, though I'm sure it must have grown since then!' The research midwife tries to reassure her:

RMW3: If you can push a baby out when you're 15, and didn't even know what labour was and were terrified, you're probably going to sail through, it will probably be so much easier this time.

J: Well, the funny thing is it only took about four hours from start to finish.

RMW3: That's right. I'm sure you'll be all right.

J: This time I should be able to get it down to an hour and a half! (*laughs*) . . . I've been threatening to phone everybody up if Jim can't get there, I'm not going on my own.

RMW3: No, well, I'll come with you if you're stuck . . . I'll tell you what we'll do, have you got . . .

J: I've got your name in there as well, I've got my diary, all the names and work numbers.

RMW3: Great. And you've got your mum's and you know everyone else's, so . . .

J: There's bound to be somebody.

RMW3: Have you got my pager number as well?

About a month after this, the problem file records that Joy rang the research midwife at 12.40 one night to say she might be in labour, with contractions every twenty minutes. After talking to her, the midwife went back to bed, 'but couldn't sleep any more, and also her son woke up and didn't want to go back to sleep! Rang again next day, all OK, quietened down after the phone call!' Joy gave birth to a normal-weight boy at 36 weeks. There were some problems with his health after birth – he had hypoglycaemia, jaundice and hypothermia, and had to be tube-fed for a while.

In total the research midwife made four home visits to Joy and spoke to her on the telephone seven times: this added up to nine and a half hours of contact. The research midwife summarized the contact:

> Joy had several major problems and seemed pleased to be able to talk about them to someone. I felt she was fairly naive about pregnancy and needed (and wanted) a lot of basic information. She was always so worried that she was 'putting you out' or phoning at an inconvenient time, I felt she was quite lonely and liked having someone to chat to.

In her postnatal questionnaire, Joy circled positive answers to the questions about the research midwife's intervention: her visits were 'just right', it was 'a good idea' to be able to contact her by phone at any time, she was 'very glad to hear her when she called'. She circled 'Don't know' against questions about the impact of the intervention on the baby's birthweight or her pregnancy experiences in general. The most helpful people during the pregnancy were her 9-year-old son and the research midwife. A year later the follow-up questionnaire recorded low emotional wellbeing, and complaints about Jim being unhelpful with the children and generally unsupportive: they had separated and got back together again; he had changed jobs and had problems at work; and they had, finally, been rehoused. Her memories of the research midwife's help were still positive: 'I loved it.'

'Money doesn't solve problems'

Name: Penny Tanner.
Age: 32.
Occupation: Part-time librarian.
Living arrangements: Husband, Lloyd (company director), one son, Sam, aged 2.
Material circumstances: Own house, paid domestic help, own car, weekly household income over £200.
Mothering history: First son born prematurely three years ago, died six hours after birth; second son born at term weighing 2840 g.
This pregnancy: Healthy girl born at term weighing 3280 g.

According to the 'problem file', when the research midwife recruited Penny for the study:

> she was very enthusiastic – fortunately allocated into INT group. RMW also delighted. Previously had baby that died at 6 hours in 1984. Another baby in 1985. Said to RMW: 'I want so much to talk about what has happened, even though I have had another baby since, I have never had the opportunity to talk about it until now.'

Penny was 17 weeks pregnant when the research midwife did her first
home visit. In the detailed account Penny gave of the circumstances
leading up to the birth and death of her previous baby, the straightforward
recitation of events is interwoven with the reliving of powerful feelings:

> I went to the toilet and that's when I lost a clot of blood, dark . . . then I knew
> it was really wrong, and I went off to hospital and got there about 3 o'clock
> . . . They didn't seem too concerned at the time. I was 36 weeks, and a
> premature baby then isn't so drastic. They gave me some injections and . . . I
> can remember they told Lloyd to go home . . . and then I just lay there
> watching the clock. It was dreadful . . . I could hear this woman screaming
> next door, it was just awful. Everytime I said something, 'I'm sure it's only a
> stomach upset . . . it's not really happening', they just stood there and looked
> at me, as if to say, 'Poor girl, she doesn't realize!' I felt so, sort of, stupid.
> Anyway, I was dozing off, but every time a contraction came I woke up again
> . . . and they were getting stronger and stronger. They gave me pethidine, I
> was as high as a kite, they couldn't wake me up to push, in the end they cut
> me . . . I can remember it was very uncomfortable . . . actually the doctor it
> was, it was a doctor, not a midwife, actually had to reach in and pull him out
> . . . I had a quick look and he went off . . . they took him off in an incubator
> into intensive care. He only weighed 3½ lb . . . very small for a nearly full-
> term, isn't it? And they took me to a room of my own [and] brought me in
> pictures of him in the incubator.

Penny is distressed here, crying gently, while she tells the midwife about
how the baby was transferred to another hospital with better intensive care
facilities:

> I haven't talked about his death for a long time . . . he had been christened . . .
> the priest had come in and said would you like him christened . . . and I
> knew that was a bad sign . . .
> He died because his lungs weren't fully developed, and they had to keep
> puncturing his chest to release the pressure . . . I can't help wondering if I
> had been in a hospital where they had the nursing facilities available, and he
> didn't have to be moved, it would have been different . . . it's always there at
> the back of my mind, wondering whether it would have been different if
> they hadn't had to transfer him to different equipment.

Penny had puzzled on what had caused her son's death, but she couldn't
think of anything, apart from shifting furniture and a general feeling that
she was unfit for motherhood:

> P: It's as if I was too greedy. My body was too greedy, if I hadn't starved it, it
> would have been all right.
> RMW2: What do you mean, starved it?
> P: Well, he was so ratty-looking and thin and weak . . . as if I hadn't been
> feeding him . . . I know it's totally irrational, but when Sam was born and
> he was so skinny as well, I thought, oh God, here we go again! I was too

arrogant ... it wasn't exactly a punishment, but that was the other thing, when we discussed having the baby and decided to get pregnant, I disagreed ... we had been married for six years ... we used the house like a hotel ... we were always out, out for the day, racing or something, visiting, anything, just not in, the only time we were home was when we were decorating ... and we decided that I was 28 and if we were going to have children, now was the time to do it. But all the way through the pregnancy there was this feeling ... I know it's the sort of thing that most women probably go through, but I wasn't totally convinced I was doing the right thing ... It was if perhaps in a way I had wished it to happen ... It's like wishing somebody dead who you have had a row with and they die, and you think, oh my God, what did I do? It's just how I feel. I've never actually told my husband that before, I don't think he'd understand. I don't think they do somehow, or, if they do understand, they don't want to tell you they understand in case they sort of feed your fears.

After the baby was born:

P: I stayed at home for a while and I cried into the sink ... I suppose it was just an acute form of baby blues ... everything getting back to normal and nothing to take your mind off it ...
RMW2: Was there anything you felt you needed in the way of support during that time you didn't have?
P: I did have a health visitor visiting me, but at that time I was being tremendously brave and I couldn't unlock anything to anybody because I would have totally collapsed ... I'm not the sort that reaches out, I'm more the sort that builds barriers, even to family, because I can't be upsetting anybody else either (*weeping*).

Penny's own guilt and self-blame resonate with her mother's history:

My mum lost a lot of children and she blamed herself, she thought she'd passed something on to me, so I couldn't talk to her ... I didn't want anyone to look after me, I wanted them to look after the people who needed it, and I don't think I need it ... What I really needed was a good friend.

Later on the research midwife asks Penny whether she has got over the baby's death now:

P: No, I can't get rid of the guilt. I rationalize it. I know it's ... totally unreasonable, and all that, but it's there, it's a feeling ... it must have been something I did ... or didn't do, and should have done or shouldn't have done ...
RMW2: What about this pregnancy?
P: I'm really happy about this one ... I'm happy I'm having it. I suppose it's because you come from a two-child family, you feel two children is right.
RMW2: When you first knew about this pregnancy, was there anything in particular you thought about?

P: Yes, my age, 32 ... and it always seems to me as soon as I get pregnant there's loads of programmes on the television that I accidentally watch, you know that start telling you all sorts of nasty things ... when I was having Sam it was scans can be dangerous and I thought, look at all those scans I had when I had Michael ... oh my God, is that wrong? ... once you lose [a child] you feel like you're on a proving ground ... you want to prove you can do it, you want that child, not possessively, but like a gift ... all during Sam's pregnancy I thought if anything happens to this one, that's it, I'm not having any more, we've got busy lives, we can cope, we won't fall apart, the marriage won't go particularly wrong, we've managed for six years, we'll be all right.

Despite this practical approach, Penny is highly anxious about the future:

I have felt this irrational fear, a friend's mother died a week ago, but that wasn't what sparked me off, because I have this totally irrational fear of being alone for a long while ... I am alone, there is no one else there, I've got this totally irrational fear of people dying on me ... I invent things to happen to people ... I have to phone my mum when she leaves here, to make sure she gets home OK ... if Lloyd's late I really panic, as soon as anybody does anything different from what they are supposed to do, I'm sure they've had an accident.

At the second home visit about three months before the expected birth, Penny is still very anxious. The focus of her concern is the effect of her lifestyle on the baby. Is it dangerous to go out to work, even part-time? What impact will the occasional drink have? This is combined with a general feeling of not being able to cope with the child she does have, and guilt at not enjoying being a mother at home:

P: I have terrible difficulty sorting problems out, stupid problems, silly problems, but they're not specific worries, they're day-to-day problems, and they stop me going to sleep. I've got several ways of dealing with it. Sometimes I make up a story and put myself in it. When I was young, it used to be fairy-tales and heroines, that's funny, isn't it? ... Stick yourself in a story, you know, Mills and Boons stuff ...
   I'm frightened very much of being alone. I'm very worried about that.
RMW2: Why are you frightened of being alone?
P: My temper's a bit short, I can't take it out on him, I have felt violent every now and again. I did more when he was younger and couldn't make himself understood. I'm very impatient. I can't cope with as much this time as I would hope. I've never been tremendously involved with small children, and everything seems to be ... too much trouble ... even just getting out of bed is too much of an effort. (*Child shouting, 'Mummy, Mummy, Mummy', all the way through the tape recording.*) ... It's really quite awful, because I'm going to work when I don't need to so that I get away from him, and I feel guilty, I want to spend time with him.
RMW2: Don't feel guilty about it.
P: It's getting worse, and, well, I've found myself thinking that I'm not living

day-to-day as I should ... the more it stretches out, this terrible feeling of not wanting to be here on my own with him, I can see it stretching into the distance and it's making me worse ... whereas if I just live for the day it would be easier ... Normally I'm active mentally and not physically, and now I've got to change round and do things with him that are physical that he can enjoy because ... he's not one for sitting down and reading a book ... he wants to be outside, and I'm not that sort of person. So I'm hopeless, I can't adjust and I don't know if I can't or won't ... I know it's me that has got to change.

(At this point the person who transcribed the tape wrote, 'Penny's voice has lowered and she sounds very depressed. The child is making an incredible amount of noise, either shrieks or calls, "Mummy, Mummy", over and over again ... not surprised she's worn down by it all!')

RMW2: Does it seem worse since you've been pregnant?

P: Yes, it's a trapped feeling, that's probably what most mothers feel when they've been at work all their lives, suddenly to be back at home with a 2-year-old, and not getting much intelligent conversation. I know I could deal with it if I could just change a little ... Taking him out for a walk ... well, walking round here would be like taking your life in your own hands anyway. It's just the doing of it, the starting ... getting into a toddler group ... whenever I've mixed with other children, he tends to get violent, but I think that's because he's not used to it.

Penny talks about the limitations put on her freedom by having a child. She is adamant that she does not resent Sam for it, 'because it was my decision to have children'. It is also *her* decision to go out to work part-time, a decision which leaves her with mixed feelings:

P: I mean, Sam to a certain extent doesn't need me ... but that's a conscious road I've taken by going to work. I've left him with his grandmother at a young age ... I do get the feeling of being rejected in favour of other people, but I can't be upset about it because it's something I've consciously chosen to do ... If I had really wanted to, I could have totally cut myself off from work and been the mother my sister is, for example ...

RMW2: But that obviously isn't you.

P: No ... I don't feel I should cut myself off ... I don't see why I should vegetate in this room for four or five years ... because I'm still a person ... I don't want to repeat what happened to my parents. We grew up, we left, and they're on their own now and they have nothing, they've stopped themselves doing things they wanted to do because of us. All right, in their case they couldn't help it, they didn't have the finances. But I have got the choice, and I don't know if it's good. I mean I'm here if he needs me, I wouldn't go away and leave him if he was ill or upset or anything like that, but as long as he's healthy and happy, I feel quite easy about leaving him with other people. I think it's good for his independence, but it does hurt, it can't help hurting me ... it's the very fierce maternal love you feel for something you've created, it's very hard to feel that, and also the fact that he doesn't need you. When he's hurt he runs to his father or granny, because they pick him up quicker than I do ... It seems to me that I can't feel envy about bits of his life that don't include me when I have consciously decided to exclude him from bits of mine, which I have done by going to work and not being like the old-fashioned mother that stays at home.

Listening to Penny's concern about her ability to be an 'old-fashioned mother' who stays at home, the research midwife feels it necessary to offer some reassurance:

> RMW2: But to look at it from a different point of view, if you stayed at home all the time, you would probably be a worse mother ... They would probably get on your nerves far more.
> P: Oh yes.
> RMW2: And you might be taking it out on them. It's probably better for the children for you to go to work, get your bit of freedom, in inverted commas, and be yourself.
> P: It's not exactly freedom, is it, it's just to have another identity. I'm just Penny in the office.
> RMW2: Exactly. Not someone's mum or somebody's wife. You are you.
> P: I have got an opinion and what I say matters, which is practically non-existent in this house.
> RMW2: But that is obviously very important to you, and you are a far better mum for doing that ... than just sitting at home with the resentment building up.
> P: Oh yes, I quite agree. But it doesn't get rid of the guilt feelings either. It's a weird combination. I think that probably every working mum ...
> RMW2: Probably, yes.

The research midwife finishes Penny's sentence for her. Penny goes on:

> P: I'm probably more concerned about his health than a lot of people. It's as if I have got this baby and he's all right, there's nothing wrong with him, so something is going to happen! (*laughs*)
> RMW2: You're a pessimist, aren't you?
> P: Yes, dreadful ... apart from losing the first baby, I've not really had anything go wrong.
> RMW2: Well, don't you think that's enough? Why should you keep on looking out for things all the time?
> P: Oh, you know, the lollypop is there and someone is going to take it away from me. But whereas before I used to worry about ... material things, they don't matter any more ... a little while ago one of the guys who works for the firm, his little boy went down with meningitis, about the same age, it's not till you have had one the same age that you think, how would I feel if it was him? He's blind now, and paralysed, and he was a perfectly happy and healthy baby boy. You just pick them up and hug them

and think, thank God, don't you? ... And every time you turn on the television you hear these things about children, because you aren't allowed to let them out of your sight because somebody might come along and take them ... somebody somewhere might be careless and ... (*laughs*)

RMW2: I think we all go through that, though.

P: Oh yes.

RMW2: Would you say you're depressed at the moment?

P: I didn't think I was until somebody said you've lost interest in your appearance, and I thought about it, and I had. I really couldn't care less. I wasn't putting my make-up on, I was scruffy, buttons were falling off blouses and I wasn't putting them on, just shoving a jumper over to cover it up, totally unlike me. Usually when I go out my hair is done and my make-up is on. I wouldn't dream of being seen out without my full regalia. I don't know if that's depression or not. Because I can make the effort when I want to. I'm not perhaps as happy as I would like, but who is? (*laughs*) ...

RMW2: Have you sat down and spoken to your mum about how you feel?

P: No ...

RMW2: Is she the sort of person you could sit and talk to? ... Sometimes it helps to talk things through, and to realize that you're not ...

P: I'd rather do it with someone like you, who knows that's what other women go through.

RMW2: That's fine, that's what I'm here for. But you don't seem to phone me up.

P: No (*laughs*). Well, it's generally 3 o'clock in the morning, and it would be such a stupid reason for phoning at 3 o'clock in the morning.

RMW2: Well, that's what the study is about.

They discuss Penny's social network, and the extent to which she can call on relatives and friends for emotional support. She describes a lack of emotional intimacy: her sister is a full-time mother ('we're totally different, we're not friends'). One woman who counted as a friend is now 'definitely a career girl, so you lose the common ground': 'I've not got a female friend ... I've never had any particular friend ... I have had several friends, but no one I've really opened up to. I don't know why, it's just the way I am.'

After this visit, the midwife noted that Penny seemed very 'depressed', and that she felt she had been of some help in allowing Penny to talk about her feelings, particularly as regards her work and leaving the children. She phoned the study secretary in London, who wrote in the 'problem' file:

RMW2 phoned. Been to do interview with Penny. Says she feels inadequate to help Penny but knows how she is feeling. The lady lives in a beautiful house – no financial worries – and says no one understands why she is so miserable. Feels guilty because she works ... Her own mother lost 4 out of 6 children so she can't speak to her. Last saw the doctor who told her to put some weight on. She said to him, 'Look, I can't eat any more than I do already', and the doctor said, 'You're a stroppy girl, aren't you?' Penny walked out.

Apart from the three main home visits, the research midwife visited a fourth time in pregnancy bearing practical information about live-in childcare – because 'Penny dislikes talking on the phone and asked me to call.' The total time (including phone contacts) the two women spent together during the pregnancy was seven hours. The lengths to which the research midwife went to ensure that Penny felt supported are reflected in a note in the 'problem file' about holiday arrangements. The four research midwives paired with each other for these, so that at any one time two of the four were 'on call' to the women in all four centres:

> RMW2 telephoned me from the airport en route to California for hols to say that she had promised Penny she would contact her before she left, but hadn't been able to. I said I would contact Penny instead. Spoke to her same day on the phone and explained RMW2 had tried to reach her – very pleased I had called. I reminded her she could call RMW3 if she wanted to.

Penny had a baby girl weighing 3280 g at term, and came home three days later. The research midwife wrote on the postnatal contact form:

> Delivery – very quick and easy. Delighted with her daughter. Has gone back to work and is employing a nanny to live in. Comment made by Penny when introducing me to a friend: 'the person who helped me through my pregnancy'.

This was confirmed by Penny's answers to the postnatal questionnaire. She described the research midwife as the second most helpful person during her pregnancy (despite the reservations expressed in the interview, her mother was the most helpful), and wrote: 'The research midwife called three or four times during my pregnancy but I needed to know she was there and on my side.' About different forms of help, Penny wrote, 'Although the physical help was most welcome, I valued the support I received mentally from the midwife the most.' In answer to the question, 'Do you think that the research has affected your experience of having a baby?', she replied, 'Initially it helped by making me consider my attitude to this baby. By being able to talk about my first baby I became happier with the expectation of this one.' The aspect of the research midwife's help she valued the most was that 'she was concerned about ME, everyone else treated me as if I as an adjunct to the baby and everything I did was seen in terms of that.' She noted that feeling she was able to telephone the midwife any time made her feel secure:

> Being able to talk to someone who understood my fears and inadequacies enabled me to voice them, and face them. Before her advent I couldn't

identify my thoughts and feelings. She always made me feel better . . . I found her visits to me helped me to rid myself of fears and feelings that I could not voice to my family, as they needed me to be well and happy so that I wasn't a worry to them. They were very supportive with practical help, but if I was upset for any or no reason this seemed to be treated as a woman being silly and not something they wished to be involved with. Even my husband seemed bored with my fears. My midwife, however, listened, understood, reassured and supported my spirits and helped me to cope with the dreadful depression that seemed to be overwhelming at times. She was a safety net.

By comparison with this, Penny did not feel her experiences of medical care were supportive. Answering a question about how medical care might be improved for women in her situation, she wrote:

Apart from following advice about smoking and diet, it seems to me that the main help is not being made to feel a nuisance if you are worried. Being carefully watched as I was with my second pregnancy brought with it extra stress, and I sometimes felt I was being protected from the real opinions of the medical staff.

One year later, in the follow-up questionnaire, Penny's good opinion of the research had not receded: 'Being lucky enough to be visited, I was able to exorcize my experience of losing my first baby, which I was never allowed to do within my family. After I poured that experience out, I feel with hindsight that I was much more relaxed.' However, Penny's other problems had not disappeared either:

Rosie was an easy baby, sleeping all night almost immediately. It is the combination of her and her brother that is very trying . . . At times I have felt that I am an extension of my family and that they are tearing me apart with their demands. I want to shout, and I sometimes do, for them to leave me alone. To restore a feeling of identity I have returned to work.

The research midwife discussed Penny Tanner's situation during several of the monthly meetings that were held during the course of the study. This is what she said on the first of these occasions:

She has a beautiful home, a lake – I'm telling you this because money doesn't solve problems – it's like a showhouse. She's got one other child, and then she got pregnant, and she thought, did I want the child? It died after six hours. They come from the East End of London originally. I think that's relevant. Anyway, obviously it was a terrible shock to her. She was numb. And then, after a few months, she wanted to talk about it, and no one would let her. Her family all said, you're over it now, forget it. Her husband told her to go and get a job – that would help her to forget it. She's never to this day discussed that baby with her husband. She doesn't know how he feels. Her parents think it's very unhealthy. I used two sides for that interview. She said it was the first time she's ever been able to talk about it, it was very therapeutic. I thought, my God, what am I doing to her? She was very upset. She said that she felt very guilty that she didn't want the baby, she made it die. Nobody told her the baby was dying. She thought her husband had been told. They'd been to visit the baby because it was doing so well. And there they were waiting to see the baby, and somebody came over and said it had died. She said the only person she could have discussed it with was her mother. But her mother had had a couple of babies who'd died, and she felt she'd passed something on to her daughter for the same thing to happen. So the one person she could have talked to, she couldn't. All the money doesn't solve problems.

'When he's crying it's my fault'

Name: Jenny Frame.
Age: 17.
Occupation: (Previously) hairdresser.
Living arrangements: Partner, Pete (plasterer), one son, Gary, aged 6 months.
Material circumstances: Council flat. No telephone or car. Weekly household income £66–85. Housing benefit.
Mothering history: One son aged 6 months, born prematurely weighing 1650 g.
This pregnancy: Healthy son born at 36 weeks, 3240 g.

Jenny was 18 weeks pregnant when the research midwife asked her if she would be willing to take part in the study. The new baby was expected on her son's first birthday.

The first home visit took place a week after the research midwife first met Jenny in the hospital antenatal clinic. They discussed Jenny's current circumstances and worries, and her son's somewhat traumatic birth. Jenny didn't express much anxiety about the child now: 'I didn't feel guilty or anything, because he's all right, even though he was so small ... I think he'd had enough of being in there!' She mentioned smoking in this context, and said that other people had told her the reason the baby had been small was because she smoked. She said she would have liked more information in general from doctors during her hospital stay, and would have liked to have been with other mothers whose babies were also in special care. Though this current pregnancy had not been planned, she was happy about it, and felt generally well, although she talked about being anxious that the previous premature birth might be repeated, and how she would cope with two babies.

The research midwife's comments on meeting Jenny were that her situation was quite difficult, and she might need a good deal of support. She identified Jenny's main needs as reassurance about the progress of the pregnancy, together with information on financial benefits. She did not feel Jenny's relationship with her partner was very stable, and noted that Jenny herself had been in care until she was 14; her own mother was dead, and she had not had a good relationship with her stepmother.

At the next home visit, Jenny was 25 weeks pregnant:

> RMW4: How do you feel about the pregnancy and the baby?
> J: I'm just waiting to have it . . . obviously I'm thinking to meself, am I gonna have it, like, the same time as Gary? . . .
> RMW4: And how are you feeling physically at the moment?
> J: Tired, irritable . . . (*laughs*) very argumentative . . . it's Pete who gets me down . . . not the little 'un! It's Pete, I don't know, he just seems to niggle me over little things . . . I feel as if he thinks that I'm not doing me housework as I should . . . I feel as if I should be doing more when I feel as if I've done enough.

They discussed Jenny's physical wellbeing in more detail, and Jenny admitted that sexually 'I have gone off it! (*laughs*) . . . we do argue about it.'

> RMW4: Does he understand that it's because you're pregnant?
> J: He says he understands . . . but I feel, I just feel as if I'm not good enough. Do you know what I mean? I don't feel nice, I feel fat and ugly and . . . you know what I mean . . . and I just want it all over with so I can go to sleep.
> RMW4: Have you got any major worries at the moment?
> J: Me gas bill! . . . it'll all be paid, you know, it's just thinking, oh, the gas bill! It does get you down, doesn't it? . . . I have to have the fire on more or less all day now because you can't put baby mittens on *all* day, because he hates them anyway and he can't play with his toys.

Jenny's main physical complaints are tiredness and headaches. One of the research midwife's responses to this is to counsel her to attend for antenatal care:

> J: I haven't been to the doctor's for three months, you know! (*laughs*) I haven't been since I went to the hospital and saw you there.
> RMW4: You should go, really.
> J: I should go, yeah, but, well I don't see the point. They don't do nothing for you. OK, they check your water and . . .
> RMW4: Do your blood pressure . . .
> J: Yeah, blood pressure, but if my blood pressure was up or something I would feel bad.
> RMW4: You should try to get along to your doctor. If it's the local doctor, the community midwives are doing most of the check-ups now, and lots of ladies prefer that because they get a chance to talk about any problems they've got, they feel they're getting a better check-up.
> J: Well, with the bloke I had before, the doctor I had before, Dr Mann, I felt as if he didn't do anything, I just went and laid down and he looked at me

for a couple of seconds and that was it . . . It's £2 on the bus to get there and back, and I have to carry him as well, because I can't get his buggy on the bus . . . It is a problem . . . carrying him, because he's a lump. He weighs about a stone now.

RMW4: So having been through what you did last time with Gary, is there anything else you'd like in the way of help or care or support for the rest of this pregnancy?

J: I'd like someone just to make sure that it won't happen again, but obviously no one can do that . . . I know I'm going to be a bit worried, you know, when it comes to the time . . .

RMW4: I think you'll feel happier once you've passed your 34 weeks.

J: If I had it now would it live?

The abruptness of the question is an indication of its importance. The midwife gives Jenny an idea of the relative risks of babies being born at different stages of pregnancy, after which the conversation moves back to her domestic circumstances:

J: With housework and things like that, yes, Pete will help . . . but as far as Gary is concerned, like . . . when he's crying it's *my* fault, he won't help as far as he's concerned . . . he baths him, but he doesn't change him because he can't change nappies . . . He's never had him by himself, he always takes him somewhere, to someone else's house . . . funny that!

RMW4: What about . . . supporting you emotionally?

J: He's terrible! He's no good at all . . . he can't talk to you nice, if you try and explain it to him he hasn't got time . . .

RMW4: What about help from family and friends?

J: Well, I see me dad, but rarely, I don't get help from him . . .

RMW4: And what about friends?

J: I haven't got none! I don't mix. If I go out, I go out with Pete.

The midwife's notes on this visit describe Jenny as being isolated and obviously under stress. In addition to the problems with Pete, the baby was not well, and 'Jenny asked if I (as a mother) ever felt like hitting my baby. I said yes, which seemed to relieve her greatly. I do not think the baby is in any danger of being hurt purposely, I just think that Jenny is surprised at herself for having such feelings. (Jenny is not yet 18 years old.)'

By the third visit, seven weeks before the expected birth, Jenny is on her own. She has asked Pete to leave; he has not been giving her any money, has been drinking heavily and has been in trouble with the police.

J: I said to him last night, what do you do in the pub, why do you have to go? He says, 'I don't know' . . . he doesn't drink in moderation, he drinks and he drinks and he drinks until he's sick and he doesn't know what he's doing . . .

RMW4: When you challenge him about his drinking, what does he say?

J: He says, 'Stop nagging' and 'I go out and work for me money and I'll spend it how I like, and if I want to go drinking, I will.'

The midwife asks her how she feels about the pregnancy now:

> J: I still want it . . . but it's a challenge . . . isn't it! (*laughs*) I mean, I'm going to prove to everybody I can do it . . . I think they're saying, Cor! she'll never be able to look after two babies.
>
> RMW4: Do you think you're getting more anxious as you get towards 34 weeks?
>
> J: I'm feeling scared, yeah! (*laughs*) I was 33 [weeks] when I had him.
>
> RMW4: Was it 33? Well, this time next week you'll be able to breathe a sigh of relief, then, won't you? (*To child, 'don't chew my shoe, it's been on all those dirty pavements.'*) And how are you feeling physically?
>
> J: I was feeling tired, but since this I'm feeling better . . . I know I've got to carry on . . . I feel free in me mind now . . . Because now I know I've made me mind up . . . OK, he's going to be popping in and visiting and all that, but at the end of the day I won't have to answer to him . . . and, I don't know, I feel as if it's going to be a lot better.

When asked if there is anything she needs in the way of help or support, Jenny says she is concerned what she will do when she goes into labour. Living on her own without a phone, it will be difficult to contact the hospital and arrange to go in. Pete's sister has a friend who lives down the road,

> and they have said if I phone them they would come and pick me up and take me to the hospital and get him as well, and take him to Doreen's. But the thing is, getting to a phone. The phone is way up over there and I can't see me, well the way I was last time I couldn't even get dressed, I felt that weak I couldn't even get dressed, so how can I put him in his buggy and push him all the way up the street, especially if it's in the middle of the night?

Jenny has contracted gonnorhoea from Pete, who at first denied and then admitted being with someone else. Although she told him to go, he keeps coming back, particularly in the evenings, drunk. He urinates in the lounge and wakes the baby up. The midwife gives Jenny some advice about how to sort out her financial situation, noting that 'The house is in her name, so at least she isn't homeless.' she called the study secretary in London after this visit, and the 'problem file' records:

> 13.4.87. RMW4 called. Been to see Jenny who has no telephone and already has a 10-month-old baby, and her boyfriend has just walked out and left her. She is 32/33 weeks pregnant. Last baby delivered at 34 weeks. How can she get in touch with someone if she goes into labour? Local phone boxes all vandalized – very anxious about getting help . . . No friends or relatives locally – only been in the area since half-way through the pregnancy. Mother dead and father remarried and doesn't want to see her. Totally alone with the toddler – only 17 years old herself! Neighbours don't have phones – very

poor area. Can we find a way of getting a phone for her? RMW3 to ask brother about renting equipment – paging system, perhaps. Ringing back later.

14.4.87. RMW3 asked RMW4 if she had suggested social services to this girl, and she said she had but the lady hadn't seen her social worker for some time. RMW4 suggested she contacts her again. Said she would. RMW4 also to find out if neighbours nearby, possibly with young children, who would be able to help i.e. telephone when Jenny needs help. Can't think of anything else. Information from RMW3's brother: BT will not rent mobile phones. Only other alternative would be installing a telephone in her home, which would cost £80 plus bills. Obviously can't afford that.

Aside from the three main home visits, the research midwife called to see Jenny twice between these. A week after the last main visit, she went again, feeling that Jenny could do with more support. Pete had moved back in, and they had decided to talk to neighbours about contacting the hospital when she went into labour. The research midwife described Jenny's main needs as 'Somebody to take an interest in her, listen to her. Information on benefits.' Two weeks later when she called again Pete was still there. He was now receiving treatment for his gonorrhoea.

A few days after this, a month early, Jenny gave birth to a boy weighing 3240 g. Pete had stayed with the little boy and Jenny had got herself to the hospital. When the research midwife visited her at home two weeks later, the baby was well, though Jenny's milk 'had dried up' and she had decided to bottle-feed. Pete was still there, drinking heavily.

Jenny's postnatal questionnaire recorded dissatisfaction with the hospital:

> I think that because I was on my own a nurse should have stayed, whereas I was left on my own a lot during labour, and after the baby was born, up on the ward. I think they are not supportive enough. Even with your second baby I was scared of him at first, but nobody helps you.

She described the research midwife as the person who had been most helpful to her throughout the pregnancy, followed by 'boyfriend occasionally', and said that of all the ways in which people could help she valued 'company' and 'being able to talk' the most. She commented that it had been helpful 'knowing there was somebody there if I needed them'.

One year later, when she filled in the follow-up questionnaire, there were no obvious problems with the children's health, though Jenny herself admitted to feeling miserable and irritable, and not very satisfied with life. Now only 18 herself, she had two children aged 1 and 2 and constant money worries. She wrote that the second baby had brought problems into her relationship with Pete:

We tend to argue about having him in bed with us and little things ...
Sometimes I felt like shaking them when they were both being naughty in
the night, and not sleeping, but I just thought to myself it won't always be like
this, and I felt better then.

'If it's a boy, I just don't think I'll keep it'

Name: Carol Slater.

Age: 32.

Occupation: (Previously) office clerk.

Living arrangements: Husband, Tom (press metal worker, unemployed), and daughter, Gabrielle, aged 3.

Material circumstances: Temporary council accommodation, as
house being renovated. No telephone or car. Household income
£36–45 per week. Receiving Family Income Supplement and
housing benefit.

Mothering history: Son born at term, LBW, fourteen years ago when
Carol was 18 and unmarried – adopted. Son born at term, LBW,
thirteen years ago, dying of sudden infant death syndrome. Daughter born term, LBW, eleven years ago, now living with Carol's first
husband. Son born preterm and VLBW, died aged 3 days. Daughter
born preterm and VLBW nine years ago, deaf and dumb due to
congenital rubella, now living in residential care. Son born, NBW,
six years ago, living with first husband. Miscarriage five years ago
at 16 weeks. Gabrielle born, NBW, three years ago.

This pregnancy: Twins born at 38 weeks – girl, 1375 g, and boy 1545
g. In special care for six weeks.

When the research midwife went to see Carol to explain the study,
according to the 'problem file':

RMW1 said she had had 45 mins chat with this lady who told her that she has
had 4 boys. CHAT TOOK PLACE BEFORE ALLOCATION MADE – (1) adopted because he
was born before she was married, (2) cot death, (3) died after 3 days, (4)
with her first husband. Also one girl at home. RMW anticipates lots of
problems.

She wrote in her notes that Carol had recently moved to this area from the
North, and was unhappy about living here. Although the purpose of the
visit was only to explain the study and ask Carol to take part in it, when she
began to talk about her problems, the midwife felt she was unable to leave
– 'I felt she wanted to talk.'

She went back to do the first interview when Carol was 16 weeks
pregnant. Her husband and her mother were there during the visit, and
her 3-year-old, who had whooping cough. The family were living in

temporary accommodation while the council renovated their house. After discussing her past history as a mother, the research midwife asked Carol if she was worried about having another small baby:

C: Yeah. I've resigned meself to the fact now.

RMW1: You are quite convinced this is going to be a small baby?

C: Yes.

RMW1: A *small* small baby or a 6 lb sort of baby?

C: I don't know . . .

RMW1: [Prophetically] You could end up with twins!

C: That's the first thing when I first went . . . it'll be small . . .

RMW1: Oh, that's the limit, it really is . . .

C: You get used to that . . . I mean, they told us she wouldn't live, didn't they? And that was before I had her . . . I mean, he were a nice doctor, weren't he . . . he [husband] just turned round and said what do you think the chances are of this one . . . and he said I don't hold out much chance . . . I was ever so upset . . .

RMW1: I don't understand that . . .

C: I had to resign meself to the fact that she weren't going to live . . .

RMW1: Let's talk a bit about this pregnancy . . . how do you actually feel about it?

C: Well, I want it to be a girl . . . everybody else wants a boy but I want a girl . . .

RMW1: So how do you feel about the fact that you are pregnant?

C: Well, we wanted another one, didn't we? We didn't plan on having one now . . . I said I would wait till she got to school . . . I mean, when I went to the doctor's he took me off the pill, didn't he? and err . . . he said, 'Oh, you don't want any more kids' . . . he says, 'Don't you think you have had enough?' And same as I said to the doctor, it's our life . . . I mean, he [her present husband] wanted two . . . she's the only one he's got . . . I have done my bit for King and Country, but he wanted another one . . . and I wanted another one . . . I wasn't going to have any more, then I kept seeing all these babies . . . all me mates were pregnant . . . and then I got pregnant and we were over the moon, weren't we? And we still are . . .

RMW1: So you are quite happy about it?

C: Oh yes. I mean, if I had twenty-two kids I wouldn't get rid of them . . . abortion is one thing I can't stand . . .

RMW1: What was the first thing you thought about when you found out you were pregnant?

C: Having a boy! That was the first thing I said to you, wasn't it? 'I wonder if it's a boy . . .'

RMW1: Are you having antenatal care at your doctor's and the hospital? Bit of both?

C: Yeah.

RMW1 And what do you feel about it so far?

C: Well, I don't know, it's only the first time I have been . . . I went to the clinic first, and then I went up to the hospital three weeks ago, and he said, Oh, we'll have to keep a close eye on this one . . . I mean, you are being referred to as a number, sort of thing . . . when he was talking to the tape recorder, he said number such-and-such ... we'll have to keep an eye on number ... you feel like a bloody robot ... or something that doesn't exist really, you are just a number to them ...

RMW1: Oh, that's dreadful ... I mean they could at least do it after you have gone out of the room ...

C: Oh, but they don't, they do it while you are there!

Later on:

RMW1: Did you say somebody had said something to you about smoking and birthweight?

C: Yes, the hospital ...

RMW1: Mr Miller?

C: Mmm.

RMW1: What did he say?

C: He said ... he was quite abrupt over that ... Do you smoke? I said yes. How many? I said as many as I want to. He said, well, how many do you smoke a day? I said about twenty. He said, do you mind packing them in? He said, completely. I said if I want to smoke I'll smoke ... He said, well, that's what's causing your small babies. I said, no it's not ... and I don't think it is.

The conversation moves from smoking to eating, which is a problem because 'we've got no gas on at the moment, the gas cooker don't work, so we've been going to me mum's for our meals, you know.'

RMW1: Oh dear!

C: We're having nothing unless it's a packet of crisps.

HUSBAND: ... you see the social don't reckon that a cooker is priority, so we just have to wait.

C: I mean it doesn't bother me, but Gabrielle isn't eating at the moment either ...

HUSBAND: ... but you know what the DHSS is like, it's because this new single payment thing stops at the end of this month, you see.

RMW1: That's right, I've not had one of those leaflets. I've been trying to get one from them for ages.

HUSBAND: ... Well, we've tried all sorts and nobody can seem to shift the DHSS.

C: I mean, we've never had anyting off of them, have we?

HUSBAND: ... see they all come here for this single payments thing now – before it comes out they stop it out of your dole money.

C: I mean, we've paid £95 for that cooker when we first moved over here. You know, when we first got here and I was working and he was working and we was without a cooker for a fortnight, weren't we, and we put so much a week away from out wages and bought that gas cooker, you know, £95, so we never got that off the social, did we? They wouldn't allow us anything because we were both working, which never bothered me, and everything we've got in here now is our own, you know.

RMW1: Yes, but when you do want something . . .

C: You can't get it. You've got to be a scrounger.

RMW1: You've just got to keep on and on and on . . . I'll give them a ring when I get home. Do you feel generally as if you haven't got any energy? (*Interruption, child crying and coughing, husband sees to child.*) You really are on tenterhooks, aren't you? Is it like this during the night as well? (*Child still coughing badly.*) Do you want to carry on, or do you want to stop?

C: No, it's all right.

RMW1: Are you sure? . . . OK, as long as you feel all right, because I mean I don't want to push you. Have you been more irritable than normal?

C: I'm always irritable.

RMW1: Are you, so you're worse than usual?

C: Especially when I'm pregnant I'm very irritable.

MOTHER: . . . oh she's terrible, terrible to live with when she's pregnant.

C: The least little thing and I snap somebody's head off, it's the same with the nursery, until they found out she had whooping cough they never bothered, and I told them yesterday she had whooping cough . . . She's the only one I've got.

HUSBAND: . . . I know.

C: I'd crack up if anything happened to her.

MOTHER: . . . a man doesn't understand like a woman does.

HUSBAND: . . . Like it's if she wakes up in the night and she'll say, quick, quick, and I'm going as quick as my legs will take.

C: And she is only in the next room you know, it's not five yards away.

HUSBAND: . . . she likes me to sleep with her at night until she goes to sleep.

C: Because I couldn't and I can't have her in the same room, you know.

RMW1: So when she hasn't got whooping cough you're not quite as on edge as you are now?

C: Oh, I am.

RMW1: You're always on edge?

C: Yeah, I'm always, you know, go and see how she is.

HUSBAND: . . . if she sleeps a little bit too long she goes to see if she is all right.

RMW1: Mind you, we do that with ours. Yo know, in the morning if they haven't woken up by, oh, I don't know, they're usually awake at 6 a.m., and if they're still asleep at 8 a.m. you go and peer at them to make sure they're OK.

C: . . . It was the same when she was born, like I've always had my kids on my side of the bed, always. When I lost the two boys and I wouldn't even have her on my side, would I, I wanted one of them mattresses [containing apnoea alarms for babies at risk of cot death] and they kept promising one and promising us one and it kept building me up, you know, oh, I'll get one tomorrow, or I'll get one next week, and one never came, they just fobbed us off with anything, didn't they, and they wouldn't give us one, and even in the morning I used to say to him, go and poke her, wake her up, even through the day, weren't it, when we were pushing her down town I would poke her.

RMW1: Peep in and make sure everything was all right.

c: You know it's stupid.

RMW1: It's not stupid . . .

RMW1: Some people do feel that they did something in pregnancy that might have caused the baby to be born smaller than usual. Do you feel like that?

c: Same as I said, really, with two of them small ones, because I weren't eating, you know, but I still don't think that makes any difference – well, it does a bit, you know, it might do, but with Paula they said I was feeding the afterbirth instead of her, because the afterbirth was 7½ lb and she was only 2 lb.

RMW1: Crikey. So is there anything you think you should be doing this time to avoid having a small baby?

c: There is nothing I can do that I haven't already done.

MOTHER: . . . well, you've eaten better up to now, haven't you?

c: Yeah.

MOTHER: . . . normally you go off food, but you come down and say, Mum, I'm starving. What have you got for breakfast?

c: You know I've never had a breakfast at your house this past fortnight!

MOTHER: . . . not this past fortnight, no.

During this visit, Carol tells the research midwife she wants to have the baby at home; she has no faith in hospitals: 'My sister, she had a small baby, it was only 3 lb, a prem. baby, and she kept it at home and put it in a fish tank, she did! At the side of the fire!' The research midwife is concerned, and indicates that she thinks Carol will be safer in hospital, but she does say that, if Carol is determined, no one can stop her giving birth at home.

Carol is 24 weeks pregnant when the research midwife calls to carry out the second interview. The family is still in temporary accommodation. Twins have been diagnosed; Carol has not been eating and has lost weight. She is smoking heavily and not talking to her husband. As the midwife reports, 'she says she can't take much more':

RMW1: Are you enjoying being pregnant?

c: Oh no.

RMW1: How do you feel about the pregnancy, about the babies now?

c: (*laughs*) I don't know, I've got used to it now, all this rigmarole with doctors and hospital that puts me off, you know, the more I go to see them, you know the more it makes me get . . . it makes me feel bad every time I go. I mean, when you're pregnant it should be a happy event, you know, the doctors should make you feel as though it's happy. To them it's just another pregnancy, they're just seeing another person.

RMW1: What sort of worries have you got, sort of in particular, either with the pregnancy or the babies?

c: Well . . . I asked him yesterday would they be all right when they're born, I said if they're born now right, if I had them now, would they live? He just weren't interested. Oh, I don't know, he said. You know, I just wanted a sort of little bit of reassurance, if you know what I mean, I mean all they have to say is, well, there's a possibility they could live, there's a possibility, you know – fifty-fifty chance that they won't live, but there's a fifty-fifty chance that they could live.

RMW1: And although you know that yourself you want somebody who is professional . . .

C: Yes, I just wanted a bit of reassurance, but you just don't get it any more, it's a waste of time asking. I used to ask at the hospital but they just didn't want to know. They said, well, we'll do all we can, if they go into the prem. unit, they'll do all they can. I said I already know that, and he said, well, what are you asking for, then?

RMW1: Do you think that you are particularly worried now? By dates you're somewhere around 28, 29 weeks, I'm not talking about the scan or anything else, but by your dates which is, you know, sort of the time you had the last two actually, but not Gabrielle, no, it was your daughter and the little one that died after three days, that's right, isn't it? . . .

C: I mean, I was worried yesterday, I said to her, I'm further on than what they say, I sat and reckoned up and I got it at 28 weeks.

RMW1: But that's if you go on your dates, well, that's what I've got down from the dates you gave me originally, although the scan date is the end of January.

C: He got it to my date yesterday as well, and the GP says, yes, she said, well, I put her down – when I first went to see her, the very first time she got me to 16 weeks, and they were 18 centimetres, and yesterday I was 30 and he said those two things coincide with my dates, she gets me to my dates, he gets my date but the scan doesn't. He said, you take no notice of that, he said, it's only because you're having twins and that they're small, so I said, well, I reckon – how big do you reckon it would be if I was only having one? Oh, I don't know.

RMW1: Normal size for 28, 29 weeks, you know, reaonable sort of size for 29 weeks probably.

C: I says, in general what size do you think, and he says it's 30 centimetres, but I said that's two, that's nothing, it doesn't mean a thing.

RMW1: That's right.

C: Which it doesn't, you know, I mean I go – like if I said like to you what size do you think they are now? And you go, well, about so big or something, you know. Yeah, well, so many inches, to me that's nothing, I just don't understand it.

RMW1: No, it's too technical, and he's not explaining it in lay terms basically.

C: Inches and feet, that's it. Centimetres is no good to me. You ask a simple question, you want a simple answer, it's only a little question, you know, it didn't take nothing for him to answer in a civil tone, but no.

RMW1: How do you feel physically?

C: Tired, I told him that yesterday, I says they give me some sleeping tablets last time I came. Who did? he said. The doctor. Why? he said. I said because I'm not getting to sleep at night. You shouldn't have had them! I said, well they're doing no good anyway, I said I can take one at 5 o'clock at night and by 4 o'clock in the morning I'm still sat there awake. He says no pregnant woman has sleeping tablets! I said, don't give me that bullshit, innit. No pregnant woman has them, he says, none of my pregnant women have any kind of tablets. And I said, well, I'm sorry.

RMW1: Some people do actually need them, not everybody . . .

C: Do you know, it really makes me wonder whether they want me to have these or not, the way they've been going about it, the way they've been treating me and speaking to me, and it's not just doctors, it's the hospital as well, they don't treat us very kindly up there, do they, you know, off-handed sort of thing, I just don't think they want us to have 'em . . . It's getting us both down, it's not just me, is it, it's getting us both down. I mean, he asked how many kids I had had, and I says to him, well, it's all down there. He says, but I'm asking you! I said, well, read it. He said, I've got a file here, he said, I can see how many you've had, and I said, well, what are you asking me for then? He said, well, why did you have four, then? And I said, well, that's my business, I couldn't give a monkey's toss whether I have twenty-two kids, that is my life, it's got nothing to do with anybody else, unless they turn round to me and say, don't have any more because it's a risk, you know, you're risking the baby's life. Then I wouldn't, but I don't give a shit whether I have twenty kids or twenty-nine kids, it's got nothing to do with anybody else, that's our life, not theirs.

RMW1: The other thing is, do the doctors realize that all your children aren't with you?

C: Yeah, I told them that yesterday, didn't I, I said we've only got Gabrielle with us, and he said, well why? And I said, well, that's my private life and I don't intend sharing it with anybody else, especially him, he's only a bloody doctor, it's nothing to do with you.

RMW1: What about the clinic?

C: It's ridiculous, innit, we just walked in. She said, get on the scales. I got on the scales, she took me blood pressure, she said, right, I want you to see your doctor now, and that was it, she ushered us out, and she gave me me notes, me files and that was it, we was in the waiting room waiting again to see him. I mean, she's supposed to be my midwife, I know you've got to see a doctor now and again, I'm supposed to see doctors up at hospital, but he only sees us in case you want a prescription, but you don't get one off of him anyway. It was all this jazz, you've got to eat meat, you've got to eat eggs and fish, and I said, well, I don't like them. You've got to eat fruit. I said, I can't afford fruit. He said to him, she's got to get plenty of vitamins down her. I said, well, are you going to pay for them?

RMW1: And wouldn't he give you any vitamin tablets?

C: No, wouldn't give me nothing. Plenty of protein, fresh fruit, you go and buy an apple, it's 10p.

RMW1: Yes, it is.

C: I'm not frightened of saying it. Me, I couldn't give a monkey's, if I haven't got money to buy it that's it, I'd rather have, you know, a bit of meat and some potatoes than I would fruit – fruit's not a meal.

RMW1: No, but do you have a pudding or anything ever?

C: No, can't afford a pudding.

RMW1: Not even at weekends?

C: No, we don't know what a pudding is. Gabrielle, she has a pudding at school when she has her dinner.

RMW1: Yes, that must help.

C: Or she'll have two dinners and two puddings because she's a pig, and then they have sandwiches and a cake perhaps at 3 o'clock.

RMW1: That must help quite a lot actually.

c: Not in a way, because she's still hungry when she comes home. I mean, it was the same when she used to come home at 12 o'clock, she used to have her dinner and two puddings and then she'd want a dinner when she came home, so we're still no better off, she's got a really healthy appetite.

RMW1: When you go into town do you ever go round the market to see if they've got things that are a bit . . .

c: I have to.

RMW1: No, but sometimes you can get fruit that's a bit cheaper, I mean have you tried? You can get bananas that are cheaper.

c: Yeah, but they're all brown.

RMW1: Yes, but they're all right, they're much better for you, my family like them like that, they won't eat yellow bananas, you know.

c: Gabrielle has to go to her Nana's for fruit, doesn't she?

RMW1: But they're not all – you know, you do find that some of the fruit down there can be cheaper.

c: I mean, when we were working, we always used to have two bowls of fruit at least, always. Can't afford it.

RMW1: That's right, obviously you've got to . . .

c: As I said, bread and milk, food in me belly comes before fruit. Just because I'd eat fruit, I can't go out and buy fruit just because I need it.

RMW1: No, but you ought to try and see if you can work things round a bit perhaps so that you do get some, perhaps even just once a week, even if you had one orange.

c: I can't even – I don't like oranges. I can't just cut down, say, well, we'll miss out on this, because there is nothing we can miss out on, you know, I mean cereal is a lot of money, but I have to buy it for Gabrielle, she has to have three or four different boxes to last her for the fortnight, then there's two milk tokens a fortnight for her, they're gone within a week because we have to . . .

RMW1: Didn't you ought to be able to claim for milk, though? You can claim for milk, I'm sure you can.

This conversation about diet is symptomatic of the strains that exist between the befriending and the health-educating role. The research midwife sympathizes with Carol's point of view, but pushes the suggestion about how to buy cheap fruit further than the flow of the conversation would otherwise take it. Unfortunately, diet is only one of a set of worries that reflect the family's impoverished circumstances:

RMW1: And now that you've accepted the fact that you are going to have two, you are relatively happy about it, are you? . . .

c: I've got over the initial shock, I've got over the big shock, I mean he's over the moon, Gabrelle is over the moon, but I mean they don't have to bring them up, it's a big step from one to three all in one go.

RMW1: Oh sure, that's right, yes.

c: I mean, anybody else doesn't have to wonder where the next meal is coming from, or if they've got a pair of shoes to their feet, you know . . .

RMW1: Would you say you've got any major worries at the moment?

C: Money worries, we've always had them, that's all.

RMW1: It's mainly money that worries you?

C: Yes, I mean it's not me, you know, I mean I can go without, that doesn't bother me, it's Gabrielle. We phoned up the Social to see if we can get her a winter coat because she's grown out of hers. I mean when we was working, when he was working, she didn't want for anything, but I phoned up to see if I could get her a pair of boots and a coat, and they said no, that's included in the giro, I mean £92 a fortnight, I mean you've got to buy for these two, you've got to buy for Gabrielle, and I mean them boots down there they cost me £19.99, I haven't got that kind of money to go out and buy.

RMW1: No, children's things are very expensive, they really are.

When they talk about how Carol is feeling about the pregnancy and the birth, she says that 'just sitting around at home' is bad for her, in that it makes her dwell on what might go wrong. She thinks of herself as naturally very active:

C: I miss work really.

RMW1: Do you?

C: Yeah, I said to him, in a way I wish I hadn't got this, I said I could be working.

RMW1: You enjoyed your work?

C: Yeah.

RMW1: What did you do?

C: I was a clerk in Timpson's.

HUSBAND: . . . well, you can go back to work when you've had 'em.

C: Oh yeah . . .

RMW1: As you've had small babies in the past, can you think of anything that would help you get through your pregnancy better that you haven't got at the moment, or something you've got that maybe you would prefer in a different way?

C: No more antenatal, no more doctors.

RMW1: Is that honestly how you feel?

C: It is.

RMW1: You feel you've been – you would get through it far better if you didn't have to go?

C: I would just rather get on with it . . . If things were more – how can I put it? – if they were more friendly towards you, you know, I mean like there was things I wanted to ask quite a few times when I've been up to hospital and I've asked them and I've got nowhere, you know, if they had just stood there for five minutes and said, right, Mrs Slater, such-and-such things are going to happen, you know, or no such-and-such thing won't happen, or if I had asked them something they'd just give me a straight answer, you know, or talked about it for a couple of minutes, it wouldn't have been so bad, but you just get pushed in, pushed around and pushed out and that's it. I felt like the four Ws up there, you whip me in, you whip me out, you wipe me and I'm whipped off.

The research midwife's concern about Carol resulted in a consultation with the London research team; she was particularly worried about Carol's reluctance to go for medical care. My own notes state:

> RMW1 says Carol isn't eating properly – when she saw her she was eating a piece of bread and butter and some chips and that was the first food she'd had for 3 days. Also smoking a lot. Hospital notes say 15–20 a day and consultant has circled this in black and written 'told to give up'. Problem at moment is focused on sex of babies. Put cot outside in rain when she knew it was twins . . . Also worried about expense. Twin prams cost £200, and there's all those forms to fill in. At end of conversation, RMW said, 'I get very involved, you know.'

The midwife's concern led her to re-visit Carol ten days later. The conversation again centred on Carol's anxiety about having another boy, about the size of the babies and about dates. The hospital said she was eight weeks earlier in pregnancy than she thought she was. Carol told the midwife she'd like to visit the special care baby unit, and the midwife suggested she ask if she could do this at her next visit.

Three weeks later Tom phoned the research midwife to say that Carol was having contractions. She visited, and advised her to call her GP. She went back a few days later to find out what had happened; Carol had not called her GP, and had decided that the cause of the contractions was that she'd walked too far. She was worried about the babies not moving very much, and about losing weight. She had also asked her health visitor about the possibility of having two cot-death bleepers, but the health visitor 'says not much chance of one, let alone two'.

At the third interview, Carol was 28 weeks pregnant (by her own reckoning). She was in hospital, because of bleeding. The research midwife took her interview schedule there, and conducted the interview by Carol's bed:

> RMW1: Would you say you're enjoying being pregnant?
>
> C: No.
>
> RMW1: Silly question. How do you actually feel about the pregnancy and about the babies now?
>
> C: I've got used to the idea now . . .
>
> RMW1: Right, so you've actually had – what? – two that were born at about this stage. I mean, although they give you 34 weeks by date, they are saying the babies are about 26 size-wise. Do you think that makes you worry more?
>
> C: It does a bit, but now I've seen the prem. unit and I'm not too bothered now . . .
>
> RMW1: Anything in your life, anything particularly difficult or unpleasant since the last time we did one of these?
>
> C: No, only coming in here.
>
> RMW1: Do you feel as if you're under stress? . . .
>
> C: I was all right until I come in here, I can't stand it.

RMW1: No, I know. Do you get on well with the other ladies, can you talk to them?

C: Yes, I've spoke to quite a few of them.

RMW1: It's just being in hospital.

C: Yes, I don't like it.

RMW1: I know you don't. How do you feel in yourself, apart from, you know, physically, how do you actually feel in yourself?

C: Just tired, really.

RMW1: Do you feel reasonably well, or would you say you don't feel very well?

C: Well, the backaches don't help, the headaches don't help. I don't feel . . .

RMW1: Full of the joys of spring.

C: I don't feel as though I can jump around, you know.

RMW1: We'll go through some of these questions that we've done before, you know, exactly the same. Do you suffer with your nerves?

C: Yeah.

RMW1: And would you say you're depressed at the moment?

C: I'm very.

RMW1: Until you came into hospital, how did you feel then, you know, if I'd come and seen you . . .

C: I wasn't too bad, you know, Gabrielle was there, I had things to do at home, it wasn't too bad, it used to take me mind off it, but in here you've got nothing to do.

RMW1: You're having headaches. Do you worry a lot?

C: Umm, I worry all the time – what mother doesn't?

RMW1: No, that's right. Do you have trouble relaxing at the moment, do you think you could be doing something all the time?

C: Well, there's nowt to do in here, is there? . . .

RMW1: How much longer is it until they're due?

C: My date is five weeks.

RMW1: Five weeks by your dates?

C: See the doctors at the clinic and the doctor here got me to my date, it's the scan that's . . .

RMW1: The scan reckons you're 26 weeks, 28 weeks, but the doctors say . . .

C: Go by my dates.

RMW1: Your dates, due five weeks?

C: Yeah.

RMW1: OK, you've just said you actually feel frightened about the delivery . . .

C: Yeah.

RMW1: But you don't know why?

C: I think it's the pain, I think everybody who is pregnant thinks what is the pain going to be like, and I've got two in here.

RMW1: But really the fact that . . .

C: I mean, I'm the only one that's got two.

RMW1: It's actually no worse than having one – well, I say that. The only thing is you deliver one and then you do get a few pains again after and you want to push again, but the initial length of labour and pain is the same as it would be anyway.

C: I'm worried about having a long labour.

RMW1: But you probably won't have such a long labour with twins because they're that much smaller.

C: I hope! (*laughs*) It'd be just my luck.

RMW1: Well, if you've got two babies that are 2 lb each that's 4 lb. Well, Gabrielle was 6 lb, so they're not actually going to be as big as Gabrielle to deliver, so they'll probably come through a lot more easily. And if you can manage another five weeks, you'll perhaps have two 3 lb babies which will be the same as Gabrielle, which would be really super.

C: Yeah . . .

RMW1: When did you actually start bleeding?

C: Oh, this is twice now. It's like a period pain, you know when you start your periods, it's like that, and then I start bleeding.

RMW1: But this time it was Monday you had a bleed, or Tuesday?

C: No, it was Friday when I started bleeding, it starts when I do me shopping or if I'm cleaning.

RMW1: Don't you, you're probably doing too much, it's warning you.

C: I mean . . .

RMW1: Yeah, I know you've got to do it, but you've just got to get . . .

C: I can't keep putting everything on Tom's shoulders.

RMW1: But he understands.

C: Oh, I know he understands, but I mean it's all right a fella helping, but they don't do it the same as a woman. You know, he does his best, I mean, if he goes round with the hoover, it's just the middle, you know, no chairs are moved, and he doesn't go under here, you know.

RMW1: Yes, I know what you mean, I know. But I think you have to sort of forget about that a bit, it's hard.

When the research midwife asks Carol about smoking (twenty a day, as throughout the pregnancy), Carol tells her about another research project on cot death in which she had been asked to take part. The ensuing conversation highlights the different role of the SSPO study compared to some others:

C: She asked me all these questions on Tuesday.

RMW1: Who?

C: Mrs Andrew, is it?

RMW1: Did she?

C: Yeah, I said what do you want to know for? I said I've already told my research midwife. She said, I'm nothing to do with her.

RMW1: Yes.

C: I said, do you mind, that's my friend!

RMW1: Thank you Carol. I've noticed she's got a list of things in clinic that she's asking people.

C: Yeah, she wanted me to open that envelope. She said, I'm dying to know what's in this envelope.

RMW1: Which envelope?

C: An envelope, it's a survey thing. I want two cot mattresses, so she says to me, there's an envelope here, she says, well, if you open it, she said, you've

got to take pot luck, it can either be weighing scales to weigh them every day
... I said, but I don't want to weigh them every day, I said, I'll take them
down to the clinic like I took Gabrielle every Thursday, I said I don't want
that, I said I want the mattresses. But why? And I said, but you know why. I
don't like her.

RMW1: Yeah, it's a bit difficult because the questions we ask for in this survey
– you know, this one that we're doing – are very similar sort of things Mrs
Andrew wants to know, and we are obviously going to pick up the same
sort of ladies, you know, we ask the same sort of ladies to help, but I've
never actually had anybody who said Mrs Andrew's asked all these
questions ... did you actually agree to take part in the cot death survey,
then?

C: I said I'd think about it ...

RMW1: I should hate to think that we've sort of pushed you doing this.

C: No, no.

RMW1: You're quite happy about it?

C: Yes, yes, she asked me that, she said you're quite happy doing this other
research, aren't you? I said, well, I wouldn't have done it if I wasn't. She
said, have you finished the course now? I said no, I said in fact she's
coming back today, I said to her, it's the last one.

RMW1: Oh.

C: I said, well, please yourself, you know where the door is, I couldn't give a
shit. Me, if I've got something to say, I'll say it ...

RMW1: Right, how do you feel generally that this pregnancy is getting along?

C: All right up to now, I think.

RMW1: How do you feel you're coping?

C: Well, it's a case of having to, innit?

RMW1: Yes, but how do you feel you've managed so far?

C: Well, I think I've done well up to now.

RMW1: I'll just go through this list and then we've actually finished. How do
you feel generally about your medical care this pregnancy?

C: A load of crap, that's putting it bluntly ...

RMW1: Tom has been OK, hasn't he, he's done a lot for you?

C: Yeah, been brilliant.

RMW1: What about friends?

C: Well, we've only got Janet and John really.

RMW1: And have they been ...

C: Yeah, they've been good.

RMW1: Do you feel as if you need other help, or do you feel that you need
more professional help from other people?

C: No, I've got this far, I'll manage on me own now, I've managed on me own
so far.

RMW1: Do you feel you've had too much from other people or ...

C: Well, nobody's helped us, you know, I mean apart from me dad and
Trudy, but as I said they're 60 to 65, they can't do a lot.

RMW1: What about domestic help?

C: What's that?

RMW1: Well, if somebody said you could have domestic help, would it make
things easier?

C: What do you mean – round me home?

RMW1: Yes.

C: Oh no, I'd rather do it meself.

RMW1: I knew you were going to say that (*laughs*). Financial help?

C: One could always do with that.

RMW1: Yes, and your housing is OK because it's being . . .

C: Well, we can't do anything about that until – I mean everything is finished now, it's just they're painting the outside of the windows, I don't think there's anything else to do in there.

RMW1: So it really is – you should be back . . .

C: All the downstairs things are done, the painting is done.

RMW1: So do you just have to wait for them to give you a date to move back?

C: I think all we're waiting for now is the inspector.

RMW1: To make sure it's OK.

C: About the wiring and decorating, yeah, make sure it's all done nice.

RMW1: So you've not got to overdo it when you do get round to moving back, just take it slowly, don't you go lifting anything or . . .

C: I know!

RMW1: But you did last time, you told me.

C: Oh, I didn't know I were having two then.

The research midwife wrote in her notes that Carol 'needs a lot of reassurance and someone with time to listen . . . Wishes she was back at work. Have arranged to take her to a twins club meeting in October. Talked about diet – GP complained about 3 lb weight gain in 2 weeks . . . Totally confused by dates.' They went to the twins club three weeks later:

> Although they offered to pick her up, she said she preferred me to take her. We went at 7.30 and returned at 10 p.m. She said they weren't at all posh and that the house was no better then hers, but felt a bit embarrassed when they started asking about previous children, especially the deaf and dumb child. Carol said she used to sign, and they have a deaf member who wasn't present but would like Carol to help if she goes again.

The research midwife visited Carol again in hospital twice. On the first of these occasions Carol told her that the hospital had said one of the babies was probably a girl. The second visit was unplanned: 'I'd gone to see someone else who'd rung me from the antenatal ward, so I couldn't avoid Carol, could I?'

The contact Carol Slater had with her research midwife totalled 10 hours 50 minutes. The twins – a boy and a girl – were born two weeks before the original date, weighing 1375 and 1545 g. They spent six weeks in special care with various problems before going home. The midwife wrote: 'My thoughts on the intervention. Possibly initially when she was feeling so down someone else around to talk to helped. Possibly she carried the babies longer than she might have done otherwise.' Carol herself expressed a good deal of anxiety about the health of the twins in her postnatal questionnaire, along with criticism of the hospital and praise for the social support intervention. About the babies she wrote:

> I was in hospital 4 weeks before having my babies and 4 weeks in hospital is not my cup of tea . . . My stay in hospital was fair up to a point but I stayed in with my babies for a while and was not very pleased, I didn't feel my babies was my own and I didn't feel like a mother to my own babies at times and I could never get to know anything from the doctors about how they was getting on. That made me mad.

Her husband and the research midwife were the most helpful people. She wrote that she was 'very happy to have helped in any way' with the research, and that she was

> very frightened at first and the research midwife helped me a lot when she came to see me . . . but for her I don't think I would have my babies with me now. She did a lot for me. Will you please thank [her] for all she has done for me and if she is ever in the area please call and see us, and I would like to thank all of you in London because without your sending the research midwife to us I would not be filling in this paper now. So to you all THANK YOU VERY MUCH from me and my 2 babies. God bless.

And in the follow-up questionnaire she wrote, painfully: 'The research midwife was a good friend to me, easy to talk to and she listened to my problems. I could do with someone like her now.'

Researching motherhood

All social research is a form of intervention in people's lives. Most is not designed, as ours was, specifically to be a positive experience for those who take part in it. One measure of our success in this objective was that, of 534 women who were asked to take part in the study, 509 agreed. How the women actually felt about the research was not considered a major 'outcome' of the study – that is, not in the quantitative terms described in chapter 9. On the other hand, if the social support intervention 'worked', it had to be via the 'mechanism' of women enjoying their contacts with the research midwives: only if they felt positive about them could they have found them supportive.

The four women who feature as case-studies in this chapter all made plain their appreciation of the research midwife's help. And, according to the quantitative outcomes outlined in the next chapter, all did well: three had normal-weight babies near term, and only one of these had health problems after birth. Carol Slater, the fourth woman, had low-birthweight twins, who had some difficulties in the postnatal period, and one of whom was later diagnosed as having a congenital heart defect; her medical and social history was especially problematic. But at one year both children were in reasonable health.

The case-study material reproduces the same narratives time after time: the bluntness of an antenatal care system that emphasizes clinical surveillance and control rather than woman-sensitive care; the unwillingness of fathers to take emotional and physical responsibility; lack of money and decent housing; social isolation and stress; mothering as hard, caring work. We can see, too, from the research midwives' and the mothers' conversations, how this intangible thing called 'social support' hovers on the margins between friendship and disinterested advice, straddles both information-giving and advocacy, tries to resist intrusive moralizing, and draws strength from the shared standpoints of supporters and supported. Both the study women and the research midwives belong to a culture that has constructed women's bodies as the objects of medical science, and has created a mismatch between motherhood as moral ideal and motherhood as social reality. What mothers are supposed to be is very different from the resources and positions they are allowed to enjoy. The fractures that result in women's everyday experiences of mothering form the cracked mirror on which the academic-technical notion of social support is pasted, slipping uneasily in and out of its jagged cracks.

9

'Real' Results

Our results confirm the findings of existing studies showing that the provision of 'social' care for pregnant women has the capacity to affect a range of pregnancy outcomes ... The mean birthweight difference we found ... suggests that our initial aim of increasing birthweight by 150 g was over-ambitious. (Oakley et al. 1990b: 160)

To do or not to do a test of significance – that is a question that divides men of good will and sound competence. (Winch and Campbell 1970: 199)

The location of the SSPO study at the margins of two different models of knowledge-production – one dealing with personal and social relations, the other with the quantification of the body in the discourse of the medical and physical sciences – had many implications for the *way* in which the study was done. The different methodologies embedded in these alternative models are usually described as quantitative and qualitative, and they are distinguished from each other in three main ways. First, with regard to the definition of data, quantitative research isolates and defines variables which constitute data, pre-specifying hypothetical relationships between variables before data collection takes place; the qualitative approach, on the other hand, is concerned with categories rather than variables, and these are expected to change their nature and definition as the research progresses. Secondly, the qualitative tradition obliges the researcher to pay some attention to the assumptions and values of those carrying out the research and collecting the data, as these are viewed as constituting part of the research data themselves; while the quantitative researcher labours in the belief that the world of personal values is separate from the world of scientific work. Thirdly, qualitative research mines the terrain while quantitative work maps it: quantitative research is geared towards the generalizability of research findings, and qualitative research to the exploration of the internal relations of, and links between, categories and processes.

In the SSPO study, these traditional methodological divisions could be summarized as follows:

Quantitative methods used:

1 An experimental research design.
2 Use of a table of random numbers to allocate subjects to intervention and control groups.
3 Pre-specified hypotheses as to relations between key variables.
4 Use of pre-coded structured research instruments.
5 Quantification of data.
6 Effectiveness of intervention assessed by means of pre-specified 'hard' outcomes.

Qualitative methods used:

1 Use of tape-recorded semi-structured interviews.
2 Attention to research participants' accounts and standpoints.
3 Analysis of processes.
4 Inclusion of 'soft' data in assessment of effectiveness of intervention.

Both approaches were built into the design of the study. There were two major areas of challenge to the conventional separation of quantitative and qualitative methods: the use of a quantitative research design (that of the randomized controlled trial) to test the effectiveness of qualitative methods (socially supportive interviewing) in improving health; and the inclusion under the heading of 'health' of both 'hard' outcomes describing aspects of physical embodiment in quantitative terms and of 'soft' outcomes relating to aspects of enselvement. Previous chapters have concentrated primarily on qualitative, case-oriented descriptions of the processes of carrying out the study. This chapter is occupied with the quantitative angle, describing the way in which quantitative research 'findings' were generated in the analysis phase of the study, and at the same time taking a self-critical look at some of the epistemological assumptions built into the notion of quantitative methods. The chapter concentrates on the example of birthweight, not because this is intrinsically more important than other aspects of women's histories of embodiment and mothering, but because of the ideological and moral importance attached to birthweight within the medical frame of reference and thus, via the medicalization of culture, within the moral frame of reference used to define women's position as mothers. (On the medical 'meaning' of birthweight see Chalmers 1979 for a critique.) In pursuing this question of what birthweight means, a series of brief excursions are taken into quite different academic domains, including medical and cultural histories of the body, and the epistemological basis of statistical significance tests.

Producing results

Contract research is not an open-ended process. Funding bodies require completion of the research by a particular date, together with production of a 'final' report which describes the study's findings. There is normally (and should be) an obligation to publish these – though who pays for the dissemination of research findings is one of many unresolved questions about this activity called research.

The main SSPO study was funded by the Department of Health from September 1985 for three years. During the three years, we needed, and were successful in negotiating, various additions to the original grant. These covered the extension of the research co-ordinator's role and the payment of overtime for the research midwives at times when their commitments to supporting the women in their interventions groups exceeded the amount of midwife time for which we had initially budgeted. We also succeeded in raising some money[1] to mail a second questionnaire to the study women on their children's first birthdays, following the earlier one at six weeks after birth, and repeating some of the same questions in order to gain a longitudinal view of the impact of our social support intervention. During 1988 the Department of Health agreed to continue a basic level of funding for an additional year (till the autumn of 1989) to permit analysis of this one-year follow-up study.

Over the last ten years there has been increasing recognition of the 'housework' underside of the research process, in the form of attention to just what interviewing, for example, is like, as opposed to how it is described in the instruction manuals. By comparison, the 'housework' of data processing and analysis remains a relatively hidden exercise. In the SSPO study, we had to confront the mammoth task of processing data as soon as these started coming in with the entry of the first woman to the study in January 1986. The projected database was large – a sample of around 500 women, with seven data-collection points, and a total of forty-five research instruments. All these had to be checked on their return to the research office, filed, coded and processed. By the end of the study we had more than 9000 separate sources of data, and a database consisting of twenty separate dBase III files with around 1500 different variables. The task at the outset was to construct a complex computerized database which would allow us to manipulate variables and test our pre-specified hypotheses[2], but would also be capable of including the coded texts of qualitative data. Traditionally, databases of this kind have been set up using mainframe computers, rather than an office-based microcomputer. However, Lyn Rajan, the research co-ordinator on the SSPO study, already had experience of analysing survey data using microcomputers, and in view of this, together with difficulties of access to university mainframe facilities, we decided to be one of the first such projects to depend exclusively on microcomputers.

Whatever type of computer technology was used, the first problem was to arrange for the entering of data. The system currently in use by many researchers was that of 'punching', which required the coded data on questionnaires to be punched on to cards, and from there entered on to a computer. It was decided to shortcut this process, and instead to enter data directly from the questionnaires. A program to do this was written for an available but ancient BBC computer. Lyn Rajan takes up the story:

> The original idea was that a postgraduate student might be sufficiently glad of the money to spend the laborious hours needed to transfer all our data to a machine-readable form. But a personal disaster suggested another option.
>
> I came back from holiday at the end of July 1986 to learn that my mother, Ethel Illman, had tripped over the flex whilst doing the ironing, and broken her leg in several places. As she has had multiple sclerosis for the past thirty years, this accident was doubly disabling; there was not enough strength in her other leg to enable her to get around with the heavy plaster cast. As a consequence, the muscles in both legs wasted, and the strength in them has never returned. She refused to stay in hospital, and so for the next six months was confined to a bed set up in their sitting-room, completely cut off from the outside world and all company save that of my father and close family.
>
> It occurred to me that she might enjoy learning how to use the computer, and that the yawning expanse of time she obviously had ahead of her could well be filled by helping us with coding the questionnaires and the data input. Somewhat hesitantly, as she hadn't been in paid employment since I arrived on the scene in the mid-forties, she agreed to give it a try. Over the next year their small living-room became a hive of industry, filled to capacity with bed, hoist and wheelchair, the BBC with its separate disk drives and processor, boxes of questionnaires, and masses of other paraphernalia. I think my father, who took over the role of chief cook and bottlewasher, sometimes despaired at getting around it all with the hoover, but he managed very well. The very traditional husband and wife roles that had been a feature of the first forty years of their marriage were reversed almost overnight, and have continued to be ever since.
>
> Their set-up is a wonderful exemplar for the use of computers by disabled people to work in their own homes. A large section of the potential workforce is out there, fully able to work, but of limited agility and unable to travel, thus deprived of both the means to earn a living, and of the dignity bestowed by economic independence, as well as of contact with others. So many tasks, both routine and creative, can now be carried out on computers, their output easily transportable either by disk or by modem using the telephone system. My mother has often said that this work saved her sanity for the two years or so it took her to get back on her feet again. She felt that she was part of a team, doing a valued job, as indeed she was . . .
>
> For years it has been considered unrewarding to retrain redundant older workers, and disabled people have been grossly under-employed. If a 60-year-old woman with MS can learn how to use Wordstar and dBase III without much difficulty, then surely other technology-enhanced skills can be learnt and utilized by other disabled people in the domestic setting and in the workplace.

This is one of many ways in which computers potentially revolutionize both the technical operations and social relations of work. They also have enormous implications for the division between quantitative and qualitative research methods. The traditional dominance of research by mainframe computer technology and its association with 'variable-oriented' research

> widened the gulf between quantitative and qualitative social scientists. Qualitative, case-oriented research appeared more and more like handicraft production (i.e. nonscience) in contrast to industrialized, variable-oriented data reduction on mainframe computers. This made ethnographic and other types of case-oriented research seem less scientific than the impersonal analysis of masses of quantitative data on mainframe computers. (Ragin and Becker 1989: 51)

But the development of microcomputers potentially banishes the distinction between industry and handicraft – as Ethel Illman found when confined to bed by illness. In intellectual terms, the microcomputer

> provides important technical means for new kinds of dialogues between ideas and evidence and, at the same time, provides a common technical ground for the meeting of qualitative and quantitative researchers. The end result may be greater attention to diversity by quantitative researchers (e.g. more detailed analyses of diverse subpopulations) and more systematic attention to diversity by qualitative researchers (e.g. more thorough examination of comparative contrasts among cases). (Ragin and Becker 1989: 54)

Though there is not as yet much evidence of this intellectual impact of microcomputers on sociological work (see Danziger 1989), there is no doubt that it was of considerable importance in allowing a blurring of the methodological divide in the SSPO study, in precisely the ways suggested by Ragin and Becker.

The first product of this home-based computer industry appears as figure 9.1. In the paper entitled 'Social support and pregnancy outcome', published in the *British Journal of Obstetrics and Gynaecology*, we accomplished the analysis, along conventional lines, of the SSPO study as a randomized controlled trial of a social support intervention in high-risk pregnancy. The paper attends to all the requirements of the quantitative method, including the reporting of the results of testing pre-specified hypotheses within the traditional hierarchy of 'hard' and 'soft' outcomes and judged by the statistical yardsticks of means, standard deviations and standard errors. It was not an easy paper to write, going through numerous revisions, and it was not easy to get it published either (see p. 328). In figure 9.1 the paper is reproduced exactly as it was published, with a few small hand corrections.

The paper concluded that social support made a difference to the health of women and their babies, though the difference it could be considered to make depended both on how health was defined and on how the data

British Journal of Obstetrics and Gynaecology
February 1990, Vol. 97, pp. 155–162

Social support and pregnancy outcome

ANN OAKLEY, LYNDA RAJAN, ADRIAN GRANT

Summary. A total of 509 women with a history of a low-birthweight (LBW, <2500 g) baby were recruited from the antenatal booking clinics of four hospitals and randomized to receive either a social support intervention in pregnancy in addition to standard antenatal care (the intervention group) or standard antenatal care only (the control group). At recruitment to the study, mean gestational age was 6 weeks, mean maternal age was 28·0 years, 86% of the women had one previous LBW baby, 11% had two and 2% had had three or more. The study population was socially disadvantaged: 77% of the women were working class, 18% had unemployed partners and 41% were smoking at booking. Social support was given by four research midwives in the form of 24-h contact telephone numbers and a programme of home visits, during which the midwives provided a listening service for the women to discuss any topic of concern to them, gave practical information and advice when asked, carried out referrals to other health professionals and welfare agencies as appropriate, and collected social and medical information. Pregnancy outcomes were assessed using obstetric case-note data (obtained for 507 women) and a postal questionnaire sent to all mothers 6 weeks after delivery (94% replied). Babies of intervention group mothers had a mean birthweight 38 g higher than that of control group babies; there were fewer very low-birthweight babies in the intervention group. The number of hospital antenatal clinic visits was the same in the two groups (mean 5·1) but more women in the control group (52%) than in the intervention group (41%) were admitted to hospital in pregnancy. Spontaneous onset of labour and spontaneous vaginal delivery were more common in the intervention group, who also used less epidural anaesthesia. The numbers of babies resuscitated at birth and babies admitted to the neonatal unit were similar in the two groups but the babies in the intervention group required less invasive methods for resuscitation and less intensive and special neonatal care. Intervention group mothers and babies were significantly healthier in the early weeks than those in the control group as judged by reported physical and psychosocial health and use of health services. Women's attitudes to the social support intervention were very positive, 80% of those who filled in the postnatal questionnaire singling out that the fact that the midwife 'listened' was important.

Figure 9.1 Publishing in the medical press

The capacity of social support to promote health has received increasing attention (Cohen & Syme 1985; Dean 1986). An individual's social relationships have been shown to be associated with health status independently of a wide range of medical and other social factors (Berkman 1984). In relation to childbearing, observational studies (Smilkstein *et al.* 1984; Nuckolls *et al.* 1972; Berkowitz & Kasl 1983) of mothers' social networks and relationships suggest that social support improves maternal and infant well-being, including birthweight, and controlled trials of social support in labour (Sosa *et al.* 1980; Klaus *et al.* 1986) provide evidence for the effectiveness of lay support during labour in decreasing perinatal problems and the need for medical interventions in labour and delivery. Furthermore, miscellaneous social interventions in pregnancy (Oakley 1988; Elbourne *et al.* 1989; Elbourne & Oakley 1990) have shown beneficial psychological and behavioural effects of such support. The present study aims to extend our understanding of the potential usefulness of social support in pregnancy by assessing the effectivenesss, in medical and psychosocial terms, of a programme of home visits provided by research midwives to women at above average risk of having a low-birthweight (LBW) baby.

Subjects and methods

Our study population was drawn from the antenatal booking clinics of four hospitals: Derby City Hospital, Pembury Hospital, Tunbridge Wells, the Royal Berkshire Hospital and the North Staffordshire Maternity Hospital in Stoke-on-Trent. The research was approved by the ethics committees in the four hospitals. Women booking for delivery at these four centres were eligible to enter the trial provided they had had at least one previous normally formed baby weighing under 2500 g following spontaneous onset of labour, were less than 24 weeks gestation with a singleton pregnancy, and were fluent in English. A sample size of at least 420 was chosen to give an 80% chance ($\alpha = 0.05$) of identifying a difference in the mean birthweight of 150 g, assuming a standard deviation (SD) of 550 g.

One research midwife was employed in each centre to recruit women and to provide the social support intervention. Between January 1986 and May 1987 a total of 534 eligible women were

informed about the study, of whom 509 agreed to participate. The midwife telephoned the coordinating centre for the random treatment allocation, which was organized in balanced blocks, stratified by centre: 255 of the women were allocated to the intervention and 254 to the control group.

The social support intervention consisted of a 'minimum package' of three home visits to be carried out at 14, 20 and 28 weeks gestation, plus two telephone contacts or brief home visits in between these times. The midwives were also asked to provide as much support as the mothers asked for, within the constraints of their own case-loads, and were supplied with radiopagers so that they could be 'on call' to the mothers 24 h a day. We designed semi-structured interview schedules to provide a basis for a flexible and open-ended communication between the midwives and the mothers, so that the mothers would feel able to discuss any topic concerning their pregnancy needs and circumstances that was important to them. The research midwives were asked to give advice or information about specific topics only if requested to do so by the mother. They did not give any clinical care, but referred women to the hospital, general practitioner, or community midwives where appropriate: other referrals, for example to social workers, were also carried out as judged necessary by the mother and midwife. Each midwife filled in a form for every contact she had with any woman she was supporting, noting who had initiated the contact, its purpose, content, length and result (e.g. action taken, if any). Parts of the three main home contacts were tape-recorded in order to generate some qualitative data on the nature of the intervention, and on women's experiences of high-risk pregnancy.

Information about the outcome of the pregnancy was obtained from hospital case-notes for 507 of the 509 women (two women who moved were lost to the study). A questionnaire was posted to the mothers from the coordinating centre 6 weeks postnatally: 477 (94%) replied, 243 (96%) in the intervention group and 234 (92%) in the control group. The base for calculating percentages hence varies depending mainly on the source of information for particular variables. Chi-squared and Student's *t*-tests were used for discrete and continuous variables respectively. Ninety-five per cent confidence intervals (CI) of the relative risks were calculated where appropriate using the method recommended by Katz *et al.* (1978).

Figure 9.1 (*continued*)

Results

The groups were comparable in important respects at trial entry, in particular with respect to the numbers having more than one previous LBW baby, 35 (14%) in the intervention group and 34 (13%) in the control group, and being currently unsupported (no living-in partner), 41 (16%) in the intervention group and 49 (19%) in the control group (Table 1). According to such criteria, the women in the study were at higher than average risk, not only obstetrically, but socially. Of the 507 women with case-note information, five sets of twins (three in the intervention, two in the control group) were diagnosed after randomization; we have excluded these from the analysis, as this is principally a trial of social support in singleton pregnancy. There were four terminations (two in each group) and 12 miscarriages (six in each group, all below 1000 g).

Of the 243 women remaining in the intervention group, 238 (98%) were seen at home at least once, and 224 (92%) at least three times (Table 2). The average time in pregnancy of the home visits was later than intended, due to later than expected booking at the four centres. At each visit fewer than half the women were referred elsewhere for professional help. Information about specific topics such as smoking was requested by a minority of mothers. One hundred and seventy mothers (70%) received more

than the minimum package of contacts with the midwife, 12 (5%) received the minimum package, and 61 (25%) less than this, the usual reason being early delivery. The most important single aspect of the research midwife's help mentioned by the mothers when they were surveyed after delivery was that the midwife listened. Most (94%) of the mothers considered the research midwife very, particularly or quite helpful (Table 2).

Table 3 summarizes the main features of pregnancy, labour and delivery. The main difference between intervention and control women antenatally was that control group women were significantly more likely to be admitted to hospital (relative risk (RR) 0·82; 95% CI 0·64–0·95). Spontaneous onset of labour (RR 1·10; 95% CI 0·98–1·23) and spontaneous vaginal delivery (RR 1·08; 95% CI 0·98–1·18) were more common in the intervention group, which also made less use of epidural anaesthesia (RR 0·69; 95% CI 0·43–1·09).

There were three stillbirths in the intervention group; two were intrapartum and associated with placental abruption (one also with a bicornate uterus) and one was antepartum at 36 weeks due to placental insufficiency (birthweight 1760 g). Of the 483 livebirths, there were five neonatal deaths (two in the intervention and three in the control group).

Birthweight and gestational age at delivery are given in Table 4. Mean birthweight of all

Table 1. Description of groups at trial entry

	Intervention (n = 254–255)		Control (n = 253–254)	
	Mean	SD	Mean	SD
Gestational age (weeks)	15·7	3·5	15·6	3·5
Maternal age (years)	27·9	4·9	28·1	5·3
	No.	%	No.	%
Women <20 years of age	9	4	10	4
Previous LBW baby: 1	220	86	220	87
2	28	11	29	11
3+	7	3	5	2
Smoking at booking	104	41	102	40
Married or cohabiting	214	84	205	81
Working class (partner's occupation)*†	194	78	178	75
Partner unemployed*†	44	18	46	19
Employed in pregnancy*†	77	30	79	34
Ethnicity Afro-Caribbean/Asian*‡	11	5	12	5

* Information provided by mother postpartum.
† n = 247–253; 235–238.
‡ n = 225; 223.

Figure 9.1 (*continued*)

Table 2. Description of the intervention

	Home contact					
	First		Second		Third	
A. Structure and content						
Number of women seen		238		235		224
Intended gestational age (weeks)		14		20		28
Actual gestational age (weeks)						
Mean (SD)	17·8	(3·3)	24·0	(4·6)	29·7	(8·5)
	No.	%	No.	%	No.	%
Referrals to:						
health professionals	44	19	58	25	51	23
welfare agencies	42	18	27	12	19	9
no referral	125	53	129	55	131	59
Information given about:						
smoking	19	8	12	5	2	1
diet	24	10	24	10	19	9
alcohol	12	5	8	3	1	<1
work	12	5	10	4	4	2
other	59	25	36	15	30	13
no 'lifestyle' information	142	60	156	66	178	80
B. Women's views†						
Women felt it important that midwife:						
listened					188	80
gave advice					154	65
saw her throughout pregnancy					131	56
gave information					131	56
was a midwife					79	33
Women considered the midwife:						
very/particularly helpful					115	50
quite helpful					102	44
Total women providing information					236	100

†Information from postnatal questionnaire.

singleton babies was 38 g higher (95% CI −72·6 to 146·6) in the intervention group. Mean gestational age was the same in the two groups.

Summary measures of the postnatal health of babies and mothers are shown in Table 5. Similar numbers of babies in the intervention and control groups were resuscitated at birth (159 and 162) and went to the neonatal unit (35 and 37) but there was a significant difference in method of resuscitation used, with intervention babies requiring less invasive methods. These babies also required less intensive and special neonatal care.

Mothers and babies in the intervention group were significantly healthier than those in the control group as judged by reported health and use of the health services (Table 5). Psychosocial measures, particularly the question 'Are you worried about your baby?' asked in the postnatal questionnaire also showed differences in favour of women who had received social support in pregnancy (Table 5).

Discussion

Our trial of social support in pregnancy was carried out on a population of highly disadvantaged women. For example, three-quarters were working-class, and the incidence of stressful life-events and chronic problems such as inadequate housing was high. These social problems were additional to the problems posed by poor obstetric history. The study was successful in terms of giving the intervention as planned. However,

Figure 9.1 (*continued*)

Table 3. Features of pregnancy, labour and delivery

	Intervention (n = 233–243) Mean	[SE]	Control (n = 225–243) Mean	[SE]
Hospital antenatal clinic visits	5·1	[0·17]	5·1	[0·17]

	No.	%	No.	%
More than one ultrasound scan in pregnancy	178	76	187	80
Antenatal cardiotocography	97	40	118	49
Antenatal hospital admission	99	41	126	52
Days in hospital Mean [SE]	7·2	[1·1]	8·3	[1·1]
Admission for threatened preterm delivery	34	14	43	18
Raised blood pressure with proteinuria*	8	8	11	11
Pregnancy-induced hypertension	22	9	23	10
Depressed in pregnancy	31	13	40	18
Onset of labour:				
spontaneous	180	74	163	68
induced	53	22	64	27
prelabour caesarean	10	4	14	6
Epidural anaesthesia	27	11	39	16
Length of labour Mean [SE]†	5·7	[0·3]	5·9	[0·3]
Type of delivery:				
spontaneous vaginal	197	81	182	75
instrumental vaginal	5	2	11	5
caesarean section	41	17	50	21

* n = 98; 104.
† n = 202; 192.

one consequence of the method of recruitment into the study that was used was a degree of 'overflow' of support to the control group, some of whom said in the postnatal questionnaire that they felt themselves to be part of the study (for example, 16 (7%) said they found the visits of the research midwife helpful, even though she had not in fact visited). This may have resulted in a narrowing of the differences found.

Our results confirm the findings of existing

Table 4. Birthweight and gestational age

	Intervention No.	%	Mean	SE	Control No.	%	Mean	SE
Birthweight, all singletons	243	100	2944	38·5	243	100	2907	40·3
Birthweight distribution (g):								
< 1500	4	2			9	4		
1500–2499	41	17			43	18		
2500–3999	194	80			184	76		
4000+	4	2			7	3		
Gestational age (weeks)			38·6	0·2			38·6	0·2
< 28	4	2			3	1		
28–32	8	3			9	4		
33–36	31	13			34	14		
37 +	200	82			197	81		

Figure 9.1 (*continued*)

Table 5. Postnatal health of baby and mother

	Intervention (n = 230–240)				Control (n = 226–243)			
	No.	%	Mean	SE	No.	%	Mean	SE
Baby								
Apgar < 7 at 5 min†	4	2			8	4		
Endotracheal intubation‡	7	5			13	8		
Respiratory distress	7	3			13	5		
To neonatal unit	35	15			37	15		
Ventilated (mean days)	8	3	5·0	1·05	13	5	6·2	1·00
Supplemental O$_2$ (mean days)	9	4	3·6	1·01	16	7	8·9	2·38
Totally/intravenously tube-fed (mean days)	13	6	6·6	2·15	13	5	18·6	3·18
Breastfed at discharge*	105	46			89	39		
Problems after discharge*	56	24			73	32		
Health service use after discharge*	138	60			156	69		
Mother	(n = 230)				(n = 226)			
Health not 'good' or 'very good'	69	30			89	39		
Hospital visit (excl. routine postnatal)	10	4			19	8		
Visit to/from GP	62	27			72	32		
Depressed after birth	92	40			107	47		
Feeling of low/no control over life	65	28			83	37		
Worried about baby	36	16			63	28		
Partner helpful:								
with other children§	190	88			168	81		
domestically¶	198	97			177	92		

* Information taken from mothers' questionnaires.
† n = 206; 215.
‡ n = 157; 155.
§ n = 205; 193.
¶ n = 217; 208.

studies showing that the provision of 'social' care for pregnant women has the capacity to affect a range of pregnancy outcomes. Previous studies include: trials of mothers holding their own case-notes (Lovell *et al.* 1987; Elbourne *et al.* 1987); continuity of care provided by midwives (Flint & Poulengeris 1987); home visits by midwives (Spira *et al.* 1981) or child health nurses (Gutelius *et al.* 1977; Olds *et al.* 1986); discussing ultrasound scans with mothers (Reading *et al.* 1982); the provision of community-based antenatal care (Reid *et al.* 1983). Two recent overviews of such studies (Oakley 1988; Elbourne & Oakley 1990) show that supported mothers are more likely than the control women to feel 'in control' during pregnancy and postpartum, to be satisfied with their medical care, not to feel unhappy after the birth, to have partners who feel involved with the baby, to be breastfeeding, to report physical well-being and to have babies with fewer worrying health problems. The effects of social support on the outcomes of mean birthweight, LBW and preterm delivery are less clear cut.

The mean birthweight difference we found in our study is of the same order as is found in controlled trials of dietary intervention in pregnancy (Rush *et al.* 1980), which suggests that our initial aim of increasing birthweight by 150 g was over-ambitious. (This aim was chosen both because it is in the region of the birthweight difference associated with maternal smoking, and because to have aimed for a lower figure would have meant increasing the sample size and therefore the costs of the study.) It is hoped that the results of a number of social support trials (Heins & Nance 1986; Heins *et al.* 1990; Stanley & Bryce 1986; Scott 1984; Hobel and Bemis 1986; Spencer & Morris 1986; Spencer *et al.* 1989) will clarify this particular question in the future. In our study we did not aim to influence the LBW rate as such, and the difference between our groups is small, though there is some suggestion of an effect on the very low-birthweight baby. On the

Figure 9.1 (*continued*)

other hand, our study does show that the benefits of social support can be manifested in the area of medical care (in pregnancy, labour, delivery and postnatally). The improved emotional well-being of the socially supported mothers in our study is consistent with the findings of other studies. Fewer physical health problems among intervention group mothers and babies after discharge from hospital may reflect the greater confidence and happiness of mothers, or real physical health effects of the social support intervention, or both. A sign test based on the 15 hypotheses of the study pre-specified in the original protocol shows that the probability of our data favouring the intervention group for 13 of these (as it does) is 0·0009. However, this needs to be interpreted conservatively as the hypotheses were not all independent.

Whatever the results of other social support in pregnancy trials, it is unlikely that social support will ever be shown to override the cumulative effects and problems of social disadvantage, many of which our research midwives encountered in giving support in this study (Buckle 1988). For example, it is known that the high rate of smoking among working-class women (observed in our study) is in part a response to the stress of caring for families in difficult circumstances (Graham 1987). In our study, and others, smoking can be linked to various indices of material conditions. For example, we found an inverse relation between income and smoking, with 56% of women living at or below supplementary benefit level smoking, as against 27% of those whose income was 300% or more of that level. Smoking in pregnancy is also associated with a depression in mean birthweight (in our study the mean birthweight of babies of smokers was 2837 g compared with 2994 g for babies of non-smokers). These considerations constrain the impact a social support intervention is likely to have. Although the policy implications of our findings must be in the direction of promoting continuity of care and a less impersonal and more sensitive antenatal service, it is important to remember that social policy changes are also needed to improve the health-denying conditions in which many mothers and babies live.

Acknowledgments

The Social Support and Pregnancy Outcome Study was funded by the Department of Health and Social Security. We should like to thank also the four midwives—Carole Galen-Bamfield, Sandra Buckle, Rosemary Marsden and Rosemary Smith—for their hard work and commitment; Sandra Stone for her absolutely invaluable administrative management of the whole study; Penrose Robertson for his computing expertise; our colleagues in the National Perinatal Epidemiology Unit, particularly Iain Chalmers and Diana Elbourne; members of the study's Steering Group (Professor Geoffrey Chamberlain, Ms Joan Greenwood, Professor Margaret Stacey, Dr Helen Sutton, Dr Donald Brooksbank and, latterly, Dr Elizabeth Wilson); Mr D. B. Garrioch, Mr J. D. Gough, Mr J. O. Greenhalf, Mr I. Johnstone, Mr I. V. Scott and Miss I. L. Waterhouse in the participating centres.

References

Berkman L. F. (1984) Assessing the physical health effects of social networks and support. *Rev Public Hlth* **5**, 413-432.

Berkowitz G. D. & Kasl S. V. (1987) The role of psychosocial factors in spontaneous preterm delivery. *J Psychosom Res* **27**, 283-290.

Buckle S. (1988) Meaningful relationships. *Nursing Times* **12**, 4647.

Cohen S. & Syme S. L. (1985) *Social Support and Health,* Academic Press, London.

Dean K. (1986) Social support and health: pathways of influence. *Hlth Promotion* **1**, 133-150.

Elbourne D., Richardson M., Chalmers I., Waterhouse I. & Holt E. (1987) The Newbury Maternity Care Study: a randomized controlled trial to assess a policy of women holding their own obstetric records. *Br J Obstet Gynaecol* **94**, 612-619.

Elbourne D., Oakley A. & Chalmers I. (1989) Social and psychological support during pregnancy. In *Effective Care in Pregnancy and Childbirth* (Chalmers I., Enkin M. & Keirse M. J. N. C., eds) Oxford University Press, Oxford, pp. 221-236.

Elbourne E. & Oakley A. (1990) An overview of trials of social support during pregnancy: effects on gestational age at delivery and birthweight. In *Advances in the Prevention of Low Birthweight* (Berendes H. W., Kessel W. & Yaffe S., eds) (in press), Perinatology Press, New York.

Flint C. & Poulengeris P. (1987) *Know Your Midwife,* Heinemann, London.

Graham H. (1987) Women's smoking and family health. *Soc Sci Med* **25**, 47-56.

Gutelius M. F., Kirsch A. D., MacDonald S., Brooks M. R. & McErlean T. M. (1977) Controlled study of child health supervision: behavioural results. *Pediatrics* **60**, 294-304.

Figure 9.1 (*continued*)

Heins H. C. & Nance N. W. (1986) A statewide randomized clinical trial to reduce the incidence of low birthweight/very low birthweight infants in South Carolina. In *Prevention of Preterm Birth* (Papiernik E., Breart G. & Spira N., eds) INSERM, Paris, 138, pp. 387-410.

Heins H. C., Nance N. W., McCarthy B. J. & Efird C. M. (1990) The South Carolina randomized trial of nurse-midwifery prenatal care. *Obstet Gynecol* (in press).

Hobel C. J. & Bemis R. L. (1986) West Area Los Angeles prematurity prevention demonstration project. In *Prevention of Preterm Birth* (Papiernik E., Breart G. & Spira N., eds) INSERM, Paris, 138, pp. 205-222.

Katz D., Baptista J., Azen S. P. & Pike M. C. (1978) Obtaining confidence intervals for the risk ratio in cohort studies. *Biometrics* 34, 469-474.

Klaus M. H., Kennell J. H., Robertson S. S. & Sosa R. (1986) Effects of social support during parturition on maternal and infant morbidity. *Br Med J* 6, 585-587.

Lovell A., Zander L. I., James C. E., Foot S., Swan A. V. & Reynolds A. (1987) The St Thomas' Hospital Maternity case notes study: a randomized controlled trial to assess the effects of giving expectant mothers their own maternity case-notes. *Pediatr Perinat Epidemiol* 1, 57-66.

Nuckolls K. B., Cassel J. & Kaplan J. H. (1972) Psychosocial assets, life crises and the prognosis of pregnancy. *Am J Epidemiol* 95, 431-441.

Oakley A. (1988) Is social support good for the health of mothers and babies? *J Inf Repro Psych* 6, 3-21.

Olds D. L., Henderson C. R., Tatelbaum R. & Chamberlin R. (1986) Improving the delivery of prenatal care and outcomes of pregnancy: a randomized trial of nurse home visitation. *Pediatrics* 77, 16-28.

Reading A. E., Campbell S., Cox D. N. & Sledmere C. M. (1982) Health beliefs and health care behaviour in pregnancy. *Psychol Med* 12, 379-383.

Reid M. E., Gutteridge S. & McIlwaine G. M. (1983) *A Comparison of the Delivery of Antenatal Care between a Hospital and a Peripheral Clinic.* Report to Health Services Research Committee, Scottish Home and Health Department.

Rush D., Stein Z. & Susser M. (1980) A randomized controlled trial of prenatal nutritional supplementation in New York City. *Pediatrics* 65, 683-697.

Scott K. (1984) Reduction of low birthweight with enhanced antenatal care. *Pediatr Res* 18, 345a.

Smilkstein G., Helsper-Lucas A., Ashworth C., Montano D. & Pagel M. (1984) Prediction of pregnancy complications: an application of the biopsychosocial model. *Soc Sci Med* 18, 315-321.

Sosa R., Kennell J., Klaus M., Robertson S. & Urrutia J. (1980) The effect of a supportive companion on perinatal problems, length of labor, and mother-infant interaction. *N Engl J Med* 303, 597-600.

Spencer B. & Morris J. (1986) The family worker project: social support in pregnancy. In *Prevention of Preterm Birth* (Papiernik E., Breart G. & Spira N., eds) INSERM, Paris, 138, pp. 363-382.

Spencer B., Thomas H. & Morris J. A. (1989) A randomized controlled trial of the provision of a social support service during pregnancy: the South Manchester Family Worker Project. *Br J Obstet Gynaecol* 96, 281-288.

Spira N., Audras F., Chapel A., Debuisson J., Jacquelin C., Kirchhoffer C., Lebrun C. & Prudent C. (1981) Domiciliary care of pathological pregnancies by midwives. Comparative controlled study on 996 women. *J Gynecol Obstet Biol Reprod* 10, 543-548.

Stanley F. J. & Bryce R. K. (1986) The pregnancy home visiting program. In *Prevention of Preterm Birth* (Papiernik E., Breart G. & Spira N., eds) INSERM, Paris, 138, pp. 309-328.

Received 31 May 1989
Accepted 4 July 1989

Figure 9.1 (*continued*)

were interpreted. The contrasts between the emotional wellbeing of the women in the intervention compared to those in the control group, together with differences in the antenatal and postnatal use of medical care and in the physical health of mothers and babies, were clearer than those relating to the quantification of the newborn as the 'product' of reproduction – specifically, birthweight.

Will the real birthweight please stand up?

Previous chapters showed how the issue of birthweight as a pregnancy 'outcome' assumed importance in the design of the SSPO study. An unquestioned assumption at the time the research was planned was that birthweight would be easy to obtain and measure: an indisputable item of 'hard' data. As each baby was born, it would be weighed, and the weight entered into hospital records: it would then be a simple matter to extract this information for research purposes. This was the model. In practice, things were different.

The kernel of the division between quantitative and qualitative research is often reduced to an opposition in the nature of the data each generates:

> Quantitative data are often thought of as 'hard' and qualitative as 'real and deep' – thus, if you prefer 'hard' data you are for quantification and if you prefer 'real', 'deep' data, you are for qualitative participant observation. What to do if you prefer data that are real, deep *and* hard is not immediately apparent. (Zelditch 1962: 566; see Brannen 1989 for a fuller discussion).

As we experienced the implications of both approaches during the course of the study, we increasingly came to understand the fusion between them 'in reality'. Birthweight is a paradigmatic example of this lack of division. Below we explore the dilemma of finding the 'real' birthweight for the babies in the SSPO study. This is followed by a step back from the specifics of this research project, to ask how and why the birthweight of babies came to be a 'vital statistic' of such importance to researchers, health professionals, parents and policy-makers. The two enterprises of chasing the real birthweight and engaging in the contingent historicity of this pursuit place us as researchers both as doers and as onlookers. Standing within one epistemological tradition, we also see our mirror images looking in at us through a one-way mirror: our 'objectivity' becomes 'their' subjectivity.

The first problem was not so much variation in the technology available for weighing in the four hospitals, but variability in social practices concerning weighing. While hospital 1 took both metric (grams) and avoirdupois (pounds and ounces) weights, hospitals 2 and 4 took the metric weight and converted it to pounds and ounces; in hospital 3 official practice was to take and record only the metric weight. In hospital 1, however, just to complicate matters, and according to the research midwife, 'In the notes there's a pink delivery sheet with a little box which has pounds and ounces and that's still filled in.'[3] But in all four hospitals parents were said to be interested only in pounds and ounces, so that, however (and whenever) the baby was weighed, the result was communicated to parents in pounds and ounces. Thus in hospital 3, where only the metric weight was supposed to be recorded, a conversion would still be done to inform the parents.

These different practices were evident in the case-notes. At least one weight in grams was recorded in the case-notes for all 483 live births; but, in addition, for 138 babies there was at least one weight in pounds and ounces. In only 20 per cent of cases did the pounds and ounces and metric weights agree within 5 g; the mean difference was 30 g (1.1 oz). These figures are shown in the first half of table 9.1. Mean birthweights calculated for the different subgroups ranged from 2868 g to 3096 g, a difference of 228 g or about 8 oz.

When the variability of different birthweights for the same baby was discussed with the midwives at one of the monthly meetings, it did not surprise them that our figures were showing sometimes as much as a 300 g difference between weights for an individual baby:

Table 9.1 Birthweight (live singleton births) in the case-notes and the postal questionnaire

Source of information	No. of cases	Mean birthweight (g)
Case-notes (N = 483)		
Weight recorded	483	2931
Recorded in grams only	345	2868
Recorded in lb and oz and grams, of which:		
The same[a]	27	3060
Different	111	3096
Postal questionnaire (N = 459)		
Weight recorded	455	2952
Recorded in grams only	5	2358
Recorded in lb and oz and grams, of which:		
The same[a]	401	2920
Different	49	2937

[a]Within 5 g.

RMW3: I can see how that happens. They put the baby on the scales and it's in kilos, and they go next door because there's one in pounds and ounces, or they go down to the ward.

RMW1: I had one the other day, there was a 40 g difference. They wrote down 6.10 in pounds and ounces but the grams one was 3000, but the midwife wrote down 3040 g. When I do the white case-notes [for the study], I write them down in pounds and ounces, then convert them. Well, Brian [her husband] did them last night.

RMW3: They round up or down if they weigh on the ward.

RMW2: Those big labour ward scales, they're very difficult to convert to pounds and ounces.

RMW1: Once the mum's been told the baby's 6.5, that's it, that's fine. The kilos are for the midwives.

AO: Do you think the pounds and ounces are more accurate?

RMW3: I think so, because that's the one the mums remember.

RMW1: I tend to disagree. Because since we've got our new scales we weigh in metric so the metric weights would probably be more accurate. But we've only been weighing in metric in the last two years. So if you're talking about the babies born in 1979 they would have been weighed in pounds and ounces and converted to metric.

RMW3: Weighed in pounds and ounces and then converted with a chart.

RMW1: We used to have real old-fashioned scales with weights – like my mum gave me as an antique!

RMW1: Some of the elderly midwives, they don't understand metrification. They say, I'll go and find a *real* pair of scales, and they march off somewhere and find them.

RMW1: They're big round ones, the modern ones. The red is the metric and the black's the pounds and ounces.

AO: Which is easier to read?

RMW3: The metric. It's round the outside ... in my hospital there are *five* different places where the baby can be weighed ... The older midwives look at the pounds and ounces to tell the mum ...

RMW1: ... now we've got big circular ones which have got the kilos and the pounds and ounces. Unless the baby lies absolutely still, which it doesn't, there's always the slight difference anyway.

The data on inconsistency and variability in birthweight are interesting in their own right, challenging as they do the notion that 'real' data are indisputable and easy to find. But the design we had chosen of the randomized controlled trial with its pre-specified outcome measures demanded that we use only one birthweight per baby in order to answer that particular bit of the question about whether or not social support promotes health. Guided by the midwives' views that the pounds and ounces weight given to the mothers would be regarded as the most important one by hospital staff, we decided to take from the case-notes the (first/only) pounds and ounces weight where there was one, doing our own (double-checked) conversion into grams for the computer database, and otherwise taking the first/only metric weight. This meant that, in 138 cases out of 483 live births, the 'real' birthweight was derived not directly from the data but by means of our choosing to operate a particular rule for generating it.

Using this 'real' birthweight, we then went on to compute a comparison of the birthweights of intervention- and control-group babies in line with our original hypothesis that the social support our study offered to intervention mothers could raise the birthweight of their babies. The first line of table 9.1 shows the answer we got for the total sample – 2931 g – and in the first line of table 9.2 this is divided by intervention and control group, showing a 50 g difference in favour of the intervention group.

The plot thickens when we take into consideration the mothers' reports of the birthweights of their babies in the postal questionnaires they were sent when the babies were 6 weeks old. On page 1 of the questionnaire the mothers were asked to write down how much their babies had weighed at birth. Their answers are shown in the second part of table 9.1. Only 4 out of the 459 women who gave birth to live babies and who answered the postal questionnaire did not provide this information. Of those who did, 11 per cent (49 out of 455) gave the answer in pounds and ounces only, while the majority – 88 per cent (401) – recorded both grams and pounds and ounces (the remaining 1 per cent – 5 mothers – replied with the metric weight only). In 73 per cent (330 out of 455) of cases for

Table 9.2 Birthweights (live singleton births) of intervention- and control-group babies according to different sources of information

Source of information	All (g)	Intervention group (g)	Control group (g)	Difference (g)
Case-notes (N = 483)				
Taking first/only lb and oz weight and converting to grams; otherwise taking first/only grams	2931	2956	2906	50
Taking first/only grams weight; otherwise first/only lb and oz and converting to grams	2940	2957	2922	35
Postal questionnaire (N = 455)				
Taking lb and oz and converting to grams; otherwise taking grams	2948	2966	2930	36
Taking grams; otherwise taking lb and oz and converting to grams	2936	2952	2921	31

which the case-notes and the postal questionnaire both recorded weight, the two sources gave different answers. Most – 98 per cent – of the discrepancies fell within a 250 g (9 oz) range, but there were some cases of much larger discrepancies, with birthweights in hospital records ranging from as much as 496 g (1 lb) less than those in the mothers' reports to as much as 824 g (1½ lb) greater. The second part of table 9.2 shows how the computation of the mean birthweights of intervention- and control-group mothers was affected by taking the mothers' answers in their various forms, rather than some version of the birthweights as recorded in the hospital case-notes: this has the effect of reducing the difference from 50 g to 36 g, and from 35 g to 31 g.

Lack of consistency in the recording and converting of birthweight suggests the falsity of the researcher's reliance on positivism to steer her/ him through the methodological quandaries thrown up by the doing of research in the 'real' world. As it happens, the different answers produced by the lack of 'hardness' about birthweight as an outcome do not much affect our interpretation of whether or not our social support intervention 'really' made a difference to how much babies weighed. But it is equally possible that taking the information from one source rather than another could have made a significant difference, even shifting the 'real' answer from one side of the conventionally accepted line of statistical significance to the other. Other conclusions about the cultural significance of birth-

Table 9.3 Birthweight groups according to hospital case-notes and postal questionnaire

Birthweight (g)	Hospital case-notes (N = 462)[a]	Postal questionnaire (N = 462)[a]
	%	%
0000–1499	2	3
1500–1749	2	1
1750–1999	4	4
2000–2249	4	4
2250–2499	8	9
2500–2749	13	12
2750–2999	16	17
3000–3249	19	19
3250–3499	16	16
3500–3749	8	7
3750–3999	6	6
4000 or more	2	2
Total	100	100

[a]The total number of cases shown in this table differs from those in tables 9.1 and 9.2, since the basis of the table is the weights of live and stillborn babies which were recorded in *both* hospital case-notes *and* postal questionnaires.

weight can be drawn from tables 9.1 and 9.2. For example, it seems clear that British mothers stick to the computation of reproductive success in pounds and ounces, whatever official clinical practice may deem the 'right' method. Even after many years of usage, the presentation of birthweight in grams does not have the same impact as it does in pounds and ounces. It is also evident from table 9.1 that babies tend to weigh more pounds and ounces than do their gram-restricted peers.

Although this analysis has focused on the *different* answers yielded by different sources of information and different procedures for recording babies' weights, it could equally be argued that the results are impressively the same. Table 9.3 shows birthweight groups in hospital records and mothers' answers (computed by taking pounds and ounces and converting this figure into grams, or taking the first/only gram weight). Elsewhere (Oakley et al. 1990c) we have argued that the broad similarity between the two categorizations implies a banishing of the traditional disregard for the 'unreliable' subjectivity of mothers. In medical language, mothers can be 'trusted' to provide epidemiologically reliable information on birthweight. In maternal language, case-notes are a reasonable approximation of the truth. Of course, whether one emphasizes the similarities or differences between different sets of 'facts' depends upon the difference that the differences can be construed to make (and/or those one wishes to construe them to make).

Quantification of the body in history

The quantification in weight within a few moments of birth of the newborn's health and vitality is very much taken for granted within both medical and social knowledge today. Indeed, for this very reason, *not* to include birthweight in our research would have seemed unreasonable. Yet, like everything else, birthweight has its own history. The 'need' to weigh babies within moments of their separation from mothers arises in a certain cultural formation. It is as much a cultural artefact as the definition through clinical psychiatric scales of unhappiness as depression, or the rating of intellectual development by means of educational tests.

In 1946, when the first national survey of births was undertaken in Britain, the collection and use of birthweight data were found to be far from straightforward matters. Birthweights were not derived from medical records for the 15,000 births in the sample week, but from questionnaires filled in by health visitors on the basis of interviews with mothers eight weeks after delivery. The health visitors were asked to check the birthweights against the maternity records, and another check was made by visiting five health authorities and comparing the birthweights obtained in 413 interviews with those recorded in the notes. Most were found to tally within 4 ounces. The report's authors struggled with another issue of accuracy: 'It is more difficult to estimate the frequency of inaccurate weighing. It is not unlikely that spring balances are sometimes faulty, that a few babies are weighed when clothed, and that weights are occasionally overstated in order to please the mother' (Joint Committee 1948: 138). By the time of the 24,000 births sampled in the 1958 survey, the quantification of birthweight was regarded as unproblematic, and its source was medical records, with mothers' information regarded as dispensable to the essentially clinical task of establishing the causes of perinatal mortality (Butler and Bonham 1963). For the third national cohort of 17,000 births sampled in 1970, birthweights were again derived from medical records. Some 'social' information was collected by midwives from mothers soon after birth (Chamberlain et al. 1978). The question of the 'accuracy' of birthweight was not addressed.

Cultural, historical and professional concerns not only affect the uses to which the quantification of embodiment in infant weight are put, but affect the very construction of birthweight as a fixed, determinable and measurable category. The increasing moral and medical significance attached to birthweight in the twentieth century can be regarded as part of the 'commodification' of human life (Rothman 1989). Babies themselves are products emerging from an assembly-line process, with the inbuilt 'quality control' of prenatal screening and testing; women are the unskilled, unpaid labourers of the production process, their identities and experiences equally subject to the quantification of embodiment rather than the valuation of enselvement that afflicts so much of our contemporary life. It is interesting to note that routine weighing of pregnant women – the ritual quantification of *their* bodies – is practised in most antenatal clinical settings today, and has been since, probably, the 1950s (see Oakley 1984), despite the fact that even viewed within the medical domain there is insufficient 'evidence' for the practice to be retained (Chalmers et al. 1989b: 1477). Much the same could be said about both routine X-rays and ultrasonography as techniques for assessing fetal size and growth before birth: though intrauterine quantification is widely practised, most of the information thus gathered cannot be used to improve the welfare of either mother or child (see Oakley 1984). A move to routine quantification is, however, almost universally taken as a sign of progress among medical professionals; indeed, the quantification of pregnant women and fetuses and of babies when born all accompany the shift from domestic to institutional reproduction.

All disciplines of knowledge must deal with the dual fact that human beings both have, and are, bodies: they are both enselved and embodied (Turner 1984). In common parlance the two are not disginguished; one does not introduce oneself by saying one's name and adding, 'and I've brought my body along, too'. Different intellectual disciplines have shown varying degrees of interest in the embodiment and enselvement of human beings. Embodiment has tended to be the preoccupation of the physical sciences and enselvement the concern of the social sciences. Indeed, it could be argued that the social sciences came into being at the point at which discourses of embodiment became inadequate to the task of explaining an increasingly complex social world (see Graham 1983). Bodies become knowledge data in different ways – through merely being counted, or by having their dimensions measured and recorded. At its simplest level, the concern with embodiment is manifested in the operation of the national census, designed to characterize particular populations with finite numbers. The earliest of these in the UK is the Domesday Survey commissioned by King William 'at Gloucester at midwinter' in 1085. The Domesday Survey was primarily a mapping of the ownership of land, but the commissioners' brief spelt out the need to count the population in the various social categories ('villagers, cottagers and slaves ... freemen') of interest at the time. Counting was regarded as a tricky business, and King William was knowledgeable enough about research methodology to build in two levels of data collection: as well as the original inquiry, a second set of commissioners were sent 'to shires they did not know, where they were themselves unknown, to check their predecessors' survey' (Thorn 1980).

Populations are notoriously unstable. People keep dying, and other people keep being born; the two may not necessarily balance. So it is important to count newly born bodies as well as dead ones, and, by including in the statistical gaze the transition points into and out of life, to arrive at a truer picture of the living. In urbanizing societies, the first regularly produced population statistics are those of death. In the first half of the sixteenth century in England, Thomas Cromwell instructed parish churches to keep records of baptisms, marriages and burials, and from 1603 deaths from plague and other diseases in the capital were published as the London Bills of Mortality. The methods used to collect these data were complex, and depended on the use of 'ancient matrons' acting as searchers; in the words of Captain John Graunt, famous for his *Observations on the London Bills of Mortality* (1665):

> When any one dies, then, either by tolling or ringing of a bell, or by bespeaking of a grave of the sexton, the same is known to the searchers, corresponding with the same sexton.
> The searchers hereupon (who are ancient matrons sworn to their office) repair to the place where the dead corpse lies, and by view of the same, and by other enquiries, they examine by what disease or casualty the corpse died. Hereupon they make their report to the parish clerk, and he, every Tuesday night, carries in an accompt of all the burials and christenings happening that week to the Clerk of the Hall. (Quoted in Farr 1885: 219).

Graunt was critical of the soundness of the data thus provided, though not in any doubt of the *principle* that the searchers *could* establish causes of death by talking to friends and relatives, as well as physicians. In 1837, when civil registration of births and deaths was established, the technique of finding out about causes of death through research in the local community was extended to the district registrars, who determined cause of death by asking any person present at death or during a final illness. Clearly this system was capable of abuse. Lack of independent certification permitted families to bury dead children as stillbirths – a stillborn child was at the time considered not to be a birth. But it was a series of cases in Essex and Norfolk in the 1840s in which family members poisoned their loved ones and then went to certify their deaths from natural causes which led to a campaign for compulsory medical certification. In an interesting passage in his *Vital Statistics* (1885) reflecting on the status of subjective accounts of death, William Farr, statistician to Britain's first Registrar-General, compared the proposed remedy of compulsory medical certification with the system then used in France, where death could be registered by declaration and without assigning a cause of death:

> The French explicitly reject women as informants, and thus must in many cases forego the best possible testimony. Women are almost always, except on the field of battle, in attendance or present at death. The wife does not forsake the husband, the mother the child, in the last moments ... The French principle is inapplicable to English women [decided Farr, not without reservation], but in England we may well avoid rushing to the other example. Why should a majority of the informants of some districts be ignorant women who sign the registers with marks...? The medical certificate is indispensable under such circumstances. (Farr 1885: 229)

Pressure to set up national statistical records came particularly from Dissenters (10 per cent of the population by 1770 (Macfarlane and Mugford 1984: 24)), whose passages through life went unrecorded in the prevailing ecclesiastical system, and from the medical and legal professions, who obviously stood to gain considerable authority by becoming the legitimated certifiers of birth and death.

In the emerging field of statistics, death remained a preoccupation for a long time. Farr's volume contained some important analyses of birth- and death-rates by occupation and social conditions. There is a long discussion of the difficulty of exactly quantifying the ages of young children (Farr 1885: 207 ff.), but no mention of birthweight, although the importance of accurate birth records receives a good deal of attention. The 1837 Act had set up a registration system, and the registration of deaths was compulsory from the outset, but the registration of births was not compulsory until 1874, and the registration of stillbirths lay outside the system until 1927 in England (1939 in Scotland and 1961 in Northern Ireland). For births, the only information required was the date of birth, the child's and the parents' names, and the occupation of the father. Birth registration and the registration of the deaths of infants remained incomplete for many years, as the idea of babies' bodies being civil entitites competed with a different set of lay beliefs about the liminal nature of infancy in which a large question mark hung over the requirement that parents need certify such uncertain embodiments to the state.

Body quantification as dead or alive is only a beginning, and it served as the sole statistical notion for a long time. Further quantification of bodies in weight and mass began seriously to be considered by physicians in the eighteenth century, though, interestingly, before that Renaissance artists had occupied themselves with how to represent the relative proportions of the human form through its different life-stages as part of the quest for the earthly, perfect image of God. Speculation and unsystematic observation remained the stuff of which an understanding of human growth was made until a French tree physiologist, George LeClerc, Count of Buffon near Dijon, promoted more systematic descriptions in his volumes of natural history published between 1749 and 1967. LeClerc's estimates of the length/height of fetuses, infants and children were based on empirical measurement and are very close to modern figures. However, as J. M. Tanner in *A History of the Study of Human Growth* observes (1981), the practice of measuring and weighing live human bodies really grew up and came of age in relation to neither art nor medicine. What was crucial was the military preference for taller rather than shorter human beings as guarantors both of physical prowess and of the superior quality of one nation's population compared to that of another. A 1779 sketch by Goethe, who was in charge of recruiting for the Prussian army at the time, shows modern techniques for recording height, including the removal of shoes and the balancing of a block aligned to a fixed rule on the recruit's head. By the time of the Boer War, when surveys of the physique and functioning of army recruits revealed many problems, regular anthropometric surveys of the population were beginning to be recommended, and some one-off studies of schoolchildren were done in the early years of the twentieth century in Britain.

As Floud and colleagues (1990) remark, it is inevitable that any historical study of height and health in Europe will draw heavily on the labours of military recruiters. Compulsory military service meant compulsory medical examination and measurement of the entire population of conscriptable adults. The fact that this means that only information about *men* was recorded does, of course, affect the generalizability of these data and their usefulness in studying body quantification in the reproductive domain.

The birth of birthweight

The more precise quantification of infant embodiment in terms of weight is a history intimately tied in with the development of obstetrics and paediatrics as the medical disciplines claiming jurisdiction over the management of birth. George LeClerc claimed average newborn weight to lie in the region of 12–14 lb (5500–6500 g), but this was the wisdom of the age rather than his own particular error. Prompted by a similar remark of Jonathan Swift in 1729 to the effect that newborn babies weighed about 12 lb, Thomas Cone, an American paediatrician, launched an inquiry into the medical history of weighing infants (Cone 1961). Before the end of the seventeenth century the only reference he could find related to the practice in Talmudic times of weighing infants and giving their body weights in coins to the poor. In 1871 the Belgian statistician Quetelet, renowned for his work on the bodily measurements of 'man', declared puzzlement as to why there was so little information about the measurements of infants. Swift's uninformed guess, like Le Clerc's, was derived from French and English medical writings, which set the average newborn weight at 10–16 lb (4500–7500 g) throughout the eighteenth century. Some of these overestimates were said to be based on empirical evidence; in 1747, Phillipson, a man-midwife, wrote to physician Theophilus Lobb to report findings collected at Lobb's instigation: 'I have according to your desire weighed a child and placenta soon after delivery: the child weighed sixteen pounds, and seven ounces, which is a large child, but have seen some larger; and the placenta weighed one pound, four ounces with the umbilical cord' (quoted in Cone 1961: 492). Another man-midwife, the famous William Smellie, reproduced these very figures in 280 courses of lectures to thousands of students. But around the mid-eighteenth century other empirical evidence collated by Roederer in Germany produced the different, and more believable, figures for average birthweight of 6 lb 12 oz (3062 g) for boys and 6 lb 5 oz (2863 g) for girls (Roederer 1763). It took fifty years for these weights to get anywhere near the textbooks, however (see Tanner 1981; 97). Though Roederer advised weighing, even in his own clinic this only became routine some eighty years later. In the UK, the practice of weighing took a leap forward when Joseph Clarke, the Master of the Dublin Lying-In Hospital from 1786 to 1793, determined to find out how far the greater size of male babies was responsible for their increased mortality (Clarke 1786). Sixty years later, James Simpson, Professor of Midwifery at Edinburgh, and famous for the introduction of chloroform anaesthesia, did likewise, commenting that male babies were also far more likely to kill their mothers because their greater size made separation from the mother more liable to be damaging (Simpson 1844). Most of the early reports of birthweight and other infant dimensions were undertaken because of a concern with the aetiology of the sex difference: the focus was not on the need for quantification of newborn weight *per se*, but on the need to explain why boy babies were more likely to die.

It is not known when post-birth weighing became the accepted practice. Cone's survey of the history of birthweight included a picture of a German engraving dated 1789 depicting the placing of a newborn baby on a pair of scales in what is clearly a well-off household. Two conditions need to be met in order for information on birthweight to become available: first of all, the weighing of babies must be regarded as necessary; secondly, the technology for weighing must exist. In many of the world's cultures, even now, the need to quantify the newborn in this way is not recognized (Richardson and Guttmacher 1967). To weigh a baby requires scales, which would have been absent in the deprived material conditions of most home births in the nineteenth century and the early decades of the twentieth. As late as 1968 in England, the midwife brought to the routine home birth spring-balance scales, a piece of equipment to which the newborn child was attached, slung in a nappy, very much resembling the stork's proverbial find behind a bush. These scales were idiosyncratic, weighing half a pound more or less depending on the way in which they were held or the child attached. Midwives were sceptical of their value.[4]

Weighing the baby is one of those many health surveillance strategies which is made easier by the concentration of health professionals and technology in institutions; a pair of scales permanently in place in the hospital delivery room facilitates the greeting of the newborn with the importance of quantification. Today, as we have seen, mothers and fathers often consider the amount their child weighs of considerable significance, though their perceptions may not agree with those of the health professionals. But for many years attempts of health professionals to quantify the weights of babies were bedevilled by the widespread belief among mothers that weighing the child was unlucky: a weighed child was one unlikely to thrive. As Janet Lane-Claypon noted in 1920, this belief implicated the quantification of bodies as social sin in itself:

> There is a superstition which is very prevalent in many parts, to the effect that if a baby is weighed it will die. The origin of this belief has, so far, it is believed, not been explained, but it seems possible that it may be a survival in an altered form of the dread of punishment similar to that visited on Israel and Judah after the numbering of the people by David. (Lane-Claypon 1920: 23)

The same superstition was found in other parts of Europe: 'If I weigh him, the poor child will never grow', said a peasant woman in Castres, France, to a doctor in 1909 (Gelis 1991: 195). A recent study of birthweight in Peru over the period 1981–6 found what is probably in part the continuation of this tradition: for one in three of the births studied there was no birthweight, and these were far more likely to be small than average-sized babies. This conclusion was reached by the creative use of a questionnaire which asked mothers not only for numerical weights but for 'subjective' perceptions of size (Morenzo and Goldman 1990).

One powerful influence on the acceptance of infantile weight as an important signifier of health in the UK came in the early 1900s with the development of the infant welfare movement. It is beautifully summed up in a well-known and much reproduced painting by the artist Jean Geoffroy of an early French clinic in 1903. The painting's three panels depict the three major functions of the clinic: in the first, the mother, about to place her child on to the scales, is watched by the doctor, his pen and notebook poised to record the results of the endeavour; the second shows the mother seated with the child being advised by the doctor on the child's health and development; in the third, the mother is collecting the sterilized milk which gave these clinics their name. 'To create a consultation for infants,' wrote one doctor at the time, 'three things suffice: a pair of scales, an apparatus for sterilizing milk, and the devotion of a doctor' (Robinson 1905: 481).

Regular weighing was instituted as part of a system of educating and regulating mothers in continental Europe, Britain and the USA in the early 1900s. Much has been written about the origins of this system, and about the ideologies and practices represented in it. Its overt goals were tied in with the continuing concern about high national rates of infant death, and with the recent discovery of the imperfect quality of young men serving as potential military recruits (see Davin 1978; Oakley 1984). Another purpose was less overt: weighing was needed as part of the move towards artificial infant feeding. As early as 1852 in Germany, Guillot advocated the advisability of regularly weighing infants to evaluate their development, and particularly noted the invaluable guide that regular weighing gave to the estimation of the quantity and quality of breastmilk. 'Scientific' nutrition of infants required quantification, and the calculation of complex formulae for the making up of feeds which would take account of the infant's age and weight. Just as the hiding of the fetus in the mother blocked the scientific gaze of obstetricians, so the containing of the infant's nutrition in the female breast frustrated the scientific claims of paediatricians. For behind the move to quantify infant development lay the emergence of a group of professionals – paediatricians – who were in the business of building up a basis for their claims to knowledge which could be held up as superior to anyone else's, and particularly mothers' (see Ehrenreich and English 1979). As the development of medicine since the seventeenth and eighteenth centuries increasingly removed talking to, and observing, the patient as techniques of diagnosis, replacing these with the 'objective' evidence of machines, so paediatrics took its place alongside other medical specialities in a system of knowledge which ranked quantifiable technological evidence as superior to all other kinds (Reiser 1978).

In Eric Pritchard's widely read *The Infant: nutrition and management* (1914), there is a whole chapter devoted to 'The determination of the quantitative food requirements of infants'. The chapter recites the findings of various experiments measuring the heat loss of babies confined in receptacles called 'calorimeters', and uses a formula containing the child's weight and skin area to determine the calorific content of the daily food required, and thus the amount of different types of milk that needs to be given. Dr Pritchard is uneasy about breastfeeding: 'If infants are breast-fed, the feedings must be given at absolutely regular intervals and at not too short intervals; the infants must not sleep in the same beds as their mothers, and they must not be fed more than once at night, preferably not at all' (Pritchard 1914: 247). Lack of regulation and insufficient rules are the causes of infant mortality, in Dr Pritchard's opinion – and it is one that informed a whole school of doctors at the time: 'Infants do not die because they do not receive enough food; they die because they are fed irregularly or too often, or because they are given too much ... they do not die because they are unloved and uncared for, they die because they are rocked and nursed and comforted too much' (Pritchard 1914: 247). Books such as Truby King's *Mothercraft* contained strict instructions for the regular weighing of babies and for assessing the normal weight gain in the early months of life: 'From one to three months, baby should gain from 6 to 8 ounces a week; from three to six months, 5 to 6 ounces a week; from six to nine months, 4 to 5 ounces a week; and from nine to twelve months, 3 to 4 ounces weekly, or about a pound a month' (King 1934: 51). The exact amounts of milk needed to reach these goals were specified, including amounts of breast milk, when test-weighing was recommended as a check on the adequacy of nutrition.

The view of both infant and mother in such regimes was mechanical; neither the baby in its calorimeter supplying data for the paediatrician nor the mother with her weighing machine worrying about her supply of milk were supposed to be affected physiologically by their emotions. Body and mind were separate. The aim was a healthy body – a healthy mind might follow. The emphasis on quantification and regulation in this philosophy of infant care extended through to the other end of the digestive system – bowel training was to be started at 3 days of life – and was one with which a whole generation of mothers must have experienced considerable difficulty.

As David Armstrong has argued, the medical surveillance of children and mothers that developed in the early twentieth century merely took into another domain – that of the child's body – what had already happened in the educational sphere. Schools, hospitals and clinics gave childhood a special status it had not had before, and justified the incursion of the state as moral guardian into the private lives of families. From this point of view, the child health clinic 'functioned as a surveillance apparatus, integrating in a hierarchy of observation the Medical Officer of Health, health visitor and mother and compiling for the body of each young child an individual dossier' (Armstrong 1983: 15). The centrality in this process of weighing the child is easily grasped: stripped of its clothes, the child, by becoming bereft of the insignia of personal identity, is rendered momentarily institutionalized, in the manner so powerfully described by Goffman (1968). The child on the scales – whether newborn in hospital or infant in the clinic – becomes the 'product' of the institution and its professional attendants.

It is only possible to guess at the effect on mothers of this persistent professional emphasis on weight. In the early French infant welfare charities, mothers were rewarded with money when their babies achieved the 'correct' weight gain (McCleary 1933: 43). The system of instructing mothers in all aspects of mothercraft was organized around weighing as the critical event in the clinic visit. Writing about the British clones of the French system, Dr G. F. McCleary noted that regular weighing was not made obligatory in the British system, as it was in the French, partly because 'In the British milk depots it was found difficult to secure the regular weighing of the babies' (McCleary 1933: 84) – the supersitition against weighing was a powerful counterforce. But in the 1930s advice manuals for mothers mentioned the fact that, while mothers had not in the past seen the importance of weighing babies, this was now coming to be accepted as normal practice. Warnings began to be made about the need *not* to weigh too much, or too often (see e.g. Langton Hewer 1932: 62).

In England from 1945 birth notifications (made normally by professional birth attendants) to local health authorities included birthweight, but birthweight data were not collected through the birth registration system until after 1960. The attempt to include the birthweight of every baby on the birth registration (made by the parent of the baby) dates from 1975. Registrars are not empowered to ask the registering parent for the birthweight, but must seek this information from the birth notification form by contacting the district health authority. In the United States, 'weight at birth' was added to the Standard Certificate of Live Birth in 1949 (Silverman 1980: 71).

These changes mean that the birthweights of most British babies appear in national statistics. There are, however, still some gaps in the system. One of these was uncovered during the writing of the research proposal for the SSPO study. In order to calculate the number of women to be included in the study, and given the objective of increasing birthweight, it was necessary to include the average weight of a British baby in the calculation. Such a figure did not exist.[5] By arranging to have a question put in the House of Commons to the Secretary of State for Social Services, the answer of 3286 grams was eventually obtained (Hansard 15 April 1985).

Birthweight as a moral category

Quantification of the infant body is intimately linked with qualitative judgements about normalcy and the role of parents (mothers) in ensuring this. Regular weighings and weight records are important in routine child surveillance work, where their practice now tends to be used to dispute the quantification of good mothering in terms of weight gain that earlier in the century paediatric professionals were keen to instil in mothers (Dingwall et al. 1983).

This is one reason why mothers have learnt to regard birthweight as important. Once data on body weight exist, there is an almost infinite series of uses to which they can be put. Most of these require the production of weight standards and the manipulation of the raw data into categories or groups held to have some intrinsic meaning. So far as weight at birth is concerned, a fundamental moral notion is that of 'normal' birthweight, with its accompanying negative category, that of 'low' birthweight.

Children's size at birth only emerges slowly as of interest in the preoccupation with the prevention of infant death that dominated the health care scene in Britain and elsewhere from the late nineteenth century on. Its first representation is in the concept of 'prematurity' or 'immaturity' which figures as a separate cause of infant death in medical writings from at least the early 1900s (see e.g. Newman 1906). For example, the *Forty-Third Report of the Local Government Board* in 1914 included infections, premature birth and injury at birth as among the chief causes of infant death. All of these, apart from infections, were considered to operate 'at or before the birth of the infant' and to account for around 1 in 5 infant deaths (Local Government Board 1914: xviii). But, in these reports and others of the time, premature birth was not defined in terms of weight. Even Eardley Holland's meticulous *The Causation of Foetal Death* (1922) was occupied with the analysis of weights of individual fetal organs to the exclusion of the analysis of birthweight of the whole baby. Holland's later *Child Life Investigations: a clinical and pathological study of 1673 cases of dead-births and neo-natal deaths* (Medical Research Council 1926, with Janet Lane-Claypon) took a length of under 35 cm, rather than birthweight, as defining premature birth. In response to German and Austrian studies of the effect of the First World War's food shortages on birthweight, an inquiry was carried out at St Thomas's Hospital in 1924 which examined birthweight in relation to the economic circumstances of mothers (Bruce Murray 1924). No relationship was found, though this is hardly surprising, as babies considered 'premature' were excluded from the analysis.

In order to clarify the confusion about the definition (or rather non-definition) of prematurity, the Finnish doctor Ylppo, at the time working in Germany, suggested in 1919 a 2500 g cut-off point for 'low' versus 'normal' birthweight. Although this cut-off point was arbitrary, it was widely taken up by the medical profession, being adopted by the American Academy of Pediatrics in 1935 (Rantakallio 1969) and by the World Health Organization in 1948 (WHO 1950). In Britain, the Annual Report of the Chief Medical Officer for England and Wales referred in 1938 to a recent statement by the Royal College of Physicians 'That in conformity with the standard in international use, an infant whose birthweight is 5 and a half lb (approximately 2500 grammes) or less, shall be considered, for the purpose of comparison of records, as either immature or prematurely born, according as the estimted period of gestation is full-time or less' (Ministry of Health 1938).

Ylppo's definition continues to constitute the definition of low birth-weight used internationally today. It entered the International Classification of Diseases produced by the World Health Organization in its ninth revision, when the definition was changed slightly to read 'less than 2500 g'. As noted earlier, there are still, today, two definitions of low birthweight in operation in Britain: the ICD convention, in which low-birthweight babies are considered to weigh less than 2500 g, and the one used by the Department of Health, which takes low birthweight as 2500 g or less. In 1980, 1990 babies in England and Wales were removed from the category of low birthweight as the arbitrary result of the adoption of the new ICD criterion (Macfarlane and Mugford 1984 (vol. 2, Tables); 172).

The nomenclatures of 'normal' and 'low' birthweight are evaluative as well as quantitative terms. At the very least, they suggest that *not* being of normal birthweight is problemtic. While the risks of death and illness faced by infants in the different birthweight groups lend some support to the problematization of low birthweight, none the less the labels attached to the different birthweight categories imply a judgement about the weights that infants *should* achieve. This ignores some important considerations, including the different birthweight distribution of different populations, and a consideration of the standpoint of mothers as the people who 'produce' babies with differently quantified bodies. For example, while all the women in the SSPO study had previously given birth to a baby classified as low birthweight, by no means all of them considered low birthweight a problem. Over half (56 per cent) said it was not a problem in itself, and a third (33 per cent) declared themselves not at all worried about the prospect of having another low-birthweight baby (see chapter 10). Some women believed that having a small baby was an advantage, because it meant an easier delivery, and a child that was easier to care for. Among those who *were* worried, many said it was not low birthweight itself that concerned them but the problems likely to follow preterm birth, particularly breathing difficulties, susceptibility to illness, and difficult feeding patterns that were disruptive of mothers' other domestic responsibilities in the early months. For example, 'As my daughter was healthy and fullterm, I felt that too much was made of the weight. If she was having trouble with her breathing, I could understand the concern' (Connie Isaacs).

Mothers' disagreement with the medical categorization of the low-birthweight/normal-birthweight division did not, however, mean that birthweight was *not* important to them. There were many examples of mothers attempting to establish how much their babies did weigh, and being frustrated and distressed by the uncertainty conveyed by health service information systems:

> The weight on the cot label for twin 1 was 2020 g, twin 2's had something tippexed out, and 1760 put next to it. I remarked and said that the weight should say 2200 g, but was told that it had been put down as 2020 g, so I must be wrong. When I saw Dr Mosley during the next round, I asked what she had meant by 'two two' as she had told me the weight at birth. Was it 2200 g or 2020 g? We both agreed that it was 2200 g, the same as the scan had suggested, and we were amazed how accurate it had been. So the weight had been put down incorrectly. It took three days before it was accepted, and only after Dr Mosley's say-so was it then changed. Had somebody bothered look in twin 2's file they would have seen his first weight put down as 1076 g and then changed to 1760 g, hence the tippex on the label. Somebody was obviously not used to grams! (Gill Fuller)

Like all statistics, those of birthweight can be, and have been, put to numerous social, medical and political uses. In the language of health policy analysis, birthweight has the status of a 'major health indicator system'. This means that the production of birthweight data for a particular population is considered to be a tool for the assessment of the effectiveness of the health care system. The reason for this is the conceptualization of birthweight as 'an objective (measurable) variable present in all the population and ... the most significant determinant for predicting the survival of the infant. Since it ... reflects the summation of events that occurred during pregnancy, controlling for birthweight allows one to look at the intrapartum and neonatal period with little concern for the medical, social and economic influences of the antenatal ... period' (McCarthy 1984: 5). The proportion of low-birthweight babies is included as one of a number of global indicators of health with which the World Health Organization intends to monitor progress towards the goal of health for all by the year 2000 (WHO 1981). The close association between low birthweight and social disadvantage, on the one hand, and between low birthweight and subsequent health in childhood and adulthood, on the other hand, make it an excellent choice for a policy target, although it might seem that an understanding of the causes of low birthweight is a necessary condition for reducing it. By the same logic, the low-birthweight rate has been used as an index of social and material deprivation (Townsend and Davidson 1982).

Birthweight data may thus play an important role in the medical profession's reiteration of its claims to expertise. A new example was recently unfolded at a Swedish conference on the 'scientific basis' of antenatal care. Charts of 'normal' growth and weight from conception through pregnancy have been available for some time, based on the dating of pregnancy by the mother's last menstrual period. The advent and increasing use of ultrasound fetal imaging for 'dating' pregnancy has imposed an assumption of standardization on individual growth patterns, so that early in pregnancy all babies are regarded as necessarily growing at the same rate: the head measurement (biparietal diameter) of one fetus at 14 weeks must be the same as that of another fetus. While the gold standard of what fetuses 'ought' to measure continues to be based on the old menstrually dated charts, adherence to the rule of non-variability with ultrasound has the consequence that a fetus smaller than the standard is deemed not have been growing as long – that is, the pregnancy is redated in order to bring fetal size into line, the baby is 'allowed' to remain *in utero* longer, and weight for age is increased, resulting in an apparent fall in the incidence of 'small-for-gestational-age' babies which is then attributed to use of the ultrasound imaging technique (Bakketeig and Magnus 1990). While nothing has really changed, it appears that something has, and erroneous conclusions may be drawn from the apparent change in the chances of babies being categorized as smaller than they 'ought' to be.

The quality of quantitative data

Theoretical definitions of birthweight must contend with all sorts of practical problems. It matters how, when, where and in what manner babies are weighed, and it matters who does the weighing, what the nature of the weighing equipment is, and how the weight is both read and recorded. The data presented from the SSPO study bear out the importance of these qualifications. Aside from the factors illuminated by our study, it is known that infants' birthweights vary with the amount of placental blood infused before weighing, which in turn will depend partly on the policy of the birth attendant concerning when after birth the umbilical cord is clamped, and how this is done: a long piece of umbilical cord plus a pair of 7-inch forceps weighs 100 g (Chamberlain, personal communication). Birthweight also varies as time elapses after birth, and the baby has a chance to eliminate waste matter and take in new. A standard list of epidemiological provisos about the 'accuracy' of birthweight goes as follows:

> Observer variation ... includes the errors introduced by the use of inaccurate scales, by inaccurate reading of the scales, and by the rounding up or down of the reading. On a worldwide basis it is extremely rare for weighing, if carried out at all, to be performed using scales that are accurate to the nearest gram. Even in the developed countries, only a minority of maternity units are likely to have such scales available and to have them regularly calibrated. Where scales of this level of accuracy are not available or staff training is poor, the tendency is to round readings up or down to the nearest 5 or 10 g, or larger round number, but this is often done at random. All studies of birthweight distribution reveal a tendency to digit preference ...

Errors introduced by rounding up or down become even larger when birthweight is expressed in pounds and ounces. (Alberman 1984: 87)

One study of perinatal practices in sixteen European countries in 1980 described a range of practices (Ierodiaconou 1980). Reports from the different countries indicated that hospital-born babies would generally be weighed naked in hospital, while other babies would be weighed by the midwife at home or, as in Portugal and Greece, in pharmacies or health centres when a few days old. Hospital scales were mostly the dial type with an accuracy of plus or minus 10 grams. In Turkey the accuracy was reported as plus or minus 200 grams both with hand-held scales at home and with hospital scales. In four countries the birthweight was entered on the birth certificate; in all countries it was entered on the mother and baby's health records. Stillbirths were weighed sometimes in six countries and 'always' in ten. It was thought that generally the 'actual' weight would be recorded in babies weighing less than 1000 g, except in Greece, where babies in that weight band might be recorded as at least 1000 g in order for the mother to obtain financial benefit from her social insurance. (Similarly, in some countries birth dates are altered for reasons of future school entry (Ierodiaconou 1980).) The unreliability of weighing procedures has a certain historical consistency. In the early reports of the maternal and child welfare movement in Britain, Janet Lane-Claypon, describing the work of health visitors in 1920, wrote:

> In a few places the visitor is provided with a hammock which can be suspended from the hook of a spring balance. The baby (usually with its clothes, since the mother does not want the trouble of undressing it) is placed in the hammock, and the weight entered on the record card. Apart from the error of the clothes, which will inevitably differ at each visit, the child rarely remains still in the hammock, and the level of the pointer oscillates on the scale, rendering it impossible to read with any degree of accuracy. Such a method of weighing is of little or no value, and weighing is best omitted from the duties of a visitor. (Lane-Claypon 1920: 23)

Half a century later, in a study of child abuse which involved documenting the work of health visitors and child welfare clinics, Robert Dingwall and colleagues noted that 'Relatively little attempt is made to obtain weights with any precision. Children are hardly ever stripped; scales are heaved around without much concern for possible effects on their accuracy and voluntary workers, in particular, often seemed very confused by metrication.' Material and ideological considerations influence weighing practices:

> clinic premises are often draughty and ill-heated. Routine undressing of children may be seen by both parents and health visitors as an unkind and intrusive act . . . Moreover, health visitors have, in the last decade or so, been

strongly influenced by paediatric concerns about overweight babies ... By playing down the significance of weight and its routine measurement, health visitors have been trying to re-educate parents on the undesirability of obesity and to reduce the competition which used to occur from week to week at clinic sessions over the extent of weight gain (Dingwall et al. 1983: 49)

In all these ways, the quantification of the human body in history, in general and in the SSPO study, is far from being the simple 'scientific' process it may seem. The research design of the SSPO study, by sharing the ideological position of quantitative science, used a vocabulary of restricted codes (the measurement of birthweight) to describe rich, complex and multilayered cultural processes which operate to ensure a social differentiation of the life chances of individuals. Birthweight is thus more a cultural symbol than an indicator of health; less an absolute amount than a relative description.

The significance of significance tests

The historial and cultural contextualization of birthweight is one strand in the approach to meaning. But it leaves untouched the question asked in the SSPO study: does social support affect birthweight? Understanding the wider meaning of birthweight does put a different gloss on the particular question, but the two approaches to meaning are framed as part of different types and levels of inquiry.

Our finding of no 'statistically significant' difference in mean birthweight between the babies of women offered social support and those of women in the control group had been predicted long before we began the research by one of the experts who commented on an early version of the proposal, David Rush (see p. 84). The difference shown in figure 9.1, table 4, was 37 g for all singleton births; this was slightly more – 50 g – for all live births (i.e. omitting the stillbirths). This result was exactly as David Rush had predicted. It would have needed a substantially bigger sample size for such a difference to be regarded as statistically significant. However, similar mean values for the birthweights of babies in the two groups are quite compatible with different *distributions* of birthweights; and different birthweight distributions would be an indication that the intervention had had an effect. Figure 9.2 shows the birthweight distributions of intervention- and control-group babies in the SSPO study, and the difference between these. One of the interesting features of the difference is that the distribution of intervention-group babies' weights is closer to that of babies nationally. This is shown in figure 9.3, and has been found by other 'social intervention' studies (see e.g. Sexton and Hebel 1984).

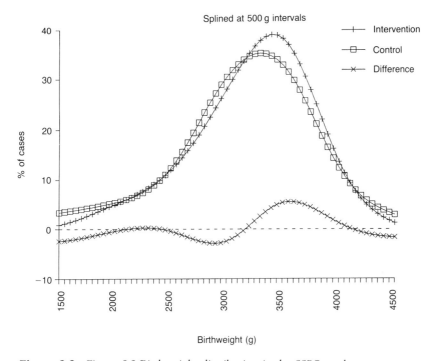

Figure 9.2   Figure 9.2 Birthweight distribution in the SSPO study

Because of this feature of our birthweight findings, we decided to seek an 'expert' opinion of what it might mean. The following answer was provided by Daphne Russell at the Health Services Research Unit in Aberdeen, who has, together with Ian Russell and colleagues, developed expertise in the analysis of birthweight and perinatal mortality data (see e.g. Wilcox and Russell 1986). Daphne Russell's opinion of our data[6] was as follows:

1   Overall, there is no significant difference between the two distributions. A Kolmogorov–Smirnov test, which is generalized enough to detect most types of difference (not just a change of mean or variance), gave a result no higher than that expected by chance (p = 0.67) – not at all close to significance. A Wald–Wolfowitz run test also gave no evidence of difference.

Because of this, *any* apparent differences between the intervention and control groups can be used only to formulate hypotheses to be examined in future experiments. Even two random samples from the same distribution will differ, and it is very easy to impose a spurious 'systematic' pattern on such random differences, if the exact nature of this pattern was not specified before inspection of the data. However, with the sample sizes here (less than 500 total) it is quite possible that a *clinically* significant change will not have produced a *statistically* significant result.

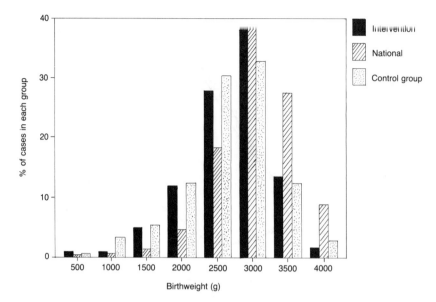

Figure 9.3 Birthweight by groups
Source: National birthweight distribution from OPCS data for 1985

2 Our Wilcox–Russell program fits parameters to a birthweight distribution on the assumption that it consists of a predominant normal distribution (mean μ, standard deviation σ with an extra 'tail' of relatively small births comprising a proportion p of the overall population). The estimates for μ, σ and p were:

Control population: $\mu = 3024$ $\sigma = 500$ $p = 0.079$
Intervention population: $\mu = 3058$ $\sigma = 481$ $p = 0.079$

Thus it appears that the intervention may slightly have increased the mean and decreased the standard deviation of the predominant normal distribution, while leaving unchanged the chance of a very small birth; but the changes are no more than would be expected in samples of this size. I have not previously used the method on samples this small; it worked well with the control sample, but there was some difficulty with the intervention sample. Comparison with simulations indicates that this may be because the intervention has changed the kurtosis ('degree of peakedness') of the predominant distribution . . .

3 I also compared the samples using $\times 2$ tests on grouped weight categories. These confirmed the findings above that there is no significant difference between the samples, but a slight hint that the intervention distribution curve may be 'flatter' in the range 2600–3500 g. However, unless there is a strong reason why the intervention may have had this 'piecemeal'

effect on birthweight (not changing low or high weights, but making a few of the babies 'due to be born at the mean weight' slightly heavier), it should be ignored.

Beyond these questions about how to interpret the statistical signifiance of data, there are questions about the use, misuse and abuse of statistical tests by social scientists and others, and more fundamental issues about the assumptions built into the design of statistical tests. The origins of statistical theory lie in the same domain as those from which the cultural concern with body quantification arose: that of the dimensions of 'man'. The Belgian statistician Quetelet not only pioneered the systematic measurement of bodies in the late nineteenth century, but was responsible for the infant science of statistics, and particularly for theories of regression and related matters (Quetelet 1871; Hogben 1970). These are not straightforward matters of science, but involve judgements about the relative importance of different substantive and policy issues (see also pp. 335–6).

Sociologists and others commonly misuse tests of statistical significance. There are a number of problems. Statistical significance, theoretical significance and (in health research) clinical significance may all differ. What is statistically significant may be so only because a proportion of all findings will be statistically significant by chance. If you do enough tests, some will yield a 'statistically significant' result. The only sound way to distinguish the randomly from the 'really' significant finding is to repeat the experiment (where appropriate). But it may still be necessary to consult the domain of *theory*: does the purported finding make sense on the level of the events/processes being described? Then there is also the problem – of findings which are theoretically significant, but which, for a variety of reasons, do not emerge as significant in the light of statistical tests.

These are pitfalls in the operation and interpretation of particular statistical tests. But the chi-square test of statistical significance has been heavily criticized, especially by medical researchers, both for its inherent limitations and for the limitations of its applicability to the analysis of randomized controlled trials. One major but often unrecognized point is that, since randomization should ensure a similar distribution of variable frequencies in both experimental and control groups, a chi-square test, which assesses whether a particular apparent difference is due to chance or not, really only functions as a test of the fairness of the randomization (Editorial 1984). Since one knows the play of chance (randomization) determined the allocation of individuals to the two groups, the test is redundant. A different problem is that significance tests give no estimate of the potential magnitude of experimental/control group differences:

> the accept/reject philosophy of significance testing based on the 'magical' p
> = 0.05 barrier remains dominant in the minds of many non-statisticians . . .
> p-values are only a guideline to the strength of evidence contradicting the

null hypothesis of no treatment difference and ... they should not be
regarded as indicating proof of treatment efficacy (Pocock 1985: 41)

For this and other reasons, the calculation of confidence intervals is often
recommended instead. Confidence intervals give information about that
range of values that is likely to include the true (but unknown) value. They
are based on the concept of hypothetical repeated studies, so that, for
example, with the principle of the commonly accepted 95 per cent
confidence interval, if the study were repeated 100 times, the confidence
interval would be expected to include the true value on 95 out of 100
occasions (Bulpitt 1987).

The social science and medical research communities are divided on
the use of statistical tests (see Morrison and Henkel (1970) for one account
of the controversy). Social scientists continue to espouse the chi-square,
while increasingly over the last ten years the medical research community
has moved to favour confidence intervals. Where statistical tests have been
used in this book, on the whole the social science convention has been
followed. The main exception is the paper reproduced as figure 9.1. The
reason why statistical tests have been used is because they are used in
similar research, not because of any 'blind' adherence to the notion that
they represent the only or best arbiter of meaning.

The tasks of knowing and of understanding require unblinkered vision.
Blinkering has many causes and many manifestations, of which the dichotomous thinking behind the conceptual templates in table A is only one.
Perhaps it is impossible both to drive a bus and to push it at the same time.
Certainly the critical stance with regard to knowledge, which demands
awareness of the ways in which both objectivity and subjectivity are
socially constructed, makes the notion of 'real results' itself merely a
theoretical construct.

10

Women at Risk

Many of the diagnostic judgements made by both experienced and inexperienced individuals will continue to be based on incomplete and imprecise characterization of individual women and babies. (Mohide and Grant 1989: 67)

The term 'risk' is ... vague and undefined. (Alexander and Keirse 1989: 346)

This chapter moves on from the case-study material for the four women presented in chapter 8 and the quantitative findings relating to pregnancy 'outcome' discussed in chapter 9 to attempt a synthesis of how all the women in the study regarded their participation in it.

A critical focus of this part of the analysis is the notion of risk. The women who took part in the SSPO study were not only exposed to the 'risk' of taking part in research,[1] they had been identified as 'at risk' in the narrowly biological sense of having already given birth to at least one baby weighing less than 2500 g. In using a quantifiable measure of risk derived from the medical domain, the study thus participated in a particular conceptualization of women and motherhood – one which prioritizes a set of meanings attached to motherhood by people other than mothers themselves. The challenge – the ethical requirement – here is to invert the analysis, and allow the women themselves to speak about their own conceptualizations of risk and mothering within a broader framework that includes the 'social' risks of material disadvantage and inadequate social support, the hazards of being identified as 'at risk' by health professionals, and any personal costs consequent on participation in the research process itself.

Although the potential benefits of using the medical risk approach have been widely publicized, its potential harm is scarcely ever mentioned; such harm must include that resulting from 'unwarranted intrusion in women's private lives, from superfluous interventions and treatments, from creating unnecessary stress and anxiety, and from allocating scarce resources to areas where they are least needed' (Alexander and Keirse 1989: 361). Clinical trials are planned, conducted and used largely by medical and academic scientists, with the subjectivity of participants taken seriously only at the point of trial entry, where there is a (limited) obligation to consider the provision of conditions for 'informed' consent. After that, it is implicit in the clinical trial methodology that evaluation of benefit lies firmly in the domain of medical science. It is not up to those who took part in the study to decide whether it was worth doing so or not, either in general, or in terms of what the trial revealed about the balance of costs and benefits attached to the treatment being tested. These aspects of the 'consumer' viewpoint are virtually unstudied within the sociology of health and illness literature, as Wynne (1989) has pointed out.

The notion of risk has been endemic for many years to the frame of reference within which doctors approach reproduction. Fundamentally, women are seen as at risk by virtue of their embodiment as women. The processes of gestation and birth are viewed as natural hazards requiring cultural management, as part of the domination of nature by 'man' (see Harding 1986). The medical claim to expertise over reproduction breeds a plethora of control strategies; doctors find ways of controlling women in the 'interests' of their and their babies' health, and must justify these in terms of arguments about the superiority of medical insights into pregnancy and childbirth (see Oakley 1984). The use of formal risk-scoring systems is one manifestation of this standpoint. With the development of computerized obstetric data banks in the 1960s, the old idea that quantification of risk could be an aid to the prediction and prevention of reproductive problems increased in popularity. Since then dozens of different systems have been advocated, used and heralded as *the* answer. Professional opinions are divided about which, if any, of these works, and why. There is widespread confusion about the kinds of risks the scoring systems are designed to predict, and about how outcomes are measured. Most of the factors included in such schemes relate to obstetric history and medical problems, though maternal age and height, and sometimes occupational class or marital status, may be added in. Of thirty-three such schemes reviewed in a 1985 US report, fifteen omitted any social factors, four included 'demographic' variables, and the remaining fourteen referred to some broad measure of socio-economic status (Institute of Medicine 1985). A ragbag of factors shelters under the 'social' heading; for instance, the widely used system of Robert Creasy and colleagues in the USA for predicting preterm birth lists as risk factors under the heading 'socio-economic status' not only low socio-economic status but also maternal age younger than 18 and older than 40, short stature, light weight, single motherhood, and two or more children at home (Creasy et al. 1980). Conceptually, the justification for including such different issues under the same heading seems bizarre. The dependence of medical definitions of risk on particular cultural standpoints is underlined by locating these historically; risk markers change over time.

Before 1973, scores included low eosinophilic counts, low pregnandiol, maternal age above 29, increasing parity, and working mothers. Ten years later, the markers have changed to include inadequate plasma volume expansion, a low level of education, receiving welfare support, psychosocial stress, previous termination of pregnancy, *in vitro* fertilization, and unknown last menstrual period; the identification of working mothers as a risk category has translated into the concern arising from research on maternal employment and reproduction which shows *not* being employed to be the risk category (Alexander and Keirse 1989).

Risk-scoring systems have the same status as any other screening test. Whether or not the test is worth using depends on its sensitivity and specificity; that is, on the extent to which it correctly identifies real problems, and its ability to avoid defining as problems factors which turn out not to be so. On average only between 10 and 30 per cent of women identified as at risk by formal risk-scoring systems do develop problems, whereas between 20 and 50 per cent of those who give birth to preterm or low-birthweight babies belong to the 'low risk' group (Alexander and Keirse 1989: 354). Indeed, the effectiveness of antenatal medical care itself is questioned when the productivity of each procedure is examined in the light of problems falsely identified or missed. An Aberdeen study which examined the records of 1907 women having babies there in 1975 found that in half the cases of perinatal death there was no identifiable risk factor at booking, a third of the women who developed pre-eclampsia (a potentially fatal condition) did so for the first time during labour or afterwards, and that 'Many problems arose in spite of routine antenatal care and were not, and could not have been, detected or prevented by it' (Hall et al. 1985: 9; see Chng et al. 1980).

No medical-risk prediction schemes include an evaluation of risk by women themselves. None consider the extent to which being called high risk becomes a self-fulfilling prophecy, in that being categorized as likely to develop problems produces the heightened stress that is known itself to lead to medical complications. What were the consequences of the medical categorization 'at risk' for the women in the SSPO study? One important question is how they felt about medical and other professional care, and how what doctors do in the cultural management of birth shaped the experience of motherhood itself. Second, there is the question of how women categorized as at risk reproductively themselves view this issue of risk. What are the 'real' risks of becoming a mother, and how are these affected by material and social circumstances? Third, there is the question of being researched: what were the costs and benefits of this to the women? Of particular concern here is the principle of random allocation, which has been criticized for its treatment of the researched as participants in 'experiments' – using 'experiment' in its derogatory, 'Auschwitz', sense (Chalmers 1983). Lastly, this chapter explores the women's own views of risk as predictors of 'outcome', contexualizing these in the framework of the social support and resources available to them in their families and communities.

'The doctors don't help'

Many different points were raised in answer to the question asked in the research: 'How did you feel about your stay in hospital before, during and after the birth, and also about the baby's care?'[2] As one woman succinctly put it in the postnatal questionnaire:

> I do feel that the attitudes of medical and other persons to a second pregnancy do not help in the prevention of another small baby. Being told to rest, not to garden, iron, hoover, carry shopping, etc., having extra scans booked when 3 months pregnant, and generally being made to feel a failure as a pregnant woman, must, I am sure, go a long way to producing further small babies (Susan Hawkins)

Assessing satisfaction with medical care is a notoriously fraught exercise (see Locker and Dunt 1978). Table 10.1 gives the responses of the intervention women in the SSPO study to questions about how medical services were perceived and used (women in the control group were not asked the same detailed questions). GP services were regarded more highly than hospital ones: in the second home interview, around one in five women described GP care as 'excellent', compared to only around one in ten who were similarly satisfied with hospital care. GP clinics require less waiting time; and care in the community has been shown to increase user satisfaction (Reid et al. 1983). In the SSPO study, there was a marked difference between GP clinics and hospital clinics care in the demands each made on mothers' time; from this point of view, in the second interview 17 per cent of women were unhappy with GP clinic care, but 39 per cent with hospital clinic care. However, the regard in which both GP and hospital care were held tended to fall as pregnancy progressed. Repeated acquaintance with the experience of receiving antenatal care produced a more critical attitude. (This comes out especially clearly in the comments of Carol Slater in chapter 8.)

The way women view the health care system is affected by their material circumstances. In the SSPO study, working-class[3] women had to wait longer for their medical care than others – 29 versus 24 minutes in GP clinics, and in hospital clinics 129 versus 114 minutes. They were also more likely to be dissatisfied with hospital waiting times and hospital care (but there were no social class differences in satisfaction with GP care).

Since the risk criterion we used in our study – that of low birthweight – is concentrated in working-class households, it could be argued that the inhospitable nature of medical care is here 'adding insult to injury'. As stress is related to poor pregnancy outcome (Oakley et al. 1982), and waiting to see the doctor causes stress, the antenatal services are in fact making more likely those adverse outcomes they were set up to reduce. In the SSPO study, the more 'adverse' the women's past history (more than one previous LBW baby, no normal-weight baby since, problems with the health and development of the previous LBW baby), the more dissatisfied they were likely to be with hospital care – and the more satisfied with GP care. Those whose last LBW child was not developing normally were most likely to be critical of their delivery and post-delivery care; 65 per cent of these mothers expressed dissatisfaction, compared with 27 per cent whose previous child was healthy. This relationship between previous adverse experiences and dissatisfaction with the health care system is partly

Table 10.1 Satisfaction with medical care: intervention women

Aspects of care	Second home interview (N = 235)		Third home interview (N = 234)		Postnatal questionnaire (N = 237)	
	Response	%	Response	%	Response	%
GP care overall[a]	Excellent	22	Excellent	13		
	Satisfactory	69	Good	44		
	Poor	9	Satisfactory	34		
	Total	100	Poor	9		
			Total	100		
Time taken at GP antenatal clinic	Happy	30				
	Don't mind	53				
	Unhappy	17				
	Total	100				
Hospital care overall[a]	Excellent	12	Excellent	6	Very good	47
	Satisfactory	76	Good	30	Good	22
	Poor	12	Satisfactory	51	Satisfactory	18
	Total	100	Poor	13	Poor	13
			Total	100	Total	100
Time taken at hospital antenatal clinic	Happy	12				
	Don't mind	49				
	Unhappy	39				
	Total	100				

[a]The format of the questions asked in the two home interviews and the questionnaire was slightly different.

explained by the inferior care experienced by those at higher 'risk'; in the SSPO study, women with two or more previous LBW babies experienced less continuity of care (they saw more care-providers) in pregnancy, and they spent significantly longer at hospital antenatal clinics (see Oakley (1991b) for details of this analysis).

The figures in table 10.1 represent a condensation of many encounters and biographies. The stories the women told about their medical care repeat well-known themes concerning impersonal treatment, inadequate information, protracted waiting times, and a general lack of consideration for other aspects of women's lives aside from their pregnancy. For example:

> You didn't ask about the doctors, most of them treated you like a nobody, didn't want to take the time to explain anything to you. I was in hospital six times, each time between 2–5 days, and each time I saw different doctors, and when I did see the same doctor twice he said, 'What are you doing here again?', and he didn't mean it as a joke, so you feel awkward from the start. They just don't know how you feel inside, sick with worry, wondering if there's something wrong with the baby, especially if you've had problems before. I had a small premature baby, then my second pregnancy ended in miscarriage, it's no wonder that I was worried when I was carrying this one. But it makes you feel worse when the doctors don't understand, or don't want to understand the fears that you feel for your unborn baby. (Liz Soldon)

One woman, Lee Stewart – a nurse herself – regularly waited forty-five minutes at her GP's antenatal clinic. She gives a detailed description of how pregnant women are 'processed' at the clinic:

> L: I didn't mind myself, but my daughter ... got a bit fed up, she wanted to keep rushing around. It wasn't too bad, they have got toys down there, but, you know, it does get a bit annoying...
> I was happy with the treatment, they obviously do everything that's necessary, but you tend to feel like ... just a number ... like a cattle market really.
> Going there, the receptionist takes your card and makes an appointment, and you have no choice about what time you go ... because I tried to explain to her a couple of times that I do shift work and it would be easier if I could get here for say 2 o'clock, so that I haven't got to rush ... I explained that I'm a nurse ... [but] I have to come when the appointment says ... so that's one drawback. And she's not a trained person, and she checks your urine ...
>
> RMW3: The receptionist does?
>
> L: ... and weight, which I'm not very happy about ... and then you go back out to the waiting area and into the corridor ... and you have to keep peering round the corner ... and when a chair is free is the time you go down ... there are six or eight chairs outside these GPs' waiting rooms, and you just have to pick your moment, and you have to be careful

because somebody can sort of nip in in front of you . . . and if you've got to keep an eye on a toddler that's running around and around in circles . . . So you go and sit up there, and then you go and see the midwife in turn, and you spent about two minutes with her, and if you have got any problems, she is in her own little office but with the door open, and there was one girl who was obviously having an awful lot of problems – social problems – and I felt really embarrassed for her, because we could all hear what the midwife was saying . . . which I didn't think was . . . I mean it wasn't anything sort of serious, but it was . . . was she going to marry the father, this sort of thing . . . and then she had to come back out and sit with the rest of us, it's a bit embarrassing. And then you go and sit outside again and wait outside the doctors' own room and then you go in for about two minutes and that's it. All that for two minutes with the doctor! A bit of a hassle really.

For women considered 'at risk' by doctors, the burden of medical advice may conflict not only with their personal circumstances but with those of clinic 'care'. When asked by the research midwife, 'Is there anything you feel you need to prevent the same thing [LBW delivery] happening again?', Rosemary Jewell replied, 'Well, the doctor says you should be resting more. But it isn't easy . . . I try, but it's a bit difficult when you've got two [children].' At her first visit to the hospital, this mother reported being very fed up:

R: The appointment was for 10 that time, and I had to wait till 1 o'clock to see the doctor. I was only there 15 minutes. I don't think it's right, really. I know there's a lot of women there . . . and I know the doctor has emergency cases sometimes, and he has to go off and that, but it is a long time to wait . . . I mean it gets warm and after a certain time you can't even get a drink . . . both times I've been there from 10 o'clock till one . . . [To go to the hospital] it costs £1.20. We get our money on that day anyway. I wouldn't be able to go if we didn't, but Wednesday is our Giro day.

RMW1: How do you feel about your treatment at the hospital?

R: . . . I went for a scan last week and I saw this – I don't know if he was a student or what he was . . . he didn't seem to say much . . . he asked me if I was all right . . . I told him I'd got pains in me legs, I think it's cramp. I got it then, when I was there, and he said there was nothing wrong with them.

RMW1: So how did you feel when you came out?

R: Well, I didn't think he was much older than me . . .

The comment about the doctor's immaturity values experience over professional expertise, and is one of the ways in which women's approaches to knowledge differ from 'professional' views (see Belenky et al. 1986).

Another woman, Kate Groves, told a story about the role of men in antenatal clinics. Her husband accompanied her to the hospital clinic sometimes, though in order to do so he had to take a day off work and lose pay. The research midwife asked if her husband actually went with her to see the doctor:

> He hasn't been, no. He was coming up with me – well, we went, he followed me up, and I don't know whether somebody said something to him, because when I turned round and they had me in the cubicle there was just me. But I knew he was behind me, because he followed me up. And whether she'd actually said something to him, that you're not allowed in these cubicles or something, I don't know. But they did fetch one bloke up, because he'd asked where his wife was, and he let rip into the doctor. He said he was bloody disgusted with this, that and the other. And I heard everything because the door was wide open, and he really was screaming and cursing at him for messing her about. And . . . the doctor must have said that her blood pressure was up or something, because he come in and he was swearing and he says to her, well, those were his exact words actually, he says, 'It's no wonder her bloody pressure is up when she's had to sit queueing all the time.' And he was really mad. And he was the only man that I saw come up (*laughs*). I never saw no more men after that at all. So whether they're actually allowed up there or not I don't know.

One woman, Holly Thompson, drew attention to a weakness in our questionnaire: the failure to ask specifically about antenatal care: 'You didn't seem to cover antenatal care very much. We could do with more visits to hospital but less waiting with not enough seats provided, once I went to hospital and couldn't sit down, it was a very small waiting room. I saw five ladies walk out because they waited so long.' Such practical issues are an important focus of discontent:

> I have had three babies and each time I was induced and a lot of people I have talked to had the same thing happen to them. I would have liked to have had one pregnancy on my own. I don't know why this is done all the time.
>
> And finally I would like to mention the labour beds are so small and narrow I wish they would improve them. The baths are huge so they must realize what the beds are like. (Sue Bird)

Alexis Walter had both praise and criticism to offer:

> Altogether I stayed in hospital for eight weeks antenatally – usually being allowed home at weekends. I was very pleased to be there – for the simple reason that if anything adverse were going to happen at least I would be near to medical attention.
>
> I found the midwives on the ward very supportive and encouraging – willing to listen to any fears and worries and to reassure me.
>
> They were also very understanding about how I felt about my previous pregnancy – and respected my wishes and feelings for privacy about it. The death of my daughter from that pregnancy was and is still very painful to me.

I did not wish every bed neighbour to know my history or personal details, and the midwives did not need to be told this.

Unfortunately, the registrars and house doctors were not so sensitive or tactful. On more than one occasion a loud-speaking doctor would blandly state details relating to my first pregnancy – with little thought as to how they might upset me. For example: 'Why did your first baby die?' 'What are you doing here – just because one baby died doesn't mean this one will! and 'Huh – it didn't take you long to get pregnant again.'

During the birth the care I received was superb. Everything I could have asked for. The midwife who delivered me was one who had worked on the antenatal ward that I was in. We knew each other quite well – she knew my history – so I did not have to answer or explain the inevitable questions yet again. It was reassuring and comforting to see a known friendly face. Everyone involved in the delivery room was kind and helpful.

Once back on the postnatal ward I felt very disappointed and let down. I arrived back there in the early hours of the morning. There was one midwife in charge supported by auxiliaries. Quite frankly the auxiliaries were just not interested. Any request – for a bedpan or pain relief etc. – was simply too great an effort for them. When my baby was brought to me in the morning (they were kept in the nursery for the first few nights) their assistance was unnecessarily rough and heavy-handed. What should have been a calm caring experience was tense and sore.

In the two days' stay on that ward, due to staff shortages and a full ward I felt unable to ask for help when I needed it. If I had gone home from there I am sure I would have given up breastfeeding within days. As it was, I was transferred to the local maternity ward where the difference in atmosphere was apparent within minutes of arriving. There were only seven beds in this ward and usually only one midwife supported by auxiliaries, but the care was superb. Instead of having to ask for help or advice, it was usually anticipated and there to take or leave. I stayed there until day 10 when I felt confident to take my baby home, even though we still had feeding problems.

I shall remember the kindness and expertise I received in both hospitals for a long time.

The contrast between care in labour and care postnatally was a common observation. Events surrounding birth tended to be described with a vivid immediacy; and, as in Mary Winter's story, were often compared with previous experiences which functioned to highlight aspects of staff behaviour this time:

During the birth I felt alone and frightened. When I went in the ward a sister told my partner I was not in labour and wouldn't have my baby tonight, so he went home. She put me on a machine to monitor my contractions which she said I was not having. I was in a great deal of pain and kept telling her I was in labour and asked to be seen by another doctor after one and a half hours and I was examined and had dilated 4 cm. I also asked for an epidural. She told me I could not have one as there was no one to give it me – they were on their tea break – so I was just left on my own again. Later I asked for a drink of water. I got one 1 hour later. The sister told me to be quiet and not make so much fuss. When I went into the delivery room she kept making me lie in a way which she wanted. It was very painful. She also told me to breath into my gas-and-air mask which she held on my mouth. I kept knocking it off and told her it was empty and was suffocating me. She didn't believe me again. (It was empty when she checked it.) After I had had my baby the afterbirth wouldn't come away. She kept pulling it and pulling caused me more pain. I told her at the time my other two births were the same and had to be removed manually. She said we don't want to disturb the doctor at this time of night, do we (2.50 a.m.), so she carried on pulling until she pulled the cord off altogether and was very angry when she had to fetch the doctors to remove it manually by epidural which took till about 5.30 a.m. This sister put me through hell, she was snappy and unpleasant. I tried to talk to her [but] most of the time she never answered me, and would not take any notice of what I was trying to tell her. She did it her way and that was that.

Over the birth of my second child I was treated different. The sister in charge of me was pleasant, she listened to what I said and talked to me, she made me feel relaxed and in control, making my delivery less painful and not so frightening. She gave me my baby to hold most of the time. But the other sister with the third child took her off me and left her screaming in a cot away from me in a corner for two hours. When I got into the ward after, things could not be better, they looked after me very well. The midwife who looked after me when I came home was very good, she was very helpful, and I don't know what I would have done without her. (Mary Winter)

What happened at the birth and immediately afterwards is viewed through the lens of subsequent experience. This is brought out very clearly in Tina Randall's discovery of her baby's health problems:

The stay in hospital for thirteen and a half hours was OK, but when I left I had more than I bargained for. When I got home the midwife came for six days, never said anything, but the baby is fine, she said. On the ninth day my own GP came to visit. She was very concerned about the health of the baby. She made me an appointment at the children's. The baby's hands, feet and mouth were still purple as when she was born. On arrival I was told some time later that I had a blue baby. They did an X-ray and it was confirmed she was a blue baby. When asked what St Mary's had said about her colour, I replied, they said she was dark due to the cord being wrapped around her neck and the purple was caused by too much blood. She was transferred to the Infirmary. She had got there on Friday 13 March and had a shunt put in on Saturday morning 14 March. I was told there was a risk involved but he said (Dr Bow) that in his opinion she was strong enough, she was 11 days old. After the operation she was a nice pink colour but she had still got some surgery ahead of her. Dr Bow said he could not understand how she had kept this little valve open for so long, usually it closes after five days. He said she must have the will to live. So all in all I am disgusted with the way St Mary's has treated my baby girl. (Tina Randall)

One woman who had a Caesarean just before Christmas had no complaints about her medical care as such:

Just before New Year I transferred from St Mary's Hospital to General where again the care was superb. But why on earth do they let people smoke in hospitals! I found it disgusting. When I compained, I was told that the health authority had to provide somewhere for mothers to smoke. In General, however, there is just one small open-plan lounge with one TV right next to the table where you eat your meals. Consequently, the smokers sat there constantly and the rest of us had to stay in our rooms all day unable to sit in the lounge or watch TV. We also had to eat our meals in a smoke-filled atmosphere. This greatly distressed me, as I had a bad chest infection and it was agony to cough. I left General with effectively a smoker's cough, which is ludicrous considering you're meant to be in a hospital to get well. (Barbara Marmot)

Commenting on the questions about her feelings during pregnancy and afterwards, Barbara went on to make a point about the need to locate such information in a social context:

I find it rather puzzling that you don't try to correlate these questions and answers with an individual's circumstances. For example, in my own case, my replies are affected more by the fact that I had two toddlers at home with me both during pregnancy and after birth – this completely drained and depressed me as I could never rest and never had any time to myself. If, however, it had been my first or even second pregnancy and I'd been sitting at home all day resting, then my answers would have been completely different. Also, if e.g. my other two children had been older and more sensible and less demanding, then again the answer would be different. An individual's circumstances would also reflect on their pregnancy, diet, problems etc., but this is not brought out by the survey, and I therefore fail to see how these questions can give any real information at all.

Is what doctors do depressing?

Women having babies are active evaluators of their medical care. As we have seen, many regard it as a far from benign influence on their passage through pregnancy to motherhood, and some identify it as having a literally depressing impact on their emotional wellbeing. The question 'is obstetric technology depressing?' has been asked and answered in a number of studies (see e.g. Elliott et al. 1984; Green 1989; Oakley 1980; for a review, see Romito 1989). Although, as Day (1982) argues, the question itself contributes unhelpfully to the dichotomous view of mind and body, of subjectivity as acted upon by the external environment, none the less an examination of the relationship between medical intervention and women's depression remains an important way of studying the effect on mothers of clinical 'care'. This is particularly so, given the high incidence of low emotional wellbeing after childbirth in medicalized societies (Romito 1989).

The rate of obstetric intervention in the births of the women in the SSPO study was higher than in more representative samples, because of the concentration of social difficulty and adverse obstetric history in the women's backgrounds. On the other hand, it was lower than in some other studies, because all the women had given birth before, and intervention rates are generally higher for first-time mothers. On the model of previous work, we added all the possible interventions together to produce an obstetric technology score,[4] and looked at how this related to the emotional wellbeing and other 'outcomes' of motherhood in the period following birth. These outcomes included: reported 'depression' in hospital after delivery, and at six weeks and one year later; enjoyment of, and control

Table 10.2 Obstetric technology and maternal wellbeing

| | Technology score group | | | |
| | 1 (N = 192) % | 2 (N = 161) % | 3 (N = 114) % | |
Aspects of wellbeing				Significance
Enjoyed birth:				
Yes	72	69	55	
Don't know	17	20	37	
No	11	11	8	p < 0.01
Total	100	100	100	
Control in labour:				
Yes	47	27	25	
Some	45	40	27	
No/don't know	8	33	48	p < 0.001
Total	100	100	100	
Depressed after birth:				
No	67	51	45	
Once or twice	26	41	32	
Some/all of the time	7	8	23	p < 0.001
Total	100	100	100	
Physical health at 6 wks:				
Very good/good	73	62	54	
Satisfactory/not good	27	38	46	p < 0.001
Total	100	100	100	
Physical health at 1 yr:				
Very good/good	65	63	49	
Satisfactory/not good	35	37	51	p < 0.05
Total	100	100	100	
Difficulty of last year, 1 yr after birth:				
Easy	12	14	10	
Fairly easy	65	57	54	
Rather/very difficult	23	29	36	p 14 0.01
Total	100	100	100	

during, birth; control over life at six weeks and a year after delivery; confidence as a mother, satisfaction with life, general life difficulty and maternal physical health at both time points; and enjoyment of the baby, relationship with the baby and perception of baby's temperament at six weeks and one year after birth. For eighteen out of twenty-two of these variables, those women who had high obstetric intervention scores felt worse. The 'significant' findings are shown in table 10.2 (see Oakley and Rajan (1990) for more details of this analysis).

Could doctors help?

Despite the evidence of the unhelpfulness of medical care, there remained a feeling among the women who took part in the SSPO study that doctors *ought* to be able to prevent low birthweight and other reproductive health problems. Indeed, women's use of medical care, and the energy they devoted to criticizing it, can only be explained in the light of their feeling that the solution to reproductive problems *should* lie with medical care. Table 10.3 shows how they answered the question in the postnatal questionnaire, 'Do you have any ideas about how the medical care of mothers who have previously had small babies might be improved?' The view that medical care ought to be able to prevent low birthweight is reflected in the most common request, which is for more monitoring (27 per cent) and better medical care (24 per cent). Next came more continuity of care, more information, and more attention to women's feelings, opinions and needs. As Bonny Howarth phrased it: '[you need] more help

Table 10.3 Suggested improvements in medical care

Improvement or other response	Intervention group (N = 237)[a] %	Control group (N = 230) %	All (N = 467)[a] %
More monitoring	26	28	27
Better medical care	25	24	24
More frequent visits/more home visits/continuity of care	20	22	21
More information	16	13	15
More attention to women's feelings/opinions/needs	14	10	12
More help/support/reassurance	11	7	9
Satisfied with care/no more can be done	7	11	9
Don't know	31	36	34

[a]Percentages do not add up to 100 as multiple answers were possible.

at the antinatal [*sic*] clinic. It's like a cattlemarket on a good day, and it's so degrading. They should treat everyone as human beings. They forget it's people like me that keep them in a job.'

Barbara Marmot, who had been in the control group, wrote a lengthy answer to the question about how mothers could be helped. This descri- bed many of the purposes of our social support intervention:

> Perhaps monitor them more at home during pregnancy. The minute you have a baby you are bombarded with visits from doctors, midwives, health visitors, but during pregnancy there's nobody . . . Somebody with problems or under stress (i.e. probably heading for a small baby) would benefit from regular visits by a friendly health visitor, would perhaps confide in her . . . If you had more home monitoring by a regular friendly face you're far more likely to tell her any problems and she could probably get you some practical help or introduce you to people in similar positions or give help, if for e.g. you've just moved into the area and don't know anyone. Antenatal checks in hospital are invariably running late with a different nurse and doctor each time . . . therefore no continuity. Also because they're always so busy you wouldn't feel encouraged to confide in anyone for half an hour even if they had time for you.
>
> Home visits during pregnancy would also provide an opportunity for personal counselling/persuading those mothers who persist in smoking and drinking to perhaps give up or at least cut down.

There was not much difference in desired improvements between the women who were offered the social support intervention and those who were not, except that those in the intervention group were somewhat more likely to say they wanted more information, more personal attention and more support generally.

Beliefs about low birthweight

The category 'mothers who have previously had small babies' may be part of the problem. Is having a small baby a problem? Although all the study women had given birth to a low-birthweight baby before, 63 per cent said low birthweight was not in itself a problem. Concern about having another LBW baby is founded on past experience; women who said it was not a problem were more likely to have had a normal-weight baby since. Those who had more than one preterm baby, who still thought a good deal about a baby that had died, and whose last baby went into special care and/or continued to have health and development problems were significantly more likely to worry in the next pregnancy. Responses to the question about the inherent problematic of LBW thus both reflect the past and predict future experiences.

Perceptions about whether LBW is a problem in itself are not related to the extent to which a concern over repeat LBW dominates the current pregnancy: 33 per cent of the study women said they had not been at all worried about having another LBW baby. The relationship between concern about a repeat LBW and perception of LBW as a problem in itself as shown in table 10.4. Again, it could be argued that these views were expressed after, and so took account of, the conclusion of the pregnancy. Women who had a healthy, normal-weight baby this time may have been reflecting this experience when they said they did not see LBW as a problem. The link between having had a normal-weight baby since the LBW one (and before the next pregnancy), on the one hand, and regarding LBW not as a problem, in itself, on the other, would suggest this. But it is likely that both processes are occurring in parallel: the reconstruction of the problem of LBW in the light of subsequent experience, and the prediction of risk – that LBW is *not* in itself a problem.

Why do women have LBW babies? The postnatal questionnaire asked the study women's views about this; it also asked about a family history of LBW on both the mother's and the father's side. Women may 'know' the reasons for LBW because they need to make sense of the event for themselves. Catrin Newby wrote, 'It may sound a little strange, but it was somehow comforting to have another small baby. This, combined with the very plausible theory about the heart-shaped uterus,[5] has eradicated the guilt I have felt since the birth of my first daughter. *I now know for sure I have done nothing wrong.*' The search for meaning and the claim to knowledge are intimately linked. Thirty-nine per cent of the study women identified a family history of LBW in the postnatal questionnaire. Twenty per cent of the 339 women who knew their own birthweight had themselves been LBW babies. Of the 239 who knew their partner's birthweight, 13 per cent said he had been a LBW baby too. These figures are considerably higher than the national one of around 7 per cent. Family history was related to birthweight in this pregnancy, with women who reported LBW babies on

Table 10.4 Worries about having another LBW baby by whether LBW was seen as a problem in itself

Worries about another LBW baby	LBW a problem (N = 157) %	LBW not a problem (N = 297) %	Significance
Not at all worried	22	39	
Slightly worried	35	38	
Worried quite a lot	26	16	
Extremely worried	17	7	p < 0.0001
Total	100	100	

both sides of the family giving birth to babies with birthweights on average 260 g lighter than those with no such history. Table 10.5 gives the categories of answers to the question about causes of LBW. There are some interesting differences. Smoking was seen as a general cause of LBW by 41 per cent of the women, but only 11 per cent thought it relevant in their own case (41 per cent of the study women smoked throughout pregnancy). A similar pattern holds for diet (22 per cent in general, 5 per cent in the woman's own case) and for drink and drugs (17 per cent compared to less than 1 per cent). Here the women may have been responding to the dominant health education message, which identifies these factors, particularly smoking, as major preventable causes of perinatal health problems (see Oakley 1989). The most consistent large category of answer in table 10.5 is heredity/small build, to which 22 per cent of women attributed a causal role in LBW in general, and 17 per cent in their own case. Significantly, only 2 per cent in general and less than 1 per cent in their own case thought poor antenatal care was to blame.

Table 10.5 Causes of LBW according to women in the SSPO study

Causes	In general (N = 424)[a] %	In woman's own case (N = 441)[a] %
Lifestyle:		
Smoking	41	11
Poor diet	22	5
Drink/drugs	17	<1
Stress	9	7
Not enough rest/working	8	3
No family support	0	<1
Biological:		
Heredity/small build	22	17
Prematurity	18	29
Problem with placenta	13	9
Reproductive/genetic abnormality	0	2
Mother's age	0	<1
Health and health care:		
General health problem	15	8
Poor antenatal care	2	<1
Induced too early	0	<1
Other, miscellaneous	2	3
Don't know	22	2

[a]Percentages do not add up to 100 as multiple answers were possible.

In the home interviews with the intervention women, the research midwives asked how they saw their pregnancy needs: table 10.6 gives their answers. The need mentioned by most – 58 per cent – of the women in relation to the birth of the previous LBW baby was for more information from doctors. (This question was not repeated for the index pregnancy, so the figure is omitted from table 10.6.) Aside from this, the major needs in the last LBW pregnancy were for more continuity of care (42 per cent) and for more sympathetic medical care (37 per cent); 23 per cent of mothers wanted more medical care, and 23 per cent wanted more financial help; these needs were closely followed by the need for help with housing, for more partner support and for more help from friends. In the current pregnancy, continuity of care ranked as the greatest need throughout the pregnancy. In second place at the first and second interviews came financial help; this was replaced by the need for more sympathetic medical care at the end of pregnancy. A significant proportion of the women would have liked more social support – at the third interview, 13 per cent wanted more help from their partners, 9 per cent from their families, and 5 per cent from their friends; 13 per cent wanted more domestic help.

The information in table 10.6 should be supplemented by that in table 10.7, which shows answers to questions about the most helpful and unhelpful people in the last pregnancy. Hospital doctors were ranked lowest of the 'most helpful' people and highest among specified 'unhelp-

Table 10.6 Self-perceived pregnancy needs

Needs	In last LBW pregnancy (N = 238)[a]		This pregnancy[a]					
			1st home interview (N = 238)		2nd home interview (N = 235)		3rd home interview (N = 224)	
	%	Rank	%	Rank	%	Rank	%	Rank
More continuity of care	42	1	35	1	40	1	33	1
More sympathetic medical care	37	2	25	3	23	3	28	2
Financial help	23	3	30	2	27	2	26	3
More medical care	23	3	20	4	12	5	14	4
Help with housing	21	4	19	5	17	4	13	5
More partner support	17	5	13	6	17	4	13	5
More help from friends	16	6	7	8	4	8	5	7
More family help	12	7	10	7	8	7	9	6
Domestic help	7	8	10	8	10	6	13	5

[a]Percentages do not add up to 100 as multiple answers were possible.

Table 10.7 Most helpful and most unhelpful people in the last pregnancy

People	Most helpful (N = 245) %	Most unhelpful (N = 241) %
Partner	43	5
Relative	17	3
Midwife	10	13
Friend	5	<1
GP	3	7
Hospital doctor/other health professional	2	17
No one	9	49
Other	11	6
Total	100	100

Table 10.8 Ways in which mothers of small babies can be helped

Ways of helping	Intervention group (N = 237)[a] %	Control group (N = 230)[a] %	All (N = 467)[a] %
More support/help from health professionals	19	22	20
Family support	12	9	10
Small clothes cheaper/ more widely available	10	11	10
Support groups	11	7	9
Help with feeding	12	5	9
More help/advice from special care baby unit	4	4	4
Better information	3	5	4
Financial help	4	3	3
Reassurance	4	2	3
Hospital accommodation	1	2	1
Help with bonding	<1	1	1
Help with transport	1	0	1

[a]Percentages do not add up to 100 as multiple answers could be given.

ful' people. GPs had a similar rating for being helpful, but midwives appeared both as relatively helpful (mentioned by 10 per cent of the women) and unhelpful (13 per cent).

Answers to a question about ways in which mothers of small babies can be helped are shown in table 10.8. One in five women said more support from health professionals was needed, and one in ten more family support. The need for practical help with the care of small babies came next, followed by requirements for better information and financial help. Women offered the social support intervention were less likely to view more support from health professionals as important, and more likely to identify both family support and 'support groups'.

Being researched

It was on to the nexus of perceptions of risk and scepticism about the medical categorization of LBW as a problem in itself that the additional resource of our social support intervention was grafted. It was intended not as yet another *deus ex machina* of a group of experts but as a response to a message that had for years resounded in the narratives of childbearing women, and which emerges from the descriptive data in the study discussed here; the need for supportive, personalized, *listening* care.

The critical quantitative data concerning the impact of being researched are given in table 10.9. This table includes information from the six-week postnatal questionnaires and from the follow-up questionnaires sent on the surviving babies' first birthdays.[6] A clearcut finding is the predominantly positive evaluation of the research by all the women who took part in the study. Most felt very good or good, glad to help or pleased in an altruistic sense ('to help others') to have participated. This finding confirms other reviews of the opinions of participants in controlled trials (see Elbourne 1987), and is linked with reports of high participation rates. In our study 509 women out of the 534 invited to take part initially agreed to do so, and response rates to the six-week and one-year questionnaires were 96 and 78 per cent respectively. These are high, given the lower participation rates expected with socially disadvantaged samples. Positive responses about the research in these questionnaires were much more likely among intervention-group women, confirming the original rationale for the study – the notion that taking part in supportive interviewing would be experienced as health-enhancing in a broad sense. Comments written by women in the intervention group include:

> I enjoyed the experience, glad to help. It made me feel useful, and having someone to talk to made me more sure of my abilities as a mother. (Maya Lester)

Table 10.9 Women's views of the research

Views	Intervention group %	Control group %	Significance
6-weeks questionnaire	(N = 237)	(N = 230)	
Feelings about taking part:			
Very good/good	58	39	
Glad to help/altruistic	24	19	
Don't know	17	39	
Apprehensive/not happy	1	3	$p < 0.0001$
Total	100	100	
Could research have affected birthweight?			
Yes	10	2	
No	74	96	
Don't know	16	2	$p < 0.0001$
Total	100	100	
Did research improve pregnancy experience?			
Yes	52	10	
No	48	90	$p < 0.0001$
Total	100	100	
1-year questionnaire	(N = 188)	(N = 174)	
Did research improve pregnancy experience:			
Yes	49	5	
No	51	95	$p < 0.0001$
Total	100	100	
Feelings about research midwife's visits:			
Positive	87	40[a]	
OK	12	40[a]	
Negative	1	20[a]	
Total	100	100	
Would have liked the midwife/someone to visit after the birth:			
Yes	47	21	
No	47	67	
Don't know	6	12	$p < 0.0001$
Total	100	100	
Memories of pregnancy and birth:			
Happy	56	45	
Mixed/unhappy	44	54	$p < 0.05$
Total	100	100	

[a]Percentages are calculated on numbers answering the particular question: these represent 2, 2 and 1 women respectively.

I felt more sure of myself knowing that I could phone the study midwife if I was worried about anything. (Liz Soldon)

I have enjoyed taking part and have felt quite special knowing I have done so. (Diane Frederick)

It has been a great help to me personally by answering my questions and giving advice when needed. I felt more settled, less worried, so I would imagine it could have kept me from having an early labour through worry. (Ellie Raymond)

The comfort and support your research midwife gave was tremendous. A fantastic help and support. We have become good friends and I value her friendship and all the help and support she gave me. (Hazel Scott)

Unsure at first but I found it helpful knowing the study midwife was only a phone call away. If I had not taken part in the study I would have worried a lot more during my pregnancy, which I feel does affect your health. (Holly Salper)

Once again, the help of the research midwife was appreciated as a contrast to medical care:

when you said I'd been picked to be in this whatsit I was quite pleased about it actually. Because you don't get a chance to talk to anybody about your pregnancy and everything . . . it makes you feel as if you *are* something and your pregnancy *is* something and not just . . .
   I know it's an everyday occurrence, but . . . it's something *special* to you . . . being in this study makes you think, well, your pregnancy *is* special, whereas normally you just go into the antenatal and you are just another person. (Lindsay Hiatt)

I enjoyed it and the visits from my research midwife. I felt as if I had someone to talk to, so it helped me to relax because I knew someone was there if I needed help. Hospitals treat you like a conveyor belt, they should tell you what's going on, you shouldn't have to ask. (Kay Wilson)

I was glad to help especially if healthier babies can be produced as an outcome. The midwife was able to reassure me especially after hospital visits. She acted as an interpreter between hospital and myself. Her advice was very useful. (Cherry Dodd)

In their comments, some women noted that the kind of support they had received as part of a research project ought to be more generally available:

I looked forward to my visits from the midwife. I enjoyed her company. Nice to know people care . . . I'd like to thank you for your interest. [With] my first baby I had nothing like this, you tend to stay in, and not have many visitors. It was a nice feeling to expect a visit from someone who is interested in you. If I do get pregnant again it would be nice to have some kind of visitor to visit me from time to time. It's a great help (like having a friend). My friends stop knowing me when I finished work so you can imagine how I valued the visits. Once again thank you. (Pat Price)

I don't feel I could have got through my pregnancy without the help of the research midwife. Just knowing she was there to reassure, advise or just listen. Support invaluable. Approachable personality . . . this kind of support I feel should be available to all women at such a vulnerable time. (Eileen MacKie)

Reassuring to know I could get in touch with someone who understands the worries of having had a small baby, detached from the doctor. It would be nice if this could be part of antenatal care in future. (Vera Grant)

Others made an important observation about the tendency of such research to induce reflection:

I didn't mind. It was nice having the research midwife to talk to. I would like to thank you for considering me to help. It has made my outlook a lot more thoughtful. I have realized just how lucky I am in a lot of ways. I hope my information wil be useful to you. (Sharon Campbell)

I don't know if I have helped but it's for something that can only do good for future LBW baby mums. I thought more about my pregnancy and my feelings, in fact, my life, which I might not have done if I had not taken part. (Isabel Lockheed)

I enjoyed it. Answering some of the questions has made me think about how lucky I am and how much help and support I have if I need it. (Jo Gove)

Others noted that it made them more sharply aware of material problems:

If it helps people who need help like we didn't get then I'm all for it. Due to circumstances I don't think it made any difference. It would be helpful if there was a service for looking after other children when there are no friends or relatives. (Jill Pope)

Some women commented that research itself has a value, even though to believe this may be an act of faith:

Hopefully very helpful as most research is helpful. (Kelly Eastwood)

Pleased to help. I'm a great believer in research, having been through university myself. (Barbara Marmot)

I think the idea is a very good idea as there are a lot of low-birthweight babies, but all I did was answer questions and fill in forms so I can't undestand how it was supposed to prevent me having a low-birthweight baby. But as I say, it is a marvellous idea and I am sure all the people working on it are doing a wonderful job. (Freda Lowry)

Some 10 per cent of intervention-group and 2 per cent of control-group women thought the research could have had an impact on their babies' birthweights; a larger number – 52 per cent of intervention and 10 per cent of control women – considered that taking part in the research had been beneficial generally. Although the women had had no contact with the research midwives after one brief postnatal visit, the positive evaluation of the research by intervention-group mothers six weeks after delivery had not 'washed out' by one year, when 49 per cent (compared with 5 per cent of control-group mothers) felt that taking part in the research had improved their experiences.

Answers to the next question in table 10.9 are somewhat surprising: 87 per cent of intervention-group women said they felt positive about the research midwives' visits, but so did 40 per cent of control-group women, who had, of course, not been visited. Their reaction may have been a reflection of the fact that they *did* feel part of a research project perceived as generally helpful to them, or a result of confusing visits from the research midwife with visits from a community midwife (or, of course, an error in completing the questionnaire). Some control-group women described their feelings about the research very positively in answers to two open-ended questions on the questionnaire:

I was happy to help in any way I could . . . I felt that people cared and were trying to help mothers with small babies. (Gill Fuller)

Very pleased because I was very worried that I was going to have the same problems I had with my first baby . . . I felt as if I was not worried because someone else cared enough about my pregnancy. (Yvonne Jardin)

I felt a little honoured in a way. (Obi Everett)

An important side-effect was referred to by one woman who noted her response to taking part in the research: 'I didn't mind, especially if it helps to understand or prevents premature birth . . . By filling in this form it helped to understand any problems I have because I had to write them down' (Jackie Goldthorpe). Several control-group women wrote 'thank you' letters:

Dear Ann Oakley,

I am pleased to have taken part in this study and I am glad to be of some help to other women in future.

I have filled in the questionnaire you have sent, I hope that it is OK. I have done as best as I could.

No doubt you have the information on me from the hospital but I think I should give you a little more information on what has happened during my pregnancy.

I was twenty-nine weeks pregnant when I went to the hospital for the routine check-up. I was admitted for bed-rest because of high BP. Despite the rest and medication blood pressure kept going up. The blood results were rising and protein in urine showing possible damage to the kidneys. I was about 28 weeks when an emergency section was carried out to deliver the baby, because blood pressure was 180 over 120.

I gave birth to a beautiful girl who weighed only 2 lb 4 oz. She was kept in SCBU for 8 wks and then she came home. She is fine and has been really well considering her size and circumstances in which she was born.

So far as my health is concerned, it is not so good. Blood pressure is still high and has been since the delivery. The doctors think that it might be because of the kidneys. I am still taking labetalol to control the blood pressure, I am being seen by the specialists about the kidneys. They have taken some blood tests and urine samples. Waiting for the results and will be seen again if there is any damage.

I think that I have told you about all that has happened. Overall it has been a very bad experience for me, but when I hold my baby in my arms I forget all that has happened and thank God that I have a very healthy baby. I hope that this information will help. Thank you for letting me take part in the study. (Maggie Lane)

Other control-group women, although happy to have taken part, were less personally engaged with the research:

I didn't mind being asked to take part. I was looking forward to doing it. (Joanna Kome)

I am quite happy to help in any way. I have enjoyed filling it out. (Erica Ellman)

Quite willing to take part if it is going to help in some way . . . I never gave it another thought from first being asked until this form arrived. (Tara Lewis)

Pleased, as I think any study into pregnancy is a good thing, as long as better care comes of it! (Moira Holland)

I think it is a helpful way of letting doctors, midwives, etc., know some of the worries of pregnancy. (Nina Hartnett)

Didn't mind. A bit puzzled as to why me. (Rose Harrison)

At the other end of the spectrum, some of the women allocated to the control group felt that their experience of taking part in the research might have been more positive had they been allocated to the intervention group:

Pleased to help . . . would have welcomed home visits from a midwife. (Patsy Rutter)

I was very pleased to help but would have enjoyed the visits and remembered a lot more. (Rachel Moffat)

Happy to [take part in the research] if it could help anyone in the future. Would have preferred to be in the group which was visited . . . it might have had a positive effect [on the pregnancy] if I'd been in the group which was visited. (Annette James)

The notion of 'relative deprivation' is relevant here. Although control-group women felt positive about the research, some also felt deprived in relation to the support given to women in the intervention group. As noted earlier, this signals a real tension between the ethics of giving everyone involved information about research, on the one hand, and the 'scientific' requirement of strictly 'controlled' conditions for research, on the other. There was also the feeling that taking part in the research may have made the women in the control group more aware of deficiencies in the services than they might otherwise have been:

I was pleased to help . . .[the research] made me much more aware of help and support or lack of during pregnancy. (Heida Lytten)

It made me think more about whether or not doctors and hospital staff help enough or not. (Holly Thompson)

[The research made me] analyse perhaps more. (Gill Fuller)

Not much apart from perhaps taking a slightly more critical look at my treatment . . . [and] feeling I would have some 'right to reply' had I been treated very badly. (Oona Strong)

This last woman felt 'pleased to have even a small interest taken in my feelings and opinions'.

In the section of the questionnaire relating to views about the research, some control-group women took the opportunity to write further comments about their pregnancies, not all of which were on topics central to the researchers' view of the research:

I was concerned at what the outcome would be. I went off my boyfriend completely during this pregnancy and my last, but since having had the baby I can't do enough to make it up to him. (Christa Mills)

I was interested. I felt upset after the birth, whilst still woozy from pethidine I was left on a labour bed nursing the baby for over half an hour and could easily have dropped her. The nurses seemed glad to get rid of us. (Janina Gardner)

I didn't mind at all ... I feel that all these ultrasound scans can cause a lot of anxiety especially if you are young and inexperienced like me. I think doctors/midwives should do the scans, they really know what they are looking for. (Stevie Dellafield)

I felt really pleased that something was being done into research for unborn babies ... it should be necessary for all pregnant women to be visited in their house at least every month of their pregnancy by trained people who can reassure them. (Amanda Douglas)

More intervention than control women would have welcomed continuity of care from pregnancy through the early months of motherhood, presumably again because the experiences of the former with the research midwives led them to identify ways in which a continuation of such care would have been welcomed. Finally, as shown in table 10.9, in response to a general question about memories of pregnancy and birth a year later, more women in the intervention group described their memories as generally happy.

The intervention women's positive assessment of the research is confirmed in table 10.10, which gives their answers to more detailed questions about the research. One woman said her partner did not like the research midwife telephoning; none said that being able to contact the midwife by phone 24 hours a day was not a good idea. Three per cent described the research midwives' visits as too long, 5 per cent said they were not long enough, and 92 per cent thought they were just right. Most found the midwives very helpful, and only one woman complained that the research midwife had not given enough help. When asked to respond to a list of attributes describing the midwives' role, 80 per cent of the women identified the midwives' listening as important, 65 per cent appreciated being able to tell them their worries and receive advice from them, 55 per cent enjoyed being visited through the pregnancy, 54 per cent valued the information given, and only 33 per cent thought it important that the research midwives had professional midwifery training. These assessments bear particularly on the policy implications of the SSPO study, and are taken up in chapter 12.

As Barbara Marmot noted (see p. 277), it is important to take into account in any overall evaluation of the research the general burden of stress and difficulty in the lives of the women who took part in the study. This was, indeed, the central challenge as the research midwives saw it. Their attempts to make a positive difference to the lives of the stressed and disadvantaged women in the intervention group were chronicled in chapter 7, which also gave a crude quantification of the extent of stress and difficulty, fleshed out by three of the case-studies in chapter 8.

Linked to the resistance to the health-promoting impact of social support posed by the women's social and economic circumstances is the extent to which they were supported by others in their families and communities. The dependence on the research midwives' help of women who felt socially isolated and/or unsupported which comes across in the transcripts of their conversations with the midwives is confirmed by

Table 10.10 Attitudes to the intervention

Attitudes	*% of women (N = 237)*
Feelings about research midwife telephoning:	
Very glad	53
Quite happy	46
Not happy	0
Partner didn't like it	1
Total	100
Feelings about 24-hr contact:	
A good idea	93
No feelings either way	7
Not a good idea	0
Total	100
Helpful that the research midwife:	
Was a midwife	3[a]
Gave advice	65[a]
Listened	80[a]
Could be told about worries	65[a]
Gave information	54[a]
Visited through pregnancy	55[a]
The research midwife's visits were:	
Too long	3
Just right	92
Not long enough	5
Total	100
Feelings about the research midwife:	
Very helpful indeed	73
Gave right amount of help	26
Didn't give enough help	1
Total	100

[a]Percentages do not add up to 100 as multiple answers were possible.

quantitative analysis. There was a good deal of variation in the extent to which women in the SSPO sample were receiving support and help within the community and from their families and friends. The figures in table 10.11 show that most of the women did not have much contact with their relatives, most said they had a few close friends, had received 'enough' general help in pregnancy, and half reported their male partners as changing nappies 'often'. These are some simple indices of the kinds of networks of support on to which our social support intervention was grafted (for more on this, and for a discussion of the 'notion' of class and

Table 10.11   Social support and social class

Social support	All (N = 465) %	Working class[a] (N = 188) %	Middle class[a] (N = 277) %	Significance
Contact with relatives:				
A lot	10	9	12	
Some	35	31	39	
Not very much	55	60	49	$p < 0.05$
Total	100	100	100	
Close friends:				
A lot	15	11	17	
A few	73	72	74	
None/other	12	17	9	$p < 0.01$
Total	100	100	100	
Help received in pregnancy:				
A lot	32	25	37	
Enough	50	53	48	
Very little	11	11	11	
None	7	11	4	$p < 0.01$
Total	100	100	100	
Partner changes nappies:				
Often	50	46	52	
Sometimes	21	21	22	
Never	29	33	26	$p < 0.0001$
Total	100	100	100	
No. of visits from research midwives:				
6 or more	12	18	10	
4–5	41	44	39	
3 or less	47	38	51	$p < 0.02$
Total	100	100	100	

[a]By housing tenure: owner-occupier = 'middle class'; rented/other = 'working class'.

its measurement in relation to women, see Oakley and Rajan 1991). Contrary to the idea that working-class women live in tightly knit communities where support from relatives is always on hand – the mythology of 'Mum' and Bethnal Green (see Young and Willmott 1957) – the working-class women in the SSPO study were less likely than middle-class women to be involved in such patterns of sociability, and therefore potentially more vulnerable in the face of stress. Their greater vulnerability was reflected in the fact that they were visited more frequently by the research midwives as part of the social support intervention – the figures are shown in the last three lines of table 10.11.

In terms of how the women perceived the midwives' help, generally high valuations were made by women reporting chronic stress and worry about the baby's health, and who lived apart from their babies' fathers. The only dimension of the midwives' proffered help that was differentiated by the women's socio-economic circumstances was the midwives' role as advice-givers, with more working-class women valuing this form of help. Women in the intervention group who led difficult lives and were worried about having another small baby were more likely to see the research as having a positive impact on the experience of pregnancy and its outcome. For the control-group women, general life difficulties and absence of friends were also associated with a higher estimation of the value of taking part in the research. Appreciation of the midwife as a listener, informant, and person to whom one can confide worries on more than a one-off basis was consistently higher among women with few or no friends. In addition, confiding in, and receiving continuity of care from, the research midwife, and the fact that she had professional training and could be reached at any time, were held in higher regard by women who were worried about having another small baby, and by those who reported a high level of general life difficulty.

Perceptions of randomness

Action research is different from other types of research in that participants are asked to consent to some kind of intervention in their lives. Of course, it can be argued that *all* research constitutes an intervention. In-depth interviewing, in particular, has the reputation of bringing about self-reflection and leading to disclosures in personal relationships that might not have occurred without it (see Brannen et al. 1991). However, as we saw in chapter 1, this function of research 'interviews' as intervention was part of the underlying rationale for the SSPO study.

As the design of the study was that of a randomized controlled trial, the women who did take part were informed by the research midwives, before they agreed to do so, about what taking part meant: a 50 per cent chance of being offered a social support intervention and a 50 per cent chance of being allocated to the control group. Some implications of this were discussed earlier (see chapter 6); the 'informed consent' guidelines used by the research midwives are reproduced in appendix I. Because of the study's design as an RCT, all the principal analyses of the study findings were pre-specified to be based on a simple comparison of the fates of women offered the social support intervention with those of women who, as a result of the operation of a table of random numbers, were not able to avail themselves of this resource (or could do so only in a limited way). Because original random allocation determined membership of the groups to be compared, how the women *perceived* their allocation status was not therefore taken into account. Some allocated to be offered the intervention did not receive it, or did so only minimally (because, for example, they miscarried or had their babies early), while others allocated to the control group felt involved in the research. There is therefore a potential clash here – between the principle of random allocation, on the one hand, and the ways in which women may or may not have perceived themselves as belonging to either randomized group, on the other. This potential conflict generates the question: what happens to the comparison of outcomes if the women's own feelings and experiences are built into the analysis?

The comparison of outcomes shown in figure 9.1, and drawn on throughout the text of this book, was achieved by attaching the variable 'allocation' to all the files in the computer database. In order to look at self-assessment of allocation, we constructed a second variable, 'perceived allocation', and re-ran the analysis. The new variable was based on two considerations: (1) women allocated to the intervention group who did not receive the intervention; (2) women allocated to the control group who felt as though they had participated in the intervention. Construction of the new variable resulted in thirteen women having their allocation changed: six women allocated originally to the intervention group moved into the control group, and seven women allocated originally to the control group entered the intervention group. The results of using the new variable, compared with the originals, are shown in table 10.12. Judged by the criterion of statistical significance, for three of the outcomes – worry about the baby, hospital admission in pregnancy, and non-spontaneous delivery – perceived allocation reduces the difference; in twentyfive the new variable makes no difference; for two outcomes – the difficulty of the last year and epidural/general anaesthesia – perceived allocation increases the difference; and in one – control over life – the difference is statistically significant for perceived allocation but not for original allocation. This suggests that taking into account research partici-pants' perception of research-group membership may significantly alter the calculation and interpretation of research findings (although from the point of view of the conventions of RCTs, such a manoeuvre may be seen to introduce 'bias').

Table 10.12 Main study outcomes by original and 'perceived' allocation

Outcomes	Original allocation			'Perceived' allocation		
	Intervention (N = 237) %	Control (N = 230) %	Significance	Intervention (N = 238) %	Control (N = 229) %	Significance
Emotional wellbeing						
At 6 weeks:						
Depressed in hospital	41	49		41	47	
Depressed since birth	11	12		10	13	
Worried about baby	16	26	p < 0.01	18	25	p < 0.1
Not enough control over life	27	34		28	36	p < 0.05
Not satisfied with life	8	10		7	11	
Not very confident as a mother	7	7		7	8	
Last year difficult	23	22		25	23	
At 1 year:						
Depressed during last year	36	31		39	34	
Depressed now	4	6		4	6	
Worried about baby	12	12		13	14	
Not very confident as a mother	5	6		6	6	
Last year difficult	25	18	p < 0.05	27	17	p < 0.01
Mixed/negative experience of motherhood	9	12		9	13	
Memories of pregnancy and birth mixed/negative	35	38		38	42	

Table 10.12 *cont.*

Outcomes	Original allocation			'Perceived' allocation		
	Intervention (N = 237) %	Control (N = 230) %	Significance	Intervention (N = 238) %	Control (N = 229) %	Significance
Women's health and health care use						
At 6 weeks:						
Admitted to hospital in pregnancy	31	53	$p < 0.0001$	36	51	$p < 0.01$
Induced onset of labour	26	33		28	33	
Non-spontaneous delivery	17	25	$p < 0.01$	18	27	$p < 0.05$
Epidural/general anaesthetic	30	35		28	37	$p < 0.1$
High obstetric technology score	37	47	$p < 0.05$	37	48	$p < 0.05$
Physical health since birth not good	6	9	$p < 0.05$	6	9	$p < 0.05$
NHS use 2 or more times	17	20		17	21	
At 1 year:						
Physical health not good	6	8		10	8	
NHS use 4 or more times	21	17		23	17	
Baby's health and health care						
At birth:						
Mean birthweight (g)	(2944)	(2907)		(2946)	(2903)	
Intubated	5	8		4	7	
To special care baby unit	15	15		15	15	
At 6 weeks:						
Problems after discharge	27	35	$p < 0.01$	28	35	$p < 0.01$
Bottlefed	53	58		52	58	
NHS use 3 or more times	15	17		11	12	
At 1 year:						
Physical health not good	24	28		26	30	
NHS use 15 or more times	17	27		30	26	

Predicting your own risk

Finally in this chapter we consider the question of risk from the standpoint of how the intervention-group women felt at the beginning of their pregnancies, and whether or not this was any guide to what happened to them. Risk is the object of formal scoring systems developed by clinicians and intended to identify on the basis of what is known at the beginning of pregnancy who will develop problems and who will not. But, if medical attempts to predict risk are, as we have seen, relatively unsuccessful, do the women's own perceptions fare any better? One of the questions the research midwives asked at the first home interview was 'How do you feel about this pregnancy now?' We included this question in the interview schedule because other research has shown that subjective health perceptions predict health problems, and even the risk of death, better than medical risk criteria (see e.g. Blaxter 1985; Kaplan and Kotler 1985). Our question was deliberately not a specific one: it did not make a distinction between physical sensations and emotional experiences, or between whether or not a pregnancy was planned, wanted or welcomed, and how it

Table 10.13 Intervention-group women's initial feelings about pregnancy and pregnancy 'outcome'

Pregnancy 'outcome'	% of women who had felt happy (N = 118)	% of women who had felt all right/ unhappy (N = 102)	Significance
Birth at less than 37 weeks gestation	16	20	
Stillbirth (number)	(1)	(2)	
Low-birthweight baby	14	23	p < 0.01
Mean birthweight (g)	(2965)	(2916)	
Baby to special care baby unit	12	20	p < 0.1
Baby had postnatal health problems	29	24	
Mother's postnatal physical health not good	24	30	
Mother depressed in hospital	39	45	
Mother had not enough control over life at 6 weeks after delivery	27	32	

was regarded by the woman now. In other words, what the question did was span the mind–body, self–embodiment, physical–psychosocial divide of table A.

Out of the women who were asked this question, 20 per cent said they felt very happy, 36 per cent said they felt happy, 33 per cent felt all right, and 5 per cent described their feelings as unhappy or very unhappy. (The remaining 6 per cent didn't know, gave mixed answers, or didn't answer the question.) The distribution of positive and negative answers according to some of the main study outcomes is shown in table 10.13. Clearly, whatever dimensions of health status this question is tapping are associated with different risks of both women and babies doing well or badly. How women feel about their pregnancies early on *is* related to what happens to them and their babies.

This is one basis for arguing that the attempt to ensure healthy pregnancy, healthy babies and healthy women (otherwise known as antenatal care) needs to allow women their own voice. Simply, how women feel about their pregnancies may be a better guide to the chances of problems developing than conventional medical risk assessments. But, because of the ways in which many women describe their experiences of receiving medical care in pregnancy, a prescription for heightened medical surveillance based on the incorporation of subjective health status would hardly be what the doctor ought to order. What is needed is a different approach altogether.

11

The Poverty of Research

It is a truism to say that a 'good' experiment is precisely that which spares us the exertion of thinking: the better it is, the less we have to worry about its interpretation, about what it 'really' means. (Medawar 1982: 82)

What it comes down to, in the end, is that the poor are likely to remain unhealthy so long as they remain poor; conversely, the way to improve their health is to improve their economic state. (Smith 1990: 350)

All research is *process*, but it is also about *results*. One of the themes of this book is that the relationship between the two is far from straightforward. Though other researchers have exposed this aspect of doing research (see e.g. Bell and Encel 1978; Bell and Roberts 1984), the disjunctiveness of the relationship is especially marked in the effort to dissolve the dichotomy of quantitative and qualitative methods. The underlying problem is that facts do not 'speak for themselves'. And 'facts' as such do not exist independently of perception and social construction.

Beyond the production of the results of research lie two other mine-ridden domains: those of the *dissemination* of research findings and of their *policy implications*. All research is political in the sense that it is about, and influenced by, relations of power. But much of it is also political in that its findings can be construed as relevant to the making of decisions about the way people live. Like research results, the policy implications of research do not simply emerge from the data. They are not born, but made; they have to be pulled out of the genuine inescapable untidiness of research, and the position of the puller affects the type of yield that is gained. Depending on viewpoint, the same piece of research can have different policy implications. But researchers themselves have an ethical obligation to say what they think the research findings mean. As developed within the feminist critique of knowledge, this moral burden lies particularly on those, like feminists, who approach the doing of research from an overt political perspective. Not to formulate views about the relevance of the research findings to the 'real' world is irresponsible, given the reason for doing the research in the first place, which was not as some ivory-tower exercise, but to advance both knowledge and understanding so as to improve the lives of those who have been particularly, or partially, bereft of these.

The SSPO study has provided the template for an exploration in this book of how research can be done in the problematic territory lying between the social and the medical, between embodiment and enselvement, between professionalized and ordinary 'lay' knowledge, between medicalized reproduction and normal childbirth, and in the difficult terrain of sex and gender with all its heavy biological and cultural baggage. The study has provided the foundations for an argument about how knowledge is constructed in a society that divides life into two: the dichotomies of table A are part of our individual socialization and endemic to how we are taught in 'educational' institutions to understand and assess the world. They are also, it has been argued here, damaging to the goal of understanding and making an impact on the quality of human life in our time. But, having used the study in this way, there is now an obligation to summarize and distil its own meanings: what did the study find, and how can what it found be sensibly translated into recommendations for action in an imperfect world which may then very well choose to ignore these?

This chapter presents an argument about both the narrow and the wider meanings of the SSPO study. It addresses the question of findings within three contexts. The first context is that of previous work on social support and health, and of the relations between social and material support; in other words, does befriending pregnant women make sense when their greatest enemy is not lack of social support but inadequate material resourcing of motherhood? The second context is the cultural treatment of women and reproduction; here the question is about the implications of the study for the routine provision of maternity care. The third context relates to the question of who listens, and attends, to the results of research; because of the problematic nature of this part of the process, the question is: does research make any difference to the 'real' world anyway?

Did it work?

The SSPO study has demonstrated the effectiveness, appropriateness and safety of a social support intervention in 'high-risk' pregnancy provided by midwives research. It has been shown to be effective in its demonstration of an impact on different pregnancy outcomes; appropriate in that very few of the 509 women who agreed to take part in the study did not feel positive about their participation in it; and safe because the data collected are reassuring on the apparent harmlessness of social support.

Taking this last point first, we saw in chapter 6 that setting up a randomized controlled trial requires uncertainty about the effectiveness, appropriateness and safety of the procedure under test. It is harder to argue uncertainty in some cases than in others, and social support may seem self-evidently 'good'. But, since other supposedly beneficial forms of help (social workers, psychotherapy, vitamin supplementation) have been shown not to be so, our starting-point was that a social support intervention of the kind we proposed had uncertain effects: it might do either good or harm. The failure to detect an adverse effect of social support may seem no news at all, but it needs to be contextualized in the origins of the study outlined in chapter 1. One main reason for undertaking a 'trial' of social support was that so many other trials of medical interventions aimed at improving the health of women and babies had come up with negative findings. Most popular among such medical interventions is drug therapy, especially with hormones, and including the infamous DES (diethylstilboestrol), which was many years later found to cause genital-tract cancers in children of treated women (see Goldstein et al. 1989). A review in 1978 of clinical strategies for the prevention of low birthweight found that none of the thirty-seven published controlled interventions in this area could point to benefits for birthweight in the absence of disabling side-effects (Hemminki and Starfield 1978); later reviews confirmed this (Anderson and Turnbull 1982; see Goldstein et al. 1989). Moreover, drug treatment for the prevention of low birthweight is not a cheap 'therapy' (Korenbrot et al. 1984). Social support as prevention for the health-damaging effects of stress is benign, whereas medical interventions, if not efficacious, may be harmful. As Mervyn Susser has noted:

> It is about forty or fifty years since the 'stress' hypothesis gathered momentum and began to displace the fashionable hypothesis of our time, which attributed ... [many] obscure ills to foci of infection. Many excellent sets of teeth and many pairs of tonsils were sacrificed to test that hypothesis. We can count ourselves lucky that the stress hypothesis does not require surgical intervention. (Susser 1987; 235).

Before the SSPO study began, fifteen hypotheses about areas that social support might affect were pre-specified (see p. 376). In terms of effectiveness, and in accordance with conventions for assessing the significance of research findings, for thirteen of these hypotheses the intervention group in the SSPO study did better, for one the control group did better, and for another no difference between the two groups was detected. The probability of this being due to chance is very low: it is, in other words, a 'statistically significant' finding. In the intervention group there were benefits for some 'outcomes' more than others. For example, more 'effect' was apparent on the physical health of mothers and babies, and on their health care use – including during childbirth itself and for babies in the immediate post-birth period – than on the birthweight of the babies or its classification as 'normal' or 'low'. The emotional wellbeing of mothers was substantially improved. Anxiety was lowered, and feelings of control enhanced. This differential effect is hardly surprising, given that there are no a priori grounds for supposing that social support affects birthweight as much as it affects maternal emotional wellbeing, or babies' use of medical care as much as their mothers' antenatal hospital admissions.

The conclusion that social support as tested in the SSPO study fulfils the three criteria of safety, effectiveness and appropriateness places it in the same category as many of the studies reviewed in chapters 2 and 3 which demonstrate that friendship, support and non-professional forms of help are at least as relevant to the production of health, and in some cases more so, than medical-risk factors and medical interventions. Friendship is important, and deficits in the social support resources already available to people may to some extent be compensated for by the introduction of 'artificial' support. There are two separate issues here. One is the substitution of artificial for natural support, while the other is the efficacy of lay, as distinct from professional, help. Although the research midwives in the SSPO study were trained midwives, their role was to act as far as possible as ordinary befrienders. This gave them some problems at times, especially when they felt that what the women wanted was a combination of friendship with clinical care – a not surprising finding, given the messages that come out of the consumer satisfaction literature (see Reid and Garcia 1989). The SSPO study midwives can point to greater success of *their* intervention than that of the clinical midwives in the French study of home visits for women with pregnancy complications (Spira et al. 1981); and, beyond the maternity care field, they can align themselves, for example, with the interviewers in the Danish study (described in chapter 3) who visited elderly people at home and succeeded in keeping them alive and out of hospital (Hendriksen et al. 1984), while social caseworkers in an American study of a similar population had precisely the opposite effect (Blenker et al. 1971).

Apart from the question of differential effects, a series of others are subsumed under the general question: does social support work? These include: is 'dose' of social support important? Are some people better at giving social support than others? What is it about social support that works, when it does? And, last but by no means least, do its effects last?

Three of these questions can be addressed by looking at the respective roles of the research midwives in the SSPO study. Some answers are suggested by the data in table 11.1. It can be seen that the differences between the birthweights of intervention- and control-group women varied from −24 g to +129 g in favour of the intervention group in the four centres; the differences in the incidences of depression and poor physical health in both mothers and babies followed broadly the same pattern, and the biggest difference in anxieties about the baby's weight at one year was also in the centre that had the greatest differences for the other outcomes. Interestingly, however, when it comes to women's reports of their experiences of taking part in the research, the women in this centre were the least likely to say it had affected them positively. More, but still the lowest percentage of the four, gave this reply at one year. The centres that did best in terms of outcomes were those in which women were most likely to say that the research midwife listened to them, and in which they appreciated being given both advice and information. However, average time spent by the research midwife did not appear to bear any relation to the differences in outcome (though it could be concluded that the best outcomes were in the centre where the research midwives spent the *least* time).

It might seem a matter of common sense that the research midwives are likely to have interpreted social support differently from one another, despite our attempts to standardize their behaviour. But this conclusion is complicated by the question of numbers. Centre 4, which looks as though it might have been more 'successful' than the others, had the largest numbers of women, and therefore the highest chance of producing statistically significant findings. This returns us to the essential question of the use and abuse of statistical tests (see pp. 262–6). However, if the differences here are 'real' (and this is one of the many important questions which could be addressed by further research), then it is interesting to note that centre 4 scored lowest on smoking advice, highest on advice on benefits, highest on referrals to health professionals, and also highest on listening and giving reassurance. Notably too, the clients of the research midwife in centre 4 were least likely to value the fact that she (like the others) had a professional midwifery training. With regard to the social characteristics of the women in the different centres, we saw earlier (table 7.1) that centres 1 and 4 had more socially disadvantaged populations than the others; the apparently superior results of centre 4 therefore cannot be explained by a more privileged population.

Sub-analysis by centre may give pointers to the next stage of social support research. And hereby hangs an important addendum: each 'trial' of any intervention can only answer a limited set of questions. These are questions about that particular intervention introduced in that particular way in that particular place and time. Generalizability to other populations is not guaranteed. It is because different interventions are different and different populations are different that research findings are not, and cannot be expected to be, uniform within the same general category of studies. Exploring data in the social support and pregnancy field, for example, Henry Heins in South Carolina found his social intervention had the biggest effect on black women with medical problems (Heins et al. 1987), while in the Western Australian study it seemed to be socially supported middle-class women who benefited the most (Bryce et al. 1991). Hereby, too, hangs the important qualification that there is no such thing as a definitive study. Knowledge is pushed forward a little at a time – inch by inch, not (usually) by quantum leaps. Ideas generate research which produces more ideas for further research. Each piece of resear is unique, making a contribution to the whole picture on the basis of sketches and blueprints provided by others.

Table 11.1 Results of the SSPO study: differences by centre

					Centre			
Study result	1 (N = 75)	Significance	2 (N = 33)	Significance	3 (N = 57)	Significance	4 (N = 83)	Significance
'Outcomes'								
Mean birthweight (g):								
Intervention	3019		2940		2865		3014	
Control	3043		2856		2861		2885	
Difference	−24		+84		+4		+129	
	%		%		%		%	
Mother depressed in hospital after birth:								
Intervention	44		32		44		40	
Control	36		54	$p < 0.1$	49		58	$p < 0.05$
Mother's physical health 'not good' 6 wks after birth:								
Intervention	37		21		37		24	
Control	42		29		40		46	$p < 0.01$
Baby had health problems at 1 yr:								
Intervention	35		35		38		22	
Control	41		43		40		41	$p < 0.08$

Table 11.1 *cont.*

	Centre							
Study result	*1 (N = 75)*	*Significance*	*2 (N = 33)*	*Significance*	*3 (N = 57)*	*Significance*	*4 (N = 83)*	*Significance*
Worried about baby's weight at 1 yr:								
Intervention	26		31		23		5	
Control	32		26		40	p < 0.09	20	p < 0.001
The intervention								
Felt that study had affected pregnancy experiences:								
At 6 wks:								
Intervention	29		39		35		24	
Control	3		0		14		0	
At 1 yr:								
Intervention	50		50		63		38	
Control	6		0		11		11	
(Intervention women only)								
Said research midwife:								
Listened	73		91		75		82	
Gave information	43		58		56		64	
Gave advice	58		58		60		78	
Average contact with research midwife (hrs)	(5.6)		(5.0)		(6.6)		(4.2)	

From here to eternity

A critical question in evaluating the success of interventions in people's lives concerns time. Some effects, noted in the short term, may 'wash out' over time; this is the case, for example, with many of the early childhood educational interventions (see Zigler and Weiss 1985). On the other hand, it is possible for effects which are not apparent in initial analyses to make their appearance later; some dietary interventions report this finding (see Oakley 1985). In the original protocol for the SSPO study we said we would stop collecting data when the postal questionnaires sent out six weeks after birth were returned. But, as we were able to raise some money to carry out another postal survey at the surviving babies' one-year birthdays, we were able to supplement this information, and look at whether social support given in pregnancy seemed to have any lasting effects.

Table 11.2 SSPO study 'outcomes' at one year: mothers' experiences

'Outcomes'	Intervention group (N = 188) %	Control group (N = 174) %	Significance
Physical health in last year:			
Very good/good	63	58	
Satisfactory/not good	37	42	
Total	100	100	
Emotional wellbeing:			
'Not depressed'	95	90	
'Depressed'	5	10	$p < 0.1$
Total	100	100	
Close friends:			
Some	82	74	
One/none	18	26	$p < 0.06$
Total	100	100	
Experience of being a mother:			
Very enjoyable/good on the whole	89	82	
Mixed/difficult/very difficult	11	18	$p < 0.09$
Total	100	100	
Worried about baby's weight:			
No	80	68	
Yes	20	32	$p < 0.01$
Total	100	100	

Some of these data are drawn on in chapter 10. Tables 11.2 and 11.3 give further information. Table 11.2 shows aspects of mothers' experiences as reported by them at one year, and divided by intervention and control group. The physical health of intervention-group mothers was better, as was their emotional wellbeing, and they were more likely to say they had close friends. Their experiences of motherhood were more positive, especially in terms of anxiety about the baby. The babies' health outcomes are shown in table 11.3: intervention-group babies were more likely to be described as very healthy at one year; they also made more use of the health services. Maternal perceptions of babies' health may well reflect mothers' positive recall of the intervention, but, on the other hand, mothers' reports matched the medical data collected directly from the case-notes after birth, suggesting that mothers described the 'real' health profiles of their babies. The apparent link between greater health and

Table 11.3 SSPO study 'outcomes' at one year: children's experiences

'Outcomes'	Intervention group (N = 188) %	Control group (N = 174) %	Significance
Physical health:			
Very healthy	68	59	
Occasionally/often unwell	32	41	$p < 0.08$
Total	100	100	
Total illness score:			
0–6	76	72	
6 or more	24	28	
Total	100	100	
Visits to GP:			
0–3	56	64	
4 or more	44	36	
Total	100	100	
Visits from GP:			
0–2	69	77	
3 or more	31	23	
Total	100	100	
Visits to health visitor:			
0–5	42	57	
6 or more	58	43	$p < 0.04$
Total	100	100	
Telephone calls to health visitor: mean (s.d.[a])	2.6 (2.2)	1.9 (1.1)	$p < 0.03$

[a]Standard deviation

more health service use may not be causal; indeed, the literature on this would suggest other interpretations (see e.g. Blaxter and Paterson 1982; Cartwright and Anderson 1981; Wolfe 1980.)

The postal survey carried out one year after birth was inexpensive and relatively easy to do. Its direct costs amounted to £1500, though entering and analysing the data took longer and cost more, and we were fortunate in securing an extension of funding from the Department of Health to make this possible. We had, however, planned a more comprehensive follow-up of the SSPO women. What we wanted to do was to look at the impact of the pregnancy support intervention over time, and to make full use of what had by now become a detailed and rich database. Unlike many such databases, ours contained not only medical information, but a wide range of social information about material circumstances and living conditions, about stress and responses to stress, about coping and emotional wellbeing, and about the complex interactions between child and adult health and the ways in which these were contextualized in the social environment. Moreover, the population of families in the SSPO study was precisely that considered by policy-makers and clinicians to form the human terrain that needed to be studied to achieve greater understanding of the links between 'socio-economic factors' and adverse reproductive outcomes.

A year before the first three-year grant from the Department of Health ran out, in July 1987, we submitted a proposal to the ESRC for a more ambitious follow-up study to the SSPO project. The project, which was called 'Social Support and Family Health', was costed at £100,000 (two part-time salaries for three years, plus fieldwork and other costs), and would run for three years. We planned to carry out a further postal survey when the children were 3 years old, and to re-interview all the intervention-group women. The study would enable us both to look at the long-term effects (if any) of our pregnancy intervention, and to analyse 'the relationship between social and material disadvantage and children's development on the one hand, and the social and material resources/ circumstances and health service use of families on the other'. Unhappily, this proposal was to fall victim of yet another internal ESRC reorganization. In November 1987 a letter informed me that the ESRC would be unlikely to communicate the result of the application for a further three months, since it had recently been decided to revamp application procedures, and that all would now be considered by a single Research Grants Board, rather than by individual subject committees. Because of this, 'We very much regret that the process of transition from the old structure to the new has caused delays in the consideration of the present round of applications. In particular, delays at the Department of Education and Science in appointing new members of Council have caused unforeseen problems in forming the new Board.' The letter apologized 'for this enforced delay and uncertainty' and reassured me that the delay should have 'no adverse consequences' on the timing of the project. A further letter came in February 1988; this said the proposal was 'an interesting one on an important subject', and that the RGB had now met but had deferred a decision about the proposal until the next meeting at the end of April:

> This is intended to allow you to respond to a number of concerns voiced by the Board and for us to discuss it with the DHSS. You should provide supplementary comments under these headings:
>
> 1 The findings and methods of the pilot and current phases of the research.
> 2 Problems in not having a control group and in using self-reporting.
> 3 Data analysis (particularly to show how the benefits of intervention can be distinguished).

This letter gave me a sense of *déjà vu*. I sent an eight-page response, reminding the ESRC that *they* had funded the pilot study and had in their possession an end-of-grant report on it, providing further details about the current phase of the research, and defending 'self-reporting' on the grounds that mothers were probably in a better position than anyone else to say what was happening to their children. Points 2 and 3 evoked the same distress as in discussions five years earlier with the ESRC (see chapter 4), who still seemed incapable of understanding the research design of a controlled trial. Thus in response to point 3 I replied;

> I find this question difficult to answer, given that our study has been designed and carried out as a randomized controlled trial precisely in order to avoid the usual problems that beset non-randomized intervention studies when it comes to the question: how can we be sure that differences between groups are due to the intervention and not to pre-existing factors that make one group different from another? All the outcomes that have been iden-tified as important in the present application ... will be analysed to see whether study allocation (intervention or control) is associated with diffe-rent patterns of outcome.

My justification did not convince, however, and the proposal was turned down two months later: 'We had another long discussion of the proposal,' said this letter, in a deceptively chatty vein, 'but felt that on balance too many doubts remained to justify funding at the level requested to follow on the current study especially in the absence of a full evaluation of that work ... We will probably invite you to consider a resubmission but when and in what format I cannot yet say.' This letter promised a synopsis of comments from the meeting, so that I would have some idea why the project had been turned down. When the synopsis arrived, it was apparent that some of the same points continued to worry board members; in particular, the use of mothers to give information about children – 'It is difficult to imagine that mothers could, in a postal questionnaire, provide complete and reliable information about events in this richly changing period of their children's lives' – and the old nightmare of research design:

> Given that low birthweight is associated with adverse sequlae and that significant difference between the birthweights of the two samples will be found, some differences in the child's health and development may well emerge. It is unclear whether it is intended to establish the extent to which any such effects are direct effects of the intervention.

There seemed little point in replying to this. The objection to applying for further funds before the current study was finished riled only slightly less than the ESRC's blindness about controlled trials. All longitudinal research suffers from the problem that extra funding needs to be sought before 'final' results are available; it is in the nature of the exercise that the activity of tracking samples through time requires a continued commitment to funding. But, because research funding operates to inhibit recognition of the importance of this, what tends to happen instead is the collection of more data from more and more newly acquired samples, in the mistaken belief that this is a more cost-effective and scientific way to proceed.

Because of uncertainty about the willingness of the ESRC to deliver the goods, we tried a number of other funding sources during the same few months. In June 1987 the Joseph Rowntree Memorial Trust turned us down ('the topic was felt to be on the margins of the Trust's interest'); in March 1988 Birthright, the research charity of the Royal College of Obstetricians and Gynaecologists (no reason given); in May the Mental Health Foundation ('a large number of applications of high scientific standard'); and in December the Health Promotion Research Trust[1] ('competition for ... resources is very fierce'). Three other organizations – Action Research for the Crippled Child, the W. K. Kellogg Foundation and the Robert Wood Foundation in the USA – said it was not worth applying. But a much smaller foundation than any of these, the Iolanthe Trust, which specializes in midwifery research, decided to award us £9000 over three years as a contribution to further work. This grant was a life-saver, and enabled us to carry out a good deal of extra analysis, even though it was not sufficient to fund the collection of extra data, as we had originally planned.

The final twist in the story is that the ESRC did eventually offer assistance for the Social Support study, though in a different guise. Under their Management of Personal Welfare Initiative, a multi-project programme of work on the interfaces between individual difficulty and both formal and informal support, we submitted a proposal for work using the database to explore issues to do with stress, service use and coping in relation to 'the health and welfare of vulnerable children', and complementing this with a study of service-providers' views. This proposal was agreed; the work started in April 1990 and is continuing today.

Poor women

Because of the way in which the sample of women who took part in the SSPO study were recruited, the majority of the women came from working-class households, and many of them were poor. We chose to select the study sample in this way because of our intention to focus on the 'problem' of low birthweight and to examine the extent to which a social process (befriending) might affect the quantification of infant embodiment, as well as health in a general (that is social *and* biological) sense, including women's experiences of motherhood. The reasoning behind this method of selecting the sample was rehearsed in earlier chapters; briefly, we thought that given such a sample we would be more likely to be able to show an effect of the social support intervention, and that such a finding would be more relevant on a policy level, *because of* the contribution that problems among this population make to the overall picture of 'preventable' reproductive illness and death.

Two-thirds of low-birthweight babies are born to women from working-class households, as against half of all babies, so the choice of low birthweight as a *biological* criterion was also the choice of material disadvantage as a *social* criterion. The overlap that exists between these two categories – of low birthweight and low social class – of course points to the unhelpful falsity of the dualism between the two sides of table A (yet again). More concretely, what it provides in discussions of issues concerning women, babies and the maternity services is a dialectical reiteration and ideological blurring: while the issues are continually forced apart by semantic differentials, yet at the same time seem to be the same, it is not clear which is the problem – the baby's weight or the woman's class. This confusion mars many social and medical texts, and many generations of weighty policy documents. Reporting in 1980, for example, the government Social Services Committee puzzled about how to distinguish the contribution of social from that of medical factors to baby deaths, themselves class-differentiated and linked to low birthweight:

> Perinatal and neonatal mortality are twice as high in the lowest socio-economic classes as in the highest ... Factors causing perinatal and neonatal mortality and handicap broadly divide into two interrelated categories:
> (a) socio-economic factors, such as lack of education, poverty, poor housing, possibly poor nutrition, unplanned pregnancy, smoking, drinking alcohol to excess, etc.
> (b) medical factors, such as lack of antenatal care, low birthewight, asphyxia during delivery or afterwards, congenital malformations, cerebral haemorrhage, etc.

While the committee accepted the difficulty of improving socio-economic conditions in the short term, it suggested:

much of the death and handicap suffered by babies of socially disadvantaged mothers can be overcome by well applied medical intervention. Important interventions we have identified are: the concentration of antenatal, intrapartum and community care on the high risk mother; improved care of the sick baby; humanizing the hospitals and clinics; persuading people to smoke less. (Social Services Committee 1980: 158–9).

Identification in such texts of the respective domains of the social and the medical is deemed important to the task of settling on appropriate remedial policies. What is social is correctable socially, while the medical must be the target of medical interventions.

Low birthweight, recognized in 1980 as a major and unhappily stable correlate of reproductive mortality rates, had, by the time of the report of the Social Services Committee nine years later, entered a class of its own. It was now recognized to be 'the most important among factors that determine mortality'. A programme of 'systematic social and medical research aimed at establishing the reasons for, and reducing the incidence of, low birthweight' (Social Services Committee 1989: ix) was recommended. The government's reply to this report accepted the need for such research, but responded to it by returning the problem to the biological domain:

> Links between low birthweight and, for example, maternal age, parity, interval between births and smoking have already been identified. However, the most important reason for low birthweight is preterm birth and this will not be satisfactorily comprehended until the mechanism of the onset of labour is better understood. It is a profoundly difficult *biological* problem. (Department of Health 1989: 5) (italics added)

In such ways the 'problems' of the official statistical categories of perinatal mortality, low birthweight and social class are batted back and forth – now you see one of them, now another. Behind the screen of the statistics which demonstrate that social deprivation, bodily deprivation and death are linked (see table 1.1), something is known to be happening; but the discursive discourse of the social and medical – the relentless argument about *which* it is – gets in the way of understanding just *what* it is.

The material poverty of the women who took part in the SSPO study emerges clearly in both the quantitative and the qualitative data drawn on in this book. Not only did many of them lack the material resources to provide for themselves and their families anything other than a health-denying quality of life, but the practical shortfalls were matched by the cultural under-resourcing of both gender and class. From the point of view of women's passages to motherhood, a classist, sexist and racist medical system (Doyal 1979) simply does not, and cannot, attend to the voices and needs of those who are perceived to be on the margins: those who are seen as being both the most needy in health terms, and the least capable of being helped because of cultural differences and patterns of resistance (expressed in the language of 'non-compliance', 'non-attendance', etc.). The poverty of the women and children in the SSPO study was part of a broader picture which can be sketched in statistical terms: in the six years before the study began, the number of people living in poverty had increased by 111 per cent, bringing the proportion of the country's children living in poverty up to nearly one in three, and doubling the proportion of low-income households made up of families with depen- dent children (Bradshaw 1990).

Two conclusions are clear, looking at obstetric history (the 'medical' domain), material and social circumstances (the 'social' domain) and the experiences of women and babies ('pregnancy outcome') in the light of our social support intervention. First, our social support intervention tended to help most those who had the most (social and/or medical) problems. Secondly, it did not help them enough to give a result which was 'statistically significant' in terms of birthweight – though statistical significance was achieved for some other important prespecified out- comes. Figures 11.1–11.3 show some of the main study outcomes by the three variables of mothers' own social support resources, their previous history of preterm labour, and household income level. The tendency for the intervention to help most those who had the most problems is clearest in figure 11.1, relating to existing social support, and least clear in figure 11.3, relating to income level.[2]

The data represented in figures 11.1–11.3 draw attention to the need to untangle the direct and indirect effects of material deprivation on pre- gnancy 'outcome'. Living in poverty has implications for health which are mediated through processes of personal identity and 'coping' strategies (see Rutter and Quine 1990). Different paradigms of welfare interpose different ways of conceptualizing the public and the private and the interrelations between these, but we are, as yet, merely at the start of a process of linking the analysis of the health and welfare effects of material conditions, on the one hand, with the language of stress, social support and coping, on the other (see Williams 1992).

Yet the research midwives' perception of the difficulty of their task – how to overcome, by providing social support, the health-defeating effects of poor material conditions with their associated high levels of life stress – also proved correct. The space for effecting change in lives such as those of Joy Digby, Jenny Frame and Carol Slater described in chapter 8 is small. This dilemma of social support interventions is perhaps best, albeit very painfully, illustrated in the story of Simone Churchill told in chapter 7. Simone's healthy baby (claimed as a 'success' by her research midwife) died at 4 months of a respiratory illness attributed by her mother to health- damaging housing. None the less, the difference befriending can make may be real (many of the SSPO women certainly thought it was). It is simply the case that the hurdles preventing the translation of this into

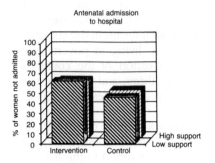

Antenatal admission
to hospital

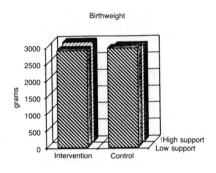

Birthweight

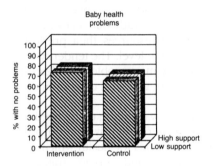

Baby health
problems

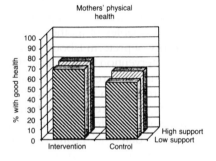

Mothers' physical
health

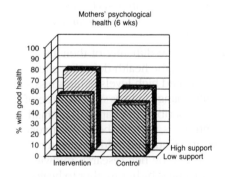

Mothers' psychological
health (6 wks)

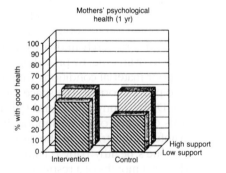

Mothers' psychological
health (1 yr)

Figure 11.1 Study outcomes by mothers' social support

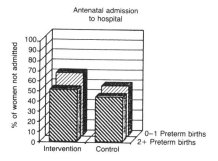

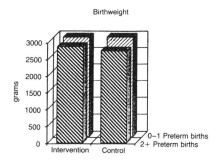

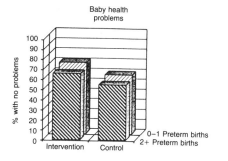

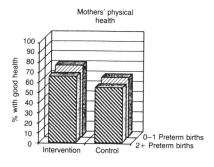

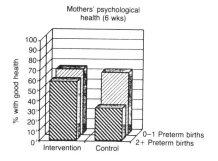

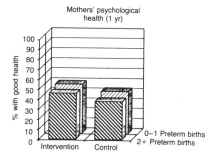

Figure 11.2 Study outcomes by mothers' history of preterm labour

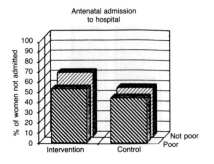

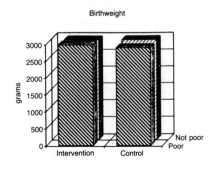

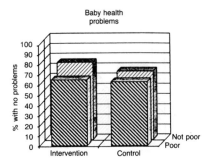

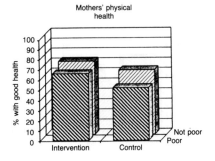

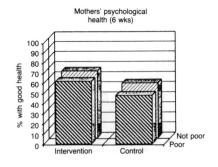

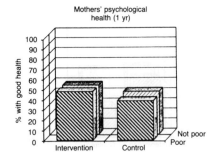

Figure 11.3   Study outcomes by income level

quantitative 'health' effects are huge. Of course, the fact that the women said they liked and benefited from the research midwives' help is important, and ought to be enough. Feeling good about something is not, however, the dominant professional definition of 'health' in our culture – though feelings, and coping, especially in relation to motherhood, are part of how non-professionals talk about their bodies, their selves, and their experiences of surviving the hassles and challenges of everyday life (Graham 1982; Cornwell 1984).

The danger is that social support may appeal in a way that direct politically driven action to improve living conditions does not. Going back to the government reports on perinatal mortality of 1980 and 1989, we can see just how the identification of the problem as part-medical, part-social, gives rise to the delineation of 'social' and then 'social support' research as a residual technical category: a box we put things into when we don't know what else to do with them. In 1980, for example, 'The Committee repeatedly sought evidence on what was known about, and what research was being carried out into, the mechanism of the links between adverse socio-economic and environmental factors and high perinatal mortality. Witnesses said little information was available' (Social Services Committee 1980: 138). A representative from the Medical Research Council admitted that his organization was 'not directly' supporting research in this field. When asked about his opposite number, the (then) Social Science Research Council, he said that so far as he knew they were not doing anything either. The Social Services Committee then concluded that 'much more work is needed in this area', specifically on issues such as diet, 'the effect of mental and physical stress', and reducing the effects of reproductive hazards such as maternal work, alcohol and smoking. Finally, they recommended that financial support for the recently established NPEU in Oxford be continued, as this was the great hope so far as unravelling 'much of the current confusion about the interaction between socio-economic and medical factors to cause death' (Social Services Committee 1980: 139).

A decade later, in its reply to the 1989 report, the government can pull out of its hat the existence of an MRC-funded study of 'risk' factors for low birthweight, a trial of cervical cerclage[3] to prevent preterm delivery, and randomized studies of aspirin to prevent pre-eclampsia and intrauterine growth retardation. There is a large white rabbit in the hat as well: 'The Thomas Coram Research Unit ... has been carrying out a randomised controlled trial to test the hypothesis that social support, provided by midwives to women at above average risk of low birthweight delivery, increases birthweight' (Department of Health 1989: 5). In such guises, researchers' 'innocent' intentions reappear, as generous, considered decisions of governments to promote the public health. The political uses to which research may be put – easy answers to obdurate problems, convenient alternatives to political action – may have nothing to do with how the researchers themselves envisaged it. Moreover, the statements in the government reports are the end-product of a process of political control in which government departments are increasingly attempting to excise from the doing and writing up of research any elements that are antipathetic to the political philosophies they espouse.[4]

Smokescreens

These considerations to do with the political construction of research on the relations between poverty and health apply generally, of course, and not only to maternity care. For both, the individualist discourse of health education, which has increasingly dominated health policy since the 1950s, provides a powerful ideological smokescreen behind which environmental constraints on achieving health are veiled as matters of individuals' irresponsible choices. Health is primarily a matter of lifestyle, not living conditions. Individuals are free to make healthy choices, and are morally culpable if they do not do so. So far as childbearing is concerned, women are blamed for choosing behaviours that damage children – smoking, alcohol, sex, stress, work, non-use of medical care – but the greatest of these is smoking. The smoking mother encapsulates the cultural problem of reproduction and of women – purity *and* danger – and provies an iron smokescreen for the concealment of the fundamental problem: that women cannot be good mothers unless motherhood (and women) is resourced and respected on an equal basis with male citizenship.

Particular discourses about maternal smoking are located within a general one: an emphasis on prevention and health that has developed over the last twenty years, and which places women in a paradoxical position within the household. They have been assigned the status of the guardians of everyone's health, and as promoters of the healthy moral order, but the health educators' rhetoric sees women at the same time as the main perpetrators of unhealthy behaviour, choosing unhealthy diets, failing to have their children immunized (Mayall 1986), and in other ways refusing to conform to the ideal of healthy behaviour. The particular discourses about smoking, linked with others about the caring, stressful work of motherhood, line the other narratives in this book. They are of special significance in a population of women 'at risk' of the main adverse consequence of pregnancy smoking – reduced birthweight (see Oakley 1989). Two out of five of the women in the SSPO study smoked throughout pregnancy; this is higher than the national average, and is to be explained in the light of the paradox that it is those whose lives are most stressful and most likely to be marked by illness and death who 'choose' to smoke. Table 11.4 shows how smoking was related to these kinds of social factors. Pregnancy smoking is associated with conditions of material disadvantage, with social stress, anxiety and indices of low control over living conditions, and with low levels of social support. All of this is missing from the predominant characterization of smoking mothers in the medical and policy literature: that mothers smoke out of ignorance of the health effects on their children, and/or from a wilful desire to harm what they (of all people) should want to protect.

The quantitative findings are supported by the accounts women themselves offer, in which smoking figures as a defence against environmental circumstances that are themselves hazardous to health. The relationship between stress and smoking was described by many of the women in the

Table 11.4 Smoking, material conditions, stress and social support in the SSPO study

Material conditions, stress & social support	Smokers (N = 183) %	Non-smokers (N = 277) %	All (N = 460) %	Significance
Income: Less than 140% of supple mentary benefit level[a]	56	44	100	
140–299%	40	60	100	
300% or more	27	73	100	p < 0.0001
Housing tenure: Rented/living with relatives	59	41	100	
Owner-occupier	32	68	100	p < 0.0001
Unemployed partner: Yes	56	44	100	
No	38	62	100	p < 0.02
Control over life: Not as much as needed/none	49	51	100	
A great deal/ as much as needed	39	61	100	p < 0.05
Worried about baby: Yes	53	47	100	
No	39	61	100	p < 0.02
'Marital' status: Not living with baby's father	69	31	100	
Living with baby's father	37	63	100	p < 0.0001
Help with other children in pregnancy: No	50	50	100	
Yes	40	60	100	p < 0.06

[a]Supplementary benefit no longer exists, but this was the measure used at the time of the study (see appendix I for supplementary benefit levels).

study. One example (from the pilot study) was Jenny Simons, who was living in one room with her 2-year-old daughter in a women's refuge, having left a marriage in which she was exposed to a great deal of both verbal and physical violence:

> JS: I went to the doctor to ask him for things to calm me down.
> AO: What did you take?
> JS: I was going to go on Valium, but in the end I thought, no, don't, and I coped. I coped without it. I was afraid that if I started anything like that, I wouldn't be able to give it up or get off it, so I went to cigarettes, and that was something I couldn't give up . . . When I'm all right I don't smoke, but when I'm under stress, I do.
> AO: How much are you smoking now?
> JS: Twenty now. I'm cutting down, but I smoke because everything I have ever wanted has been ruined, I haven't got anything else left now.

The other main feature of women's accounts of smoking is, as Hilary Graham (1976; 1987) has shown, the link with the caring and health-promoting work women do in the private space of the household. In Graham's study of low-income households, 28 per cent of mothers reported using smoking as a coping strategy (Graham 1986). Two of the women in the SSPO pilot study, both full-time carers of their children, said:

> I'd love to pack up, but as soon as I get . . . if the kids play up or something, I have a cigarette to calm me down. (Jane Mellors).

> I keep trying to put on weight,[5] and I sit here smoking, and eating cream buns at the same time (*laughs*), which is rather bad. I mean, the worry of it causes me to smoke, but knowing that the smoking can produce a small baby, or presuming that it can, makes it a vicious circle . . . I have tried [to give up smoking]. I've been to a hypnotherapist . . . I've been to an acupuncturist, that was quite good, for a whole 24 hours I didn't have one cigarette. It nearly killed me, and then it all got too much, I got steamed up about something or other, got quite hysterical and lit a cigarette. I had one that day, two the next and six the next and I was back to square one again. (Susie Hawkins)

The health consequences for women of caring work are highlighted with particular poignancy in a population of women who have already experienced what is said to be an adverse consequence of smoking, the production of a low-birthweight baby. If the conventional health education model is to be believed by such women, then what they are being asked to confront is the paradox that it is in the very activity of caring that they damage those for whom they care. Dominant discourses about reproductive mortality and morbidity identify the effect of maternal smoking on babies, and particularly on birthweight, as the major single health effect of women's smoking – as much more important than the health hazards of smoking to women themselves, which are rarely mentioned (Gabbe 1984). Pregnancy smoking has been attached to a large category of both short- and long-term health effects in children. These include more hospital admissions in infancy, more bronchitis and pneumonia, more delayed motor development, increased risk of sudden infant death syndrome, and increased risk of childhood and teenage cancer (the latter via a mechanism named 'transplacental carcinogenesis' (Everson 1980; Stjernfeldt et al. 1986; Stevens et al. 1988); longer-term effects include reduced height and impaired social adjustment among 7-year-olds (Davie et al. 1972), retardation in reading, maths and general intellectual ability at ages 7 and 11 (Butler and Goldstein 1973), and lower qualifications obtained by the age of 23 (Fogelman and Manor 1988).

These links between pregnancy smoking and later health effects in children are disputed by some, and are evidently far from simple (for a recent review see Lumley 1991). It is, for example, considerably more dangerous to have a smoking mother if you are going to be a working-class baby (Rantakallio 1979). Smoking fathers and other smokers in the environment of fetal growth are dangerous too, but their culpability is hidden. The health education message is uncompromisingly simple: *all* maternal smoking in pregnancy is dangerous to *all* babies. Smoking fills the gap of ignorance about the unknown causes of low birthweight, as noted by the Secretary of State for Social Services replying in 1988 to a parliamentary question about 'the main known factors in prematurity and low birthweight in babies': 'The cause of prematurity or low birthweight in babies is in most cases not known. Apart from clinical factors of various kinds relating to the pregnancy, it is becoming increasingly clear that smoking by pregnant women ... may be important' (Hansard, 14 June 1988). Going further back, 'Evidence suggests', stated the DHSS in its 1977 document, 'that persuading expectant mothers not to smoke cigarettes *would do more to reduce infant mortality in the UK than any other single action*' (Department of Health and Social Security 1977: 33). On the other side of the Atlantic, the US Institute of Medicine report in 1985 *Preventing Low Birthweight* argued that 'Smoking is *one of the most important preventable determinants of low birthweight.*' (Institute of Medicine 1985: 67). A recent Swedish study (Cnattingius et al. 1988: 259) concluded that even (or especially) in that country, where perinatal mortality is so low – less than 7 per thousand compared with 9 in the UK – cigarette smoking in pregnancy may be *'the most important preventable risk factor for late fetal death'*.

This view of women's smoking in pregnancy, which attributes it with such power as a determinant of adverse outcome for babies, results in pregnant women's subjection to 'massive anti-smoking publicity' (Cnattingius et al. 1988: 261). A recent example comes from Bolton Maternity Hospital in the form of a leaflet handed out to women in antenatal clinics.

IS YOUR BABY DYING FOR A SMOKE?

All women hope to give birth to a healthy and beautiful child, one that will have a happy life and bring joy to its parents.

The doctors and midwives of Bolton Maternity Hospital wish to emphasise to all our pregnant patients that cigarette smoking before and during pregnancy has many bad effects on both the baby and the pregnant mum.

These complications are all commoner in women smokers:-
Miscarriage.
Ectopic pregnancy.
Premature birth.
Stunted growth in the womb.
Haemorrhage in pregnancy.
Irregular heart beat in labour.
Stillbirth.
Death within a few days of birth.
Mental Handicap.

Following complicated birth the baby may suffer long term defects of learning ability, development of personality, and achievement at school.

We think that each year in Bolton about 600 babies are damaged by cigarette smoking.

In Bolton smoking now kills more children than heroin and cocaine abuse, more than in home or road accidents and causes more mental handicap than infections such as German Measles, Listeria, Toxoplasmosis & food poisoning; and more brain damage than birth injuries.

The unborn child is the ultimate example of the passive smoker, forced to inhale what its mother smokes.

Think, at birth your baby is actually 9 months old, and has been an involuntary smoker for that time. As its mother you naturally want to protect your baby from harm; that protection must begin before the baby's actual birthday.

For the sake of your child, if not for yourself, you should give up smoking.

Wednesday, March 13, 1991

Figure 11.4 Bolton Maternity Hospital leaflet

It is reproduced in figure 11.4. Its message is appallingly simple, heavily medicalized and socially decontextualized: mothers who smoke are deliberately harming their babies.

Interventions designed to lower smoking which are moralizing and/or didactic do not result in lowered pregnancy smoking. Those that are socially supportive have some impact (see e.g. Macarthur et al. 1987; Lumley and Astbury 1989, for a review). The SSPO study was not aimed at reducing smoking, though an element in our original thinking was that support from research midwives might result in some women reducing smoking because they wanted to. At the time of the six-week postal questionnaire, there were some differences in smoking habits between intervention and control women: intervention women smoked less. By the one-year follow-up this difference had increased, reaching 'conventional' levels of statistical significance ($p < 0.05$): 61 per cent of intervention mothers and 51 per cent of control mothers were non-smokers; at the other end of the smoking scale, 15 per cent of intervention but 20 per cent of control mothers reported smoking sixteen or more cigarettes a day.

Getting the message across

The SSPO study belongs to a larger category of studies, some of which were briefly reviewed in chapter 3, and all of which test the capacity of some non-clinical intervention to improve health. The studies reviewed in chapter 3 demonstrate the falsity of the notion that the only domain the social can affect is the social. 'Social' interventions promote physical health. They promote psychological, emotional and social manifestations of health as well, which is hardly surprising, given the inappropriateness of the Cartesian mind–body dualism to the way in which most people experience living in their bodies.

This applies to health in general, as well as to health in the reproductive domain. Systematic reviews of social interventions in reproduction referred to in chapter 3 show that some indices of reproductive health appear to be more sensitive to the impact of social interventions than others. Specifically, health care use and psychosocial dimensions of health seem easier to affect than birthweight. Most social interventions in pregnancy increase the birthweight of babies of supported women, though not enough to move the difference into the 'statistically significant' domain; this is true not only of our study but of the London 'Know Your Midwife' (Flint and Poulengeris 1987) and client-held case-note (Lovell et al. 1987; Elbourne et al. 1987) interventions, the Birmingham linkworker study (Dance 1987), the South Carolina and Western Australia home-visiting studies (Heins et al. 1990; Bryce et al. 1991), and the Scottish trial of community-based antenatal care (Reid et al. 1983). It is most unlikely that these are freak findings. Rather, what they suggest is that the capacity for affecting birthweight by means of a short-term (pregnancy) intervention is limited. Birthweight is shaped by long-term factors relating to the mother's own health in adulthood and childhood, and including biological influences deriving from her own physical constitution (see Illsley and Mitchell 1984). It is also, as we have seen, affected by the social stresses to which mothers are exposed; there is no shortage of these in class-differentiated societies where class inequalities in health are pronounced, and widening (Marmot and McDowall 1986; Smith et al. 1990), and where financial benefits and other material support for mothers are seen as expensive and unnecesary investments in a present and future dominated by unemployment, economic recession and the general collapse of the infrastructure of capitalism.

The relevance of social support to health demonstrated in this book has to be interpreted within this context. The health-promoting effects of social support cannot cancel the health-damaging effects of poverty (see also Infante-Rivard et al. 1989; Main et al. 1985; Stein et al. 1989). There are no 'quick fixes' for the ways in which poverty damages health. This is a politically uncomfortable message in capitalist post-welfare societies. Precisely because of this, studies of social support may be used to fulfil the equally politically uncomfortable function of arguing that all we need to do to make things better – to lower death-rates, raise the birthweights of babies, reduce the health service burden of social problems, and so on – is to provide the instant remedy of social support. Social support, as Lisa Berkman (1984) said, is the chicken soup of the folk remedy; or, perhaps more appositely, the Angel Delight of the supermarket shelves, whipped up quickly into a froth of saccharine sweetness which dulls the tongue to more ordinary bitter tastes. The pseudo-technical language of social support as distinct from the 'lay' formulation of friendship is probably important here – seeming, as it does, to provide a professional justification for 'folk' wisdom. It dresses up what most people know into something that a few have recently discovered.

The 'poverty' of research derives in part from the limitations of research as an exercise, and in part from the poverty of the people it studies. So far as the former is concerned, with the research design of the controlled trial as described in this book, for example, the methodology of 'control' is usually interpreted to mean, not only that selection bias will be excluded, but that the laboratory condition of 'no contamination' will be replicated in the social world. What is made to happen to the experimental group in a study will not be allowed to affect the control population. But in practice, of course, people do talk to other people. If they find themselves sitting next to each other in antenatal clinics, women randomly allocated to an experimental group are likely to tell those allocated to a control group what is going on. A powerful example of this in the general health field was an RCT of health screening for the elderly in Finland, which failed to test the effectiveness of this form of health surveillance because a local media campaign raised the rate of follow-up examinations in the control group to a figure that was 10 per cent higher than the rate in the experimental group (Antilla and Isokoski 1985).

What research interventions can be expected to accomplish in the field of reproductive care is framed within the double vision of a culture which accords motherhood ideological importance while refusing to confront what it is about motherhood that makes it difficult: the unsupported labours of love; the poverty of caring; the struggle to work, in the home and outside it; the stress of trying to hold the social relations of families together. None the less, certain simple messages are clear. First, the provision of sympathetic, listening support through continuity of care, which is what women have been requiring whenever anyone has thought to ask them, is a more effective way to promote their health and that of their babies than most of the medical interventions carried out in the name of antenatal 'care'. It is what women want; it works; and it is safe and inexpensive. Second, the implication from the SSPO study and others like it is that supportive care in pregnancy is best provided by women to women. The reason is not the biology of sex but the culture of gender, and the differences in professional training and ideology between midwives on the one hand and obstetricians on the other. Women generally work harder at close relationships, and are more sympathetic and skilled listeners (Spender 1980), though men, including male obstetricians, can to some extent be trained to improve these skills (Weihs and Chapados 1986). Midwifery is about caring for mothers as whole people, and giving personalized attention and help. It is about respecting and encouraging normalcy, not about justifying expensive and health-damaging interventions. Thus, in the present climate, the best way to 'translate' the findings of the SSPO study into action is to give more responsibility for antenatal care to midwives, and to reorganize the antenatal care system so that a small group of midwives provides care to each woman, instead of the barrage of new faces that now greets most of them. Territory is important, too. One of the valued aspects of the SSPO intervention was that midwives took care to the home; this enabled them to see the women in their normal environments, and better to understand the stresses on them. By contrast, staff in hospital and other clinics have only a partial view, and may thus tend to underestimate the problems of poverty, be short on practical help and even 'blame' the poor for being poor (see Reid et al. 1983). A good deal of antenatal care could safely be carried out at home, and the expense of a domiciliary system would be easily counterbalanced by the savings in the expense of high-technology care in pregnancy and afterwards that would be made by helping women to feel 'at home' in their bodies, and confident and capable carers of their children-to-be. It should also be noted in this context that some of the social interventions reviewed in this book have been tested on high-risk and some on low-risk women, but it does not seem to make a great deal of difference to the findings which group is selected. In other words, the effectiveness of social support is not restricted to women who have few problems anyway. On the contrary, it seems to help most those who are in difficulty. And those who are not probably need very little intervention of any kind – either medical or social.

To argue for socially supportive care on grounds of cost is both important and dangerous. It is important because suggestions about improving the social support capacities of existing health care professionals and organizations are likely to be seen as 'expensive add-ons to the present system' and 'quite out of step with much current discussion about health services, which seeks to minimize costs' (Haggerty 1980; 398). It is dangerous because advocacy of social support may translate into the manipulation of people's social support resources, and this may appear to be an easier and politically more acceptable strategy for improving health than tackling the root material causes of health problems (Wortman 1984). As regards cost, it does not seem to be the case that social support is expensive as an alternative to more standard forms of care. In the London 'Know Your Midwife' study, the care used by intervention-group women was estimated to cost about 25 per cent less than that used by women receiving ordinary care. In our own SSPO study, the probable saving in the cost of antenatal hospital admissions, less use of special care for babies, and lower Caesarean and epidural analgesia rates was in the region of £120,000 and equivalent to the amount of money provided to fund the study.

Dissemination of the findings of social support trials is handicapped by the threat these pose to two groups in particular. Most obviously, the documentation of social support as health-promoting threatens clinical standing and expertise. If listening to women's worries, visiting them at home and providing continuity of care are shown to be beneficial, then where does this leave obstetricians, who generally speaking do none of these things?[6] A negative response from the obstetrical establishment lies behind the non-publication of papers about social support in clinical journals; our own was turned down by the *Lancet* and by the *British Medical Journal* on grounds of 'irrelevance to clinical practice'. Discussing studies of client-held case-notes, Lovell and colleagues (1987: 610) reported that although this issue 'generates considerable heat in the medical profession . . . it is also seen as a trivial issue'. One senior registrar in the study for which Lovell was responsible 'remarked that researching the effects of access to obstetric records was "of no interest to obstetricians".' The same response was evident with a recent further study from the Klaus and Kennell team who pioneered work on the value of social support in labour. A paper reporting this study in the *Journal of the American Medical Association* had the word 'social' changed to 'emotional' support in its title (Kennell et al. 1991a), and elicited a fairly hostile, nitpicking correspondence (see Kennell et al. 1991b; Gevirtz and Marx 1991). As John Kennell remarked of the study findings, 'These obstetric outcome differences are impressive to many physicians, but the response from US obstetricians has been inaudible' (Kennell, personal communication).

The same could be said of UK obstetricians and the SSPO study. Presentation of the study findings to clinical audiences has commonly met with the following responses: because midwives provided the intervention, the study has shown the benefits of *professional* support, if it has shown anything; the possibility cannot be ruled out that the intervention women did better because they were referred to health professionals more often (in fact they were not); the samples were not representative, and neither were the four centres where the study was done; because you're a woman and a sociologist and a feminist the study was biased from the start; you ought to show confidence intervals on your slides; what do you mean by social support anyway?; what is wrong with obstetricians adding this to what they already do?; and if, as you contend, social support 'works' then how on earth does it do so?

The 'how' is an important question. In the SSPO study all our documentation of the processes of giving and receiving the social support intervention suggests that the following pathways were significant: first, by providing a listening ear, the research midwives helped the intervention women to cope better with stress, and to gain more confidence as individuals, as mothers and as users of the health care system. Thus, although the babies of intervention and control mothers were equally likely to go to the neonatal unit after delivery, intervention mothers' babies spent much less time there. The probable explanation was that babies were admitted on the basis of their mothers' obstetric histories, rather than because of their own conditions, and intervention mothers were more likely to ask for their babies to be released sooner. Supporting evidence for this was that by the end of the study some of the doctors the women were seeing were complaining that their clientele had become distinctly more 'stroppy' recently. The finding that intervention women's partners became more helpful domestically may be traced to the same heightened assertiveness on the part of intervention women to secure the kind of help *they* felt they needed. A second, related, pathway was the efforts of the research midwives to help the women in the intervention group to make more *appropriate* use of health care. This lies behind the finding of fewer antenatal hospital admissions in the intervention group, but more health care use of various kinds after delivery. The research midwives were concerned both to protect intervention women from 'unnecessary' medical procedures and to help them obtain 'necessary' ones. By comparison with these two mechanisms of effect, the giving of practical help, such as baby clothes or advice about welfare benefits, was probably less important in itself than as a demonstration of the basic position the research midwives adopted: that of being 'with woman' in the original sense of the term 'midwife'. It was because of this fundamental alignment of standpoints – woman and midwife – and the consequent legitimation of the mothers' points of view, that women offered the support intervention were able to build up and draw on their own resources of initiative, control and support, and by maximizing these to achieve more for themselves and their babies than would otherwise have been the case.

The second major group to exhibit hostility to the SSPO study has been women opposed to the ethics of, and the need for, 'experimental' research on women. Indeed, the view of experimental research as inherently unethical is central to the feminist critique of knowledge (see Spallone and Steinberg 1987; Birke 1986). This replicates the 'Auschwitz' view of research (see I. Chalmers 1983) and, like it, misses the absolutely crucial point that controlled experimentation is preferable to the uncontrolled experimentation that goes on under the heading of routine practice – whether in medical, educational, social welfare or other fields. Most of the interventions introduced into people's lives have ridden on the back of professionals' claims of clearcut benefits, not founded on the basis of controlled evaluations that have established their effectiveness, appropriateness and safety. This is a far more dangerous situation than the setting up of controlled trials. Indeed, the frequency with which doctors have imposed on people experiments of an uncontrolled nature has been one of the strongest objections raised by the women's health movement in Europe and North America over the last twenty years (Ruzek 1978). From this viewpoint, women are important beneficiaries of the advocacy of controlled evaluation. One example is the treatment of breast cancer, a disease affecting one in twelve women in the UK at some point in their lives. Analysis of the results of trials of breast cancer treatments has shown that 'conservative' treatments are superior to 'radical' treatments, both in ensuring survival and in maintaining the quality of life. Randomized trials of drug therapy show important differences in the effectiveness of these treatments in older and younger women. They also provide evidence that short courses of some treatments are as effective as longer courses – a major consideration given the sometimes unpleasant side-effects of these (Consensus Development Conference 1986; Early Breast Cancer Triallists' Group 1992). But while the women's health movement has been sceptical of the need for such evaluation, and rightly hostile to the way in which some of it has been carried out,[7] there has also been a tendency to demonstrate an uncomfortable certainty about the benefits of other procedures, including screening programmes and 'alternative' forms of treatment. For example, the frequently heard demand for universal cervical screening ignores significant questions concerning the ethics, efficacy and adverse effects of screening (Robinson 1987). For example, too, opposition to a proposed trial of vitamin supplementation in pregnancy on the grounds that vitamins are known to be beneficial (see Micklethwait et al. 1982) disregarded significant evidence that vitamin supplementation can have harmful effects.

The position of relatively powerless social groups, such as working-class class pregnant women, raises acute questions about the ethics of both controlled experimentation (research) and uncontrolled experimentation (everyday practice). These questions lead to requirements for the highest standards of information and consent. In the research domain, the need for fully informed consent[8] may compromise the chances of demonstrating the efficacy of interventions, as, indeed, it did with the SSPO study. However, this conflict between ethics and science merely highlights the essential dilemmas of knowledge. The question of how we can know something if it is only by treating people badly is also a question about the opposition between objectivity and subjectivity. This opposition returns us to the realms of philosophy – to models of knowing and understanding underlying particular research practices.

12

Models of Knowing and Understanding

> But one obstacle remains. Even after the two domains of the ethical and the epistemological are set apart, some argue that the latter should have priority. It is useless to be overly concerned with truthfulness, they claim, so long as one cannot know whether human beings are capable of knowing and conveying the truth in the first place ... Once again, the exalted and all-absorbing preoccupation with 'truth' then comes to nourish the reluctance to confront falsehood. (Bok 1980: 9)

This book began with three aims: first, the simple telling of a story about a research project; second, a reflexive articulation of the *process* of undertaking research; and, third, addressing questions to do with the *status* and *gendering* of sociological *knowledge* itself. Like the imposition of a division between qualitative and quantitative methodology, the separability of the three aims is theoretical rather than practical. Few stories can be simply told. Because it concerns a research enterprise that straddles the two knowledge domains of the social and the medical, the story of this one inhabits the double hermeneutics of its ideological space. It moves backwards and forwards from one domain to the other, uncomfortable with each but unable to let go of either in the effort to create its own original merging of the two. In this, the book's narrative resembles the fate of women under patriarchy – living their own lives but as men see them, and forging, if they are lucky and/or sufficiently determined, an existence which is their own novel (qualitative) creation rather than mere mechanistic (quantitative) survival. As Kate Millett said, now many years ago, the challenge is to create 'a world we can bear out of the desert we inhabit' (Millett 1969: 363).

So *Social Support and Motherhood* has told a story, but/and in a self-conscious way. Addressing the third aim, of exploring traditional ssumptions about knowledge, has been implicit throughout most of the text, perhaps even uneasily so, in a disjunctive leapfrogging between the different textual modes of description and analysis; and between the central conundrum of quantitative and qualitative approaches to the generation and presentation of research data. Thus, while chapters 6 and 9 address directly the two methodological questions of the status of RCTs as tools for researching women's (people's) health, and the subjectivity of objective data, chapters 7, 8 and 10 combine the presentation of narratives of detail from the women and the midwives who took part in the study with the process both of analytic induction, as celebrated in accounts of qualitative research logic, and of hypothetico-deduction and 'simple' enumeration, as recognized within the quantitative model (see Bryman 1988). In chapter 11, which interprets and debates the findings of the study in the context of dominant discourses of health, use is made, again, both of material yielded by the focus on individual standpoints and by the elision of these into composite, general variables.

The fact that it may not be easy to read a book presented in this way (and it has certainly not been easy to write it) is, of course, testimony to the very novelty of the enterprise of combining different modes of inquiry. This is essentially an enterprise of *improvisation*. Some things seem to work, others which do not are discarded in favour of another strategy. 'Negative' cases which dispute any emerging consensual interpretation result in revisions being made to that interpretation. Procedurally, this process parallels how others have described the analysis of interview and case-study materials (see e.g. Turner 1981). Certain key features of this type of work, including the account of the SSPO study presented here, deserve to be drawn out, though from the standpoint of retrospective interpretation with its well-known 'effort after meaning' rather than from any a priori epistemological position. Common parlance calls this 'the wisdom of hindsight'.

Whereas the last chapter examined what the SSPO project can be said to have achieved in the way of research 'findings', the focus of this one broadens the framework of discussion to questions about the status of knowledge and methodologies of inquiry. It tries to locate the SSPO study within the paradigm of the cultural turning-point referred to earlier – as an instance in the reworking of approaches to knowledge which characterizes intellectual debate in the latter part of the twentieth century. One way to approach this broader task from the specifics of the SSPO study is to ask what kind of methodology it is that combines the approach of an RCT with that of 'qualitative' interviews, themselves conceived of as an agentic intervention in people's lives, and which 'tests' the hypothesis that friendship improves wellbeing, but by approaching the evaluation of how people are through a discursive reductionism into separate, quantifiable indices. Is this feminist sociology or 'blind' adherence to the logic of masculinist scientific inquiry? And, even if using such an approach can be said to illuminate some discrete issues relating to women and reproduction, what, if anything, does it have to say about the universe of sociological work and the meta-ethics of different forms of inquiry?

Ways of knowing

In *Women's Ways of Knowing*, Mary Belenky and her colleagues retell the story of an interview carried out by the Russian psychologist A. R. Luria (1981) with illiterate Russian peasants. Luria asked his interviewees to solve some problems which involved going beyond their own immediate experience, such as: 'In the far north, where there is snow, all bears are white. Novaya Zemlya is in the far north. What colour are the bears there?' Their answers were along the lines of: 'We don't talk about what we haven't seen' and 'If you want an answer to that question, you should ask people who have been there and seen them' (Belenky et al. 1986: 26).

Such an answer seems reasonable enough. Indeed, it encapsulates the basic logic behind social-scientific research, which involves the systematic description of other people's experiences. In the use of the pronoun 'we', the Russian peasants' response also appeals to a commonality of perspective – the interior cultural frame of reference of a particular community. What it does not do, of course, is to move on from the importance of personal experience to generalizable, conceptual thought; it does not step outside one specific cultural frame of reference to the universe of alternative and potentially different others. Because of these limitations, we deem the peasants' responses pre-modern and non-scientific. The knowledge systems of the developed world set absolute standards against which the centrality of the personal, practical viewpoint appears as relatively inferior, outmoded and even *childlike*.

Knowing

Behind the conventional, commonsense view of knowledge in developed societies are certain assumptions, among which the following are critical:

1 Knowing involves *representational* naming. That is, *concepts* are developed by *abstracting* from experience, then forming a representational currency for organizing and communicating it.
2 To name is to *classify*. That is, in naming objects and places and events and people, we organize the perceived world into *categories*.
3 Classified units are *equivalent* to one another. That is, by belonging to the same category as each other, these units all have identical status.
4 Classificatory and conceptual schemes allow the deduction, induction and enumeration of *facts*. Essential to this fact-deducing process is the possibility of bypassing repeated empirical observation as a basis of making statements about the world.
5 Facts exist. That is, facts are *absolutely true*, and *only absolutely true facts count as knowledge*.

These assumptions underlie everyday uses and abuses of the term 'knowledge'. For example, the view that knowledge is constituted of objectively evident facts is intrinsic to a nationally standardized and examinable education system. In this sense, a restricted view of knowledge is a requisite of large-scale bureaucratic society.

Historians, philosophers and scientists of various kinds have traced the cultural origins of this view of knowledge to the proclamations and practices of certain key thinkers from the seventeenth century on – Descartes, Bacon, J. S. Mill and others (see Medawar 1982). The modern view of knowledge represents the triumph over the older method of induction proposed by Mill as a way of establishing knowledge. A good deal could be (and has been) said about just what is intrinsic to this view of knowledge and what is not – a question which overlaps with the question of how the components of the scientific method can themselves be described. From the standpoint of the argument here, three matters are crucial. First, it was within this discourse about the hypothetico-deductive method that the emphasis on experimentation as a way of knowing was born – not in the Baconian sense of 'doing' something to nature in order to see what happens, but in the sense of doing something to test a hypothesis about what might be true about it. Second, it is central to this approach that the position of the knower/scientist/researcher is logically, but not personally, defined. Knowledge is the object of human endeavour, but the personal background, characteristics and inclination of the knower are regarded as independent of what is known. Thirdly, however, and in contrast to this, wherever the procedures of science or knowledge-gaining are examined in detail, they are shown to reveal a very different picture: one in which the art of imagining what might be true and what could be known are essential episodes in the process of constructing knowledge. Theory is imaginative construction – a story. The point is to discover whether the story describes 'real life'.

The danger of setting up something called 'knowledge' and then criticizing it from a different standpoint is that of trying to discredit what is anyway unreal: a 'straw' (wo)man. That is why the 'real' nature of scientific inquiry must be appreciated, both as an activity linked closely to the imaginative visions of the artist or the novelist, and as an enterprise bound by the social and cultural locations within which it occurs (Rose 1986). Science and knowledge are socially produced; that is, they are subject to the very influence of social processes and partialities that their common-sense representations would dismiss as quite beyond their frames of reference.

Four examples (out of many possible ones) illustrate this. The first links back to the discussion of statistical tests in chapter 9. Between 1900 and 1914 in Britain there was controversy among statisticians about how best to measure statistical association. The core debate was between Karl Pearson and his pupil, George Udny Yule. Pearson espoused views prominent at the time about the importance of genetic endowment in determining individuals' social fates. While Pearson's programme of work was concerned with showing the power of biological inheritance, Yule worked on subjects such as pauperism (for eugenicists a symptom of hereditary degeneracy), focusing on topics such as the impact of administrative reforms on the incidence of pauperism. Pearson's perception of biological continuity, and his definition of the goal of statistical work as being about the construction of a predictive and eugenically based mathematical theory of descent, was reflected in a perception of an underlying continuity between variables. This led Pearson to specify certain statistical procedures with which Yule, from a non-eugenicist standpoint, did not agree. 'The different cognitive interests of Pearson and Yule led to their two positions being incommensurable ... Their concepts of "measuring association" were different: for Pearson it meant seeking to establish an underlying correlation; for Yule, seeking in a looser sense to measure the dependence of the given nominal data' (Mackenzie 1978: 52).

The second example comes from the work of anthropologist Jack Goody (1977), in his study of the LoDagaa of northern Ghana. Anthropological work throws important light on the culturally and temporarily specific 'nature' of knowledge. In his study Goody shows how the taxonomy of binary division handicaps understanding of different cultural modes of thought and the changes in these over time. The same is true of methodological procedures. Studying the LoDagaa of northern Ghana, Goody asked someone to count for him, so he could find out about procedures for counting: 'the answer was "count what?" For different procedures are used for counting different objects. Counting cows is different from counting cowries' (Goody 1977: 13). As Goody observes, the LoDagaa's counting habits cannot be dismissed as evidence of lack of abstract thought. They have an abstract numerical system; but the ways in which they use these concepts are embedded in daily living. The decontextualization of knowledge may give rise to false dichotomies which are no aid to understanding the nature of knowledge itself.

Third and fourth are two examples from the SSPO study. The first is represented in table 12.1. This shows disagreement between the research midwives and the women allocated to be offered social support about this central enterprise of the project. In 64 per cent of situations where the women considered the midwife had been helpful, the midwives took the same view, but in 36 per cent of cases the midwives felt they had not been helpful when the women thought they had been. In 49 per cent of cases where the women had found the midwives not helpful, the midwives thought they had been. Similar discrepancies obtained with respect to the perception of the women's stress levels. Judgements about the stress the women were under exemplify a tendency for midwives to underestimate the women's stress, or for women to feel that their lives were more difficult than they might be perceived to be. Such dissonances, apart from

Table 12.1 SSPO intervention-group women's assessments of stress and helpfulness in relation to views of research midwives

| Helpfulness | Midwife said she was: | | | |
	Helpful	Not helpful	All	Significance
% of cases[a] where woman said midwife was:				
Helpful	64	36	100	
Not helpful	49	51	100	p < 0.06

| Stress | Midwife said woman had: | | | |
	Low stress	High stress	All	Significance
% of cases[a] where woman said she had:				
Low stress	51	49	100	
High stress	70	30	100	p < 0.01

[a]Number of cases = 209.

forming the 'really interesting' (that is, requiring the invention of an explanation) stuff of research, contextualize the 'scientific' testing of hypotheses about social support within the personal social locations of people as non-laboratory subjects. Not only do they not all see the same thing, but it is easy for *us* to see how their relative visions spring from the platform of both different and shared political positions: an identity as women which tends to the self-effacing self-evaluations of 'unimportant people' (Miller 1976); the research-attributed roles of supporter, faced with stress-promoting social disadvantage, and supported, groaning under the selfsame burden.

During discussion of some of the differences between centres described in chapter 11, one of the research midwives proposed the theory that her 'ladies' might be doing better than others because they lived in a place with a geographically stable population and a strong sense of community and family support. This provides our fourth example of a discontinuity between the notion of knowledge as an abstract attainable reality, and the untidy world of understanding the moral equivalence of different viewpoints. Here, however, the different positions in question are those of qualitative and quantitative research methods themselves. What the midwife suggested by way of an explanation seemed to be backed up by what some of the women in her intervention group said. We decided to put her hunch to the (statistical) test. A chi-square and lamda statistic showed that the two variables of geographical area and social support score were independent; one variable was not a good predictor of the other. But as the researcher[1] put it:

> This doesn't mean the midwife's hunch is necessarily wrong, just that it is not borne out by analysis of the quantitative data using those particular measures (it might be worth disaggregating the support variable).
>
> Cross-checking with other statements from the midwives and women may indicate an inconsistency between intuitive understandings of what support is . . . and the level of support to be found associated with area according to the quantified data (assuming of course that the support variable *is* a measure of 'support').
>
> More work needs to be done on this question . . .

Understanding

There have been two major sources of challenge to the orthodox model of knowledge since the 1950s: one from within the social sciences, and one that emerged from the political movement for the liberation of women. The crux of both concerns the effective *partiality* of what is known, and the difference between *knowing* and *understanding*. The epistemological challenge encapsulates, but is broader than, the famous contrast between quantitative and qualitative research methods. Indeed, the framing of the quantitative/qualitative division forms a particular case within the epistemological challenge, and is therefore best approached as such: that is, it is helpful first to grasp *why* the challenge to knowledge posed by recent pluralist ideologies and practices should so persistently be reduced to the contrast between quantity and quality.

The origins of the social sciences lie in the fertile, but uneasy, combination of the politics of social reform with the pursuit of universal laws underlying social relations, following the example of the physical sciences. Thus, while the methodology of inquiry within early social science was largely borrowed from existing procedures, the objects to which it was to be applied, and the goals of the inquiry itself, departed from standard positivist practice. Seen as a European movement, the rise of social science is not a unified phenomenon; some of the key intellectual figures, including Comte and Durkheim, promoted the physical science model, while others argued for a different approach. As Wolf Lepenies (1988) has argued, a significant factor in the 'physicalization' of sociology was the competing representation of subjectivity by literature; while sociology was concerned with fact, novelists and poets dealt with feelings. Novelists such as Balzac regarded themselves as in competition with sociology in terms of the understanding of society they offered. Thus, Balzac's *Comédie Humaine* was originally entitled *Etudes Sociales*, but, whatever it was called, it was regarded as providing a *sociological* understanding before Durkheim began his own sociological work (Lepenies 1988: 4–6). The battle lines were drawn between 'sociology [as] a discipline characterized by cold rationality, which seeks to comprehend the structures and laws of motion of modern industrial society by means of measurement and computation and in doing so only serves to alienate man [*sic*] more effectively from himself and from the world around him', and, on the opposite side, 'a literature whose intuition can see farther than the analyses of the sociologists and whose ability to address the heart of man [*sic*] is to be preferred to the products of a discipline that misunderstands itself as a natural science of society' (Lepenies 1988: 13). Following the logic of this division of labour, it is not surprising to find the intellectual crises of male 'sociologists' such as Comte and J. S. Mill resulting in an 'emotionalization' of their life and work, set in train, in each case, by women.

The struggle of sociology to find a place for itself next to the competing claims of literature was an uneven one, and there were those, such as Weber, who did not yield to a physical model. Weber's well-known insistence on *verstehen* as the prerequisite for an 'objective science of the subjective' (Bauman 1978: 72), and his dismissal of abstract general laws as a goal of intellectual activity on the grounds of their being the least valuable because necessarily the most content-free (Weber 1903–17), came close to stating the art of the novelist in 'scientific' form.

Weber agreed with the German psychologist Dilthey's emphasis on the need to appreciate 'the experienced whole', the general goal being understanding rather than explanation *per se*, and achieved through identification or empathy, with similarity of experience between studier and studied being critical to the success of the enterprise. But, although this historical stress on the divergences between the social and natural sciences constitutes a developed set of observations and not an isolated warning, it was the physical science model of social inquiry that came to dominate the language of methodology. Within the mainstream pedagogy of the social sciences in the 1940s, the epistemological pluralism of the nineteenth-century texts has become a dogmatic mechanical model. Even today, the methodological texts prioritize the model of large-scale data gathering and analysis, considering other approaches such as interviews and participant observation as secondary and problematic – methods to be treated with considerable caution (see e.g. Denzin 1970).

The reasons for this monotheistic epistemology have to be sought in the social relations of social scientists themselves. The elevation of the enumerative social survey, for example, can be traced to men's pursuit of questions about how society works when faced with the anxiety-inducing changes of nineteenth-century capitalism (Graham 1983). This search for understanding was represented as a discourse of 'knowing', and so drew on and into itself the quantitative logic of capitalism: a repetition of premises about classification, counting and the equivalence of enumerated units. The hegemony of this perspective within a gendered, male-dominated culture ensured the exclusion of any other standpoint (including women's) describing and interpreting the dynamics of social change. It is no accident that the historical moments in which positivism is prioritized as the epistemological base of social science are also those in which the cultural privatization of women is marked (Klein 1946).

The challenge to the physical science model of social science put by such developments as phenomenology and symbolic interactionism in the 1960s has much in common with the resistance to accepted knowledge flowing from the politics of the women's movement. It is also distinctively different. The German philosopher Alfred Schutz (first translated into English during this period) extended Weber's notion of *verstehen* in contending that the core of the social science enterprise should be accessing the constructs that individuals use for organizing their place in the world. While molecules and atoms do not subjectively experience the world of nature, social reality is made up of many different subjectively experienced realities, so that 'The thought objects constructed by the social scientist ... have to be founded upon the thought objects constructed by the common-sense thinking of men [*sic*], living their daily life within the social world' (Schutz 1962: 59). It is essential to avoid the intellectual creation as social science's project of 'a fictional non-existing world constructed by the scientific observer' (Schutz 1962: 8).

The implications of symbolic interactionism for the status of social-scientific inquiry are similar to those of phenomenology, though the nature of the subjective process is conceptualized differently, in particular by an emphasis on *interpreting* the social world rather than constructing sensible perceptions of it. Central to the interpretation process is a dialogue between who we are and who we think other people think we are. In a self-reflexive history of social science epistemologies, texts from phenomenology and symbolic interactionism and the various 'sub-schools' these have spawned are valuable in legitimating the use of the qualitative approach as the methodological 'underdog' of social science. But this, too, is a process which reflects the gendering of culture, and of intellectual work specifically; for by far the most substantive challenge to the physical science model in recent years has come from feminist social scientists. The downplaying of the feminist contribution may well be (like many) a sin of omission rather than commission, and conducted from the 'best' of motives – the desire to select as intellectual defence the most academically respectable texts. This is, of course, a chicken-and-egg affair: intellectually the feminist standpoint will continue to be less respectable than the masculinist one so long as it is awarded this status (in masculinist writings).

Women's ways

Knowledge – what counts as knowledge – has different social functions. Most trivially, it is important to those whose work lies in the knowledge-production domain: academics, intellectuals, professionals of one kind or another. Secondly, knowledge is power. That is, it is deployed as a means of social control – as a way of putting and keeping people in their place. Because of the social-control function of knowledge, who 'owns' it is crucial. Those who do not own knowledge are vulnerable to being controlled by those who do. In and of itself, knowledge, of course, also tends to reproduce the power relations dominant culturally. Hence the linguistic/social origins of the word 'real' referred to earlier – 'of, or pertaining to, the king' (Frye 1989: 79).[2] In so far as knowledge is intended to be a representation of social reality (as the physical science model would have us believe), what is known is the world *from one particular standpoint.* That the particularity of this standpoint is hidden by an implicit assumption of universality is only to be expected, given the premise of (in)visible bias woven into the logic of mainstream knowledge – as long as you do not *ac*knowledge it, it is not there (see Wright Mills 1959: 21).

A more subtle manifestation of the power of knowledge lies in the discourses which comprise it. The ways in which these construct normative social identities and practices can have a profound impact on individual experience. To take an example central to the themes of this book, what is 'known' about motherhood may be broken down into various prescriptive descriptions of who mothers are and what they do – in the delineation of the 'good' mother, for instance, or in that of the 'working mother', or in that of the 'depressed' mother (the disjunction between these three seeming to rule out that 'real' mothers may be all of these at the same time). In turn, the representation of such notions in practices affecting mothers – for example, in the treatment practices of health professionals, or in employment practices – puts limits on mothers' experiences and the ways in which they are able subjectively to organize these.

The association between knowledge and power means that any political or cultural movement of a social group which challenges the status quo will, if only by default, also be entering into an epistemological dispute. Thus, in the most recent history of contemporary capitalist societies, the political representation of the rights of black people, of women, of those who do not subscribe to a normative heterosexuality or of those who are not able-bodied has had to speak both to the actual organization of power in society and to the incorporation of this into what 'is known'. There are various levels on which the argument can proceed and has proceeded. The initial stance is likely to be one of identifying more or less simple exclusion: the fact that the position of black people or women is not included as a particular area of knowledge. Within sociology, the exclusion of women from stratification theory (see e.g. Crompton and Mann 1986) or from the study of political institutions and power (see e.g. Stacey and Price 1981) is a good example of this. Social 'minority' groups also commonly find themselves represented in knowledge as a special case. Thus the sociology of work includes female employees as exemplars of nonvocational or non-professional work orientation (as 'working mothers', 'employed wives', etc.) but not as general instances of the general class of workers. Or, within the sociology of the professions, those in which women predominate will, by virtue of this fact, be deemed 'semi-professions' (Etzioni 1969).

From the identification of exclusion, it is a relatively small step to a critique of the subject areas within sociology as themselves discriminatorily gendered. Critics are helped on this path by the very obvious over-representation of women in areas concerning private life – notably the sociology of the family and marriage, where men flit in and out of their roles as instrumentally provident husbands and fathers, while women occupy the centre of the domestic stage. In its intellectual and social organization, sociology itself is male. But the paradox, noted at the beginning of the long journey of this book, is that the enterprise of sociology is female in its original conception: the knowledge or wisdom (*logos*) of a friend (*socius*); that expressive role accorded women in the functionalist paradigm of the family; or, in more contemporary terms, women's functions as kin-keepers (Young and Willmott 1957), as managers of emotion (Zaretsky 1976), as friends and helpers to one another (Raymond 1986), and, as we have seen in this book, as 'social supporters' in the new technical language of the depoliticization of welfare (Williams 1992). The female enterprise of articulating, guarding and negotiating social relations was, under the impetus of the anomic anxiety of nineteenth-century capitalism, transformed into an academic specialism of men. In Britain, where early twentieth-century sociology absorbed and rewrote the agenda of social 'work' as well as 'knowledge' (Wootton 1959), this masculine intellectual colonialism is even more striking. The appropriation of women's social labours in this way allowed the reproduction within sociological discourse of the central cultural schema of rational man and his counterpart irrational woman – in other words, the bipolar dimensions of table A.

The gendering of methodology

It was on to this framework of unequal division that the specialized discourse of quantitative versus qualitative methodologies came to be grafted in the postwar period. Phenomenology, ethnomethodology and symbolic interactionism as new intellectual movements within the social sciences entailed procedures of inquiry that were different from the enumerative large-scale procedures of the survey method; but their intellectual pretensions were more all-embracing than this, extending to the revisioning of sociological knowledge itself. When feminist social scientists embarked on their own projects of reappraisal, they began with more modest visions – of how to undo some of sociology's worst misogynies and how to correct its central standpoint by attending to that of women. It was here that the insistence on 'qualitative' methodology came in. But the relationship of this term and the epistemology it defends with the project of feminism is complex. On the one hand, it may seem self-evidently true that, in order to shift the basic orientation of sociology away from a male-dominated viewpoint, it is essential for pragmatic reasons to choose an approach to the collection of new data that will permit more than the enumeration of responses – that will, in fact, allow for a recitation of the 'quality' of experience. Only in this way will it be possible, for example, to 'hear' that housework is alienating manual labour (Oakley 1974), the appropriation by a capitalist economic system of women's labour power in the service of social reproduction (Delphy 1980), rather than an aspect of women's expressive role in marriage. Thus the 'qualitative' study of housework, which is one way of viewing the private heterosexual relations of the family, may lead to an alteration in both traditional conceptions of work and those of family life and heterosexuality. Similarly, attending to women's accounts of motherhood results in the hearing of something that is very different from enshrined sociological typifications of this condition. What is heard emphasizes the hard experience of caring (Graham 1986), the pervasive universalist capabilities of maternal thinking (Ruddick 1989), the psychic roots and perpetuation of maternity in the gender-divided familial processes of child socialization (Chodorow 1978), and the fragmentation and commodification of maternal experiences by an 'objective', 'scientific' health care system (Rothman 1989). Or it can only be by an insistence on the need to listen to 'inside' accounts that an alternative standpoint on the typification of mental illness can be heard; the voice of reason within the depressed mother, for example, explaining how and why in the vital work of producing children she has lost a sense of wellbeing and of who she is, not because of some inherent flaw in her own or women's collective personality, but because of the psychic and bodily damage inflicted by a system that cares more about itself than about her (see Romito 1989).

However, if it is evidently true that correction of bias requires attention to the quality of others' narratives, the discourses surrounding qualitative methodology have a more sinister aspect. For, in so far as the feminist reform of sociology is seen to demand a qualitative methodology, women are returned to their expressive roles: his the hard, enumerative data; hers the soft, qualitative stuff of which the feminine expressive role is fashioned. The repetition of this archaic formula should alert us to the impropriety of the paradigm: quantitative *or* qualitative. Whereas the feminist critique has not been imaginative about the ways in which quantitative research can serve the end of a sociology for women,[3] the 'reality' is that, wherever the distinction between the two approaches is closely examined, a process of elision is seen to occur. Nothing that is 'qualitative' cannot be enumerated, and the process of quantification is a qualitative one. To disentangle the objective from the subjective, fact from feeling, 'warrantable' knowledge from grounded understanding, is easier in theory than in practice because the division between the two is one of the best examples we have of a theoretical construct.

The wisdom of hindsight

So, putting all these different strands together, what can be said 'with the wisdom of hindsight' about the logic of inquiry pursued in the SSPO study, as a case-study in the forging of an alternative, non-dichotomous, discourse of knowledge?

1   There is no single right way to present such an inquiry. There are ways that would offend the data by being wrong, but the choice of how best to do it *is* a matter of choice. Thus:

2   The standpoint of the researcher(s) is critical. Her/his/their subjectivity is an integral part of the discourse of meaning within which the research design and results are located. This is a strength, not a weakness, provided that researcher subjectivity is a self-conscious and reflexive process, being seen to constitute part of the research data themselves. All research (all knowledge) incorporates/is affected by the stance of the researcher (knower). It is the failure to understand and explicate this that is dangerous, not the obverse.[4]

3   The primary goal of scientific research is not *knowing* but *understanding*. Knowledge without understanding does not permit the application of research findings to human action. In the health field, which has been dominated by the 'knowing' model, policies to promote people's health that are formulated on the basis of research findings have largely failed because they have been devoid of understanding of the how and why of interconnections between 'variables'. Process is not the handmaid of causality. The identification of cause requires an understanding of process and of interpretative frameworks.

4   Experimental research, a model 'borrowed' from the natural sciences, is possible and user-friendly within the social sciences. Moreover, it is desirable as a way of answering both policy-relevant and theoretical questions about social relations and the nature of human action. Many topics within such fields as education, health, welfare, politics, work and the family would benefit from the use of a research design which 'holds constant' some variables while others are changed, and ensures equal distribution of both known and unknown biases between different research groups. The 'blindness' of such a research design is a disguise needed to permit a different way of seeing. It should not be an excuse for the researcher to remain unaware of his/her own role in the research (Belenky et al. 1986: 26). Nor should it be taken to legitimate withholding

full information about research from those who are asked to participate in it.

5   Such research is compatible with – indeed, demands as part of its project of understanding – attention to the standpoint of *all those who take part in it*. In the case of the SSPO study, this includes the London-based research team, the research midwives who provided the social support intervention and the women who participated in the study by agreeing to random allocation to social support or control group. While the traditional product of such research within the medical model emphasizes the quantification of enumerative, non-subjective data, the use of procedures which incorporate other standpoints provides a model of understanding rather than merely a way of knowing. It also attends to ethical concerns about the objectification of research participants and the use of experimental research on social 'minority' groups. Thus:

6   The *knowledge* demand for quantifiable data that ignores subjective standpoints must be combined with the *understanding* to be obtained by attention to subjective narrative. Thus also:

7   It is out of the dialectic between the two that research 'findings' are produced, and within which they are located. This applies both to the forms in which they become written texts, and to other forms of dissemination.

This is a different way of reaching a similar conclusion to that of Mary Belenky and her colleagues in *Women's Ways of Knowing*. Listening to the accounts of 135 women they talked to about personal experiences and views of knowledge, the research team derived a hierarchy of ways of knowing, beginning with *silence* (the knower is voiceless and effectively subject to the authority of others), and ending with *constructed knowledge*, which is organized around an integration of what is known intuitively and what is known as received knowledge. Constructed knowers see all knowledge as contextual and as a product of both the pursuit of objectivity and the incorporation of subjective standpoints. This stance on knowledge requires the abandonment of 'the habit of thinking in dichotomies' (see pp. xiii–xiv). The tendency to construct oppositonal categories has been traced by Whitbeck (1989) to the domination of knowledge practices by *men's* experiences – specifically, here, the differentiation of opposites occurring between mothers and sons in nuclear family-based child socialization. Whitbeck points out that the model of mother–daughter relations would have different consequences for how knowledge is constructed – those of 'mutual realization'. Constructed knowers in Belenky and colleagues' scheme also display a high tolerance for internal contradiction and ambiguity (Belenky et al. 1986: 137). A related distinction that emerged from a study of individual women's standpoints was that between separate and connected knowing. In separate knowing, the self and what is to be known are logically and emotionally separate: the knower plays 'the doubting game … separate knowers … are like doormen at exclusive clubs. They don't want to let anything in unless they are pretty sure it is good' (Belenky et al. 1986: 104). But connected knowers perceive a link between themselves as knowers and what it is that they know: they play 'a believing game'. The two sorts of knowers deal with the need for objectivity – for avoiding simply projecting the content of one's own head on what is known – in different ways. While separate knowers suppress the self and deny the importance of personal values and so forth, connected knowers believe that the 'best' knowledge comes from personal experience, which means developing procedures based on empathy for gaining access to what others know. Many of the women Belenky and colleagues talked to had an interesting answer to the question 'Why be objective?' Their answer was that it is impossible to *help* someone without the objectivity that comes from understanding how he or she sees their own situation.

The distinction between separate and connected knowing developed by Belenky and colleagues is paralleled by the one argued here, between knowing and understanding. One implication of both distinctions for the enterprise of social science research is that the logic of the relations between hypotheses, data and findings must attend to the perspectives of all members of the research. Another is that the social relations of researcher and researched form a self-conscious process; these constitute not so much an instrument of data collection as the procedure for turning knowledge into understanding. Through attending to the viewpoints of research participants, researchers develop an empathic understanding of the processes under investigation which cannot be obtained from research strategies that insist on the absence or invisibility of social relations. Some aspects of the relevance of this to our SSPO study will be obvious. Our research deliberately deployed the social relations of researchers and researched (those of the research midwives with the women enrolled in the intervention part of the study) as a device for accessing the standpoints of both, and providing narrative material which could be built into the generation of the research findings. We used the qualitative material from the interviews the midwives carried out to illuminate processes whose meaning would otherwise be confined to the production of statistically significant relationships between variables.

At the same time, the social relations of the women with the research midwives had another function, that of constituting an experiment designed to test hypotheses about the promotion of health. The relations between the midwives and the women were our experiment. While not pretending that the SSPO study was ethical in every way, or the perfect example of how to tackle the conventional orthodoxy of the quantitative/ qualitative dilemma (this would, indeed, be far from the truth), no one agreed to take part in our research except on the basis of as full information *as we could give them* about the risks and implications of doing so. We also tried to build into the evaluation of the success of the experiment the perspectives of the women and the midwives on whether the support proposed, offered, given and received did 'in fact' make any difference. An important part of the analysis of this question in earlier chapters was the perspective of the women who were not offered support but who, by virtue of the ethical requirement that they both knew and understood the research project of which they were a part, may well have interpreted their role as much to be befriended as to be researched.

The relations of reproduction: understanding women

Finally, one must not detach the question of methodological procedures from the substance of the research: what is to be both known and understood. Here, too, we are on somewhat novel ground. The SSPO study occupied the discursive space between medical conceptualizations of women and their reproductive bodies, on the one hand, and sociological notions of the role of friendship in reproductive health promotion, on the other. The two disciplinary perspectives were integrated in the original plan of the research to form the question: what happens to women's bodies and lives if social support is added to medical care in an effort to promote health? The research design gave prominence at different points to the two approaches. A medical definition of risk was taken to generate the research sample – one which proved interestingly at odds with the views of many of the women themselves and also, to an extent, their social supporters. (Such findings are as much a result of the research as mean birthweight or differences in emotional wellbeing, and draw attention to the importance of reconceptualizing 'serendipitous' research findings.) Conversely, the social support intervention specified relied heavily on sociological notions of the interview which would be (indeed were) unrecognizable in the medical domain. In producing and writing up the findings we began with the medical – the *British Journal of Obstetrics and Gynaecology* paper reproduced as figure 9.1 – but extended our repertoire to include papers in sociological journals contributing to the literature on social class and social support. Sociologists do not read the *BJOG*, and doctors do not read *Sociology*. One-half of the products of the study will thus be inaccessible to each audience. This means that each will have a partial knowledge and understanding of the totality of what constituted the SSPO project.

The original question was one about the impact of social support on the biological process and social relations of reproduction. Pregnancy, as has often been said, presents a unique opportunity for researchers. It has an identified beginning and a discrete end (hence the language of pregnancy 'outcome'), which are both contained in a relatively short space of time. Research on pregnancy can be longitudinal in a temporally collapsed meaning of that term. Secondly, though pregnancy puts women under the lens of medical surveillance, it is not in itself a state of illness; researchers therefore have the opportunity to examine the potential disjunction between objective categories and subjective perception: to explore narratives of professional control and individual resistance. Thirdly, any study of reproduction is 'about women' and thus about the biologization of culture and the gendering of biology. The field of potential insights is enormous. Fourthly, and taking reproduction as a species of a genus rather than the other way around, a study such as ours is concerned with the cultural logic of both embodiment and enselvement: the fact that we are and have bodies, and are and are seen to have selves.

Among the greatest dilemmas of our time are two which arise out of the location of women and bodies on the borders of nature and culture. The first is the containment of women's emancipation within the confines of capitalism's division between public and private lives. Can women be both people and mothers; can mothers be people? The question is oversimplified but 'real'. The second major dilemma concerns the cultural management of bodies in general. What is health? Is it important? Who knows about health? Perhaps more saliently in terms of the themes of this book, who understands it?

Appendix I

Study Guidelines

Below are reproduced the guidelines written for the research midwives who took part in the SSPO study. These cover how the midwives introduced the study to the women they were recruiting to take part, and compilations of the research evidence related to topics women in the intervention group might ask about in the course of pregnancy. These latter guidelines were produced in 1985, and so may have been superseded by new data published since. In the case of the guidelines on poverty and financial benefits, supplementary benefit has, of course, been replaced by income support, and other state benefits have also changed.

How to seek informed consent when recruiting women for the study

In this hospital we are taking part in a London University research study which is trying to help women have healthy and successful pregnancies. In particular its aim is to help women who have given birth to low-birthweight babies in the past. (Many low-birthweight babies are perfectly healthy, but some do have problems, and it's these we're concerned about.) Part of the study consists of providing a personal midwife for mothers during pregnancy. We're asking you whether you would be prepared to take part in this study. However, I should say now that it's entirely up to you to decide whether you want to or not, and your antenatal care in the hospital will be exactly the same whether or not you choose to take part in the study. Before you decide I would like just to tell you a little more about what the study involves. If you want to interrupt and ask me any questions please do so, or else I will answer any questions you have at the end.

All the mothers who agree to take part in the research will be asked to fill in quite a detailed questionnaire after delivery. This will be a postal questionnaire, so it won't involve anyone actually interviewing you, but it will provide us with a lot of very helpful information about the kinds of things that happen to mothers in pregnancy. In addition to this, half the women who agree to take part will be visited at home three times during pregnancy by a research midwife who will listen to any individual problems, will try to provide any help needed and will collect some information on women's needs and circumstances during pregnancy. We think that this may help women to have better and healthier pregnancies, but, because this is one of the first such studies in this country, we really don't know whether it will help, or how mothers may feel about it. At the end of the study, we will look at how the women in the home-visiting part of the study did compared with those who didn't have home visits but just filled in a questionnaire after delivery.

Because it is important to be sure whether or not the home-visiting programme works, we will toss a coin to decide which mothers will receive the home visits and which will not. This means that you won't be able to choose whether or not you will be in the home-visit group. This may sound an odd way of making this kind of decision, but the difficulty with mothers themselves choosing to be in the home-visit group is that, in order to find out whether this kind of extra help works, we have to compare it with standard antenatal care in a way that we know isn't influenced by other factors. The only way to be sure of this is to ask half of you to have the home visits and half of you not to, leaving the decision about who is in which group up to chance.

It is entirely up to you whether or not you agree to help with this research. We feel it is important research because quite a lot of babies born in this country are born weighing less than they should, and we don't really know how to prevent this. So we would be glad if you could agree to help. As I said, your care at this hospital will of course be *exactly* the same whether or not you agree to take part. The home visits by the midwives are an 'extra' on top of ordinary antenatal care.

If you agree to take part we will let you know as soon as possible which group you are in.

Alcohol: guidelines from the research evidence

About half of women and three-quarters of men aged 18–65 in Britain drink alcohol twice a week or more. One in ten young women (18–24) take more than three drinks daily. In recent years drinking among women has increased. Reliable figures for drinking during pregnancy are hard to find: it seems that around three-quarters of pregnant women probably drink at least some alcohol during pregnancy (meaning about three to four glasses of wine or two pints of lager or their equivalent per week). It is common for women to 'go off' alcohol in early pregnancy because it makes them feel sick, but later in pregnancy alcohol may not have the same effect.

The idea that alcohol is bad in pregnancy has been around for a long time. In the early 1970s a group of American researchers drew attention to something they called the 'fetal alcohol syndrome' – a cluster of congenital malformations associated wtih heavy maternal drinking in pregnancy. Partly as a result of their work, people became very interested in the harmful effects of alcohol on the fetus, and many health professionals began to recommend that pregnant women should drink no alcohol at all.

It is a matter of common sense that heavy drinking is bad for anyone – women and fetuses included. Women who are heavy drinkers (five to six drinks a day) do seem rather more likely to give birth to babies with problems, including a lowered birthweight. There is some evidence that 'binge' drinking in pregnancy particularly may not be a good idea. However, whether or not a specific 'fetal alcohol syndrome' exists is not clear. The original research in the 1970s was based on very small numbers of children whose mothers were extremely socially disadvantaged. They had many associated problems, including possible dietary deficiencies and illicit drug use. Much the same is true of alcohol as is true of smoking in pregnancy: both heavy drinking and heavy smoking are associated with perinatal problems, including lowered birthweight, but both are also associated with other factors harmful to health, including poverty and poor diet and the use of certain drugs. It is therefore difficult to say how important alcohol on its own is as a cause of perinatal problems.

There is no clear evidence that light or moderate drinking in pregnancy is harmful. (Although, of course, there is also no evidence that such drinking is absolutely safe.)

It is not easy to define 'light' or 'moderate' drinking, but most of the studies agree that five or fewer drinks per week are not associated with an increased risk of problems, and some studies point to a level of up to two drinks a day as being all right.

Just to confuse the picture further, health professionals know, and some pregnant women may also know, that alcohol used to be given intravenously in attempts to stop preterm labour.

This study
Women with a history of low-birthweight delivery may be anxious about many aspects of their behaviour in terms of possible harm to the baby. Since alcohol in pregnancy is in the news a lot these days, they may ask whether or not it is safe to drink in pregnancy, and especially whether or not drinking decreases the baby's birthweight.

> IF WOMEN DO NOT RAISE THESE QUESTIONS, PLEASE DO NOT DO SO EITHER: AS WITH SMOKING, WAIT TO BE ASKED.

If you are asked, follow the guidelines set out above. The main message is that there is no evidence that light or moderate drinking is bad for the baby. But heavy drinking is not sensible either for mother or baby, and it is also sensible to avoid 'binge' drinking. As with smoking, it is important to remember both the reasons why pregnant women may do it, and the broader social and political context. Alcohol is a prop in times of stress, and it is, moreover, socially acceptable as such. MPs, doctors and the stars of television soap operas will use alcohol, and it has been said that the government is more dependent on alcohol than any alcoholic – taxes and excise duty on alcohol bring in no less than £4000 million a year.

Diet: guidelines from the research evidence

The idea that the diet of pregnant women is important for the health of their babies is an idea with an immediate appeal to common sense. It seems obvious that what pregnant women eat influences the wellbeing of their babies. However, what is much more difficult is to say just *how* a mother's diet affects her baby.

Severe malnutrition reduces fertility and increases many perinatal complications, including the incidence of low birthweight. This level of malnutrition is found under famine conditions and would be unusual in industrialized countries today. More relevant questions have to do with the possible effects and prevention of mild to moderate malnutrition, the implications for pregnancy outcome of dietary restriction programmes and specific questions to do with particular components of diet, including vitamins and substances such as tea and coffee.

Dietary supplementation: any effect?

There have been many intervention studies which have focused on adding to pregnant women's ordinary diet in an attempt to reduce perinatal problems. Although wonderful results have sometimes been claimed, the way many of these studies were done makes their findings difficult to interpret, because it is impossible to know whether the change of diet or some other factor was responsible for the apparent improvement. Studies of dietary supplementation which have used a randomized design, and are therefore easier to interpret, have come up with interesting and sometimes surprising findings. One of the best known of these studies was done in New York in the 1970s. This study found that a high-protein supplement in pregnancy was associated with *lower* birthweight and *more* preterm delivery. A balanced protein-calorie supplement on the other hand was associated with *higher* birthweight and *less* preterm delivery.

This finding, which is echoed in other studies, has led people to be cautious about advocating simple changes in diet as a way of automatically improving pregnancy outcome. However, it is important to remember that diet also has a *long-term* effect on health. How pregnant women eat in their own childhoods influences their biological capacity as mothers. And to say that it is difficult to prove a link between dietary supplements in pregnancy and healthier babies is not of course to say that diet in general shouldn't be better. On the contrary, there is evidence that the diets of many people (men, women and children) in Britain today are inadequate and need to be improved.

In studies giving pregnant women either fairly directive nutritional advice and/or lower-protein-density supplements, the average increase in mean birthweight is about 50 g (2 oz). This is a fairly small effect, and it is interesting that the effect is the same whether whole families or individuals are counselled – in other words, it is possible that some dietary interventions in pregnancy work because of their social support effect.

Dietary restriction
Pregnant women used to be advised to restrict weight gain during pregnancy. There is some evidence that women who do this have lower-birthweight infants than women who don't.

Vitamins
It's very likely that, as with other elements of diet, vitamins are important in promoting healthy pregnancy. But this doesn't mean that vitamin *supplementation* is always a good thing. In controlled trials, there is no evidence that iron supplements in pregnancy are followed by healthier babies. Extra vitamin B6 appears to reduce women's appetites, although there is also evidence that it is good for their teeth. Extremely high doses of vitamin C during pregnancy have been associated with scurvy in the newborn baby. The study recently mounted by the Medical Research Council to look at any effect of vitamin supplementation before and after conception on neural-tube defects met with antagonism from the 'consumer' organizations, who argued the case in favour of vitamins already proven. This is a good example of the power of the argument that vitamins, being 'natural', must somehow be good. The studies that gave rise to the MRC trial did appear to show that women with a history of having babies with neural-tube defects who were given a multivitamin and iron preparation were less likely to have another such infant than women with a similar history, who did not take the preparation. However, there were indications in the study that the two groups of women were not very similar and probably ran different risks of having this complication in any case.

In short, there is no evidence that women having normal adequate diets give birth to healthier babies if they take additional vitamins in pregnancy. No known vitamin is the magic answer to the problem of preventing low birthweight.

Tea and coffee
According to figures in a recent Scottish study, one in two pregnant women drink one to four cups of coffee a day, and one in seven drink between five and nine cups a day. Tea drinking is even more common – over half the women in this study drank one to four cups of tea a day and one in five drank between five and nine cups.

Both heavy tea drinkers and heavy coffee drinkers have an increased risk of perinatal problems, but there is really no evidence that either tea or coffee is responsible for this. It is more likely to be the case that women with an increased risk of problems also drink more tea or coffee than average. Some research does suggest a link between tea drinking and anencephaly, but this is only a suggestion. Birthweight doesn't seem to be affected by tea or coffee drinking independently of other factors.

This study
There are remarkably few clear answers emerging from this mass of research on diet and pregnancy. Nevertheless, women anxious about having another low-birthweight baby may want to be told how to improve their diets – or they may ask whether poor diet is a cause of low birthweight.

IF YOU ARE ASKED SUCH QUESTIONS, PLEASE USE THE INFORMATION GIVEN ABOVE AS A GUIDE TO YOUR ANSWERS. DON'T OFFER DIETARY ADVICE – WAIT TO BE ASKED.

The only exception to this concerns women who smoke a lot – the smoking guidelines suggest discussing with them the possibility of eating more, since it seems that heavy smoking could be a bad thing in pregnancy partly because it depresses women's appetites and weight gain. Some general points to bear in mind when talking about diet are:

1 A 'good' diet is important in pregnancy (even if we don't know exactly which components of diet are related to exactly which pregnancy outcomes).
2 A 'good' diet is important for the mother, as well as for the baby. Indeed, it is possible for the baby to be OK even when the mother isn't eating properly. The reasons for eating well in pregnancy have to do with women's health, as well as with that of their babies.
3 What is a good diet? Rather than giving diet sheets with lists of precise accounts of the required foods, it would seem sensible to suggest guidelines, namely:

Some protein (meat, cheese, fish, eggs, nuts, etc.) every day.
Fresh fruit and vegetables every day.
Bread in diffferent varieties, brown, white and wholemeal.
Milk (or yoghurt) every day, either fresh or in cooked foods.
Fresh, raw and lightly cooked food is generally better than food pre-pared by prolonged cooking. Grilling (for instance, of fish fingers and bacon) is better than frying.

PLEASE STRESS THE GOOD FOODS RATHER THAN LISTING THE BAD ONES

This may be difficult when you have a fairly good idea that a woman is eating a grossly imbalanced diet, (i.e. a lot of fried/starchy/poor-quality convenience foods). In fact what is important is not the quality of individual foods, but the overall diet. 'Bad' foods are acceptable within the context of a diet that provides a reasonably wide range of nutrients. Despite the British emphasis on the need to eat meat, vegetarian diets, for example, are normally quite adequate – though certain 'cult' diets (for instance that of the Rastafarians) are not.

Women, particularly working-class women with a history of low birth-weight, are constantly being told what *not* to do. So the aim of this study is to emphasize the positive things that can easily be done to make women feel better about their pregnancies.

4   If a woman wants to take vitamin pills, the answer is that these won't do any harm (provided she is not talking about enormously high doses). Part of wanting to take extra vitamins is wanting to do everything possible to look after oneself and one's baby. This feeling should be encouraged.
5   A varied diet is more likely to fill nutrient needs than a monotonous one, and is better from this point of view than dietary supplements.

Medicines and drugs: guidelines from the research evidence

Although current medical advice is *against* taking unnecessary medicines and drugs in pregnancy, many pregnant women do take medicines for one reason or another. In a recent American study 70 per cent of pregnant women reported having taken at least one drug at some point in pregnancy. Most of these were non-prescription drugs (analgesics, antacids and cold/allergy preparations). Among the prescribed drugs, the most frequently used were analgesics and tranquillizers. Comparable British data show that about two-thirds of pregnant women report using one or more drugs during early pregnancy (either prescribed or over-the-counter preparations). About 1 per cent admit to having used drugs such as cannabis and heroin.

Two different issues need to be borne in mind when discussing the effects of drugs and medicines taken in pregnancy. One is the possibility that drugs taken early in pregnancy could result in babies with congenital malformations. The other is the possible effect on the growth and vitality of the fetus of drugs taken in later pregnancy. In addition, the whole question of drug-taking in pregnancy needs to be set in the context of a society in which women, in general, are pill-takers. In any one year, for instance, one in five British women will take some form of mood-altering drug (tranquillizers, anti-depressants and sedatives).

It is hard to make definite statements about the effect (if any) on women and their babies of most commonly used drugs and medicines. Large, carefully controlled studies are needed to be sure whether these substances affect pregnancy, and such studies are difficult to do and complicated to interpret. One reason is that women who take the occasional aspirin for headaches in pregnancy, for example, may also be involved in other potentially harmful activities (e.g. smoking) and situations (e.g. poor/overcrowded housing). It's difficult to control for the effect of these other factors in order to be clear about the impact of the drugs as such. It's therefore not possible to say that such medicines definitely do no harm. On the other hand, there isn't any evidence to suggest that occasional use of medicines such as aspirin or paracetamol or commonly used treatments for indigestion or constipation are harmful to the baby. (There is even a suggestion that aspirin may be helpful in preventing pre-eclampsia!) There is also no evidence that these drugs or prescribed drugs such as Valium are specifically associated with low birthweight (due to either preterm delivery or intrauterine growth retardation), although it is the case that regular medication with relatively large amounts of Valium prior to delivery may make babies sleepy and cause a 'withdrawal syndrome'.

Evidence on the effects of illicit drugs including cannabis and heroin is even more difficult to come by. However, the fetal-growth-retarding effects of maternal heroin use are fairly well documented; these babies also suffer neonatal withdrawal symptoms and respiratory depression. There appears to be little evidence about the effect on pregnancy outcome of regular or occasional cannabis use (aside from the suggestion that use in early pregnancy may increase the risk of congenital malformations).

This study
The most likely way for the topic of medicine/drugs to come up in your contacts with the study women is for women to say that they are worried about taking/having taken common over-the-counter preparations such as analgesics during pregnancy. This is a frequently reported worry in studies of pregnancy. It's perfectly OK to be reassuring in such cases. So far as we know, this sort of drug use doesn't harm babies at all. Another possibility is that women under stress will report using/having used central nervous system drugs including tranquillizers, anti-depressants and sedatives. It is not a good idea to take these in early pregnancy because of the risk of congenital malformations, and maternal use at the end of pregnancy may result in a baby with respiratory depression.

Otherwise, it's a matter of discussing with the women the advantages and disadvantages of taking such drugs. Although there is much more of an awareness now about the dangers of drug-taking in pregnancy, many doctors do continue to prescribe drugs such as Valium, and women take them in good faith that their health will be improved by them. Some questions to explore in talking about this with a woman who has been given such a prescription are: How does the drug make her feel? How does she feel about taking it? Does it help her to cope with her problems, or does it make coping more difficult? Might there be some alternative to taking the drug, such as counselling, or some other form of support? In some places there are now self-help groups for women who are, or have been, taking tranquillizers, anti-depressants, etc. There are also Community Mental Health Units which can help.

All of these avenues should be explored, but the most important response is to allow the woman to talk about her own feelings – those that led her to take the drug and those she has about taking it. It would be counter-productive to add to the guilt and worry experienced by an already stressed woman who's been prescribed a drug such as Valium and who feels she needs the drug in order to survive.

It isn't likely that you will be seeing a woman who is taking 'hard' drugs such as heroin and who is willing to discuss this. If you do, it is most important to preserve the woman's trust in you and assure her that you will not instantly inform her GP or hospital consultant. She will, however, need specialist help, and we will be able to provide contact names and addresses so that you can secure appropriate help for her.

If specific queries about particular drugs arise, please refer these to us and we will attempt to find the answers.

Poverty and health guidelines from the research evidence

It seems obvious that being poor might be expected to put at risk the health of pregnant women and their children. It can be expected to do this in a number of related ways:

1 Living in poverty may mean that people cannot afford things that are necessary to maintain health, such as good food, warm clothing, reasonable housing, fuel, and so on, both currently in the pregnancy and in their past.
2 Additionally it may mean that people are constantly anxious about how they will pay future bills and be able to afford the additional cost of a new child.
3 Being poor may also mean that people are socially isolated, unable to pay the cost of travel, to have or use a telephone or to join in social events.

There is no one way of drawing the line below which people can be said to be living in poverty, but in the United Kingdom the rate of supplementary benefit is normally taken as a semi-official poverty line, because it represents the government's estimate of the minimum income necessary to meet the costs of living. There are no up-to-date figures for the number of people living on such low incomes and none at all for the number of pregnant women involved. However, we do know that in 1981 there were 2.8 million people living on incomes below the level of supplementary benefit, and a further 4.8 million people receiving supplementary benefit.

Forty per cent of these 7.6 million people were in families with dependent children. It has been estimated that by 1983 the total number of people living on incomes at or below supplementary benefit level had increased to 9 million.

Life on low incomes
There is considerable evidence that living on incomes at around the level of supplementary benefit may put health at risk. One study of sixty-five families living on supplementary benefit found that at least a third said they were never or only 'now and again' able to buy cheese, fresh vegetables, fresh fruit, fresh meat, butter and fresh fish. Additionally, those families who were adequately fed were more likely to be in debt. Another study based on interviews with 1800 people living on benefit found that three out of five parents were missing a standard item of clothing, such as a warm coat or a change of shoes. This study also found that around a quarter of the families with children felt they had gone cold during the winter of 1982–83 because they could not afford fuel.

Pregnancy can be expected to put additional strains on family budgets. There is little information about the experience of pregnancy on low incomes, but it has recently been estimated that the cost of a week's menu for pregnant women based on hospitals' diet sheets can come to as much as a third of the weekly budget for a couple and a half of that for single women. The pre-birth costs of basic equipment and clothing for the baby are also considerable, and trying to meet them may cause a fair amount of anxiety. One manufacturer's list of equipment for a baby's first year, quoted in the *Daily Mirror*, adds up to almost £450, including some secondhand equipment.

Layette	£52.35
Nursery furniture	£77.73
High chair	£28.49
Feeding accessories	£15.33
Pushchair	£62.45
Pram	£94.95
Safety devices (home and car)	£43.29
Playpen, toys, etc.	£72.90
Total:	£447.49

It is also important to recognize that within families it appears to be women who are more likely to take the brunt of low incomes. Studies have suggested that women may cut back on their own food consumption to ensure that partners and children do not go short. Similarly, research suggests that domestic heating may be reduced during the day when women are home alone or with children, to economize on fuel. Recently there has also been increasing attention to the possibility that, within families which do not have low incomes, women may live in 'poverty amidst plenty', with weekly allowances inadequate to meet the family expenditure for which they are seen to be responsible.

Poverty and health during pregnancy
There is in fact very little research which has looked directly at the possible relationships between low income and the health of pregnant women and their children. Analyses of perinatal mortality data and the distribution of low-birthweight babies by occupational social class show the now familiar pattern of a higher incidence in lower occupational classes. But income, housing conditions, place of residence and other material circumstances are only some dimensions of social class, and others, such as smoking behaviour, maternal age, height and parity, have been argued to explain all or some of these social class differences.

Studies do, however, suggest that the effects of poverty on diet are important. A recent research project in London, for example, found that pregnant women in a deprived area had deficient diets compared with those in a more affluent area. Average calorie intake for the poorer women was 1689 – almost a slimming diet – compared to 2044 for the more affluent women. The amount of essential fatty acids needed for the development of all membranes, particularly important in pregnancy, was lower in the poorer women. Poor diets in childhood may have a long-term adverse effect on the outcomes of women's subsequent pegnancies. Research also indicates that women with high levels of anxiety and stress have a greater proportion of pregnancy complications and perhaps of physical abnormalities in children (see 'stress guidelines'). Poverty may be a cause of such anxiety.

This study
It is important that you are sensitive to the possibility that some women in the study may be living on very low incomes. This may be because they and their families are receiving social security, or because the parents are low paid. It is worth remembering that in 1979 the DHSS estimated that 20 per cent of people living on an income below the level of supplementary benefit were in families where there was at least one income from *full-time* work. Financial difficulties may also be caused by the unemployment of older children or because a woman does not get enough money from her husband.

Many people find it particularly difficult to talk about financial problems. While therefore, in line with the other guidelines, you are not expected to probe into family income (except for one or two questions in the home-contact schedules), it is important that you make it obvious that you are aware of the financial constraints on the choices women make about work or diet, for example, or how they spend their time. This will at least provide an opportunity for them to discuss these problems if they wish. On the other hand you shouldn't be surprised if some women are aggressively aware of their rights to social security benefit or that some women are so numbed by the conditions they live in that they seem hard and 'uncaring'.

IF FINANCIAL PROBLEMS ARE RAISED BY THE WOMEN YOU SHOULD PAY PARTICU-
LAR ATTENTION TO THE FOLLOWING POINTS:

1   Many people do not claim all the benefits they are entitled to. Many benefits are available – see the attached sheet, though these may change as a result of a major government review in 1985. Entitlement is often difficult to calculate, and some people may be ashamed to claim even if they know about them. Some benefits are particularly likely to be unclaimed, espe-cially by people in low-paid jobs, who may be entitled to free milk and vitamins, housing benefit, family income supplement or one-parent benefit.

All means-tested benefits have to be claimed and there is sometimes no form. Women have to write a letter to claim a one-off payment (see attached sheet) for maternity clothes or baby items. This may not be easy for people who rarely write letters. 'Automatic' benefits like free milk for pregnant women are not paid until the woman or her partner notifies the DHSS office that she is pregnant. This should happen as soon as the pregnancy is confirmed. Women need to know about these benefits early.

You are not expected to be an expert on social security benefits, but it would help if you familiarized yourself with the range of benefits that are currently available and knew what expert advice is available locally. Almost all areas have Citizens Advice Bureaux which will help, and some have specialist Welfare Rights Centres. Social service departments may also be able to help. Sending people to DHSS offices for advice is probably not the most appropriate response. They are often not very pleasant places, queues may be long, and the staff harassed and unable to find the time to give careful advice. When you are discussing benefits it is important to remember that people have a legal right to these benefits. They are not charity.

2   In some areas there may be special facilities available for people who are on social security or low paid – subsidized transport facilities, for example, or reduced fees for access to leisure facilities. Information about these is normally available from Citizens Advice Bureaux, from the local authority or from local community centres.

3   In many areas there are also independent charities providing secondhand clothes, for example. If you do suggest that women make use of these, or of subsidized access to facilities, you should be sensitive to the fact that using secondhand clothes, etc., may be experienced as degrading, and the procedure for obtaining these often involves obtaining a letter from a professional such as a social worker or health visitor or showing a special card. You may not be in a position to change these procedures, but you can share the women's anxieties and discuss with them any worries they have about using them.

4   Although some women may live in households whose overall income doesn't seem low, this income isn't always shared out equally between family members. It might, therefore, sometimes be appropriate to discuss with a woman in this situation the possibility of her talking to her partner about increasing her share of the family income. You could suggest to her that with the new baby coming she would be justified in doing this because of the extra expense.

Benefits related to having a baby

Maternity grant. A grant of £25 is made to virtually all women having a baby, for help with the cost of baby things, such as a pram, nappies, etc. The basic condition is that the women must have been in Great Britain for 182 days of the 52 weeks immediately prior to the actual or expected date of birth. The grant will not be paid until the 11th week before the expected date of birth and if claimed more than 3 months after the birth will not normally be given.

Maternity allowance. A benefit for women who have worked before their pregnancy, worth £29.15 a week for up to 18 weeks, based on a woman's own National Insurance contributions.

Maternity pay. Not strictly a state benefit but performs a similar function to maternity allowance (at a higher level and for a shorter period) for some women who have been working. Employers are required by law to pay it to pregnant women who have worked continuously for the same employer for two years full-time or five years part-time. The amount is nine-tenths of normal weekly pay, reduced by the full amount of the maternity allowance (whether it is received or not). This means that women on lower earnings receive a lower proportion of their normal pay than women on higher earnings. Some employers are more generous and provide above the legal minimum.

Free prescriptions and dental treatment. Available to all women while they are pregnant and for a year after the baby is born, as well as to all children under 16. All the members of families on supplementary benefit, Family Income Supplement and with incomes just above the supplementary benefit level (who qualify on grounds of 'low income') are entitled anyway.

Free milk and vitamins. Once universal, this benefit is now available only to families on supplementary benefit, Family Income Supplement and 'low incomes': pregnant and nursing mothers in such families are entitled for themselves, and their children are entitled until they are 5 years old.

Child benefit. £7.00 a week for all children.

One-parent benefit. An extra £4.55 a week on top of child benefit (only one payment per family).

Unemployment benefit. Paid to individuals who are available for work and have made, or been credited, with the required National Insurance contributions. (This is quite a complicated calculation normally made by the DHSS. Expert advice will have to be sought if their decision seems unfair.) The benefit is worth £30.45 per week for a single claimant, and £49.25 for a couple. No additions are available other than child benefit.

Supplementary benefit. A means-tested, family-based benefit available primarily to people who have no other source of income, though some people receive supplementary benefit to 'top up' other benefits because they are below the level of supplementary benefit. It is intended to cover all day-to-day needs (except housing, which is separately provided for); people with savings over £3000 excluded. Weekly rates are:

Husband and wife	£47.85
Single householder	£29.50
18 or over	£23.60
16–17	£18.20
1–15	£15.10
0–10	£10.10

Extra weekly payments are available, for example for homes that are especially difficult to heat; and £2.20 weekly addition is paid automatically when there is one child under 5 years old (no extra if there is more than one child). One-off payments are also available in certain circumstances, but savings of over £500 are taken into account. The one-off payments include payments to cover the cost of clothing for a woman who is pregnant or has had a baby; the cost of furniture which, in relation to babies, would include a high chair and a safety gate (although not necessarily new ones); and the cost of a 'sufficient' amount of things necessary for a newborn baby, such as nappies, a cot, etc.

Supplementary benefit entitles claimants to certain other benefits, for example free prescriptions, and, for pregnant women, free milk and vitamins (see above).

Family Income Supplement. A weekly benefit for people with children who have low earnings from full-time paid employment. The amount of help depends on family size as well as earnings.

Housing benefit. Means-tested help with housing costs available from your local authority. It can be claimed by anyone living in a dwelling as their home who has to pay rent and/or rates. The amount of help depends on size of family, weekly income and rent/rate levels.

NOTE: FURTHER DETAILS ARE AVAILABLE FROM *THE MATERNITY RIGHTS HANDBOOK* (PENGUIN, 1984), *THE NATIONAL WELFARE BENEFITS HANDBOOK* AND *THE RIGHTS GUIDE TO NON-MEANS-TESTED BENEFITS* (CHILD POVERTY ACTION GROUP, 1984).

Sex: guidelines from the research evidence

The possible effects on the unborn baby of maternal sexual activity have been discussed for a long time. Until the 1950s sex in pregnancy was widely condemned as being bad – although there was no evidence one way or the other. Since then the idea that sex in pregnancy is not harmful, and may even be a good thing, has become more fashionable – again without evidence. In fact many surveys have shown that, whatever they are advised to do, most pregnant women decrease their sexual activity progressively throughout pregnancy. Many men and women report that sexual activity in pregnancy is highly problematic for a variety of reasons.

In the late 1970s work by an American researcher was interpreted as showing that babies of women who had intercourse once a week or more in the month before delivery ran an increased risk of dying, particularly as a result of amniotic fluid infections and preterm delivery. There are many problems with these data, including the fact that the information about sexual activity used in the analysis was unreliable. Furthermore, there are other studies which contain exactly opposite findings, including the conclusion that *not* having intercourse may be associated with increased risk to the baby.

One major problem about the relationship between sexual activity during pregnancy and potential effects on the baby is that it is unclear which aspect of sexual activity might be important. For example, semen contains prostaglandin which, if placed around the cervix, could start preterm labour. Mechanical pressure on the cervix might be significant. Orgasm in the woman is sometimes associated with uterine contractions. Nipple stimulation may release oxytocin, which can affect the uterus. (In a controlled trial, nipple stimulation has been found to be a good way of hastening the onset of labour.) Thus, if sexual activity is suspect, there may be grounds for advising pregnant women against masturbation in pregnancy, and also against such practices as vaginal examination by a doctor or midwife and massage of the nipples in preparation for breastfeeding!

This study
Women who have delivered preterm in a previous pregnancy are especially likely to mention the possible hazards of sexual activity and ask for advice on this.

PLEASE DO NOT RAISE THE SUBJECT UNLESS THE MOTHER REFERS TO IT

Some such reference may be indirect – a woman may indicate she is worrying about whether or not she should have sex (and whether or not having sex in the previous pregnancy was what caused the baby to have been born early and/or small). It is necessary to be sensitive to any sign of anxiety about this, even if it isn't spelt out. *If it's on her mind, encourage her to talk about it.* So far as the advice angle is concerned, your main guidelines are:

1 Women (and men) should do what they feel happy about.
2 There is no obligation to be sexually active during pregnancy. On the other hand, if a couple enjoy sex and are not worrying about it, and there are no obvious 'contra-indications' (such as vaginal bleeding during or after intercourse) then there are no strong reasons to advise against it, except possibly during the last few weeks.
3 Women who have experienced preterm delivery may well be happier not having intercourse in late pregnancy. This is particularly likely to be true of women who find that intercourse or orgasm causes noticeable contractions and/or uterine irritability.

Smoking: guidelines from the research evidence

In the UK as a whole about one in three people smoke. Between a quarter and a half of all pregnant women smoke at some time in pregnancy. The evidence about the effects of smoking in pregnancy is confused and somewhat contradictory. Many studies have shown that smoking in pregnancy is associated with slightly lighter and slightly less healthy babies as compared to the babies of non-smoking mothers. On average, babies of mothers who smoke weigh 150–250 g (5–9 oz) less. Some, but not all, studies show that the more cigarettes that are smoked, the lighter is the baby, but this effect is slight.

    A lot of factors are associated with lowered birthweight, and it is difficult to be certain how much of the fall in birthweight is actually due to smoking. The difference in birthweight associated with smoking is smaller than that associated with other factors such as working-class versus middle-class occupations, or the mother's height. Of course these other 'risk' factors are themselves associated; for instance, smoking is two to three times more common among people with manual, as compared with non-manual, occupations.

Some researchers have argued that birthweight differences between the babies of smoking and non-smoking mothers are due to innate biological differences in the mothers. One piece of evidence in favour of this point of view is that there are larger differences between smoking and non-smoking mothers in terms of low birthweight than in perinatal mortality. There are also other differences between the two groups of women – for example, non-smokers seem to plan pregnancies more and drink less coffee and alcohol.

If smoking causes lower birthweight, it may do so either directly (by restricting the amount of oxygen available to the fetus) or by other means, particularly by lowering the mother's appetite, so that she eats less and gains less weight in pregnancy.

Health education

It is commonly believed that women should be advised not to smoke in pregnancy and that when properly informed and advised they won't do so. However, not all anti-smoking education campaigns have been evaluated – we don't know whether or not they work. In carefully done studies that are large enough to answer the question, it appears to be only sensitively and sympathetically given advice that succeeds in persuading mothers not to smoke. Just telling pregnant women that they mustn't smoke for the sake of the baby doesn't help, and may only make mothers feel guilty. On the other hand, advice on cutting down in the context of understanding why a woman smokes, and what her particular problems are, is much more likely to succeed.

Most women know that the health education message is against smoking in pregnancy. But knowing this doesn't seem to be enough to change their behaviour. Since many women who smoke worry about smoking, insensitive health education campaigns may actually do more harm than good.

Why do mothers smoke

As well as knowing that smoking is said to be bad for babies, many women also know from personal experience that heavy babies can be born to heavy smokers and light babies to non-smokers. Research has shown that smoking is often an important way of coping with stress for many women. This is particularly true of women living in difficult circumstances with lots of social problems. Smoking isn't a sign of irresponsibility towards the fetus, but rather of the responsibility women feel towards their families, which means that it is important for them to be able to cope with the

strains of daily life. It is important also to remember that pregnant women
smoke in a context in which many other people turn to cigarettes when
life gets difficult. Smoking is still a socially acceptable habit and the power
of the tobacco industry has so far ensured that it remains so.

This study
Many women who have already had a low-birthweight baby will continue
to smoke throughout the next pregnancy. Most will be aware of the
medical debate about the harmful effects of smoking on babies, although
some will ask for information about this. If you are asked for information,
please follow the guidelines given above.

DO NOT OFFER INFORMATION ABOUT SMOKING AND PREGNANCY – WAIT FOR
WOMEN TO ASK

Some women may smoke during your visits and, while not mentioning the
subject directly, may indicate some tension about smoking. In these
circumstances it may be helpful to say that your role is not to advise them
against smoking, but rather to talk about some of the stresses they may
have that they feel are relieved by smoking. It is possible that this approach
might lead to a reduction in smoking – if so, we should pick this up in the
quesionnaire answers.

Since part of the potentially harmful effect of smoking on the fetus may
be due to poor diet, it is probably worth exploring with women who
smoke (and who raise the issue of smoking) the quality and quantity of
their food intake and then suggesting some improvements in this (see diet
guidelines).

A recent review of the evidence about smoking and pregnancy pointed
out that about one in ten smokers actually smoke more heavily during
pregnancy because of 'greater tension' and that many smokers spend the
whole of pregnancy 'in a state of guilt and inadequacy' about smoking. The
authors of this review comment that 'We do not know what the effects of
such chronic stress and anxiety might be on the course of pregnancy and
labour, or on the ultimate relationship with the child.'

Stress: guidelines from the research evidence

The idea that stress is bad for pregnant women is an old one. Those who
have cared for pregnant women have always suspected that stress is bad
for babies and/or their mothers. In the eighteenth and nineteenth centuries stress was even blamed for causing all kinds of congenital malformations!

Modern scientific knowledge about the effects of stress on pregnancy
outcome is a good deal more precise than this about just how maternal
stress can affect babies. The word 'stress' comes from the same linguistic

root as 'distress' and refers to 'the overpowering pressure of some adverse force or influence'. In the 1980s the lives of many people can justifiably be described as rather full of such experiences, and pregnant women with a history of low-birthweight delivery may well be under a variety of general stresses, as well as living through the particular stress of worrying about another low-birthweight delivery.

Stress, pregnancy and health
Research has shown that both preterm delivery and low birthweight are associated with stressful life events and situations such as mental break-down, family illness, unemployment and housing problems. Women who deliver preterm or have small babies at term have more of this kind of stress in their lives than women without such obstetric complications. One recent study showed that 'objective life events' (such as husbands becoming unemployed) were significantly associated with low-birthweight delivery and that this association was independent of the women's social class.

There are many studies which appear to demonstrate that anxious mothers, or mothers with mental health problems, are more likely to have complicated pregnancies and deliveries and give birth to babies with problems than non-anxious mothers. The design of these studies makes it difficult to say just what kind of role maternal anxiety plays in relation to reproductive problems, since both the anxiety and the pregnancy compli-cations, for example, could be influenced by another factor (for example, stressful life events).

When it comes to working out the processes underlying the relationship between stress and reproductive difficulty, such as low birthweight, there isn't a great deal of sound evidence to draw on. Emotional states in humans and animals certainly affect endocrine function. In particular, psychological stress produces an increase in catecholamine levels, which have a variety of physiological effects on different body organs and systems including the uterus itself. However, while the exact mechanisms may be unclear, there is no doubt that stress can sometimes have measurable physiological effects.

Stress and social support
The idea that social support helps people to cope with stress is one of the main hypotheses behind the present study. Research is quite convincing on the stress-reducing function of social support. People under stress (whether pregnant women, unemployed men, busy midwives or harassed researchers) can feel considerably less stressed when they are receiving social support from those around them.

Some studies describe the impact of social support on mothers and babies. Among those experiences which seem to be affected by social support are mothers' use of analgesia, the length of their labours, the chance of having an instrumental delivery, and the risk of feeling unhappy or depressed after the birth. In these ways, and quite independently of any other factors, extra social support seems to improve the experience of pregnancy, delivery and early motherhood. In the field of health more generally, people's social relationships have been shown to be an important independent influence on their chances of remaining healthy, or becoming ill.

This study

Many of the mothers in this study may be under all sorts of stress and some of them may talk about it explicitly. Sometimes you may be asked a specific question about the effect of stress on the unborn baby (and/or on the risk of preterm labour). This sort of question is not easy to handle. In responding to it, and the more general question of how important stress is, the following suggestions would appear to make sense against the backdrop of existing research evidence:

1   Stress does seem to be one among many factors associated with low birthweight, but how significant stress is compared to the other factors we don't really know.
2   If a woman is under stress there may be very little she can do directly to reduce it, and she should certainly not feel guilty about subjecting her fetus and herself to problems she can't avoid. It's rather like the standard advice to 'just relax' when being examined in an antenatal clinic, which usually succeeds in making one feel more tense: so telling women to take life more easily when their circumstances are particularly difficult isn't really a great help.
3   What probably does help is encouraging people to talk about their problems. Just talking is important, but it may also help people to define the problems more clearly and also possibly think of ways in which they can exercise more control over some aspects of their lives.
4   Is it therefore possible to work out ways of reducing stress by helping a woman to feel more in control? One example would be to enable women to have more information about state financial benefits for which they are eligible; knowing and exercising one's rights can also make one feel generally better about one's situation.
5   You may not feel you are able to make much impact on the levels of stress some women are under, but you may in fact be preventing things from becoming worse! The effects of social support in stressful situations can sometimes help to prevent depression developing. A large research project in London some years ago found some factors which definitely seemed to protect women from becoming depressed when their lives became difficult. These factors included both having a close supportive relationship with another adult, and having some kind of job outside the home.
6   While the idea that stress is a factor associated with low birthweight

and other such complications can be a difficult one for women to handle (because of their relative powerlessness to affect the stress they are under), it is, nevertheless, an idea that makes a lot of sense to many women. It corresponds with their daily experiences of being pregnant, feeling often tense and nervous, and worrying about the baby. It can therefore actually help to hear someone else support the idea that stress is important, and is a *real* experience, even if we don't know precisely whether or how it affects the baby.

Work: guidelines from the research evidence

Whether or not mothers, including pregnant women, should work has provided many people for many years with something to talk, argue, write and advise about. Much of this discussion has focused on paid employment. However, in talking about the importance of or otherwise of work in pregnancy, it is necessary to include not only paid work but also the unpaid housework and childcare mothers do at home.

If work is either bad or good for pregnant women and their babies, there are a number of different aspects of work that might be important, including:

1 The physical activity involved in it.
2 Direct hazards of work (for example, working with X-ray equipment or dangerous chemicals, either in the work place or in the home).
3 The effect of paid work in raising household income and alleviating poverty.
4 The emotional, psychological and social consequences of work – for example, in increasing a woman's self-confidence or bringing her into contact with friendly and supportive workmates (or not doing so, in the case of housework).
5 The implications of paid work for attendance at antenatal clinics and maternity benefit.
6 The combination of paid and unpaid work – women's 'double burden'.

About 80 per cent of women having their first babies are employed during pregnancy, and so are more than 20 per cent of those having subsequent children. There is no evidence that employment in itself is dangerous for mother or baby. Some studies in fact suggest that employed women have fewer perinatal problems than their non-employed counterparts.

Preterm birth is less common among employed women. Although general social differences between women who are employed during pregnancy and those who are not explain some of this effect, it remains even when these differences are taken into account. Employed women's babies do not have lower birthweights than those of non-employed women – indeed, birthweight seems to be higher in this group. While, overall, employment may be associated with fewer problems, it seems that there is a sub-group of employed women who do not enjoy this advantage – working-class women doing jobs that involve heavy physical activity, often in low-income families.

There are no studies which give reliable data on the possible effects of housework, or on the combined effects on pregnancy of women's employment status and domestic responsibilities.

Recent research, especially some done in France, has identified some characteristics of work that do not appear to be good for babies (or their mothers). Although 'work' in this research meant employment, many of the findings also apply to housework. The negative aspects of work were:

1 Standing for prolonged periods of time in late pregnancy.
2 Physically tiring work, especially work involving lifting.
3 A long working week (over 42 hours).
4 Long journeys to and from work.
5 Working in a noisy, hot environment.
6 Working with vibrating machines.
7 Work involving mental stress (for example, frequent repetition of tasks).

This study
If a womain raises with you the question of work during pregnancy, it is worth discussing with her the various issues involved, i.e. the economic benefits/costs of employment/non-employment, the kinds of physical activity involved, and specific aspects such as the length of her journey to and from work. If she raises the subject she is concerned about it.

PLEASE DON'T RAISE IT YOURSELF

Some women won't be employed, and not all those who are will be anxious about any possible effects on their babies. There may also be questions about domestic work. Lifting children, for example, or carrying heavy shopping (two particularly heavy domestic tasks) may well be of concern to a woman who has given birth preterm in a previous pregnancy.

IN DISCUSSING THE SUBJECT OF WORK WITH ANY WOMAN WHO RAISES IT, PLEASE TRY TO FOLLOW THESE GUIDELINES:

Paid work:

1 The most important thing is how a woman feels about working. If she is happy about it and doesn't find it unduly tiring or uncomfortable,

there is no reason why she should be concerned about any bad effects on her baby. Under the 1980 Employment Act all women should be allowed time off work without loss of earnings to attend for antenatal care.

2   If a woman wants to work, but finds her job tiring or unpleasant from the point of view of her pregnancy, it might be worth discussing with her the possibility of changing the nature of her job (either at the same workplace or to a different one). Employers are generally more conscious these days of the needs of pregnant women than they used to be. Some firms provide rest rooms and are willing to adjust work hours so that getting to and from work is less exhausting.

3   Just as there is evidence that employment is good for health, there is also evidence that unemployment can be bad for health. If a woman who doesn't already have children to care for is thinking of giving up her job and staying at home in pregnancy because she thinks this will be good for the baby, it might perhaps be a good idea to talk to her about how she feels at home all the time. Worry about the outcome of pregnancy can become quite all-consuming when there isn't a great deal else to do. Likewise a woman who isn't employed and who is spending many anxious hours at home worrying about her pregnancy might benefit from the suggestion of a part-time job. (The mental health and social support effects of employment hold for part-time as well as full-time jobs.)

Unpaid domestic work:

1   Much of this is tiring and particularly so in pregnancy. Are there ways of reducing the amount done – for instance, by doing housework routines less often or by eating the healthier convenience foods rather than elaborately prepared meals?

2   One of the greatest needs of pregnant women who have young children to look after is probably to have some domestic help. Middle-class women may be able to afford paid help, but it is much more likely to be a case of using neighbourhood and family resources. Is it possible to think of ways of involving other people more? Day care (nursery or childminder) for existing children may also need to be thought about.

Many women may not see their domestic responsibilities as problems from the viewpoint of their pregnancies. *So again, please only discuss these kinds of issues if the woman herself raises them, or gives some indication that she is worried about them.*

Appendix II

Publications from the Social Support and Pregnancy Outcome Study

1   Oakley, A. (1985) Social support and perinatal outcome. *Internatonal Journal of Technology Assessment in Health Care*, 4 (1): 843–54.
2   Oakley, A. (1985) Social support in pregnancy: the 'soft' way to increase birthweight? *Social Science and Medicine*, 21 (11): 1259–68.
3   Knowleden, C. (1987) Pregnancy Home Visiting Study. *National Childbirth Trust Newsletter, Crowborough and District Branch*, 818 (Autumn): 6–7.
4   Oakley, A. (1988) Is social support good for the health of mothers and babies? *Journal of Reproductive and Infant Psychology*, 6: 3–21.
5   Oakley, A., Elbourne, D., and Chalmers, I. (1986) The effects of social interventions in pregnancy. In G. Breart, N. Spira and E. Papiernik (eds), *Proceedings of a Workshop on Prevention of Preterm Birth – new goals and new practices in prenatal care*. Paris, INSERM.
6   Elbourne, D., Oakley, A., and Chalmers, I. (1989) Social and psychological support during pregnancy. In I. Chalmers, M. Enkin, and M. J. N. C. Keirse (eds), *Effective Care in Pregnancy and Childbirth*, Oxford, Oxford University Press.
7   Oakley, A. (1989) Can social support influence pregnancy outcome? *British Journal of Obstetrics and Gynaecology*, 96: 260.
8   Oakley, A., and Rajan, L. (1988) The social support and pregnancy outcome study. *Research and the Midwife Conference Proceedings 1988*: 37–58.
9   Oakley, A. (1989) Who cares for women? Science versus love in midwifery today. *Midwives' Chronicle and Nursing Notes* (July): 214–21.
10 Buckle, S. (1989) Interview. *Midirs Information Pack* (August): 11.
11 Buckle, S. (1988) Meaningful relationships. *Nursing Times*, 12 (84): 46–7.
12 Marsden, R. (1988) Pregnancy home visiting study. *Midwives' Chronicle and Nursing Notes* (March): 86–7.
13 Oakley, A. (1989) Smoking in pregnancy – smokescreen or risk factor? Towards a materialist analysis. *Sociology of Health and Illness*, 11 (4): 311–35.
14 Oakley, A. (1989) Who's afraid of the randomized controlled trial? Some dilemmas of the scientific method and 'good' research practice. *Women and Health*, 15 (2); 25–9.
15 Report in *Nursing Times* (1989), 85 (2): 24–30.
16 Oakley, A. (1990) Who's afraid of the randomized controlled trial? Some dilemmas of the scientific method and 'good' research practice. In H. Roberts (ed.), *Women's Health Counts*, London, Routledge & Kegan Paul.
17 Oakley, A., Rajan, L., and Grant, A. (1990) Social support and pregnancy outcome: report of a randomized trial. *British Journal of Obstetrics and Gynaecology*, 97: 155–62.
18 Rajan, L. and Oakley, A. (1990) Infant feeding practices in mothers at risk of low birthweight delivery. *Midwifery*, 6: 18–27.

19 Rajan, L., and Oakley, A. (1990) Low birthweight babies: the mother's point of view. *Midwifery*, 6: 73–85.

20 Oakley, A., and Rajan, L. (1990) Obstetric technology and maternal emotional wellbeing: a further research note. *Journal of Reproductive and Infant Psychology*, 8: 45–55.

21 Oakley, A., Rajan, L., and Robertson, P. (1990) A comparison of different sources of information on pregnancy and childbirth. *Journal of Biosocial Science*, 22: 477–87.

22 Oakley, A. (1989) Pregnany Home Visiting Study (letter). *Midwives' Chronicle and Nursing Notes* (August): 258.

23 Bedside manner and healthy babies. Report in *The Women's Letter* (1990), 3 (4): 3.

24 Oakley, A., and Rajan, L. (1991) Social class and social support – the same or different? *Sociology*, 25 (1): 31–59.

25 Rajan, L. (1989) Social support and pregnancy outcome. *Nursing Times*, 85 (21): 56–7.

26 Oakley, A., and Rajan, L. (1991) The social support and pregnancy outcome study. In H. Berendes, S. Kessel, and S. Yaffe (eds), *Advances in the Prevention of Low Birthweight: an international symposium*. Washington, DC, National Center for Education in Maternal and Child Health.

27 Elbourne, D., and Oakley, A. (1991) An overview of trials of social support during pregnancy. In H. Berendes, S. Kessel, and S. Yaffe (eds), *Advances in the Prevention of Low Birthweight: an international symposium*, Washington, DC, National Center for Education in Maternal and Child Health.

28 Oakley, A. (1991) Using medical care: the views and experiences of high-risk mothers. *Health Services Research*, 26 (5): 651–69.

29 Oakley A. (1992) Getting at the oyster: one of many lessons from the Social Support and Pregnancy Outcome study. In H. Roberts (ed.), *Women's Health Matters*, London, Routledge & Kegan Paul.

Notes

Chapter 1   Social Origins

1   The idea of a fourth perinatal mortality survey was turned down by the Department of Health in October 1979.
2   See Stinson and Stinson (1983). The same judgements do not seem to be applied to fathers.
3   Calculated on the basis of live births only.
4   The title of this section is taken from Finch (1984: 74).

Chapter 3   Sickness in Salonica and Other Stories

1   This raises interesting questions about the role of wives in medical research.
2   See note 1.
3   Allocation method in the Runnerstrom study was by case-note number, and complicated deliveries were excluded from the analysis. These are possible sources of bias (see Elbourne and Oakley 1991).
4   These are dubious assumptions. See Oakley (1984) and Oakley (1985) for reviews of the evidence.

Chapter 4   Eve in the Garden of Health Research

1   The term actually describes a class of which the oyster is one member.
2   There was a strike of power workers at the time.
3   See the distinction made by Ditton and Williams (1981) between 'fundable' and 'doable' research.
4   Raymond Illsley (personal communication).

Chapter 5   A Bite of the Apple

1   All the names used to identify the study women, their families and other 'real' people throughout this book are pseudonyms.

2 Smoking to help cope with the emotional stress of confronting a child's death, when that death has been attributed by medical staff to smoking, draws attention to the paradox for women that smoking is both health-damaging and health-protecting.

3 Like other researchers blessed with the disguise of 'Dr', I was aware that the midwives and women attending the clinic may have thought I myself had a medical background. This may aid, or impede, the process of gaining a sample. But its practical and ethical implications are rarely discussed.

Chapter 6 Who's Afraid of the Randomized Controlled Trial?

1 The use of titles, as always, is significant.

2 The former consideration posed rather more moral problems than the latter; the low pay and status of midwives within the maternity services was a recurrent theme of research team discussions throughout the study.

3 The Department of Health was funding work on ethnicity and maternity care under the heading of 'The Asian Mother and Baby Campaign'. There seemed to be a general feeling that as a consequence it was not important to highlight ethnicity in other studies. This is, of course, very regrettable.

4 The postal questionnaire designed to be sent six weeks after delivery.

5 The questions about income and living arrangements were asked for the purpose of gaining information about the women's material and social circumstances to be used in the analysis of the impact of the social support intervention.

6 I am indebted to Iain Chalmers for pointing out to me that 'ethical' committees (often so called) may or may not be ethical. The correct term is 'ethics committees'.

7 The Department of Health has recently issued guidelines attempting some standardization (see Department of Health 1991).

8 Sandra Stone's official designation. Needless to say, it does not accurately describe her role.

9 The four research midwives are referred to as RMW1, RMW2, RMW3 and RMW4.

10 The extracts from this file used in this and other chapters have been edited slightly for the sake of brevity and clarity, but otherwise appear in their original formats.

11 She was included in the analysis as if she had received the intervention, following the usual conventions in the analysis of controlled trials (see Schwarz et al. 1980).

12 The research midwives referred to the women in the study as their 'ladies'.

13 The follow-up survey was not part of the original study design. See pp. 308–10.

Chapter 7 'One of Mummy's Ladies'

1 Some women were not interviewed because of difficulties setting up and keeping appointments, and because of hospital admissions and other pregnancy complications.

2 Class was here defined on the basis of occupation (the partner's where there was one, otherwise the woman's own). See Oakley and Rajan 1991 for a discussion of women and class.

3 Cushing's syndrome is a condition of excess production by the adrenal cortex of cortisol, causing a collection of symptoms including fatty swellings, abdominal distension, amenorrhoea, general weakness and usually high blood pressure. Causes of the condition are genetic, tumours, and excess intake of steroid drugs.

4 See pp. 48–9. There was one point in the allocations when one of the midwives felt able to predict the pattern.

5 This was to some extent determined by the three semi-structured interview schedules the midwives were using for these visits, which decreased in length.

6   One reason for this might have been that she continued to work there as a midwife part-time during the study.

7   See appendix I.

8   The research midwives were provided with identification cards they could show to the women.

9   Getting the research midwives' expenses paid on time through the university bureaucracy was a major hassle throughout the study.

10   Motherhood was not a selection criterion for the jobs! See chapter 6, p. 131.

Chapter 9   'Real' Results

1   Thanks to the Institute of Education Research Fund.

2   This is an important point. In the design of RCTs, results obtained through testing pre-specified hypotheses are more robust than those secured through unplanned posthoc explorations of the data ('data-dredging'). Our fifteen pre-specified hypotheses were that intervention compared with control group families would have been higher mean birthweight, longer gestational age, less preterm delivery, fewer physical health problems in pregnancy, better psychological health in pregnancy, shorter labours, less analgesia, fewer obstetric interventions, less postnatal depression, more confidence as mothers, less neonatal medical care, better postnatal maternal physical health, better postnatal infant health, more satisfaction with medical care, and happier mother–baby relationships.

3   Discussion during a monthly meeting of the research team.

4   These observations derive from the birth of my second child at home in 1968.

5   A proxy for it could be obtained by using birthweight data from the Hospital Inpatient Enquiry (a 10 per cent sample of all hospitalization episodes).

6   Communicated by letter to the author.

Chapter 10   Women at Risk

1   The default assumption is that participating in social research is harmless (whereas taking part in medical research may not be). Textbooks of research methods give insufficient attention to this important question.

2   As well as discussing their experiences of hospital and GP care during the home interviews, many women wrote accounts of these when they filled in their postnatal questionnaires. Some of the questions were open-ended, and we invited the women to write as much as they wanted. Some questionnaires were returned with extra pages stapled on, or with accompanying letters, or simply with amplifications of various answers inscribed on the backs of the questionnaire pages.

3   'Working class' is here defined by housing tenure: it refers to women living in rented accommodation.

4   The 'obstetric technology score' is a measure of the number and extent of the medical interventions received at birth. For a detailed description, see Oakley and Rajan (1990).

5   A malformation in which the womb is divided into two (technically, 'bicornuate uterus').

6   As all the postnatal questionnaires were sent from, and returned directly to, the London research office, it is unlikely that the women filled in the questionnaires thinking that their answers would be read by the midwives whose role they were being asked to evaluate.

Chapter 11   The Poverty of Research

1   This application was preceded by a good deal of discussion about the ethics of asking a funder supported by tobacco revenue for research money. It was pointed out that any government funding can be classified in the same way.
2   Analysis of the data in terms of these subgroups was planned before the study began.
3   This is a procedure which involves putting a temporary stitch in the neck of the womb to provide a mechanical obstruction to preterm delivery.
4   Association of Department of Health and Department of Social Security funded Researchers, London.
5   Susie had been told by a doctor at the hospital antenatal clinic that she wasn't putting on enough weight.
6   Except in their private practices, which is significant.
7   Much of the opposition has centred on the issue of partial or misleading information.
8   This is an ideal-type concept; see Alderson (1990) for a discussion.

Chapter 12   Models of Knowing and Understanding

1   Deborah Hickey, working on the ESRC-funded stage of the research now in progress.
2   This is one derivation. The *OED* also gives a derivation from the Latin *res*, 'thing'.
3   An argument for the importance of quantitative experimental work in this context was put in relation to women's health in chapter 11.
4   Awareness of the political and ethical aspects of the research process leads to *greater*, not *less*, rigour in the doing of research (including, particularly, experimental research), because of the reflexivity that is focused on every stage in the research process.

References

Adams, S. O., Barr, G. D., and Huenemann, R. L. (1978) Effects of nutritional supplementation in pregnancy I: Outcome of pregnancy. *Journal of the American Dietary Association*, 72: 144–7.

Ader, A., Kreutner, A., and Jacobs, H. L. (1963) Social environment, emotionality and alloxan diabetes in the rat. *Psychosomatic Medicine*, 25: 60–8.

Adler, H. M., and Hammett, B. O. (1973) The doctor–patient relationship revisited: an analysis of the placebo effect. *Annals of Internal Medicine*, 78: 595–8.

Advisory Board for the Research Councils (1989) *Contract Researchers – the Human Resource*. ABRC Science Policy Studies no. 3. Brighton, Institute of Manpower Studies.

Alberman, E. (1984) Low birthweight. In M. Bracken (ed.), *Perinatal Epidemiology*, New York, Oxford University Press.

Alberoni, F. (1983) *Falling in Love*. New York, Random House.

Alderson, P. (1990) *Choosing for Children: parents' consent to surgery*. Oxford, Oxford University Press.

Alexander, S., and Keirse, M. J. N. C. (1989) Formal risk scoring during pregnancy. In Chalmers et al. (1989a).

Allan, G. (1979) *A Sociology of Friendship and Kinship*. London, Allen & Unwin.

Allan, G. (1989) *Friendship: developing a sociological perspective*. Hemel Hempstead, Harvester Press.

Anderson, A., and Turnbull, A. (1982) Effect of oestrogens, progestogens and betamimetics in pregnancy. In M. Enkin and I. Chalmers (eds), *Effectiveness and Satisfaction in Antenatal Care*, London, Spastics International Medical Publications.

Antilla, S., and Isokoski, M. (1985) Unexpected control-group behaviour in an intervention study (letter). *Lancet*, 5 January: 43.

Armstrong, D. (1983) *Political Anatomy of the Body*. Cambridge, Cambridge University Press.

Arney, W. R. (1982) *Power and the Profession of Obstetrics*. Chicago, Chicago University Press.

Association of University Teachers (1989) *The Case for Increased Investment in our Universities*. London, AUT.

Badura, B. (1985) Social support as a factor in heart disease. Unpublished background paper for the Health Promotion programme of the WHO Regional Office for Europe.

Bakketeig, L. S., Hoffman, H. J., and Harley, E. E. (1979) The tendency to repeat gestational age and birth weight in successive births. *American Journal of Obstetrics and Gynecology*, 135 (8): 1086–103.

Bakketeig, L. S., and Magnus, P. (1990) Small-for-gestational-age (SGA) definitions and associated risks. Unpublished paper presented at State-of-the-Art Conference on the Scientific Basis of Antenatal Care Routines, Gimo, Sweden, 21–23 May.

Banta, D. (1984) Health education by professionals during pregnancy. Unpublished paper presented at Interregional Conference on Appropriate Technology for Prenatal Care, Washington, DC.

Barker, D. J. P., Osmond, C., Golding, J., Kuh, D., and Wadsworth, M. E. J. (1989) Growth in utero, blood pressure in childhood and adult life, and mortality from cardiovascular disease. *British Medical Journal*, 298: 564–7.

Barrera, M. (1981) Social support in the adjustment of pregnant adolescents: assessment issues. In Gottlieb (1981a).

Bauman, K. E., Bryan, E. S., Dent, C. W., and Joch, G. G. (1983) The influence of observing carbon monoxide level of cigarette smoking by public prenatal patients. *American Journal of Public Health*, 73 (9): 1089–91.

Bauman, Z. (1978) *Hermeneutics and Social Science*. London, Hutchinson.

Beecher, H. K. (1955) The powerful placebo. *Journal of the American Medical Association*, 24 December 1602–6.

Beels, C. C. (1981) Social support and schizophrenia. *Schizophrenia Bulletin*, 7: 58–72.

Belenky, M. B., Clinchy, B. M., Goldberger, N. R., and Tarule, J. M. (1986) *Women's Ways of Knowing*. New York, Basic Books.

Bell, C. (1984) The SSRC: restructured and defended. In Bell and Roberts (1984).

Bell, C., and Encel, S. (eds.) (1978) *Inside the Whale*. Sydney, Pergamon.

Bell, C., and Roberts, H. (eds) (1984) *Social Researching: politics, problems, practice*. London, Routledge & Kegan Paul.

Bell, R. (1981) *Worlds of Friendship*. Beverly Hills, Cal., Sage Publications.

Bendelow, G. (1992) Gender differences in perceptions of pain: towards a phenomenological approach. Unpublished PhD thesis, University of London.

Benson, P. R. (1989) The social control of human biomedical research: an overview and review of the literature. *Social Science and Medicine*, 29 (1): 1–12.

Berger, P. L., and Luckman, T. (1971) *The Social Construction of Reality*. Harmondsworth, Penguin.

Berkman, L. F. (1984) Assessing the physical health effects of social networks and social support. *American Review of Public Health*, 5: 413–32.

Berkman, L. F., and Breslow, L. (1983) *Health and Ways of Living: the Alameda County Study*. New York and Oxford, Oxford University Press.

Berkman, L. F., and Syme, S. L. (1979) Social networks, host resistance and mortality: a nine year follow-up study of Alameda County residents. *American Journal of Epidemiology*, 109: 186–204.

Berkowitz, G. D., and Kasl, S. V. (1983) The role of psychosocial factors in spontaneous preterm delivery. *Journal of Psychosomatic Research*, 27 (4): 283–90.

Bernard, J. (1973) *The Future of Marriage*. New York, Souvenir Press.

Bernstein, B. (1984) A note on the position of funded research staff. Unpublished paper, London, Institute of Education.

Berrueta-Clement, J. R., Schweinhart, L. J., Barnett, W. S., Epstein, A. S., and Weikart, D. P. (1984) *Changed Lives: the effects of the Perry Preschool Program on youths through age 19*. Ypsilanti, MI, High/Scope.

Berry, K., and Wiehl, D. G. (1952) An experiment in education during pregnancy. *Milbank Memorial Fund Quarterly*, 39: 119–51.

Bibby, J., Boyd, N., Redman, C. W. E., and Luesley, D. M. (1988) Consent for vaginal examination by students on anaesthetised patients. *Lancet*, 12 November (letter): 1150.

Birke, L. (1986) *Women, Feminism and Biology*. Brighton, Wheatsheaf Books.

Blank, G., McCartney, J. L., and Brent, E. (eds) (1989) *New Technology in Sociology: practical applications in research and work*. London, Transaction Publishers.

Blaxter, M. (1985) Self definitions of health status and consulting rates in primary care. *Quarterly Journal of Social Affairs*, 1: 131–71.

Blaxter, M., and Paterson, E. (1982) *Mothers and Daughters: a three generational study of health attitudes and behaviour*. London, Heinemann.

Blazer, D. (1982) Social support and mortality in an elderly community population. *American Journal of Epidemiology*, 115: 684–94.

Blenker, M., Bloom, M., and Nielsen, M. (1971) A research and demonstration project of protective services. *Social Casework*, 52: 483–99.

Blondel, B., Bréart, G., and Llado, J., (n.d.) Prevention of preterm deliveries by home visiting midwives: results of a French randomized controlled trial (unpublished).

Bloom, J. R. (1990) The relationship of social support to health. *Social Science and Medicine*, 30 (5): 635–7.

Bloom, J. R., and Spiegel, D. (1984) The effect of two dimensions of social support on the psychological wellbeing and social functioning of women with advanced breast cancer. *Social Science and Medicine*, 19: 888–91.

Bok, S. (1980) *Lying: moral choice in public and private life*. London, Quartet Books.

Bott, E. (1971) *Family and Social Network*. Rev. edn, London, Tavistock.

Bourne, H. R. (1971) The placebo – a poorly understood and neglected therapeutic agent. *Rational Drug Therapy*, 5 (11): 1–6.

Boyle, M. H., Torrance, G. W., Sinclair, J. C., and Horwood, S. P. (1983) Economic evaluation of neonatal intensive care of very-low-birth-weight infants. *New England Journal of Medicine*, 308 (22): 1330–7.

Bracken, M. (1987) Clinical trials and the acceptance of uncertainty. *British Medical Journal*, 294: 1111–12.

Bradshaw, J. (1990) *Child Poverty and Deprivation in the UK*. London, National Children's Bureau.

Brahams, D. (1983) Informed consent does not demand full disclosure of risks. *Lancet*, 2 July: 58.

Brannen, J. (1989) Combining qualitative and quantitative approaches. Training seminar sponsored by the Department of Health. London, Thomas Coram Research Unit.

Brannen, J., Dodd, K., and Oakley, A. (1991) Getting involved: the effects of research on participants. Unpublished paper, British Sociological Association Conference, Health and Society.

Brannen, J., and Wilson, G. (eds) (1987) *Give and Take in Families: studies in resource distribution*. London, Unwin Hyman.

Brill, N. Q., Koegler, R. R., Epstein, L. J., and Forgy, E. W. (1964) Controlled study of psychiatric outpatient treatment. *Archives of General Psychiatry*, 10: 581–95.

British Medical Association (1981) Local ethical committees. *British Medical Journal*, 282: 1010.

Brody, H. (1977) *Placebos and the Philosophy of Medicine*. Chicago, University of Chicago Press.

Brown, G. W., and Harris, T. (1978) *Social Origins of Depression*. London, Tavistock.

Brown, M. A. (1986) Social support during pregnancy: a unidimensional or multidimensional construct? *Nursing Research*, 35 (1): 4–9.

Bruce Murray, M. (1924) *The Effect of Maternal Social Conditions and Nutrition upon Birthweight and Birth Length*. Medical Research Council Report, no. 81. London, HMSO.

Bryce, R. L., Stanley, F. J., and Garner, J. B. (1991) Randomized controlled trial of antenatal social support to prevent preterm birth. *British Journal of Obstetrics and Gynaecology*, 98: 1001–8.

Bryman, A. (1988) *Quantity and Quality in Social Research*. London, Unwin Hyman.

Bulpitt, C. J. (1987) Confidence intervals. *Lancet*, 28 February: 491–7.

Butler, N. R., and Bonham, D. (1963) *Perinatal Mortality*. Edinburgh, E. and S. Livingstone.

Butler, N. R., and Goldstein, H. (1973) Smoking in pregnancy and subsequent child development. *British Medical Journal*, 4: 573–5.

Calhoun, J. B. (1962) Population density and social pathology. *Scientific American*, 206 (2): 139–48.

Cameron, C. S., and Graham, S. (1944) Antenatal diet and its influences on still births and prematurity. *Glasgow Medical Journal*, 1420: 1–7.

Capra, F. (1983) *The Turning Point*. New York, Bantam Books.

Carpenter, J., Aldrich, K., and Boverman, H. (1968) The effectiveness of patient interviews. A controlled study of emotional support during pregnancy. *Archives of General Psychiatry*, 19: 110–12.

Cartwright, A., and Anderson, R. (1981) *General Practice Revisited*. London, Tavistock.

Cassel, J. (1976) The contribution of the social environment to host resistance. *American Journal of Epidemiology*, 104 (2): 107–23.

Ceci, S. J., Peters, D., and Plotkin, J. (1985) Human subjects: review, personal values, and the regulation of social science research. *American Psychologist*, 40: 994.

Chalmers, I. (1979) Perinatal health: the search for indices. *Lancet*, 2: 1063–5.

Chalmers, I. (1981) Evaluation of perinatal practice: the limitations of audit by death. In R. Chester, P. Diggory, and M. B. Sutherland (eds), *Changing Patterns of Childbearing and Childrearing*. London, Academic Press.

Chalmers, I. (1983) Scientific inquiry and authoritarianism in perinatal care and education. *Birth*, 10 (3): 151–64.

Chalmers, I. (1989) Evaluating the effects of care during pregnancy and childbirth. In Chalmers et al. (1989a).

Chalmers, I., Enkin, M., and Keirse, M. J. N. C. (eds) (1989a) *Effective Care in Pregnancy and Childbirth*. Oxford, Oxford University Press.

Chalmers, I., Enkin, M., and Keirse, M. J. N. C. (1989b) Effective care in pregnancy and childbirth: a synopsis for guiding practice and research. In Chalmers et al. (1989a).

Chalmers, I., Oakley, A., and Macfarlane, J. A. (1980) Perinatal health services: an immodest proposal. *British Medical Journal*, 1: 842–5.

Chalmers, T. C. (1983) The control of bias in clinical trials. In S. H. Shapiro and T. A. Louis (eds), *Clinical Trials: issues and approaches*, New York, Marcel Dekker.

Chalmers, T. C., Celano, P., Sacks, H. S., and Smith, H. (1983) Bias in treatment assignment in controlled clinical trials. *New England Journal of Medicine*, 1 December: 1358–61.

Chamberlain, G., Howlett, B., Philipp, E., and Masters, K. (1978) *British Births 1970*. London, Heinemann.

Chard, T., and Richards, M. (eds) (1982) *Benefits and Hazards of the New Obstetrics*. London, Spastics International Medical Publications.

Chng, P., Hall, M., and MacGillivray, I. (1980) An audit of antenatal care: the value of the first antenatal visit. *British Medical Journal*, 281: 1184–6.

Chodorow, N. (1978) *The Reproduction of Mothering*. Berkeley, University of California Press.

Clarke, J. (1786) Observations on some causes of the excess of the mortality of males above that of females. *Philosophical Transactions of the Royal Society of London*, 76: 349–64.

Cnattingius, S., Haglund, B., and Merik, O. (1988) Cigarette smoking as risk factor for late fetal and early neonatal death. *British Medical Journal*, 297: 258–61.

Cobb, S. (1976) Social support as a moderator of life stress. *Psychosomatic Medicine*, 38 (5): 300–14.

Cochrane, A. L. (1972) *Effectiveness and Efficiency*. London, Nuffield Provincial Hospitals Trust.

Cochrane, A. L. (1979) 1931–1971: A critical review with particular reference to the medical profession. In G. Teeling-Smith and N. E. J. Wells (eds), *Medicines for the Year 2000*, New York, Basic Books.

Cochrane, A. L. (1984) Sickness in Salonica: my first, worst, and most successful clinical trial. *British Medical Journal*, 289: 1726–7.

Cochrane, R., and Robertson, A. (1973) The life events inventory: a measure of the relative severity of psychosocial stressors. *Journal of Psychosomatic Research*, 17: 135–40.

Cogan, R., and Winer, J. L. (1982) Effect of childbirth educator communication skills training on postpartum reports of parents. *Birth*, 9: 241–4.

Cohen, S., and Syme, L. (eds) (1985) *Social Support and Health*. New York, Academic Press.

Cohen, S., and Wills, T. A. (1985) Stress, social support and the buffering hypothesis. *Psychological Bulletin*, 98 (2): 310–57.

Colebrook, L., and Kenny, M. (1936) Treatment with prontosil of puerperal infections. *Lancet*, 5 December: 1319–26.

Cone, T. (1961) The history of weighing the newborn infant. *Pediatrics*, September: 490–8.

Consensus Development Conference (1986) Treatment of primary breast cancer. *British Medical Journal*, 293: 946–7.

Corea, G. (1985) *The Mother Machine*. New York, Harper & Row.

Cornwell, J. (1984) *Hard-Earned Lives*. London, Tavistock.

Coronary Drug Project Research Group (1980) Influence of adherence to treatment and response of cholesterol on mortality in the coronary drug project. *New England Journal of Medicine*, 303: 1038–41.

Court Report (1976) *Fit for the Future: the Report of the Committee on Child Health Services*. London, HMSO.

Cousins, N. (1989) *Head First: the biology of hope*. New York, E. P. Dutton.

Creasy, R. K., Gummer, B. A., and Liggins, G. C. (1980) System for predicting spontaneous preterm birth. *Obstetrics and Gynecology*, 55: 692–5.

Crompton, R., and Mann, M. (1986) *Gender and Stratification*. Cambridge, Polity Press.

Dance, J. (1987) A social intervention by linkworkers to Pakistani women and pregnancy outcome (unpublished).

Danziger, J. N. (1989) *Waiting for the Revolution: the use of microcomputers by social scientists*. In Blank et al. (1989).

D'Arcy Hart, P. (1991) Randomized controlled clinical trials (letter). *British Medical Journal*, 302: (25 May) 1271–2.

Davidson, S. (1979) Massive psychic traumatization and social support. *Journal of Psychosomatic Research*, 23: 395–402.

Davie, R., Butler, H. R., and Goldstein, H. (1972) *From Birth to Seven*. London, Longman.

Davies, J. M., and Rose, M. (1977) Intramuscular diazepam in labour. *British Journal of Anaesthesia*, 49: 601–4.

Davin, A. (1978) Imperialism and motherhood. *History Workshop*, 5: 9–65.

Dawson, J. (1986) Randomized trials and informed consent in neonatal medicine. *British Medical Journal*, 292: 1373–4.

Day, S. (1982) Is obstetric technology depressing? *Radical Science Journal*, 12: 17–45.

Dean, K. (1986) Social support and health: pathways of influence. *Health Promotion*, 1 (2): 133–50.

Delphy, C. (1980) A materialist feminism is possible. *Feminist Review*, 4: 79–105.

Denzin, N. (1970) *Sociological Methods: a sourcebook*. London, Butterworths.

Department of Health (1989) *Perinatal, Neonatal and Infant Mortality: Government reply to the first report from the Social Services Committee, session 1988–1989*. London, HMSO.

Department of Health (1991) *Local Research Ethics Committees*. London, Department of Health.

Department of Health and Social Security (1977) *Reducing the Risk; safer pregnancy and childbirth*. London, HMSO.

DiMatteo, M. R., and Hays, R. (1981) Social support and serious illness. In Gottlieb (1981a).

Dingwall, R., Eekelaar, R. J. and Murray, T. (1983) *The Protection of Children*. Oxford, Basil Blackwell.

Ditton, J., and Williams, R. (1981) The fundable versus the doable. Unpublished paper, Department of Sociology, University of Glasgow.

Donovan, J. W. (1977) Randomized controlled trial of anti-smoking advice in pregnancy. *British Journal of Preventive and Social Medicine*, 31: 6–12.

Doucet, H., Baumgarten, M., and Infante-Rivard, C. (1989) Low birth weight and household structure. *Developmental and Behavioral Pediatrics*, 10 (5): 249–52.

Doyal, L. (1979) *The Political Economy of Health*. London, Pluto Press.

Dudley, H. A. F. (1983) The controlled clinical trial and the advance of reliable knowledge: an outsider looks in. *British Medical Journal*, 287: 957–60.

Dunst, C. J., and Rheingrover, R. (1981) An analysis of the efficacy of infant intervention programs with organically handicapped children. *Evaluation and Program Planning*, 4: 287–323.

Durkheim, E. (1952) *Suicide: a study in sociology*. London, Routledge & Kegan Paul.

Early Breast Cancer Triallists' Group (1992) Systemic treatment of early breast cancer by hormonal, cytotoxic or immune therapy. *Lancet* 339: 1–15.

Economic and Social Research Council (1984) *Newsletter*, 51 (March).

Editorial (1982) Sir Keith and the SSRC. *Times Higher Education Supplement*, 15 January.

Editorial (1984) A fair trial? *British Medical Journal*, 289: 336–7.

Ehrenreich, B., and English, D. (1979) *For Her Own Good: 150 years of the experts' advice to women*. London, Pluto Press.

Elbourne, D. (1987) Subjects' views about participation in a randomized controlled trial. *Journal of Reproductive and Infant Psychology*, 5: 3–8.

Elbourne, D., and Oakley, A. (1991) An overview of trials of social support during pregnancy. In H. Berendes, S. Kessel and S. Yaffe (eds), *Advances in the Prevention of Low Birthweight: an international symposium*, Washington, DC, National Center for Education in Maternal and Child Health.

Elbourne, D., Oakley, A., and Chalmers, I. (1989) Social and psychological support during pregnancy. In Chalmers et al. (1989a).

Elbourne, D., Richardson, M., Chalmers, I., Waterhouse, I., and Holt, E. (1987) The Newbury Maternity Care Study: a randomized controlled trial to assess a policy of women holding their own obstetric records. *British Journal of Obstetrics and Gynaecology*, 94: 612–19.

Elliott, A. A., Anderson, M., Brough, D. I., Watson, J. P., and Rugg, A. J. (1984) Relationship between obstetric outcome and psychological measures in pregnancy and the postnatal year. *Journal of Reproductive and Infant Psychology*, 2 (1): 18–32.

Epstein, C. (1985) The politics of stress: public visions, private realities. *The American Journal of Psychoanalysis*, 45 (3): 282–90.

Etzioni, A. (ed.) (1969) *The Semi-Professions and Their Organization*. New York, Free Press.

Evans, F. J. (1974) The power of a sugar pill. *Psychology Today*, April: 55–61.

Everson, R. (1980) Individuals transplacentally exposed to maternal smoking may be at increased cancer risk in adult life. *Lancet*, 19 July: 123–7.

Fader, R., and Beauchamp, T. L. (1986) *A History and Theory of Informed Consent*. New York, Oxford University Press.

Faderman, L. (1981) *Surpassing the Love of Men: romantic friendship and love between women from the Renaissance to the present*. London, Junction Books.

Faris, R., and Dunham, H. (1939) *Mental Disorders in Urban Areas*. Chicago, University of Chicago Press.

Farr, W. (1885) *Vital Statistics*. London, Edward Stanford.

Farran, D. C. (1990) Effects of intervention with disadvantaged and disabled children: a decade review. In Meisels and Shonkoff (1990).

Farrant, W. (1980) Stress after amniocentesis for high serum alphafetoprotein concentrations. *British Medical Journal*, 1: 452.

Faulder, C. (1985) *Whose Body Is It? The troubling issue of informed consent*. London, Virago.

Ferguson, J. H. (1953) Effect of stilboestrol on pregnancy compared to the effect of a placebo. *American Journal of Obstetrics and Gynecology*, 65: 592–601.

Field, T., Sandberg, D., Quetel, T. A., Garcia, R., and Rosario, M. (1985) Effects of ultrasound feedback on pregnancy anxiety, fetal activity and neonatal outcome. *Obstetrics and Gynecology*, 66: 525–8.

Finch, J. (1984) 'It's great to have someone to talk to': the ethics and politics of interviewing women. In Bell and Roberts (1984).

Fischer, J. (1973) Is casework effective? A review. *Social Work*, January: 5–20.

Fitzgerald, J. P. B. (1955) The effect of promethazine in nausea and vomiting of pregnancy. *New Zealand Medical Journal*, 54: 215–18.

Flint, C., and Poulengeris, P. (n.d.) *The Know Your Midwife Scheme*. Unpublished report, London.

Flint, C., and Poulengeris, P. (1987) *Know Your Midwife*. London, Heinemann.

Floud, R., Wachter, K., and Gregory, A. (1990) *Height, Health and History*. Cambridge, Cambridge University Press.

Fogelman, K. R., and Manor, O. (1988) Smoking in pregnancy and development into early adulthood. *British Medical Journal*, 297: 1233–6.

Forrest, G. C., Standish, E., and Baum, J. D. (1982) Support after perinatal death; a study of support and counselling after perinatal bereavement. *British Medical Journal*, 285: 1475–9.

Fox, J. (1988) Social network interaction: new jargon in health inequalities. *British Medical Journal*, 297: 373–4.

Frank, J. D. (1983) The placebo is psychotherapy. *The Behavioral and Brain Sciences*, 6: 291–2.

Frye, M. (1989) To see and be seen: the politics of reality. In Garry and Pearsall (1989).

Gabbe, S. (1984) Reproductive hazards of the American life style. In G. Chamberlain (ed.), *Pregnant Women at Work*, London, Macmillan.

Gaddum, J. H. (1954) Walter Earnest Dixon Memorial Lecture. *Clinical Pharmacology: proceedings of the Royal Society of Medicine*, 47: 195–204.

Garcia, J., Kilpatrick, R., and Richards, M. (eds) (1988) *The Politics of Maternity Care*. Oxford, Oxford University Press.

Garry, A., and Pearsall, M. (eds) (1989) *Women, Knowledge and Reality*. Boston, Unwin Hyman.

Gelis, J. (1991) *History of Childbirth*. Cambridge, Polity Press.

Gennser, G., Rymark, P., and Isberg, P. E. (1988) Low birth weight and risk of high blood pressure in adulthood. *British Medical Journal*, 296: 1498–1500.

Gevirtz, C. M., and Marx, G. F. (1991) Continuous emotional support during labor (letter). *Journal of the American Medical Association*, 266 (11): 1509.

Gilligan, M. (1980) Perinatal mortality enquiries at district level. In I. Chalmers, and G. McIlwaine (eds), *Perinatal Audit and Surveillance*, Proceedings of the Eighth Study Group of the Royal College of Obstetricians and Gynaecologists, London, RCOG.

Ginzler, M., Davies, J., McPherson, K., and Black, N. (1990) Ethics committees and health services research *Journal of Public Health Medicine*, 12: 190–6.

Goffman, E. (1968) *Asylum: essays on the social situation of mental patients and other inmates*. New York, Anchor Books.

Goldblatt, P. (1989) Mortality by social class 1971–85. *Population Trends*, 56: 6–15.

Goldstein, P. A., Sacks, H. S., and Chalmers, T. C. (1989) Hormone administration for the maintenance of pregnancy. In Chalmers et al. (1989a).

Goody, J. (1977) *The Domestication of the Savage Mind*. Cambridge, Cambridge University Press.

Gordon, R. E., and Gordon, K. K. (1960) Social factors in the prevention of postpartum emotional problems. *Obstetrics and Gynecology*, 15: 433–8.

Gore, S. (1978) The effect of social support in moderating the health consequences of unemployment. *Journal of Health and Social Behaviour*, 19: 155–65.

Gottlieb, B. H. (1978) Development and application of a classification scheme of informal helping behaviour. *Canadian Journal of Behavioral Science*, 10: 105–15.

Gottlieb, B. H. (ed.) (1981a) *Social Networks and Social Support*, Beverly Hills, Cal., Sage Publications.

Gottlieb, B. H. (1981b) Preventive interventions involving social networks and social support. In Gottlieb (1981a).

Gottlieb, B. H. (1981c) Social networks and social support in community mental health. In Gottlieb (1981a).

Grad, B. (1963) A telekinetic effect on plant growth. *International Journal of Parapsychology*, 5: 117–33.

Graham, H. (1976) Smoking in pregnancy: the attitudes of expectant mothers. *Social Science and Medicine*, 10: 399–405.

Graham, H. (1982) Coping: or how mothers are seen and not heard. In S. Friedmann and E. Sarah (eds), *On the Problem of Men*, London, The Women's Press.

Graham, H. (1983) Do his answers fit her questions? In E. Garminikow, D. Morgan, J. Purvis, D. Taylorson (eds), *The Public and the Private*, London, Heinemann.

Graham, H. (1986) *Caring for the Family*. London, Health Education Council.

Graham, H. (1986) *Women, Health and the Family*. Brighton, Harvester Press.

Graham, H. (1987) Women's smoking and family health. *Social Science and Medicine*, 25; 47–56.

Graham, H., and Oakley, A. (1981) Competing ideologies of reproduction: medical and maternal perspectives on pregnancy and birth. In H. Roberts (ed.), *Women, Health and Reproduction*, London, Routledge & Kegan Paul.

Grant, A. (1989) Monitoring the fetus during labour. In Chalmers et al. (1989a).

Green, J. M. (1989) Who is unhappy after childbirth? Results of a prospective study. Unpublished paper presented to the Ninth International Psychosomatic Obstetrics and Gynaecology Conference, Amsterdam.

Gross, W. B. (1972) Effect of social stress on occurrence of Marek's disease in chickens. *American Journal of Veterinary Research*, 33 (11): 2275–9.

Guillemin, J. H., and Holmstrom, L. L. (1986) *Mixed Blessings: intensive care for newborns*. New York, Oxford University Press.

Guillot, N. (1852) Klinische bemerkungen über Ammen und Säuglinge. *J. Kinderkr.* 19: 113–25.

Gutelius, M. F., Kirsch, A. D., MacDonald, S., Brooks, M. R., and McErlean, T. (1977) Controlled study of child health supervision: behavioural results. *Pediatrics*, 60 (3): 294–304.

Hack, M. H. and Fanaroff, A. A. (1986) Changes in the delivery room care of the extremely small infant: effects on morbidity and outcome. *The New England Journal of Medicine*, 314: 660–4.

Hagberg, B., Hagberg, G., and Olow, I. (1984) The changing panorama of cerebral palsy in Sweden. *Acta Paediatrica Scandinavica*, 73: 433–40.

Haggerty, R. J. (1980) Life stress, illness and social support. *Developmental Medicine and Child Neurology*, 22: 391–400.

Hall, M., Macintyre, S., and Porter, M. (1985) *Antenatal Care Assessed*. Aberdeen, Aberdeen University Press.

Hammersley, M. (1989) *The Dilemma of Qualitative Methods: Herbert Blumer and the Chicago tradition*. London, Routledge & Kegan Paul.

Harding, S. (1986) *The Science Question in Feminism*. Milton Keynes, Open University Press.

Hart, N. (1986) Inequalities in health: the individual versus the environment. *Journal of the Royal Statistical Society*, 3: 228–46.

Hartsock, N. (1984) *Money, Sex and Power*. Boston, Mass., Northeastern University Press.

Hauser-Cram, P. (1990) Designing meaningful evaluations of early intervention studies. In Meisels and Shonkoff (1990).

Heinonen, K., Hakulinen, A., and Jokela, V. (1988) Survival of the smallest: time trends and determinants of mortality in a very preterm population during the 1980s. *Lancet*, 23 July: 204–7.

Heins, H. C., Nance, N. W., and Ferguson, J. E. (1987) Social support in improving perinatal outcome: the Resource Mothers Program. *Obstetrics and Gynecology*, 69 (10): 1–4.

Heins, H. C., Nance, N. W., McCarthy, B. J., and Efird, C. M. (1990) A randomized trial of nurse-midwifery prenatal care to reduce low birthweight. *Obstetrics and Gynecology*, 75 (3): 341–5.

Helsing, K., Szklo, M., and Comstock, G. (1981) Factors associated with mortality after widowhood. *American Journal of Public Health*, 71: 8029.

Hemminki, E., and Kojo-Austin, H. (1989) Problems of multidisciplinary research in health care – the case of birth services. *Acta Sociologica*, 32 (3): 253–60.

Hemminki, E., and Starfield, B. (1978) Prevention and treatment of premature labour by drugs: review of controlled clinical trials. *British Journal of Obstetrics and Gynaecology*, 85: 411–17.

Henderson, S., Byrne, D. G., and Duncan-Jones, P. (1981) *Neurosis and the Social Environment*. Sydney, Academic Press.

Hendriksen, C., Lund, E., and Stromgard, E. (1984) Consequences of assessment and intervention among elderly people; a three year randomized controlled trial. *British Medical Journal*, 289: 1522–4.

Henry, J. P. (1986) Mechanisms by which stress can lead to coronary heart disease. *Postgraduate Medical Journal*, 62: 687–93.

Henry, J., Meehan, J., and Stephens, P. (1967) The use of psychosocial stimuli to induce prolonged hypertension in mice. *Psychosomatic Medicine*, 29: 408.

Herron, M. A., Katz, M., and Creasy, R. K. (1982) Evaluation of a preterm birth prevention program. *Obstetrics and Gynecology*, 59: 52.

Herxheimer, A. (1988) The rights of the patient in clinical research. *Lancet*, 12 November: 1128–30.

Hinkle, L. E. (1980) The effect of exposure to culture change, social change, and changes in interpersonal relationships on health. In D. Mechanic (ed.), *Readings in Medical Sociology*, New York, Free Press.

Hirsch, B. J. (1980) Natural support systems and coping with major life change. *American Journal of Community Psychology*, 8: 159–72.

Hochschild, A. R. (1975) The sociology of feeling and emotion: selected possibilities. In M. Millman, and R. M. Kanter (eds), *Another Voice: feminist perspectives on social life and social science*, New York, Anchor Books.

Hogben, L. (1970) The contemporary crisis or the uncertainties of uncertain inference. In Morrison and Henkel (1970).

Holahan, C. J., and Moos, R. (1981) Social support and psychological distress: a longitudinal analysis. *Journal of Abnormal Psychology*, 90: 365–70.

Holland, E. (1922) *Report on the Causation of Foetal Death*. Reports on Public Health and Medical Subjects, no. 7. London, HMSO.

Holmes, T. H., and Rahe, R. H. (1967) The social readjustment rating scale. *Journal of Psychosomatic Research*, 11: 213–18.

Home, E. (1794) *A Short Account of the Author's Life by his Brother-in-law Everard Home*. Reproduced F. A. Willius and T. E. Keys, *Cardiac Classics*, St Louis, C. V. Mosby, 1941.

Honzak, R., Horackova, E., and Culik, A. (1972) Our experience with the effect of placebo in some functional and psychosomatic disorders. *Activitas Nervosa Superior (Prague)*, 14: 184–5.

Horrobin, D. (1978) *Medical Hubris*. Edinburgh, Churchill Livingstone.

House, J. S., and Kahn, R. L. (1985) Measures (and concepts) of social support. In Cohen and Syme (1985).

House, J. S., Robbins, C., and Melzner, H. L. (1982) The association of social relationships and activities with mortality: prospective evidence from the Tecumseh Community Health Study. *American Journal of Epidemiology*, 116 (1): 123–40.

Ierodiaconou, E. (1980) Perinatal practices in the European region: report of the perinatal study group. Unpublished report, World Health Organization, Regional Office for Europe, Copenhagen.

Illich, I. (1975) *Medical Nemesis*. London, Calder & Boyars.

Illsley, R. (1967) The sociological study of reproduction and its outcome. In Richardson and Guttmacher (1967).

Illsley, R., and Mitchell, R. G. (eds.) (1984) *Low Birth Weight: a medical, psychological and social study*. Chichester, John Wiley.

Ince, M. (1986) Science for all. *New Society*, 27 June.

Infante-Rivard, C., Filion, G., Baumgarten, M., Bourassa, M., Labelle, J., and Messier, M. (1989) A public health home intervention among families of low socioeconomic status. *Children's Health Care*, 18 (2): 102–7.

Institute of Medicine (1985) *Preventing Low Birthweight*. Washington, National Academy Press.

Joint Committee of the Royal College of Obstetricians and Gynaecologists and the Population Investigation Committee (1948) *Maternity in Great Britain*. Oxford, Oxford University Press.

Kahn, R., Antonucci, T. (1980) Convoys over the life course: attachment, roles and social support. In P. B. Baltes and O. Brim (eds), *Life-Span Development and Behavior*. Boston, Mass., Lexington Press.

Kaplan, G. A., and Camacho, T. (1983) Perceived health and mortality: a nine year follow up of the human population laboratory cohort. *American Journal of Epidemiology*, 117: 292–304.

Kaplan, G. A., and Kotler, P. L. (1985) Self reports: predictive of mortality. *Journal of Chronic Diseases*, 38 (8): 195–201.

Kehrer, B. H. and Wohin, C. M. (1979) Impact of income maintenance on low birthweight: evidence from the Gary experiment. *Journal of Human Resources*, 14: 434–62.

Keller, E. F. (1983) *A Feeling for the Organism: the life and work of Barbara McClintock*. New York, W. H. Freeman.

Keller, E. F. (1989) Feminism and science. In Garry and Pearsall (1989).

Kennell, J., Klaus, M., McGrath, S., Robertson, S., and Hinkley, C. (1991a) Continuous emotional support during labour in a US hospital: a randomized controlled trial. *Journal of the American Medical Association*, 265 (17): 2197–201.

Kennell, J., Klaus, M., Robertson, S., and Hinkley, C. (1991b) Continuous emotional support during labor (letter). *Journal of the American Medical Association*, 266 (11): 1509–10.

Killien, M. G., and Shy, K. (1989) A randomized trial of electronic fetal monitoring in preterm labor: mothers' views. *Birth*, 16 (1): 7–12.

King, A. G. (1955) The treatment of pregnancy nausea with a pill. *After Office Hours* 332–8.

King, T. (1934) *Mothercraft*. London, Simpkin, Marshall.

Klaus, M. H., Kennell, J. H., Robertson, S. S., and Sosa, R. (1986) Effects of social support during parturition on maternal and infant morbidity. *British Medical Journal*, 6 (September): 585–7.

Klein, V. (1946; repr. 1971) *The Feminine Character: history of an ideology*. London, Routledge & Kegan Paul.

Korenbrot, C. C., Aalto, L. H., and Laros, R. K. (1984) The cost effectiveness of stopping preterm labor with beta-adrenergic treatment. *The New England Journal of Medicine*, 310 (11): 691–6.

Kotelchuck, M., Schwartz, J. B., Anderka, M. T., and Finison, K. S. (1984) WIC participation and pregnancy outcomes: Massachusetts statewide evaluation project. *American Journal of Public Health*, 74 (10): 1086–92.

Lane-Claypon, J. (1920) *The Child Welfare Movement*. London, G. Bell.

Langton Hewer, J. (1932) *Our Baby for Mothers and Nurses*. Bristol, John Wright & Sons.

Laqueur, T. (1990) *Making Sex: body and gender from the Greeks to Freud*. Cambridge, Mass., Harvard University Press.

Larson, C. P. (1980) Efficacy of prenatal and postpartum home visits on child health and development. *Paediatrics*, 66: 191–7.

Leavy, R. L. (1983) Social support and psychological disorder: a review. *Journal of Community Psychology*, 11: 3–21.

Lenrow, P. B. and Burch, R. W. (1981) Mutual aid and professional services: opposing or complementary? In Gottlieb (1981a).

Lepenies, W. (1988) *Between Literature and Science: the rise of sociology*. Cambridge, Cambridge University Press, and Paris, Editions de la maison des Sciences de l'Homme.

Levin, B. W. (1990) International perspectives on treatment choice in neonatal intensive care units. *Social Science and Medicine*, 30 (8): 901–12.

Levine, J. D., Gordon, N. C., and Fields, H. L. (1978) The mechanism of placebo analgesia. *Lancet*, 2: 654–7.

Lewis, C. A. (1960) *The Four Loves*. London, Geoffrey Bles.

Lin, N., Simeone, R. S., Ensel, W. M., and Kuo, W. (1979) Social support, stressful life events and illness: a model and an empirical test. *Journal of Health and Social Behaviour*, 20: 108–19.

Little, B. C., Hayworth, J., Benson, P., Hall, F., Beard, R. W., Dewhurst, J., and Priest, R. (1984) Treatment of hypertension in pregnancy by relaxation and biofeedback. *Lancet*, 21 April: 865–67.

Locker, D., and Dunt, D. (1978) Theoretical and methodological issues in sociological studies of consumer satisfaction with medical care. *Social Science and Medicine*, 12: 283–92.

Loftus, E. F., and Fries, J.F. (1979) Informed consent may be hazardous to health. *Science*, 204: 11.

Local Government Board (1914) *Forty-Third Report of the Local Government Board 1913–14*. Supplement 1913–14. London, HMSO.

Lovell, A., Zander, L. I., James, C. E. J., Foot, S., Swan, A. V., and Reynolds, A. (1986) *St Thomas's Maternity Case-Notes Study: Why Not Give Mothers Their Own Notes?* London, Cicely Northcote Trust.

Lovell, A., Zander, L. I., James, C. E., Foot, S., Swan, A. V., and Reynolds, A. (1987) The St Thomas's Hospital maternity case-notes study: a randomized controlled trial to assess the effects of giving expectant mothers their own maternity case-notes. *Pediatric and Perinatal Epidemiology*, 1: 57–66.

Lowe, M. (1970) Effectiveness of teaching as measured by compliance with medical recommendations. *Nursing Research*, 19 (1): 59–63.

Lumley, J. (1988) The prevention of preterm birth: unresolved problems and work in progress. *Australian Paediatric Journal*, 24: 101–11.

Lumley, J. (1991) Stopping smoking – again. *British Journal of Obstetrics and Gynaecology*, 98: 847–9.

Lumley, J., and Astbury, J. (1989) Advice for pregnancy. In Chalmers et al. (1989a).

Luria, A. R. (1981) *Language and Cognition*, New York, Wiley.

Macarthur, C., Newton, J. K., Knox, E. G. (1987) Effect of anti-smoking health education on infant size at birth: a randomized controlled trial. *British Journal of Obstetrics and Gynaecology*, 94: 295–300.

McAuley, D. M., O'Neill, M. P., Moore, J., and Dundee, J. W. (1982) Lorazepam premedication for labour. *British Journal of Obstetrics and Gynaecology*, 89: 149–54.

McCarthy, B. J. (1984) The use of birthweight in perinatal surveillance and evaluation. Unpublished paper presented at AMRO/EURO interregional conference on Appropriate Technology for Prenatal Care, Washington, DC, 26–30 November.

McCleary, G. F. (1933) *The Early History of the Infant Welfare Movement*. London, H. K. Lewis.

McCord, J. (1981) Consideration of some effects of a counselling programme. In S. E. Martin, L. B. Sechrest and R. Redner (eds), *New Directions in the Rehabilitation of Criminal Offenders*, Washington, DC, National Academy Press.

McCord, J. (1982) The Cambridge–Somerville Youth Study: a sobering lesson on treatment, prevention and evaluation. In A. J. McSweeny, W. J. Freeman and R. Hawkins (eds), *Practical Program Evaluation in Youth*, Springfield, Ill., Charles C. Thomas.

McDonald, C. J., Mazzuca, S. A., and McCabe, G. P. (1983) How much of the placebo 'effect' is really statistical regression? *Statistics in Medicine*, 2: 417–27.

Macfarlane, M., and Mugford, M. (1984) *Birth Counts: statistics of pregnancy and childbirth*. London, HMSO.

McGuire, J. C., and Gottlieb, B. H. (1979) Social support groups among new parents: an experimental study in primary prevention. *Journal of Clinical Child Psychology* (Summer): 111–15.

Macintyre, S. (1976) To have or have not – promotion and prevention in gynaecological work. In M. Stacey (ed.), *The Sociology of the NHS*, Sociological Review Monograph 22, Staffordshire, University of Keele.

Mackenzie, D. (1978) Statistical theory and social interests. *Social Studies of Science*, 8: 35–83.

McKeown, T. (1976) *The Modern Rise of Population*. New York, Academic Press.

McKinlay, J. B. (1981) From 'Promising Report' to 'Standard Procedure': seven stages in the career of a medical innovation. *Millbank Memorial Fund Quarterly*, 59 (3): 374–411.

McLanahan, S. S., Wedemeyer, N. V., Adelberg, T. (1981) Network structure, social support, and psychological wellbeing in the single-parent family. *Journal of Marriage and the Family*, 43: 601–12.

Madge, N., and Marmot, M. G. (1987) Psychosocial factors and health. *The Quarterly Journal of Social Affairs*, 3 (2): 81–134.

Main, D. M., Gabbe, S. G., Richardson, D., and Strong, S. (1985) Can preterm deliveries be prevented? *American Journal of Obstetrics and Gynecology*, 151 (7): 892–8.

Malseed, J. (1987) Research note: straw men: a note on Ann Oakley's treatment of textbook prescriptions for interviewing. *Sociology*, 21 (4): 629–31.

Marmot, M. G., and McDowall, M. E. (1986) Mortality decline and widening social inequalities. *Lancet*, 2 August; 274–6.

Marmot, M. G., Shipley, M. J., and Rose, A. G. (1984) Inequalities in death: specific explanations of a general pattern. *Lancet*, ii: 1003–6.

Martin, E. 1987. *The Woman in the Body*. Boston, Beacon Press.

Maughan, B., and Rutter, M. (1985) Education: improving practice through increasing understanding. In Rapoport (1985).

Mayall, B. (1986) *Keeping Children Healthy*. London, Unwin Hyman.

Mayall, B., and Foster, M.-C. (1989) *Child Health Care*. London, Heinemann.

Medawar, P. (1982) *Pluto's Republic*. Oxford, Oxford University Press.

Medical Research Council (1926) *Child Life Investigations: a clinical and pathological study of 1673 cases of dead-births and neo-natal deaths* (by E. Holland and J. Lane-Claypon). London, HMSO.

Meisels, S. J., and Shonkoff, J. P. (eds) (1990) *Handbook of Early Childhood Intervention*. Cambridge, Cambridge University Press.

Mercer, A. (1985) Smallpox and epidemiological-demographic change in Europe: the role of vaccination. *Population Studies*, 39: 287–307.

Meyer, R. J., and Haggerty, R. J. (1962) Streptococcal infections in families. *Pediatrics*, 29: 239–49.

Micklethwait, P., Jenkins, C. C., Flanagan, G. L., Mansfield, R., Beech, B., Wynn, A., and Wynn, M. (1982) Letter to the *Observer*, 25 July.

Miller, J. B. (1976) *Toward a New Psychology of Women*. Boston, Beacon Press.

Miller, P. M., and Ingham, J. G. (1976) Friends, confidants and symptoms. *Social Psychiatry*, 11: 51–8.

Millett, K. (1969) *Sexual Politics*. London, Rupert Hart-Davis.

Ministry of Health (1929) Ante-natal clinics: their conduct and scope. Reprinted in Departmental Committee on Maternal Mortality and Morbidity, *Interim Report*, London, HMSO, 1930.

Ministry of Health (1938) *Annual Report of the Chief Medical Officer of Health for the Year 1937*. London, HMSO.

Mitchell, J., and Oakley, A. (eds) (1986) *What is Feminism?* Oxford, Basil Blackwell.

Mohide, P., and Grant, A. (1989) Evaluating diagnosis and screening during pregnancy and childbirth. In Chalmers et al. (1989a).

Morenzo, L., and Goldman, N. (1990) An assessment of survey data on birthweight. *Social Science and Medicine*, 31 (4): 491–500.

Morrison, D. E., and Henkel, R. E. (eds) (1970) *The Significance Test Controversy*. Chicago, Aldine Publishing Company.

Myles, M. F. (1981) *Text Book for Midwives*. 9th edn. Edinburgh, Churchill Livingstone.

Myrdal, G. (1969) *Objectivity in Social Research*. New York, Pantheon.

National Perinatal Epidemiology Unit (1978) *Annual Report*. Oxford, NPEU.

National Perinatal Epidemioogy Unit (1979) *Annual Report*. Oxford, NPEU.

Neilson, J., and Grant, A. (1989) Ultrasound in pregnancy. In Chalmers et al. (1989a).

Nelson, N., Enkin, M., Saigal, S., Bennett, K. J., Milner, R., and Sackett, D. L. (1980) A randomized clinical trial of the Leboyer approach to childbirth. *New England Journal of Medicine*, 208: 655–60.

Neuberger, J. (1991) *Ethics and Health Care: the role of research ethics committees in the United Kingdom*. Research Report 13, London, King's Fund Institute.

Newman, G. (1906) *Infant Mortality: a social problem*. London, Methuen.

Newns, B., Drummond, M. F., Durbin, G. M., and Culley, P. (1984) Costs and outcomes in a regional neonatal intensive care unit. *Archives of Disease in Childhood*, 59: 1064–7.

Newton, R. W., and Hunt, L. P. (1984) Psychosocial stress in pregnancy and its relation to low birthweight. *British Medical Journal*, 288: 1191–3.

Newton, R. W., Webster, P. A. L., Binn, P. S., Maskrey, N., and Phillips, A. B. (1979) Psychosocial stress in pregnancy and its relation to the onset of premature labour. *British Medical Journal*, 2: 411–13.

Nolan, T., Zvagulis, I., and Pleiss, B. (1987) Controlled trial of social work in childhood chronic illness. *Lancet*, 22 August: 411–15.

Norbeck, J., and Tilden, V. (1983) Life stress, social support and emotional disequilibrium in complications of pregnancy: a prospective multivariate study. *Journal of Health and Social Behaviour*, 24: 30–46.

Nuckolls, K. B., Cassel, J., and Kaplan, J. H. (1972) Psychosocial assets, life crises and the prognosis of pregnancy. *American Journal of Epidemiology*, 95: 431–41.

Oakley, A. (1972) *Sex, Gender and Society*. London, Maurice Temple Smith.

Oakley, A. (1974) *The Sociology of Housework*. London, Martin Robertson.

Oakley, A. (1979a) *Becoming a Mother*. Oxford, Martin Robertson.

Oakley, A. (1979b) Comments on the desirability and proposed study design of a fourth national perinatal survey from a social science persepctive. Report submitted to the Department of Health and Social Security, London, May (unpublished).

Oakley, A. (1980) *Women Confined: towards a sociology of childbirth*. Oxford, Martin Robertson.

Oakley, A. (1981a). Interviewing women: a contradiction in terms? In H. Roberts (ed.) *Doing Feminist Research*, London, Routledge & Kegan Paul.

Oakley, A. (1981b) Normal motherhood: an exercise in self-control? In B. Hutter and G. Williams (eds) *Controlling Women*, London, Croom Helm.

Oakley, A. (1984) *The Captured Womb: a history of the medical care of pregnant women*. Oxford, Basil Blackwell.

Oakley, A. (1985) Social support in pregnancy: the 'soft' way to increase birthweight? *Social Science and Medicine*, 21 (11): 1259–68.

Oakley, A. (1986) Feminism, motherhood and medicine – who cares? In Mitchell and Oakley (1986).

Oakley, A. (1988) Is social support good for the health of mothers and babies? *Journal of Reproductive and Infant Psychology*, 6: 3–21.

Oakley, A. (1989) Smoking in pregnancy – smokescreen or risk factor? Towards a materialist analysis. *Sociology of Health and Illness*, 11 (4): 311–35.

Oakley, A. (1991a) Eugenics, social medicine and the career of Richard Titmuss in Britain 1935–50. *British Journal of Sociology*, 42 (2): 165–194.

Oakley, A. (1991b) Using medical care: the views and experiences of high-risk mothers. *Health Services Research*, 26 (5): 651–69.

Oakley, A., Macfarlane, J. A., and Chalmers, I. (1982) Social class, stress and reproduction. In A. R. Rees and H. Purcell (eds), *Disease and the Environment*, Chichester, John Wiley.

Oakley, A., McPherson, A., and Roberts, H. (1990a). *Miscarriage*. Rev. edn. Harmondsworth, Penguin.

Oakley, A., and Rajan, L. (1990) Obstetric technology and maternal emotional wellbeing: a further research note. *Journal of Reproductive and Infant Psychology*, 8: 45–55.

Oakley, A., and Rajan, L. (1991) Social class and social support – the same or different? *Sociology*, 25 (1): 31–59.

Oakley, A., Rajan, L., and Grant, A. (1990b) Social support and pregnancy outcome: report of a randomized trial. *British Journal of Obstetrics and Gynaecology*, 97: 155–62.

Oakley, A., Rajan, L., and Robertson, P. (1990c) A comparison of different sources information about pregnancy and childbirth. *Journal of Biosocial Science*, 22: 477–87.

Odent, M. (1986) *Primal Health*, London, Century Hutchinson.

Olds, D. L., Henderson, C. R., Tatelbaum, R. and Chamberlin, R. (1986) Improving the delivery of prenatal care and outcomes of pregnancy: a randomized trial of nurse home visitation. *Pediatrics*, 77 (1): 16–28.

Orth-Gomer, K., and Unden, L. A. (1987) The measurement of social support in population surveys. *Social Science and Medicine*, 24 (1): 83–94.

Palmer, E. L. (1973) Formative research in the production of television for children. In National Society for the Study of Education *Yearbook for 1973 on Early Childhood Development*, Chicago, University of Chicago Press.

Papaioannou, A. (1982) Informed consent after randomisation (letter). *Lancet*, 9 October: 828.

Papiernik, E., Breart, G., and Spira, N. (eds) (1986) *Prevention of Preterm Birth: new goals and new practices in prenatal care*. Paris, INSERM.

Papiernik-Berkhauer, E. (1980) Prediction of the preterm baby. *Clinical Obstetrics and Gynaecology*, 11: 315–19.

Park, L. C., and Covi, L. (1965) Nonblind placebo trial: an exploration of neurotic outpatients' responses to placebo when its inert content is disclosed. *Archives of General Psychiatry*, 12: 336–45.

Pascoe, J. M., Chessare, J., Baugh, E., Urich, L., and Ialongo, N. (1987) Help with prenatal household tasks and newborn birth weight: is there an association? *Journal of Developmental and Behavioral Pediatrics*, 8 (4): 207–12.

Pascoe, J. M., and Earp, J. A. (1984) The effect of mothers' social support and life changes on the stimulation of their children in the home. *American Journal of Public Health*, 74 (4): 358–60.

Pascoe, J. M., Loda, F. A., Jeffries, V., and Earp, J. A. (1981) The association between mothers' social support and provision of stimulation to their children. *Developmental and Behavioral Pediatrics*, 2 (1): 15–24.

Patel, C., Marmot, M. G., Terry, D. J., Carruthers, M., Hunt, B., and Patel, M. (1985) Trial of relaxation in reducing coronary risk: four year follow up. *British Medical Journal*, 290: 1103–6.

Patulin Clinical Trials Committee (1944) Clinical trial of patulin in the common cold. *Lancet*, 16 September: 373–5.

Paykel, E. S., Emms, E. M., Fletcher, J., and Rassaby, E. S. (1980) Life events and social support in puerperal depression. *British Journal of Psychiatry*, 136: 339–46.

Peller, S. (1947–8) Mortality, past and future. *Population Studies*, 1: 405–56.

Peoples, M. D., Grimson, R. C., and Daughtry, G. L. (1984) Evaluation of the effects of the North Carolina Improved Pregnancy Outcome Project; implications for state-level decision-making. *American Journal of Public Health*, 74 (6): 549–54.

Peoples, M. D., and Siegel, E. (1983) Measuring the impact of programs for mothers and infants on prenatal care and low birthweight: the value of refined analyses. *Medical Care*, 21 (6): 586–604.

Peters, D., and Ceci, S. (1982) Peer-review practices of psychology journals: the fate of published articles submitted again. *The Behavioral and Brain Sciences*, 5: 187–255.

Phillips, O. C., Lyons, W. B., Campbell, C., and Frazier, T. M. (1960) Trilafon analgesia during labour. *Obstetrics and Gynecology*, 15 (2): 182–7.

Phoenix, A. (1991) *Young Mothers?* Cambridge, Polity Press.

Platt, J. (1976) *Realities of Social Research: an empirical study of British sociologists*. London, Sussex University Press.

Pocock, S. J. (1985) Current issues in the design and interpretation of trials. *British Medical Journal*, 290: 39–42.

Porritt, D. (1979) Social support in crisis: quantity or quality? *Social Science and Medicine*, 13A: 715–21.

Potelaikhoff, A., and Carruthers, M. (1981) *Real Health*. London, Davis Poynter.

Powell, T. G., Pharoah, P. O. D., and Cooke, R. W. I. (1986) Survival and morbidity in a geographically defined population of low birthweight infants. *Lancet*, 8 March: 539–43.

Powers, E., and Witmer, H. (1951) *An Experiment in the Prevention of Delinquency: the Cambridge–Somerville Youth Study*. New York, Columbia University Press.

Prioleau, L., Murdock, M., and Brody, N. (1983) An analysis of psychotherapy versus placebo studies. *The Behavioral and Brain Sciences*, 6: 275–310.

Pritchard, E. (1914) *The Infant: nutrition and management*. London, Edward Arnold.

Puffer, R. R., and Serrano, C. V. (1987) *Patterns of Birthweights*. Scientific Publication no. 504, Washington, DC, Pan-American Health Organization.

Quetelet, L. A. (1971) *Anthropométrie ou mesure des différentes facultés de l'homme*. Brussels.

Ragin, C. C., and Becker, H. S. (1989) How the microcomputer is changing our analytic habits. In Blank et al. (1989).

Rantakallio, P. (1969) Groups at risk in low birth weight infants and perinatal mortality. *Acta Paediatrica Scandinavica*, suppl. 193: 1–71.

Rantakallio, P. (1979) Social backgrounds of women who smoke during pregnancy and influence of these factors on the offspring. *Social Science and Medicine*, 13A: 423–9.

Rapoport, R. M. (ed.) (1985) *Children, Youth and Families – the Action–Research Relationship*. Cambridge, Cambridge University Press.

Ratcliffe, H. L. (1962) Environment, behaviour and disease. In E. Sellar and J. M. Sprague (eds), *Progress in Physiological Psychology*, New York, Academic Press.

Raymond, J. G. (1986) *A Passion for Friends: toward a philosophy of female affection*. Boston, Beacon Press.

Reading, A. E., Campbell, S., Cox, D. N., and Sledmere, C. M. (1982) Health beliefs and health care behaviour in pregnancy. *Psychological Medicine*, 12: 379–83.

Reid, M., and Garcia, J. (1989) Women's views of care during pregnancy and childbirth. In Chalmers et al. (1989a).

Reid, M. E., Gutteridge, S., and McIlwaine, G. M. (1983) *A Comparison of the Delivery of Antenatal Care between a Hospital and a Peripheral Clinic*. Report to Health Services Research Committee, Scottish Home and Health Department, Glasgow, Scotland.

Reiser, S. J. (1978) *Medicine and the Reign of Technology*. Cambridge, Cambridge University Press.

Rhinehart, L. (1972) *The Dice Man*. London, Grafton Books.

Richards, M. P. M. (1980) Is neonatal care overused? *Birth and the Family Journal*, 7 (4): 225–7.

Richards, M. (1983) The limits of randomized controlled trials: comment. *Birth*, 10 (3): 164–5.

Richardson, S. A., and Guttmacher, A. F. (eds) (1967) *Childbearing: its social and psychological aspects*. Baltimore, Williams & Wilkins.

Riley, E. M. D. (1977) 'What do women want?' The question of choice in the conduct of labour. In Chard and Richards (1982).

Robinson, J. (1987) Cervical cancer – doctors hide the truth. In S. O. Sullivan (ed.), *Woman's Health: Spare Rib reader*, London, Pandora Press.

Robinson, J. (1988) *A Patient Voice at the GMC*. London, Health Rights.

Robinson, L. (1905) Consultations for infants in France. *The Practitioner* (October): 479–88.

Roederer, J. G. (1763) *Opuscula Medica: de temporum in graviditate et partu aestimatione*. Göttingen, Bossigelius.

Romito, P. (1989) Unhappiness after childbirth. In Chalmers et al. (1989a).

Rose, A., Lewontin, R. C., and Kamin, L. J. (1984) *Not in Our Genes*. Harmondsworth, Penguin.

Rose, H. (1986) Women's work: women's knowledge. In Mitchell and Oakley (1986).

Rothman, B. K. (1989) *Recreating Motherhood: ideology and technology in a patriarchal society*. New York, W. W. Norton.

Roy, A. (1978) Vulnerability factors and depression in women. *British Journal of Psychiatry*, 133: 106–10.

Ruddick, S. (1989) *Maternal Thinking*. London, The Women's Press.

Runnerstrom, L. R. (1969) The effectiveness of nurse-midwifery in a supervised hospital environment. *Bulletin of the American College of Nurse Midwives*, 145: 40–52.

Rush, D. (1984) Some comments on the Massachusetts WIC evaluation. *American Journal of Public Health*, 74 (10): 1145–9.

Rush, D. (1989) Effects of changes in protein and calorie intake during pregnancy on the growth of the human fetus. In Chalmers et al. (1989a).

Russell, J. (n.d.) The current debate on pregnancy and childbirth: assumptions, ideologies and definitions. Unpublished paper, Department of Social Administration, University College, Cardiff.

Rutter, D. R., and Quine, L. (1990) Inequalities in pregnancy outcome: a review of psycho-social and behavioural mediators. *Social Science and Medicine*, 30 (5): 553–67.

Ruzek, S. B. (1978) *The Women's Health Movement*. New York, Praeger.

Sackett, D. L. (1989) Rules of evidence and clinical recommendations on the use of anti-thrombotic agents. *Chest* 95: 25–45.

Sagan, L. A. (1987) *The Health of Nations*. New York, Basic Books.

St Leger, A., Cochrane, A., and Moore, F. (1978) The anomaly that wouldn't go away. *Lancet*, II: 1153.

Sandhu, B., Cooke, R. W. I., Stevenson, R. C., and Pharoah, P. O. D. (1986) Cost of neonatal intensive care for very-low-birthweight infants. *Lancet*, 15 March: 600–3.

Schaefer, C., Coyne, J. C., and Lazarus, R. S. (1981) The health-related functions of social support. *Journal of Behavioral Medicine*, 4 (4): 381–405.

Schutz, A. (1962) *Collected Papers I: The problem of social reality*. The Hague, Martinus Nijhoff.

Schwarz, D., Flamant, R., and Lellouch, J. (1980) *Clinical Trials*. London, Academic Press.

Sebeok, T. A. (1983) Psychotherapy and placebo: 'sticks and stones will break my bones, but can words never harm me?' *The Behavioral and Brain Sciences*, 6: 300.

Sexton, M., and Hebel, J. R. (1984) A clinical trial of change in maternal smoking and its effect on birth weight. *Journal of the American Medical Association*, 215: 911–15.

Shafi, M. I., Constantine, G., Rowlands, D. (1988) Routine one-stage ultrasound screening in pregnancy (letter). *Lancet*, 1 October: 804.

Sherwin, S. (1989) Philosophical methodology and feminist methodology: are they compatible? In Garry and Pearsall (1989).

Shonkoff, J. P. (1984) Social support and the development of vulnerable children. *American Journal of Public Health*, 74 (4): 310–12.

Silverman, W. A. (1980) *Retrolental Fibroplasia: a modern parable*. New York, Grune & Stratton.

Silverman, W. A. (1985) *Human Experimentation: a guided step into the unknown*. Oxford, Oxford University Press.

Simkim, P., and Enkin, M. (1989) Antenatal classes. In Chalmers et al. (1989a).

Simpson, J. Y. (1844) Memoir on the sex of the child as a cause of difficulty and danger in human parturition. *Edinburgh Medical and Surgical Journal*, 62: 387–439.

Slater, J., and Depue, R. A. (1981) The contribution of environmental events and social support to serious suicide attempts in primary depressive disorder. *Journal of Abnormal Psychology*, 90: 275–85.

Slome, C., Wetherbee, H., Daly, M., Christenseu, K., Meglen, M., and Thiede, H. (1976) Effectiveness of certified nurse-midwives. *American Journal of Obstetrics and Gynecology*, 124 (1): 177–182.

Smilkstein, G., Helsper-Lucas, A., Ashworth, C., Montano, D., and Pagel, M. (1984) Prediction of pregnancy complications – an application of the biopsychosocial model. *Social Science and Medicine*, 18(4): 315–21.

Smith, D. E. (1987) *The Everyday World as Problematic*. Milton Keynes, Open University Press.

Smith, D. E. (1979) A sociology for women. In J. A. Sherman and E. T. Beck (eds), *The Prism of Sex: essays on the sociology of knowledge*. Madison, Wisc., University of Wisconsin Press.

Smith, G. D., Bartley, M., and Blane, D. (1990) The Black Report on socioeconomic inequalities in health 10 years on . *British Medical Journal*, 301: 373–7.

Smith, M. L., and Glass, G. V. (1977) Meta-analysis of psychotherapy outcome. *American Psychologist*, 32: 752–60.

Smith, R. (1988) International comparisons of funding and output of research: bye bye Britain. *British Medical Journal*, 296: 409–12.

Smith, T. (1990) Poverty and health in the 1990s. *British Medical Journal*, 301: 349–50.

Snow, H. (1893) *Cancer and the Cancer Process*. London, Churchill.

Social Research Association (1980) *Terms and Conditions of Social Research Funding in Britain: report of the working group*. London, Social Research Association.

Social Science Research Council (1981). *A Change in Structure for Charging Circumstance*. London, SSRC.

Social Services Committee (1980) *Second Report from the Social Services Committee. Perinatal and Neonatal Mortality*. London, HMSO.

Social Services Committee (1988–1989). *First Report. Perinatal, Neonatal and Infant Mortality.* London, HMSO.

Sosa, R., Kennell, J., Klaus, M., Robertson, S., and Urrutia, J. (1980) The effect of a supportive companion on perinatal problems, length of labor and mother–infant interaction. *New England Journal of Medicine*, 303: 596–600.

Spallone, P., and Steinberg, D. L. (eds) (1987) *Made to Order: the myth of reproductive and genetic progress.* Oxford, Pergamon Press.

Spence Cagle, C. (1984) Changed interpersonal needs of the pregnant couple: nursing roles. *Journal of Obstetrics and Gynecology and Neonatal Nursing*, 13: 56.

Spencer, B., and Morris, J. (1986) The family worker project: social support in pregnancy. In Papiernik et al. (1986).

Spencer, B., Thomas, H., and Morris, J. A. (1989) A randomized controlled trial of the provision of a social support service during pregnancy: the South Manchester Family Worker Project. *British Journal of Obstetrics and Gynaecology*, 96: 281–8.

Spender, D. (1980) *Man Made Language.* London, Routledge & Kegan Paul.

Spiegel, D., Bloom, J. R., Kraemer, H. C., and Gottheil, E. (1989) Effect of psychosocial treatment on survival of patients with metastatic breast cancer. *Lancet*, 14 October: 888–901.

Spira, N., Audras, F., Chapel, A., Debuisson, E., Jacquelin, J., Kirchhoffer, C., Lebrun, C., and Prudent, C. (1981) Surveillance à domicile des grossesses pathologiques par les sages-femmes. *Journal Gynécologie, Obstétriques, Biologie et Reproduction*, 10: 543–8.

Stacey, M. (1982) Quoted in the *Times Higher Education Supplement*, 2 April.

Stacey, M. (1988) *The Sociology of Health and Healing.* London, Unwin Hyman.

Stacey, M., and Homans, H. (1978) The sociology of health and illness: its present state, future prospects and potential for health research. *Sociology*, 12 (2): 281–307.

Stacey, M., and Price, M. (1981) *Women, Power and Politics.* London, Tavistock.

Stanley, F. J. (n.d.) Prevention of preterm birth. Unpublished protocol.

Stanley, F. J., and Atkinson, S. (1981) Impact of neonatal intensive care on cerebral palsy in infants of low birthweight (letter). *Lancet*, 21 November: 1162.

Stanley, F. J., and Bryce, R. L. (1986) The pregnancy home visiting program. In Papiernik et al. (1986).

Stanley, F. J. and Watson, L. (1992) Trends in perinatal mortality and cerebral palsy in Western Australia, 1967 to 1985. *British Medical Journal* 304: 1658–63.

Stein, A., Cooper, P. J., Campbell, E. A., Day, A., and Altham, P. M. E. (1989) Social adversity and perinatal complications: their relation to postnatal depression. *British Medical Journal*, 298: 1073–4.

Stevens, R. J., Becker, R. C., Frumpson, G. L., Lanz, L. J., and Tolan, C. J. (1988) Postnatal sequelae of parental smoking during and after pregnancy. *Journal of Reproductive and Infant Psychology*, 6: 61–81.

Stinson, R., and Stinson, P. (1983) *The Long Dying of Baby Andrew.* Boston, Little Brown.

Stjernfeldt, M., Beglund, K., Lindsten, J., and Ludvigsson, J. (1986) Maternal smoking during pregnancy and risk of childhood cancer. *Lancet*, 14 June: 1350–2.

Stone, I. (1972) *The Healing Factor: vitamin C against disease.* New York, Grosset and Dunlap.

Strobino, D. M., Chase, G. A., Kim, Y. J., Crawley, B. E., Salim, J. H., and Baruffi, G. (1986) The impact of the Mississippi Improved Child Health Project on prenatal care and low birthweight. *American Journal of Public Health*, 76 (3): 274–6.

Surtees, P. G. (1980) Social support, residual adversity and depressive outcome. *Social Psychiatry*, 15: 71–80.

Susser, M. (1981) Widowhood: a statistical life stress or a stressful life event. *American Journal of Public Health*, 71: 793–5.

Susser, M. (1987) *Epidemiology, Health and Society: selected papers.* New York: Oxford University Press.

Szreter, S. (1988) The importance of social intervention in Britain's mortality decline c. 1850–1914: a re-interpretation of the role of public health. *Society for the Social History of Medicine*, 38: 1–37.

Tanner, J. M. (1981) *A History of the Study of Human Growth*. Cambridge, Cambridge University Press.

Thoits, P. A. (1982) Conceptual, methodological and theoretical problems in studying social support as a buffer against life stress. *Journal of Health and Social Behaviour*, 23: 145–59.

Thomas, E. (1988) Cited in *Observer*, 9 October.

Thomas, K. B. (1987) General practice consultations: is there any point in being positive. *British Medical Journal*, 294: 1200–92.

Thomson, M. E., and Kramer, M. S. (1984) Methodologic standards for controlled clinical trials of early contact and maternal–infant behaviour. *Paediatrics*, 73 (3): 294–300.

Thorn, F. (1980) *Domesday Book, 29 Rutland*. Chichester, Phillimore.

Timm, M. M. (1979) Prenatal education evaluation. *Nursing Research*, 28 (6): 338–42.

Totman, R. (1979) *Social Causes of Illness*. London, Souvenir Press.

Townsend, P., and Davidson, N. (1982) *Inequalities in Health*. Harmondsworth, Penguin.

Turner, B. A. (1981) Some practical aspects of qualitative data analysis: one way of organizing the cognitive processes associated with the generation of grounded theory. *Quality and Quantity*, 15: 225–47.

Turner, B. S. (1984) *The Body and Society*. Oxford, Basil Blackwell.

Tyrer, P., Murphy, S., Kingdom, D., Brothwell, J., Gregory, S., Seivewright, N., Ferguson, B., Barczak, P., Darling, C., and Johnson, A. L. (1988) The Nottingham study of neurotic disorder: comparison of drug and psychological treatments. *Lancet*, 30 July: 235–40.

University Grants Committee (1989) *Report of the Review Committee on Sociology*.

Voysey, M. (1975) *A Constant Burden*. London, Routledge & Kegan Paul.

Waldenstrom, U., Axelsson, O., Nilsson, S., Eklund, G., Fall, O., Lindberg, S., and Sjodin, Y. (1988) Effects of routine one-stage ultrasound screening in pregnancy: a randomized controlled trial. *Lancet*, 10 September: 586–8.

Walkerdine, V., and Lucey, H. (1989) *Democracy in the Kitchen*. London, Virago.

Weber, M. (1903–17) *The Methodology of the Social Sciences*. Repr. New York, Free Press, 1949.

Webster, C. (n.d.) Oxford and the origins of social medicine. Unpublished paper.

Weihs, K., and Chapados, J. T. (1986) Interviewing skills training – a study. *Social Science and Medicine*, 23 (1): 31–4.

Weinberger, S. L., Hiner, W. M., and Tierney, W. M. (1986) Improving functional status in arthritis: the effect of social support. *Social Science and Medicine*, 23 (9): 899–904.

Welin, L., Svardsudd, K., Ander-Peciva, S., Tibblin, G., Tibblin, B., and Larsson, B. (1985) Prospective study of social influences on mortality. *Lancet*, 20 April: 915–18.

Wellman, B. (1979) The community question. *American Journal of Sociology*, 84: 1201–231.

Whitbeck, C. (1989) A different reality: feminist ontology. In Garry and Pearsall. (1989)

Wilcox, A. J., and Russell, I. T. (1986) Birthweight and perinatal mortality III: toward a new method of analysis. *International Journal of Epidemiology*, 15 (2): 188–96.

Wilcox, B. L. (1981) Social support, life stress and psychological adjustment: a test of the buffering hypothesis. *American Journal of Psychology*, 9: 371–86.

Williams, F. (1992) Structural inequalities and the management of personal welfare: a selective literature review and assessment. Unpublished paper prepared for the Economic and Social Research Council Management of Personal Welfare Initiative.

Winch, R. F., and Campbell, D. T. (1970) Proof? No. Evidence? Yes. The significance of tests of significance. In Morrison and Henkel (1970).

Windsor, R. A., Cutter, G., Morris, J., Reese, Y., Manzella, B., Bartlett, E. E., Samuelson, C., and Spanos, D. (1985) The effectiveness of smoking cessation methods for smokers in public health maternity clinics: a randomized trial. *American Journal of Public Health*, 75 (12): 1389–92.

Wolf, S. (1959) Placebos. *Association for Research in Nervous and Mental Disease Research Publications*, 37: 147–61.

Wolfe, B. L. (1980) Children's utilization of medical care. *Medical Care*, 18: 1196.

Woolhandler, S., and Himmelstein, D. U. (1985) Militarism and mortality. *Lancet*, 15 June: 1375–8.

Wootton, B. (1959) *Social Science and Social Pathology*. London, Allen & Unwin.

World Health Organization (1950) *Expert Group on Prematurity Final Report*. Technical Report series no. 27. Geneva, WHO.

World Health Organization (1981) *Global Strategy for Health for All by the Year 2000*. Geneva, WHO.

World Health Organization (1984) The incidence of low birth weight: an update. *Weekly Epidemiological Record*, 59: 205–11.

Wortman, C. B. (1984) Social support and the cancer patient. *Cancer*, 53: 2339–60.

Wright Mills, C. (1959) *The Sociological Imagination*. New York, Oxford University Press.

Wynne, A. (1989) Is it any good? The evaluation of therapy by participants in a clinical trial. *Social Science and Medicine*, 29 (11): 1289–97.

Yanover, M. J., Jones, D., and Miller, M. D. (1976) Perinatal care of low-risk mothers and infants. *New England Journal of Medicine*, 94 (13): 702–5.

Ylppo, A. (1919) Zur Physiologie, Klinik, und zum Schicksal der Frühgeborenen. *Zeitschrift für Kinderheilkunde*, 24: 1–110.

Young, M., and Willmott, P. (1957) *Family and Kinship in East London*. London, Routledge & Kegan Paul.

Zaretsky, E. (1976) *Capitalism, the Family and Personal Life*. London, Pluto Press.

Zelditch, M. (1962) Some methodological problems of field studies. *American Journal of Sociology*, 67: 566–76.

Zigler, E., and Weiss, H. (1985) Family support systems: an ecological approach to child development. In Rapoport (1985).

Zimmer, E. Z., Divon, M., Vilensky, A., Sarna, Z., Peretz, B. A., and Paldi, E. (1982) Maternal exposure to music and fetal activity. *European Journal of Obstetrics and Gynaecological and Reproductive Biology*, 13: 209–13.

Index

Note: SSPO study is used as an abbreviation for Social Support and Pregnancy Outcome study; pilot study refers to the Social Factors and Pregnancy Outcomes project.